Risk Management Principles and Practices

Risk Management Principles and Practices

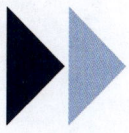

Edited by
Michael W. Elliott, CPCU, AIAF, MBA

1st Edition • 1st Printing

The Institutes
720 Providence Road, Suite 100
Malvern, Pennsylvania 19355-3433

© 2012
American Institute For Chartered Property Casualty Underwriters

All rights reserved. This book or any part thereof may not be reproduced without the written permission of the copyright holder.

Unless otherwise apparent, examples used in The Institutes materials related to this course are based on hypothetical situations and are for educational purposes only. The characters, persons, products, services, and organizations described in these examples are fictional. Any similarity or resemblance to any other character, person, product, services, or organization is merely coincidental. The Institutes are not responsible for such coincidental or accidental resemblances.

This material may contain Internet Web site links external to The Institutes. The Institutes neither approve nor endorse any information, products, or services to which any external Web sites refer. Nor do The Institutes control these Web sites' content or the procedures for Web site content development.

The Institutes specifically disclaim any implied warranties of merchantability or fitness for a particular purpose. No warranty may be created or extended by sales representatives or written sales materials.

The Institutes materials related to this course are provided with the understanding that The Institutes are not engaged in rendering legal, accounting, or other professional service. Nor are The Institutes explicitly or implicitly stating that any of the processes, procedures, or policies described in the materials are the only appropriate ones to use. The advice and strategies contained herein may not be suitable for every situation.

Information which is copyrighted by and proprietary to Insurance Services Office, Inc. ("ISO Material") is included in this publication. Use of the ISO Material is limited to ISO Participating Insurers and their Authorized Representatives. Use by ISO Participating Insurers is limited to use in those jurisdictions for which the insurer has an appropriate participation with ISO. Use of the ISO Material by Authorized Representatives is limited to use solely on behalf of one or more ISO Participating Insurers.

This publication includes forms which are provided for review purposes only. These forms may not be used, in whole or in part, by any company or individuals not licensed by Insurance Services Office, Inc. (ISO) for the applicable line of insurance and jurisdiction to which this form applies. It is a copyright infringement to include any part(s) of this form within independent company programs without the written permission of ISO.

1st Edition • 1st Printing • October 2012

Library of Congress Control Number: 2012949966

ISBN 978-0-89463-613-4

Foreword

The Institutes are the trusted leader in delivering proven knowledge solutions that drive powerful business results for the risk management and property-casualty insurance industry. For more than 100 years, The Institutes have been meeting the industry's changing professional development needs with customer-driven products and services.

In conjunction with industry experts and members of the academic community, our Knowledge Resources Department develops our course and program content, including Institutes study materials. Practical and technical knowledge gained from Institutes courses enhances qualifications, improves performance, and contributes to professional growth—all of which drive results.

The Institutes' proven knowledge helps individuals and organizations achieve powerful results with a variety of flexible, customer-focused options:

Recognized Credentials—The Institutes offer an unmatched range of widely recognized and industry-respected specialty credentials. The Institutes' Chartered Property Casualty Underwriter (CPCU) professional designation is designed to provide a broad understanding of the property-casualty insurance industry. Depending on professional needs, CPCU students may select either a commercial insurance focus or a personal risk management and insurance focus and may choose from a variety of electives.

In addition, The Institutes offer certificate or designation programs in a variety of disciplines, including these:

- Claims
- Commercial underwriting
- Fidelity and surety bonding
- General insurance
- Insurance accounting and finance
- Insurance information technology
- Insurance production and agency management
- Insurance regulation and compliance
- Management
- Marine insurance
- Personal insurance
- Premium auditing
- Quality insurance services
- Reinsurance
- Risk management
- Surplus lines

Ethics—Ethical behavior is crucial to preserving not only the trust on which insurance transactions are based, but also the public's trust in our industry as a whole. All Institutes designations now have an ethics requirement, which is delivered online and free of charge. The ethics requirement content is designed specifically for insurance practitioners and uses insurance-based case studies to outline an ethical framework. More information is available in the Programs section of our website, www.TheInstitutes.org.

Flexible Online Learning—The Institutes have an unmatched variety of technical insurance content covering topics from accounting to underwriting, which we now deliver through hundreds of online courses. These cost-effective self-study courses are a convenient way to fill gaps in technical knowledge in a matter of hours without ever leaving the office.

Continuing Education—A majority of The Institutes' courses are filed for CE credit in most states. We also deliver quality, affordable, online CE courses quickly and conveniently through our newest business unit, CEU.com. Visit www.CEU.com to learn more.

College Credits—Most Institutes courses carry college credit recommendations from the American Council on Education. A variety of courses also qualify for credits toward certain associate, bachelor's, and master's degrees at several prestigious colleges and universities. More information is available in the Student Services section of our website, www.TheInstitutes.org.

Custom Applications—The Institutes collaborate with corporate customers to use our trusted course content and flexible delivery options in developing customized solutions that help them achieve their unique organizational goals.

Insightful Analysis—Our Insurance Research Council (IRC) division conducts public policy research on important contemporary issues in property-casualty insurance and risk management. Visit www.ircweb.org to learn more or purchase its most recent studies.

The Institutes look forward to serving the risk management and property-casualty insurance industry for another 100 years. We welcome comments from our students and course leaders; your feedback helps us continue to improve the quality of our study materials.

Peter L. Miller, CPCU
President and CEO
The Institutes

Preface

Risk Management Principles and Practices is the assigned textbook for the ARM 54 course in The Institutes' Associate in Risk Management (ARM) designation program. This text provides learners with a broad understanding of risk management and the risk management process.

The course starts with an enterprise-wide perspective of risk by applying risk management concepts to four major categories of risk: hazard (insurable), operational, financial, and strategic. The enterprise-wide risk management process is contrasted with the traditional risk management process, which applies solely to insurable risk. Risk identification and analysis tools and techniques, including risk registers and risk mapping, are discussed in detail.

The text describes global risk management standards and guidelines, including *ISO 31000 Risk Management–Principles and Guidelines*, developed by the International Organization for Standardization, and *COSO Enterprise Risk Management–Integrated Framework*, developed by the Committee of Sponsoring Organizations of the Treadway Commission.

The latter part of the course emphasizes financial risk, including financial leverage, liquidity risk, and capital investment risk. Risk oversight, monitoring, and assurance are discussed from the perspectives of governance and internal control.

The Institutes are grateful to the insurance professionals who contributed to this text. Their assistance during the review and development stages helped ensure that the text reflects current industry practices. We are particularly grateful to Kristina Narvaez, MBA, and Kathleen J. Robison, CPCU, AU, ARM, AIC, CPIW.

We are also grateful to the individual members of the Risk and Insurance Management Society (RIMS) and the Public Risk Management Association (PRIMA) who gave us feedback on the relative importance of various topics included in the course.

For more information about The Institutes' programs, please call our Customer Service Department at (800) 644-2101, e-mail us at customerservice@TheInstitutes.org, or visit our website at www.TheInstitutes.org.

Michael W. Elliott

Contributors

The Institutes acknowledge with deep appreciation the contributions made to the content of this text by the following persons:

Michael M. Barth, PhD, CPCU, AU

Richard Berthelsen, JD, CPCU, AIC, ARM, AU, ARe, MBA

Laura J. Partsch, JD

Judith M. Vaughan, CPCU, AIC

Contents

Assignment 1
Introduction to Risk Management ... 1.1
The Risk Management Environment ... 1.3
Benefits of Risk Management ... 1.9
Risk Management Objectives and Goals ... 1.14
Basic Risk Measures ... 1.19
Risk Classifications ... 1.23
Enterprise Risk Management ... 1.29
Summary ... 1.34

Assignment 2
Risk Management Standards and Guidelines ... 2.1
Introduction to Risk Management Standards and Guidelines ... 2.3
ISO 31000 Risk Management—Principles and Guidelines ... 2.8
COSO Enterprise Risk Management—Integrated Framework ... 2.13
Solvency II and Basel II and III Regulatory Standards ... 2.18
Summary ... 2.22

Assignment 3
Hazard Risk ... 3.1
The Nature of Hazard Risk ... 3.3
Loss Exposures ... 3.8
Commercial Insurance Policies ... 3.16
Summary ... 3.25

Assignment 4
Operational, Financial, and Strategic Risk ... 4.1
Operational Risk ... 4.3
Operational Risk Indicators ... 4.8
Financial Risk ... 4.13
Value at Risk and Earnings at Risk ... 4.18
Regulatory Capital ... 4.20
Economic Capital ... 4.26
Strategic Risk ... 4.31
Summary ... 4.34

Assignment 5
Risk Management Framework and Process ... 5.1
Modeling an Enterprise-Wide Risk Management Framework and Process ... 5.3
Designing and Implementing an Enterprise-Wide Risk Management Framework and Process ... 5.9
Comparing the Enterprise-Wide Risk Management Process With the Traditional Risk Management Process ... 5.15
Applying the Enterprise-Wide Risk Management Framework and Process ... 5.22
Summary ... 5.31

Assignment 6
Risk Identification — 6.1
Introduction to Risk Identification — 6.3
Team Approaches to Risk Identification — 6.8
Risk Registers — 6.12
Risk Maps — 6.17
Identifying Loss Exposures — 6.21
Identifying Risk — 6.29
Summary — 6.35

Assignment 7
Risk Analysis — 7.1
Introduction to Risk Analysis — 7.3
Probability Analysis — 7.5
Characteristics of Probability Distributions — 7.11
Trend Analysis — 7.17
Analyzing Event Consequences — 7.23
Analyzing Loss Exposures — 7.28
Summary — 7.38

Assignment 8
Risk Treatment — 8.1
Risk Treatment — 8.3
Introduction to Risk Financing — 8.6
Summary — 8.10

Assignment 9
Financial Statement Risk Analysis — 9.1
Purpose of Financial Statements — 9.3
Balance Sheet — 9.4
Income Statement — 9.8
Statement of Changes in Shareholders' Equity and Statement of Cash Flows — 9.13
Supplemental Sources of Financial Information — 9.17
Income Statement Trend Analysis — 9.23
Analyzing Liquidity Risk — 9.25
Capital Structure — 9.29
Financial Leverage — 9.32
Operating Leverage — 9.35
Summary — 9.39

Assignment 10
Capital Investment and Financial Risk — 10.1
Present Value and Discounting — 10.3
Present Value of an Annuity — 10.5
Present Value of Unequal Payments — 10.7
Net Present Value — 10.9
Evaluating Capital Investment Proposals — 10.11
Evaluating Cash Flows From Treating Hazard Risk — 10.17
Using Call Options to Limit Financial Risk — 10.23
Summary — 10.27

Assignment 11
Monitoring and Reporting on Risk — 11.1
Board Risk Oversight — 11.3
Internal Controls Support to Risk Monitoring — 11.9
Internal Audit Support to Risk Monitoring — 11.16
Risk Assurance to Evaluate Risk Management Performance — 11.20
Risk Management Monitoring and Reporting — 11.24
Summary — 11.27

Segment A

Assignment 1
Introduction to Risk Management

Assignment 2
Risk Management Standards and Guidelines

Assignment 3
Hazard Risk

Assignment 4
Operational, Financial, and Strategic Risk

Direct Your Learning

Introduction to Risk Management

Educational Objectives

After learning the content of this assignment, you should be able to:

▸ Describe risk management and the risk management environment.

▸ State the benefits of risk management for an organization and the economy.

▸ Summarize various objectives and goals for managing risk.

▸ Explain how basic risk measures apply to the management of risk.

▸ Explain how the following classifications of risk apply and how they help in risk management:

- Pure and speculative risk
- Subjective and objective risk
- Diversifiable and nondiversifiable risk
- Quadrants of risk (hazard, operational, financial, and strategic)

▸ Describe the concept of enterprise risk management.

Outline

The Risk Management Environment

Benefits of Risk Management

Risk Management Objectives and Goals

Basic Risk Measures

Risk Classifications

Enterprise Risk Management

Summary

Introduction to Risk Management

THE RISK MANAGEMENT ENVIRONMENT

After the 2008 financial crisis, international regulatory agencies required improvements in risk management processes and disclosures. Risk management organizations, such as the Risk and Insurance Management Society (RIMS), conducted conferences and published discussions on the evolution of risk and risk management in the context of the financial crisis and other significant risk events.

Traditionally, risk management has been applied to the risks associated with accidental losses. However, risk management is increasingly being used in other contexts. The definitions of risk and risk management have broadened considerably to include all risks of the organization and the potential effects of those risks on the organization's objectives. The understanding of the risk management environment has also evolved to consider the interconnections between internal and external risks.

Risk and Risk Management Defined

Merriam-Webster defines risk as "the possibility of loss or injury: peril."[1] This is the traditional definition used by insurance and risk management professionals. However, the definition of risk has evolved, and various definitions of risk are now being used in different risk management texts and standards. See the exhibit "Definitions of Risk."

In his book *Against the Gods: The Remarkable Story of Risk*, Peter L. Bernstein writes, "The word 'risk' derives from the early Italian *risicare*, which means 'to dare.' In this sense, risk is a choice rather than a fate."[2] He further states, "When we take a risk, we are betting on an outcome that will result from a decision we have made, though we do not know for certain what the outcome will be." Bernstein's statements about risk reflect the definition to be used during this discussion: "Uncertainty about outcomes that can be either negative or positive." This definition reinforces Bernstein's concept that risk is a choice, not merely something that might happen.

The traditional concept of risk, inherent to insurance, is that risk is a hazard that could happen to an individual or organization. Fire or wind could destroy a home or a business. The homeowner or business owner viewed risk in a negative sense, as a possibility of loss.

1.4 Risk Management Principles and Practices

Definitions of Risk

Definition of Risk	Source
Effect of uncertainty on objectives	ISO 31000:2009 (International Organization for Standardization)*
The possibility that an event will occur and adversely affect the achievement of objectives	COSO ERM:2004 (Committee of Sponsoring Organizations of the Treadway Commission)**
An uncertain future outcome that can either improve or worsen your position	RIMS***
The probable frequency and probable magnitude of future loss	Risk Management Insight****
Exposure to a proposition of which one is uncertain	CFA Institute*****

*International Organization for Standardization, "Risk Management—Principles and Guidelines," ISO 2009 (Geneva, Switzerland: International Organization for Standardization, 2009), p. 1.

**Committee of Sponsoring Organizations of the Treadway Commission, Enterprise Risk Management—Integrated Framework, 2004, p. 124.

*** Carol Fox, "The ERM Tipping Point," Risk and Insurance Management Society, www.rmmag.com/MGTemplate.cfm?Section=RMMagazine&NavMenuID=128&template=/Magazine/DisplayMagazines.cfm&MGPreview=1&Volume=58&IssueID=360&AID=4431&ShowArticle=1 (accessed February 14, 2012).

**** An Introduction to Factor Analysis of Information Risk (FAIR), Risk Management Insight LLC, November 2006, www.riskmanagementinsight.com/media/docs/FAIR_introduction.pdf (accessed February 17, 2012).

***** Glyn A. Holton, "Defining Risk," Financial Analysis Journal, vol. 60, no. 6, 2004, CFA Institute, http://riskexpertise.com/papers/risk.pdf.

[DA08643]

The evolved concept of risk as "uncertainty about outcomes that can be either negative or positive" provides a much broader understanding. A homeowner deciding to purchase a home or a business owner deciding to go into business faces a variety of risks. The value of the home could rise or fall, and the business may profit or fail. The homeowner or business owner may or may not be able to sell the investment if the need arises. The home's neighborhood or the business's market environment could decline or improve. The risks to the homeowner or business owner include the traditional hazard risks, but they are more comprehensive. The homeowner or business owner should understand the risks in the context of the objectives for buying a home or going into business.

The definition of risk management has evolved along with the definition of risk. The website *Business Dictionary* defines risk management as "the identification, analysis, assessment, control, and avoidance, minimization, or elimination of unacceptable risks."[3] This reflects the traditional concept of risk as negative. Newer definitions include positive as well as negative attributes of risk. See the exhibit "Definitions of Risk Management."

Definitions of Risk Management

Definition of Risk Management	Source
Coordinated activities to direct and control an organization with regard to risk.	ISO 31000:2009*
The identification, assessment, and response to risk to a specific objective.	COSO ERM:2004**
Strategic risk management is a business discipline that drives deliberation and action regarding uncertainties and untapped opportunities that affect an organization's strategy and strategy execution.	RIMS***

*International Organization for Standardization, "Risk Management—Principles and Guidelines," ISO 2009 (Geneva, Switzerland: International Organization for Standardization, 2009), p. 2.

**Committee of Sponsoring Organizations of the Treadway Commission, "Appendix: COSO Enterprise Risk Management Framework," 2004, www.erm.coso.org, p. 4 (accessed February 22, 2012).

***Risk and Insurance Management Society, "RIMS Defines an Emerging Discipline," www.rims.org/aboutRIMS/Newsroom/News/Pages/SRMDefinition.aspx (accessed February 22, 2012).

[DA08644]

In *Against the Gods*, Bernstein states, "The essence of risk management lies in maximizing the areas where we have some control over the outcome while minimizing the areas where we have absolutely no control over the outcome and the linkage between effect and cause is hidden from us." This concept reflects our definition of risk management: "The process of making and implementing decisions that enable an organization to optimize its level of risk." This definition reflects an organization managing risks, both positive and negative, to meet its objectives. This is the definition that will be used throughout this discussion of risk management.

To return to the example of a start-up business, the business owner must decide on objectives and then apply risk management to the risks that could affect the achievement of those objectives. Positive risks might include exceeding sales objectives or attracting investor interest. Although these risks are positive, they still need to be managed. Exceeding sales objectives would require additional products. Attracting investor interest might involve relinquishing some management control. Negative risks include the traditional hazard risks (fire and wind) and traditional legal risks (product liability), as well as operational risks such as the inability to obtain materials for the products or to distribute the products efficiently and cost-effectively.

Risk Management Environment

The evolution in the definitions of risk and risk management has occurred as a result of recognition of the increasing variety, number, and interaction of risks facing organizations. Recent risk management theory includes the concept of a holistic approach to risk management. Organizations now realize that it is important to manage all of their risks, not just those that are familiar or easy to quantify. Risks that seem insignificant have the potential to create significant damage or opportunity when they interact with other events. A holistic approach helps organizations to develop a true perspective on the significance of various risks.[4]

These are the high-level categories of risk:

Hazard risk
Risk from accidental loss, including the possibility of loss or no loss.

- **Hazard (or pure) risks**
- Operational risks
- Financial risks
- Strategic risks

These categories can be broken down into subcategories such as project risk, financial reporting risk, and process risk. Over time, all of these risks become part of an organization's overall risk portfolio, which has its own individual **risk profile**.

Risk profile
A set of characteristics common to all risks in a portfolio.

The evolution of risk management has occurred in part because of high-profile failures of large organizations during the late twentieth and early twenty-first centuries, followed by the global financial crisis. In the first part of the twenty-first century, the failure of Enron and its accounting firm, Arthur Andersen, was the catalyst for the 2002 Sarbanes-Oxley Act, which contains requirements for risk management controls to be disclosed and discussed by public companies and their registered auditors in annual financial statements. Rating agencies such as Standard & Poor's now require financial organizations to implement and monitor their risk management programs. In 2009, the United States Securities and Exchange Commission issued rules requiring public corporations to disclose information about risk and risk management, including the board's role in risk oversight.

At the same time that regulators in the U.S. were requiring improved financial risk management and disclosure, there was also an international movement in this direction. A 2004 Forum on Asian Insolvency Reform, sponsored by the World Bank and the Organization for Economic Co-operation and Development (OECD), discussed the evolution of risk management in China. The European Union has been working to adopt the Solvency II and Basel III standards for risk management in financial organizations. Although risk management of accidental losses is historically the most widely practiced type of risk management, the 2011 tsunami in Japan revealed a need for a reevaluation of earthquake, flood, and nuclear power risk management. This catastrophe also pointed out a need for many organizations to evaluate and manage their supply-chain risk.

In large part because of trends in technology, globalization, and finance, the risk landscape has changed dramatically. Organizations operate in a global environment where they face hazard risks such as earthquakes and floods, political risks such as terrorism, economic risks such as a recession, and financial risk such as currency exchange rates. Ironically, risk has also increased because of certain techniques employed to manage some of these risks, such as derivatives to manage exchange rate or supply cost risks. Interconnection of these risks adds to their complexity and potential effect on organizations. See the exhibit "Risk Interconnection Map."

Along with the rapidly evolving external risk management landscape, organizations face increasing changes in their internal risk management environment. In addition to regulations requiring improved risk management processes, compliance, and reporting, organizations face newer types of risk, such as computer attacks, and magnified consequences of traditional risk, such as reputational risk resulting from an event because of the rapid spread of information on the Internet.

In its 2011 report on global risks, the World Economic Forum concluded that the "interconnections between risks require us to better understand the systems behind risks as well the risk context" and that "it is no longer sufficient to simply assess operational risks in the corporate context."[5] Bernstein states in his conclusion to *Against the Gods*:

> ...the science of risk management sometimes creates new risks even as it brings old risks under control. Our faith in risk management encourages us to take risks we would not otherwise take. On most counts that is beneficial, but we must be wary of adding to the amount of risk in the system. Research reveals that seatbelts encourage drivers to drive more aggressively. Consequently, the number of accidents rises even though the seriousness of injury in any one accident declines. Derivative financial instruments designed as hedges have tempted investors to transform them into speculative vehicles... involving risks that no corporate risk manager should contemplate. The introduction of portfolio insurance in the late 1970s encouraged a higher level of equity exposure than had prevailed before. In the same fashion, conservative institutional investors tend to use broad diversification to justify higher exposure to risk in untested areas—but diversification is not a guarantee against loss, only against losing everything at once.[6]

The challenge for risk management professionals is to navigate the evolving risk management environment and develop processes that will guide their organizations toward meeting their objectives. This challenge now involves a holistic approach and recognition of the interconnections of external and internal risks within a rapidly changing landscape.

1.8 Risk Management Principles and Practices

Risk Interconnection Map

[Diagram: Risk Interconnection Map showing four Centres of Gravity — Rising greenhouse gas emissions (green), Critical systems failure (purple), Global governance failure (orange), Unsustainable population growth (red), and Chronic fiscal imbalances (blue) — with interconnections to numerous other risks including Irremediable pollution, Persistent extreme weather, Militarization of space, Proliferation of orbital debris, Unprecedented geophysical destruction, Failure of intellectual property regime, Unforeseen negative consequences of regulations, Failure of climate change adaptation, Unintended consequences of climate change mitigation, Water supply crises, Extreme volatility in energy and agriculture prices, Rising rates of chronic disease, Mismanaged urbanization, Massive incident of data fraud or theft, Mineral resource supply vulnerability, Pervasive entrenched corruption, Hard landing of an emerging economy, Land and waterway use mismanagement, Cyber attacks, Terrorism, Critical fragile states, Backlash against globalization, Mismanagement of population aging, Food shortage crises, Massive digital misinformation, Failure of diplomatic conflict resolution, Unmanaged migration, Unintended consequences of nanotechnology, Major systemic financial failure, Prolonged infrastructure neglect, Severe income disparity, Vulnerability to pandemics, Entrenched organized crime, Rising religious fanaticism, Unilateral resource nationalization, Vulnerability to geomagnetic storms, Widespread illicit trade, Unintended consequences of new life science technologies, Species over-exploitation, Diffusion of weapons of mass destruction, Chronic labour market imbalances, Ineffective drug policies, Antibiotic-resistant bacteria, Unmanageable inflation or deflation, Recurring liquidity crises]

Source: World Economic Forum

Analysis of the 2012 Global Risks Map reveals four risks as playing significant roles in connecting the Centres of Gravity to each other. These four Critical Connectors, which link the main clusters of the system, are highlighted as black dots in the diagram. They are:

- Severe income disparity (economic)
- Major systemic financial failure (economic)
- Unforeseen negative consequences of regulation (economic)
- Extreme volatility in energy and agriculture prices (economic)

Weak Signals are defined as risks which are most loosely connected in the network, based on how many links they have and how often these were selected by survey respondents. The top five Weak Signals are:

- Vulnerability to geomagnetic storms (environmental)
- Proliferation of orbital debris (technological)
- Unintended consequences of nanotechnology (technological)
- Ineffective drug policies (societal)
- Militarization of space (geopolitical)

They have almost without exception received relatively low-impact and low-likelihood scores, and in most cases exhibit a significant variation in how survey respondents perceive them, particularly among the different regions.

World Economic Forum's Global Risks 2012 report, www.weforum.org/reports/global-risks-2012-seventh-edition [DA08796]

BENEFITS OF RISK MANAGEMENT

In a 2008 speech, Ben Bernanke, Chairman of the United States Federal Reserve, stated that a significant factor in causing the 2008 financial crisis was risk-management weaknesses at large global financial institutions. He continued, "Given the central role of effective, firm-wide risk management in maintaining strong financial institutions, it is clear that supervisors must redouble their efforts to help organizations improve their risk-management practices."[7]

Traditionally, organizations have recognized the benefits of risk management for hazard risks. Organizations' risk-management techniques, primarily risk mitigation and risk transfer, benefit not only the individual organization, but also the overall economy. For example, insurance can prevent a business failure after a catastrophe and the unemployment that could result from such a failure.

There are also broader risks within individual organizations and the economy. Some of these risks are positive, such as opportunity risk when an organization expands or develops a new product. These risks can result in growth for organizations as well as for the overall economy. However, in the wake of large-scale and well-publicized business failures, such as Enron, and the global financial crisis, many economists are concerned that organizational risk management has not been effective for the broader scope of risks beyond traditional hazard risks. Additionally, Ben Bernanke and other economists believe that risk management must expand to address **systemic risk** in the economy.

Systemic risk
The potential for a major disruption in the function of an entire market or financial system.

Benefits for an Organization

All organizations face various risks simply by operating. Many risks result in a negative outcome only, such as the possibility of accidental loss, and could prevent an organization from meeting its objectives. Other risks can have either a positive or negative outcome, such as a new product or a financial investment, and could help an organization meet its objectives. There are various benefits to any organization in managing these risks.

Reduce Cost of Hazard Risk

In risk management, an organization's **cost of risk** associated with a particular asset or activity is the total of these:

- Costs of accidental losses not reimbursed by insurance or other outside sources
- Insurance premiums or expenses incurred for noninsurance indemnity
- Costs of risk control techniques to prevent or reduce the size of accidental losses
- Costs of administering risk management activities

Cost of risk
The total cost incurred by an organization because of the possibility of accidental loss.

Risk management aims to reduce the long-term overall cost of risk for the organization without precluding or otherwise interfering with the organization's achieving its goals or engaging in its normal activities. The reduction in the overall cost of risk can increase the organization's profits (or, for a not-for-profit organization, reduce the budget it needs for a particular activity). Risk management also supports safety while minimizing the financial effect of safety measures on the organization's productivity.

Reduce Deterrence Effects of Hazard Risks

The fear of possible future losses tends to make senior management reluctant to undertake activities they consider too risky. Consequently, the organization is deprived of potential benefits. Risk management reduces the deterrence effects of uncertainty about potential future accidental losses by making these losses less frequent, less severe, or more foreseeable. The resulting reduction in uncertainty benefits an organization in these ways:

- Alleviates or reduces management's fears about potential losses, thereby increasing the feasibility of ventures that once appeared too risky
- Increases profit potential by greater participation in investment or production activities
- Makes the organization a safer investment, and, therefore, more attractive to suppliers of investment capital through which the organization can expand

Many new products and manufacturing processes have become attractive only when better ways of preventing and paying for accidental losses have reduced related uncertainty.

Like an organization's senior managers, those who would provide the organization with funds seek assurances: stockholders or other investors seek assurance that their equity is safe and will generate future income; creditors seek assurance that the money they have loaned will be repaid on time with interest. The security sought by these sources of new capital rests, at least partly, on confidence that the organization will prosper despite any accidental losses that might befall it. Consequently, an organization's ability to attract willing investors depends to a significant degree on the effectiveness of its risk management program to protect investors' capital against the cost of accidental losses.

Reduce Downside Risk

Downside risks, including losses and failures, are an inevitable aspect of any type of business or speculative risk. For example, a company has downside risk whenever it introduces a new product. A financial institution has downside risk every time it makes a loan or an investment. Operational risk is a part of an organization's processes, and the downside risks include delays, errors, cost increases, and the failure of any aspect of the operation. Reducing downside risk provides similar organizational benefits as reducing the deterrence effects of hazard risks.

To reduce downside risks, organizations can use stop-loss limits. This technique has been used successfully in financial firms to reduce market risk, but it also applies to other types of risk. In operational risk, for example, an organization can have triggers in place whenever operations hit a predetermined stop-loss limit. Management can then review what happened and determine the best course of action in view of the organization's risk appetite.[8]

Manage the Downside of Risk

Although it cannot eliminate downside risk, risk management can help an organization meet its objectives. See the exhibit "Example of Risk Management Failure at Metallgesellschaft."

Example of Risk Management Failure at Metallgesellschaft

In 1992, an American subsidiary of Metallgesellschaft (MG), Metallgesellschaft Refining and Marketing (MGRM), began using a strategy of agreements to sell petroleum products at prices above the current market price over a ten-year period. MGRM hedged these long-term commitments by purchasing short-term energy futures. Their theory was, if oil prices dropped, the fixed-price positions would gain while the futures positions would lose money. Conversely, if oil prices rose, the futures positions would gain while the fixed-price positions would lose. However, when oil prices actually dropped, MGRM had margin calls on the futures positions, which resulted in a cash flow crisis. MG bailed out MGRM at a cost of more than $1 billion.

The risk management failure included failure to recognize funding risk and a mismatch between long and short positions.

James Lam, Enterprise Risk Management: From Incentives to Controls, John Wiley & Sons, Inc., 2003, pp. 12-13. [DA08659]

However, as illustrated in the example of MG and its subsidiary, MGRM, the risk management strategy used must be well thought out so that the risk management itself does not increase risk. Hedging is an example of a risk-management technique that can be used to manage downside risk resulting from market volatility, but it must be well designed and executed.

Intelligent Risk Taking

Successful organizations usually take risks to grow and increase profit. This type of risk can create a positive or a negative outcome. Decisions regarding new opportunities should be based on the organization's risk appetite, which is "the total exposed amount that an organization wishes to undertake on the basis of risk-return trade-offs for one or more desired and expected outcomes."[9]

A benefit of risk management includes providing the organization with a framework to analyze the risks associated with an opportunity and then to manage those risks. For example, an organization might consider whether to expand into a new product line. Risk management can help the organization decide if the potential rewards are greater than the downside risks. If the organization decides to go forward with the new product line, risk management can assist in designing a process to manage the associated risks.

Maximize Profitability

Risk management can help an organization achieve the optimal risk-adjusted return on capital. If an organization does not take enough risk, its capital may be underutilized. However, if an organization takes on too much risk, it may exceed its capability to withstand potential losses.

Risk management provides an organization information to evaluate the potential risk-adjusted return on its activities and to manage the risks associated with those activities. For example, an organization may consider whether to increase its dividend to shareholders versus investing in a new product. Although the same amount of capital may be considered for each option, the risk-adjusted return will not be the same. Risk managers can help the organization evaluate the risks and potential return of each option and their effects on the organization meeting its objectives.

Holistic Risk Management

Traditional risk management was conducted in silos within an organization. For example, a manufacturing organization would typically have the risk-management function manage hazard risk, the finance function manage financial risks such as credit and exchange-rate risk, the operations function manage operational risks such as equipment failures, and the information technology function manage cyber risk. This fragmented approach can miss critical risks to the organization and fails to provide senior management with a picture of the organization's risk portfolio and profile.

In the example of the manufacturing organization, the risk-management function may not be aware of the age and condition of equipment in the plants if this equipment is not insured. Operations may not be aware of the risks presented by some of the older equipment, and its request to senior management for a capital expenditure for new equipment may be turned down. A piece of machinery then malfunctions and causes a fire, rendering the plant unusable for a year and delaying production.

An integrated, holistic approach that manages risk across all levels and function within an organization presents a more complete picture of an organization's risk portfolio and profile. This picture allows for better decisions and improved outcomes for senior management. In the example of the manufacturing organization, if there was a complete understanding of the risks the equipment presented, senior management may have allocated capital to replacing the equipment instead of making a different investment.

Legal and Regulatory Requirements

Because of the failure of large organizations, such as Enron, and the financial crisis, legislation and regulation in the U.S. require public companies to use and report on risk management. In 2009, the Securities and Exchange Commission (SEC) approved a rule requiring corporate disclosure about risk. The Sarbanes-Oxley Act of 2002 requires both the management of public companies and their auditors to assess and report on financial risk and controls. The Dodd-Frank Act of 2010 requires that financial bank holding companies and certain other public companies have a risk committee, and at least one member of the committee must be a risk-management expert. Basel III and Solvency II in Europe also have risk-management requirements for financial firms and insurers.

One of the benefits of risk management is that organizations with effective risk-management programs will be able to comply with the recent regulatory requirements. Additionally, external auditors will be able to report on these risk-management processes to satisfy the reporting requirements.

Benefits for the Economy

The economy at both local and national levels incurs certain costs associated with risk and its management, as well as uncertainty about future losses. For example, a major hurricane can have widespread effects on the national economy, not just on individual organizations. Beyond a single loss occurrence like a hurricane, the cumulative effect of many smaller losses also adversely affects the national and local economies. For example, many retail stores in a shopping mall would suffer reduced sales if one of the anchor stores were closed because of an accidental loss. Depending on the magnitude of the loss and the length of time required for the anchor store to recover, the local community may sustain lost jobs, reduced tax revenue, and an overall reduction in the quality of life that was enjoyed when the mall was fully operational and thriving.

An economy's cost of risk management includes the resources consumed by or devoted to combating losses. For example, uncertainty throughout the economy causes organizations to be more risk averse. This in turn causes allocation of the economy's resources away from assets or activities that seem to be too risky so that the economy is not as productive as it might otherwise be. Consequently, average living standards can be reduced. Risk management benefits the entire economy by reducing waste of resources, improving allocation of productive resources, and reducing systemic risk.

Reduced Waste of Resources

Any economy possesses a given quantity of resources with which to produce goods and services. If an accidental loss reduces those resources, such as when a fire or an earthquake demolishes a factory or destroys a highway, that economy's overall productive resources are reduced. Risk management prevents or minimizes the waste of these productive resources.

Whenever there is a risk that accidental losses may occur, some portion of the economy's resources must be devoted to risk management. Allocating such resources is a cost because the resources cannot be used for other purposes that could promote growth. However, without such resources the economy would suffer even more in the event of an accidental loss.

Improved Allocation of Productive Resources

Risk management also improves the allocation of productive resources because, when economic uncertainty is reduced for individual organizations, allocating productive resources is improved. Risk management makes those who own or run an organization more willing to undertake formerly risky activities because they are better protected against the downside of risk. That greater willingness frees senior managers, workers, and suppliers of financial capital to pursue activities that maximize profits, returns on investments, and ultimately wages. Such a shift increases overall productivity within an economy and, on balance, improves everyone's average standard of living.

Reduced Systemic Risk

The Dodd-Frank Act, Solvency II, and Basel III all have the purpose of reducing systemic risk. If a systemically important organization does not have an effective risk-management program, that organization's risks can result in failure not only for the organization but also for the economy.

Not only did the financial crisis of 2008-2009 cause widespread negative consequences, such as recessions and high unemployment, it also caused many organizations to become risk averse and, therefore, afraid to invest their capital because of uncertainty. The benefits of risk-management programs at systemically important organizations include reducing systemic risk and reassuring investors and the public about reasonable risk taking that can provide economic growth.

RISK MANAGEMENT OBJECTIVES AND GOALS

A structured, logical, and appropriate program is the foundation on which an organization's entire risk management effort rests.

The support of an organization's senior management is essential to an effective risk management program. To gain that support, a risk management professional should design a program with objectives and goals that align with the organization's overall objectives. In some circumstances, a trade-off will be necessary between organizational objectives and risk management goals.

Risk Management Objectives

Each organization should align its risk management objectives with its overall objectives. Common objectives for risk management are balancing risk and reward and supporting decision-making. These objectives should reflect the organization's risk appetite and the organization's internal and external context. Objectives can emphasize certain goals, such as business continuity, protection of reputation, or growth. See the exhibit "Example of an Organization's Risk Management Objectives: Zurich's Enterprise Risk Management."

Example of an Organization's Risk Management Objectives: Zurich's Enterprise Risk Management

Mission and Objectives of Risk Management

The mission of Zurich's Enterprise Risk Management is to promptly identify, measure, manage, report and monitor risks that affect the achievement of our strategic, operational and financial objectives. This includes adjusting the risk profile in line with the Group's stated risk tolerance to respond to new threats and opportunities in order to optimize returns.

Our major Enterprise Risk Management objectives are to:

- Protect the capital base by monitoring that risks are not taken beyond the Group's risk tolerance
- Enhance value creation and contribute to an optimal risk-return profile by providing the basis for an efficient capital deployment
- Support the Group's decision-making processes by providing consistent, reliable and timely risk information
- Protect our reputation and brand by promoting a sound culture of risk awareness and disciplined and informed risk taking

© Zurich Insurance Company [DA08642]

Risk management objectives can emphasize certain goals in order to align the risk management program with the organization's risk philosophy and to help the organization meet its overall objectives.

Risk Management Goals

The risk management program should have goals to manage the risks that an organization will face. These goals should be incorporated into the risk management framework and the process designed to meet a particular organization's objectives. These are typical risk management goals:

- Tolerable uncertainty
- Legal and regulatory compliance
- Survival
- Business continuity
- Earnings stability
- Profitability and growth
- Social responsibility
- Economy of risk management operations

Tolerable Uncertainty

A typical risk management goal is tolerable uncertainty, which means aligning risks with the organization's risk appetite ("the total exposed amount that an organization wishes to undertake on the basis of risk-return trade-offs for one or more desired and expected outcomes").[10] Managers want to be assured that whatever might happen will be within the bounds of what was anticipated and will be effectively addressed by the risk management program.

Risk management programs should use measurements that align with the organization's overall objectives and take into account the risk appetite of senior management. For example, **value at risk (VaR)** can be used to analyze various financial portfolios with different assets and risk factors. VaR can be calculated quickly and easily to determine risk factor returns on a portfolio.

Value at risk
A threshold value such that the probability of loss on the portfolio over the given time horizon exceeds this value, assuming normal markets and no trading in the portfolio.

Legal and Regulatory Compliance

An important goal for risk management programs is to ensure that the organization's legal obligations are satisfied. Such legal obligations are typically based on these items:

- Standard of care that is owed to others
- Contracts entered into by the organization
- Federal, state, provincial, territorial, and local laws and regulations

A risk management professional has an essential role in helping the organization manage regulatory risk and the potential for liability.

Survival

For risk management purposes, an organization can be viewed as a structured system of resources such as financial assets, machinery and raw materials, employees, and managerial leadership. The organization generates income for its employees and owners by producing goods or services that meet others' needs. Many risks can threaten the survival of an organization. Traditionally, hazard risk, which could destroy an organization's facilities or cause injury to employees or customers, was viewed as the major threat to an organization's survival. Risk management professionals use techniques such as loss control and risk transfer to manage hazard risks.

However, the risks that organizations face are much broader than hazard risk. These risks include financial risks such as the value of assets (for example, the organization's stock value), competition, supply-chain risks, and technology (vulnerability to computer attacks and ability to keep pace with technological developments). Survival of an organization depends on identifying as many risks as possible that could threaten the organization's ability to survive and managing those risks appropriately. It also depends on anticipating and recognizing emerging risks, such as those related to climate change.

Business Continuity

Continuity of operations is a key goal for many private organizations and an essential goal for all public entities. Although survival requires that no risk occurrence (no matter how severe) permanently shut down an organization, the goal of continuity of operations is more demanding. To be resilient, an organization cannot interrupt its operations for any appreciable time. When an organization's senior management sets business continuity as a goal, its risk management professionals must have a clear, detailed understanding of the specific operations for which continuity is essential and the maximum tolerable interruption interval for each operation.

These are the steps an organization should take to provide business continuity and, therefore, resiliency:

- Identify activities whose interruptions cannot be tolerated
- Identify the types of accidents that could interrupt such activities
- Determine the standby resources that must be immediately available to counter the effects of those accidents
- Ensure the availability of the standby resources at even the most unlikely and difficult times

Earnings Stability

Earnings stability is a goal of some organizations. Rather than strive for the highest possible level of current profits (or, for not-for-profit organizations, surpluses) in a given period, some organizations emphasize earnings stability over time. Striving for earnings stability requires precision in forecasting fluctuations in asset values; liability values; and risk management costs, such as costs for insurance.

Profitability and Growth

An organization's senior management might have established a minimum amount of profit (or surplus) that no event should reduce. To achieve that minimum amount, risk management professionals must identify the risks that could prevent this goal from being reached, as well as the risks that could help achieve this goal within the context of the organization's overall objectives. For example, an organization concerned that a disaster preventing a key supplier from delivering parts will cause a supply-chain risk could develop a backup plan that might not only avoid this risk but also provide an opportunity to sell the backup parts to other companies.

An organization might measure profitability for its various units on a risk-adjusted basis. For example, high-risk investments require higher expected profits to account for the risk involved. By measuring profit on a risk-adjusted basis, the organization can efficiently deploy its capital.

Most organizations set goals for growth. Emphasizing growth—for example, enlarging an organization's market share, the size and scope of its activities or products, or its assets—might have two distinctly opposing effects on its risk management program: the reduction of the potentially negative consequences of risk versus supporting the organization's entrepreneurial risk-taking. Those effects depend on managers' and owners' tolerance for uncertainty. It is essential that risk managers understand growth goals in the context of senior management's risk appetite. Risk managers should also advise senior management of the potential risk in different growth strategies that the organization considers. For example, before the financial crisis, many financial organizations became highly leveraged in order to achieve growth. Although this strategy provided significant short-term growth, it ultimately caused the failure of several prominent firms.

Social Responsibility

Social responsibility is a goal for many organizations. It includes the organization's ethical conduct as well as the philanthropic commitments that the owners of the organization have made to the community and society as a whole. Beyond the altruistic interests of the organization's owners, many organizations justify pursuing the objective of social responsibility because such activities enhance the organization's reputation. Risk management professionals should consider an organization's societal commitments when developing its risk management program.

Economy of Risk Management Operations

Risk management should operate economically and efficiently; that is, an organization generally should not incur substantial costs for slight benefits gained. Risk management programs should be operated economically and efficiently.

One way to measure the economy of a risk management program is through benchmarking, in which an organization's risk management costs are compared with those of similar organizations. The Risk and Insurance Management Society (RIMS), a global organization of risk management professionals, conducts an annual benchmarking survey, in partnership with

Advisen, that organizations can use to compare their cost of hazard risk with other organizations in their industry. The benchmark survey combines expenditures for risk assessment, risk control, and risk financing, as well as the administrative costs of risk management programs. These costs are then related to revenue so that comparisons can be made between organizations and industry sectors.

Trade-Offs Among Goals

Although an organization's risk management objectives and goals are interrelated, sometimes they are not consistent with one another. For example, to obtain tolerable uncertainty, the risk management professional may have to advise senior management that a growth goal may not be achievable without adjusting either the risk appetite or the growth strategy. Legality and social responsibility goals may conflict with the economy of operations goal. Some externally imposed legal obligations, such as safety standards dictated by building codes, are nonnegotiable. Therefore, costs associated with these obligations are unavoidable. Other nonlegal obligations, such as charitable contributions, may be negotiable. However, while meeting social responsibility may raise costs in the short term, it can have worthwhile long-term benefits that make the costs acceptable.

In working with others regarding the trade-offs among organizational goals, a risk management professional must consider the likely effects of alternative risk treatment techniques and the costs and benefits of each. The interests and concerns of the various groups affected by an organization's risk management program should also be considered.

The way in which a risk management department is structured, how it cooperates with other departments, and how it handles communication of information are all relevant in enabling risk management professionals to respond to the goals and concerns of the organization and of affected parties.

BASIC RISK MEASURES

The physicist Lord Kelvin said, "To measure is to know" and "If you cannot measure it, you cannot improve it." Risk management requires measures of risk in order to both know the nature of risks and manage them to help an organization meet its objectives.

Although it is not possible to measure all the risks that could potentially affect an organization's ability to meet its objectives, quantifying those risks that can be measured should form the basis of risk assessment. Additionally, ongoing measurement provides benchmarks to monitor and evaluate the success of an organization's risk management program.

These are the basic measures that apply to risk management:

- Exposure
- Volatility
- Likelihood
- Consequences
- Time horizon
- Correlation

Exposure
Any condition that presents a possibility of gain or loss, whether or not an actual loss occurs.

Exposure provides a measure of the maximum potential damage associated with an occurrence. Generally, the risk increases as the exposure increases, assuming the risk is nondiversifiable. For example, if a bank underwrites mortgages to subprime borrowers, the credit risk increases as the amount of subprime mortgages increases because the exposure to default increases. An insurer that writes homeowners policies in coastal areas increases its exposure to windstorms as its coastal book of business increases. In these examples, the exposure can be quantified based on the amount of mortgages or policy coverage issued. Other exposures, such as the risk of a data breach or reputational risk, are not as easily quantified. However, even if an exposure cannot be readily quantified, there should be an attempt to qualitatively measure its effect on the organization to effectively manage the risk. For example, the effect of reputational risk could be measured in terms of its potential influence on an organization's stock price, customer loyalty, and employee turnover.

Volatility
Frequent fluctuations, such as in the price of an asset.

Volatility provides a basic measure that can be applied to risk. Generally, risk increases as volatility increases. Volatility can often be quantified. For example, VIX, the Chicago Board Options Exchange Market Volatility Index, provides a measure of stock market volatility. The volatility of energy prices, for example, is a major risk for many organizations. Utility companies, airlines, trucking companies, and other types of organizations that are highly dependent on fuel use strategies such as hedging to manage the risk associated with volatility in the price of oil. However, organizations that may be only indirectly affected by energy price volatility, such as retailers whose customers have less disposable income when gas prices rise, may also want to assess and manage this risk through inventory and pricing adjustments.

The likelihood of an occurrence is a key measure in risk management. The ability to determine the probability of an event mathematically is the foundation of insurance and risk management.[11] The term "likelihood" is used rather than "probability" because probability analysis relies on the **law of large numbers**. Although insurers and some other organizations can use the law of large numbers to accurately determine the probability of various risks, most organizations need to determine the likelihood of an occurrence without the benefit of a probability analysis of large numbers.

Law of large numbers
A mathematical principle stating that as the number of similar but independent exposure units increases, the relative accuracy of predictions about future outcomes (losses) also increases.

For example, a bank can probably determine and quantify the likelihood of default on a loan based on credit scores and other factors in the bank's extensive data. However, it would be more difficult for the bank to determine the likelihood of a cyber attack in which customer data are taken, resulting in liability. It would be even more difficult for the bank to predict the likelihood of a terrorist attack that could be catastrophic. Similarly, it is easier to determine the likelihood that certain risks undertaken to improve an organization's performance will have a positive outcome than it is for others. If a bank decides to issue credit to borrowers with slightly lower credit scores than its current borrowers, the bank probably has sufficient data to determine the likelihood of a positive outcome. However, if the bank decides to expand into a new and unfamiliar region, it may be more difficult to predict the likelihood of a successful outcome.

The relationship between likelihood and consequences is critical for risk management in assessing risk and deciding whether and how to manage it. Therefore, organizations must determine to the extent possible the likelihood of an event and then determine the potential consequences if the event occurs.

Consequences are the measure of the degree to which an occurrence could positively or negatively affect an organization. The greater the consequences, the greater the risk. In assessing the level of risk, the risk management professional must understand to the extent possible both the likelihood and the consequences. If there is a low likelihood of an occurrence with minor consequences, it may not be necessary for an organization to actively manage the risk. For example, a bank may decide that the likelihood of employees taking office supplies for personal use is low, and the consequences if this occurs are minor. Therefore, the bank may decide not to manage this risk.

Risks with high likelihood and minor consequences should usually be managed through an organization's routine business procedures. For example, there is a significant likelihood that a customer will be a few days late in making a loan payment. The consequences of payments that are a few days late are relatively minor. However, the bank should manage this risk through normal business procedures such as late charges or sending reminder notices if the payment is not received by the due date.

Risks with potentially major consequences should be managed even if the likelihood of their occurrence is low. For example, the risk of a fire at a bank, although unlikely, must be managed. Risks with significant likelihood and major consequences require significant, continuous risk management. For example, an international bank faces exchange rate risk that is likely and that could result in considerable losses. The bank may use hedging strategies and other techniques to modify this type of risk.

The **time horizon** of an exposure is another basic measure that is applied in risk management. A risk's time horizon can be measured in various ways. The time horizon associated with an investment risk, such as a stock or bond, can be determined by specified bond duration or by how quickly a stock can be traded. Longer time horizons are generally riskier than shorter ones. For example, a thirty-year mortgage is usually riskier for a bank than a fifteen-year

Time horizon
Estimated duration.

mortgage. A business strategy that involves purchase of real estate and building new structures is not as easily reversed as one that involves only a new advertising campaign and is therefore riskier.

Although an organization may have little or no control over the time horizon of a risk, the organization should evaluate and manage this risk just as it would manage other risks over which it has no control, such as weather-related risks. For example, diversification in financial investments can help manage the risks associated with the time horizon of those investments. An insurance company that matches the durations of its assets (investments) and liabilities (loss reserves) neutralizes the risks associated with time horizon. When real estate prices are highly volatile, an organization may defer an expansion strategy that involves a long time horizon, such as purchasing or building new facilities.

Correlation
A relationship between variables.

Correlation is a measure that should be applied to the management of an organization's overall risk portfolio. If two or more risks are similar, they are usually highly correlated. The greater the correlation, the greater the risk. For example, if a bank makes mortgage loans primarily to the employees of a local manufacturer and business loans primarily to that same manufacturer, the bank's loan risks are highly correlated. The failure of the manufacturing business would likely be catastrophic for the bank's entire loan book of business. If a manufacturer contracts with three major suppliers in the same earthquake-prone region in Asia, the manufacturer's supply-chain risks are highly correlated. Diversification is a risk management strategy that can reduce the risk of correlation.[12]

Risk management professionals should evaluate all of these measures and their overall effect on an organization's risk portfolio. Highly correlated risks with a high likelihood, major consequences, high volatility, and significant exposure over a long time horizon should be a key focus of risk management. The global financial crisis that started in 2007 resulted in part from the failure to recognize or address this type of risk. Subprime mortgages represented highly correlated risk to the same types of risky borrowers, large exposure with major consequences, high volatility due to fluctuations in their market value (and in the market value of the underlying real estate collateral), and a long time horizon because of their duration. Therefore, it is essential that organizations apply these basic measures when assessing their risk.

Apply Your Knowledge

An insurer decides to achieve growth in its auto insurance line by offering a discount to its homeowners insurance customers who also purchase auto insurance. Which of the following risk measures is or are likely to increase as a result of this business decision? Select all that apply.

a. Exposure
b. Volatility
c. Time horizon
d. Correlation

Feedback: a. and d. The insurer increases its exposure to its existing customer base by offering discounted auto insurance to its homeowners customers. The insurer also increases its risk correlation because it insures the same customers for both the homeowners and auto lines. Presumably, the insurer can manage its risk volatility through diversification, and its time horizon for risk is largely limited by the length of the auto and homeowners policy terms.

RISK CLASSIFICATIONS

Classifying the various types of risk can help an organization understand and manage its risks. The categories should align with an organization's objectives and risk management goals.

Classification can help with assessing risks, because many risks in the same classification have similar attributes. It also can help with managing risk, because many risks in the same classification can be managed with similar techniques. Finally, classification helps with the administrative function of risk management by helping to ensure that risks in the same classification are less likely to be overlooked.

These classifications of risk are some of the most commonly used:

- Pure and speculative risk
- Subjective and objective risk
- Diversifiable and nondiversifiable risk
- Quadrants of risk (hazard, operational, financial, and strategic)

These classifications are not mutually exclusive and can be applied to any given risk.

Pure and Speculative Risk

A **pure risk** is a chance of loss or no loss, but no chance of gain. For example, the owner of a commercial building faces the risk associated with a possible fire loss. The building will either burn or not burn. If the building burns, the owner suffers a financial loss. If the building does not burn, the owner's financial condition is unchanged. Neither of the possible outcomes would produce a gain. Because there is no opportunity for financial gain, pure risks are always undesirable. See the exhibit "Classifications of Risk."

In comparison, **speculative risk** involves a chance of gain. As a result, it can be desirable, as evidenced by the fact that every business venture involves speculative risks. For example, an investor who purchases an apartment building to rent to tenants expects to profit from this investment, so it is a desirable speculative risk. However, the venture could be unprofitable if rental price controls limit the amount of rent that can be charged.

Pure risk
A chance of loss or no loss, but no chance of gain.

Speculative risk
A chance of loss, no loss, or gain.

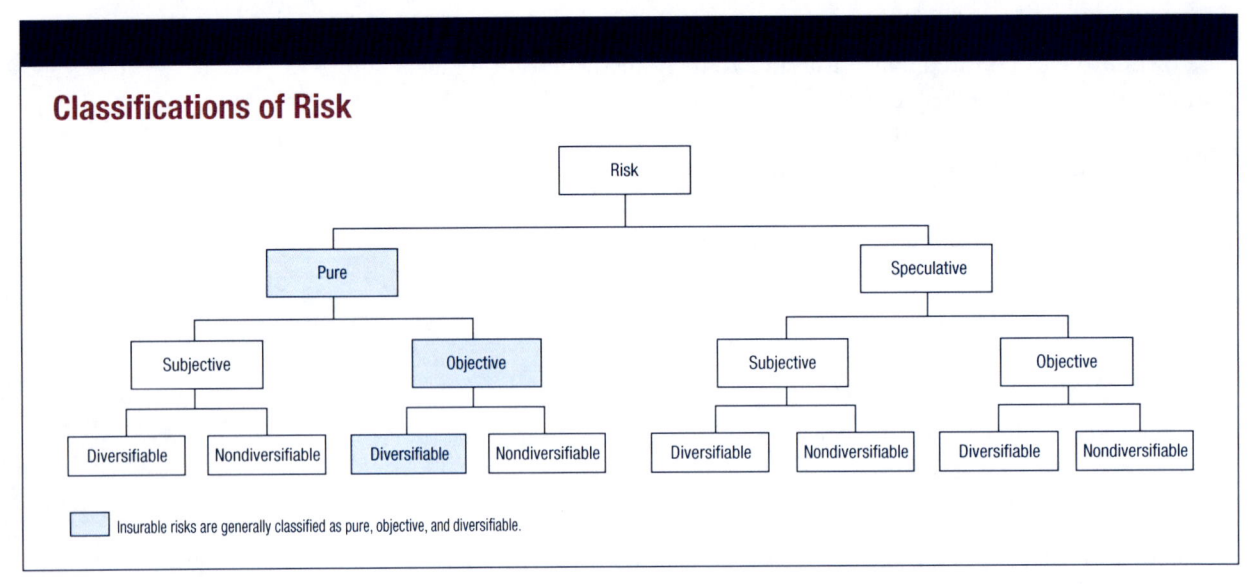

Classifications of Risk

```
                              Risk
                    ┌──────────┴──────────┐
                   Pure                Speculative
              ┌─────┴─────┐         ┌─────┴─────┐
          Subjective   Objective  Subjective   Objective
           ┌──┴──┐      ┌──┴──┐    ┌──┴──┐      ┌──┴──┐
      Diversifiable  Nondiversifiable  Diversifiable  Nondiversifiable  Diversifiable  Nondiversifiable  Diversifiable  Nondiversifiable
```

☐ Insurable risks are generally classified as pure, objective, and diversifiable.

[DA02396]

Certain businesses involve speculative risks, such as these:

- Price risk—Uncertainty over the size of cash flows resulting from possible changes in the cost of raw materials and other inputs (such as lumber, gas, or electricity), as well as cost-related changes in the market for completed products and other outputs.

- **Credit risk**—Although a credit risk is particularly significant for banks and other financial institutions, it can be relevant to any organization with accounts receivable.

Credit risk
The risk that customers or other creditors will fail to make promised payments as they come due.

Financial investments, such as the purchase of stock shares, involve a distinct set of speculative risks. See the exhibit "Speculative Risks in Investments."

Insurance deals primarily with risks of loss, not risks of gain; that is, with pure risks rather than speculative risks. However, the distinction between these two classifications of risk is not always precise—many risks have both pure and speculative aspects.

Distinguishing between pure and speculative risks is important because those risks must often be managed differently. For example, although a commercial building owner faces a pure risk from causes of loss such as fire, he or she also faces the speculative risk that the market value of the building will increase or decrease during any one year. Similarly, although an investor who purchases an apartment building to rent to tenants faces speculative risk because rental income may produce a profit or loss, the investor also faces a pure risk from causes of loss such as fire.

To properly manage these investments, the commercial building owner and the apartment owner must consider both the speculative and the pure risks. For example, they may choose to manage the pure risk by buying insurance or taking other measures to address property loss exposures. The speculative risk might be managed by obtaining a favorable mortgage and maintaining the property to enhance its resale value.

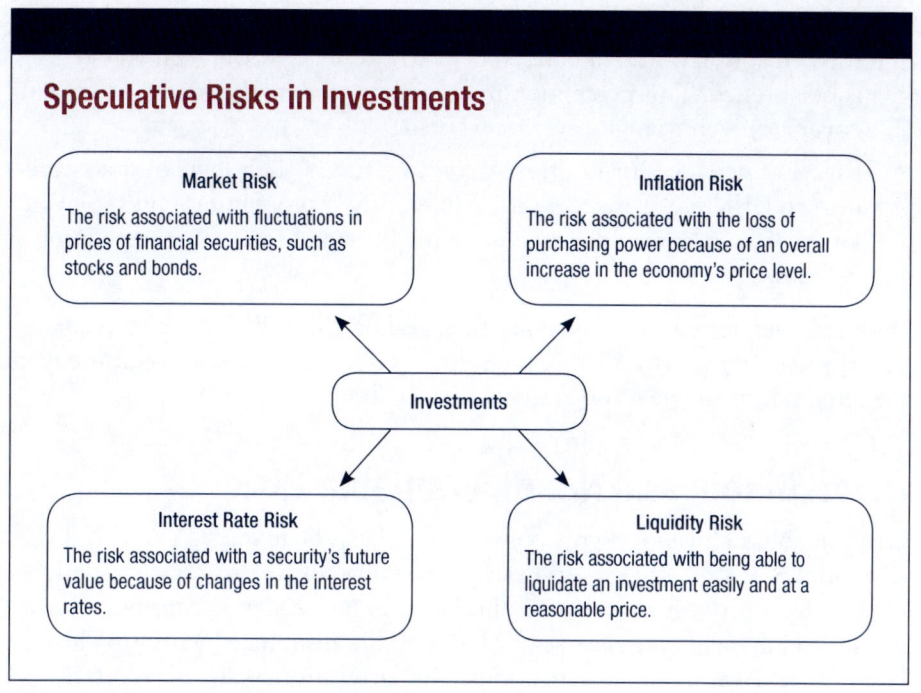

Speculative Risks in Investments

Market Risk
The risk associated with fluctuations in prices of financial securities, such as stocks and bonds.

Inflation Risk
The risk associated with the loss of purchasing power because of an overall increase in the economy's price level.

Investments

Interest Rate Risk
The risk associated with a security's future value because of changes in the interest rates.

Liquidity Risk
The risk associated with being able to liquidate an investment easily and at a reasonable price.

[DA02398]

Subjective and Objective Risk

When individuals and organizations must make a decision that involves risk, they usually base it on the individual's or organization's assessment of the risk. The assessment can be based on opinions, which are subjective, or facts, which are objective.

Because it is based on opinion rather than fact, **subjective risk** may be quite different from the actual underlying risk that is present. In fact, subjective risk can exist even where **objective risk** does not. The closer an individual's or organization's subjective interpretation of risk is to the objective risk, the more effective its risk management plan will likely be.

The reasons that subjective and objective risk can differ substantially include these:

- Familiarity and control—For example, although many people consider air travel (over which they have no control) to carry a high degree of risk, they are much more likely to suffer a serious injury when driving their cars, where the perception of control is much greater.
- Consequences over likelihood—People often have two views of low-likelihood, high-consequence events. The first misconception is the "It can't happen to me" view, which assigns a probability of zero to low-likelihood events such as natural disasters, murder, fires, accidents, and so on. The second misconception is overstating the probability of a low-likelihood event, which is common for people who have personally been exposed to the event previously. If the effect of a particular event can be severe,

Subjective risk
The perceived amount of risk based on an individual's or organization's opinion.

Objective risk
The measurable variation in uncertain outcomes based on facts and data.

such as the potentially destructive effects of a hurricane or earthquake, the perception of the likelihood of deaths resulting from such an event is heightened. This perception may be enhanced by the increased media coverage given to high-severity events.

- Risk awareness—Organizations differ in terms of their level of risk awareness and, therefore, perceive risks differently. An organization that is not aware of its risks would perceive the likelihood of something happening as very low.

Both risk management and insurance depend on the ability to objectively identify and analyze risks. However, subjectivity is also necessary because facts are often not available to objectively assess risk.

Diversifiable and Nondiversifiable Risk

Diversifiable risk is not highly correlated and can be managed through diversification, or spread, of risk. An example of a diversifiable risk is a fire, which is likely to affect only one or a small number of businesses. For instance, an insurer can diversify the risks associated with fire insurance by insuring many buildings in several different locations. Similarly, business investors often diversify their holdings, as opposed to investing in only one business, hoping those that succeed will more than offset those that fail.

Examples of **nondiversifiable risks** include inflation, unemployment, and natural disasters such as hurricanes. Nondiversifiable risks are correlated—that is, their gains or losses tend to occur simultaneously rather than randomly. For example, under certain monetary conditions, interest rates increase for all firms at the same time. If an insurer were to insure firms against interest rate increases, it would not be able to diversify its portfolio of interest rate risks by underwriting a large number of insureds, because all of them would suffer losses at the same time.

Systemic risks are generally nondiversifiable. For example, if excess leverage by financial institutions causes systemic risk resulting in an event that disrupts the financial system, this risk will have an effect on the entire economy and, therefore, on all organizations. Because of the global interconnections in finance and industry, many risks that were once viewed as nonsystemic (affecting only one organization) are now viewed as systemic. For instance, many economists view the failure of Lehman Brothers in early 2008 as a trigger event: highlighting the systemic risk in the banking sector that resulted in the financial crisis. Not understanding the systemic nature of risk posed by the securitization of mortgage obligations was at the root of AIG's risk management failure in writing a large number of collateralized debt obligations to back the securitizations—the high correlation and systemic risk were not recognized or managed.

Diversifiable risk
A risk that affects only some individuals, businesses, or small groups.

Nondiversifiable risk
A risk that affects a large segment of society at the same time.

Quadrants of Risk: Hazard, Operational, Financial, and Strategic

Although no consensus exists about how an organization should categorize its risks, one approach involves dividing them into risk quadrants:

- Hazard risks arise from property, liability, or personnel loss exposures and are generally the subject of insurance.
- Operational risks fall outside the hazard risk category and arise from people or a failure in processes, systems, or controls, including those involving information technology.
- Financial risks arise from the effect of market forces on financial assets or liabilities and include **market risk**, credit risk, **liquidity risk**, and price risk.
- Strategic risks arise from trends in the economy and society, including changes in the economic, political, and competitive environments, as well as from demographic shifts.

Hazard and operational risks are classified as pure risks, and financial and strategic risks are classified as speculative risks.

The focus of the risk quadrants is different from the risk classifications previously discussed. Whereas the classifications of risk focus on some aspect of the risk itself, the four quadrants of risk focus on the risk source and who traditionally manages it. For example, the chief financial officer traditionally manages financial risk, and the risk manager traditionally manages hazard risk. Just as a particular risk can fall into more than one classification, a risk can also fall into multiple risk quadrants. For example, embezzlement of funds by an employee can be considered both a hazard risk, because it is an insurable pure risk, and an operational risk, because it involves a failure of controls. See the exhibit "Risk Quadrants."

Organizations define types of risk differently. Some organizations consider legal risks as operational risk, and some may characterize certain hazard risks as operational risk. Financial institutions generally use the categories of market, credit, and operational risk (defined as all other risk, including hazard risk). Each organization should select categories that align with its objectives and processes.

> **Market risk**
> Uncertainty about an investment's future value because of potential changes in the market for that type of investment.
>
> **Liquidity risk**
> The risk that an asset cannot be sold on short notice without incurring a loss.

Apply Your Knowledge

The New Company manufactures electronic consumer products. The company's manufacturing plant is highly automated and located in the United States. However, it purchases components from three companies in Asia. The majority of its sales are in the U.S., but European sales represent a growing percentage.

Describe the types of risk New Company would have in each of the four risk quadrants.

Risk Quadrants

Hazard Risk
Arises from property, liability, or personnel loss exposures
- Property risk
- Legal risk
- Personnel risk
- Consequential loss

Operational Risk
Arises from people, processes, systems, or controls
- People risk
- IT risk
- Management oversight
- Business processes

Financial Risk
Arises from the effect of market forces on financial assets or liabilities
- Market risk
- Credit risk
- Price risk
- Liquidity risk

Strategic Risk
Arises from trends in the economy and society
- Economic environment
- Political environment
- Demographics
- Competition

Pure Risk | Speculative Risk

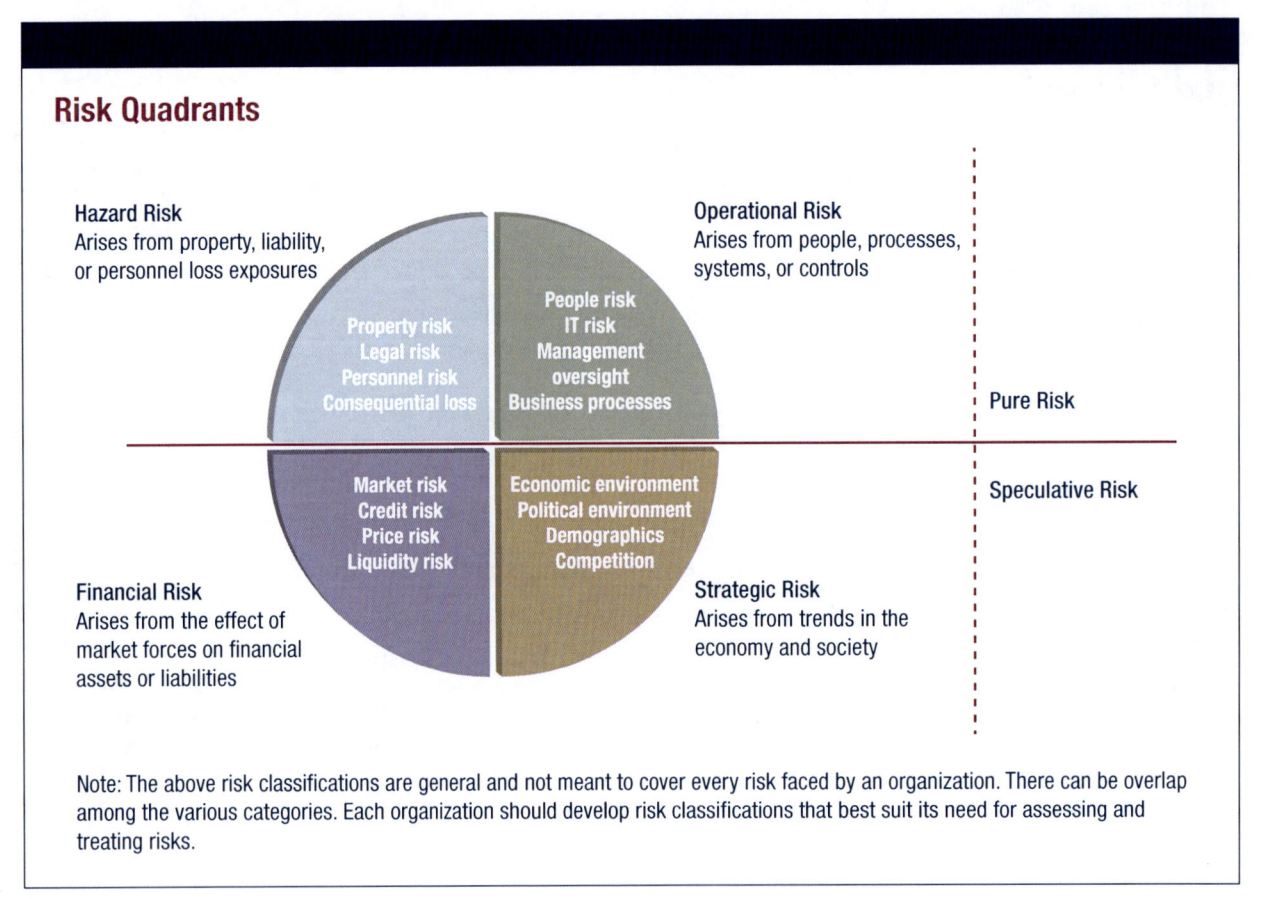

Note: The above risk classifications are general and not meant to cover every risk faced by an organization. There can be overlap among the various categories. Each organization should develop risk classifications that best suit its need for assessing and treating risks.

[DA08677]

Feedback: In the hazard risk quadrant, New Company would have property damage risks to its plant and equipment resulting from fire, storms, or other events. It would also have risk of injury to its employees and liability risks associated with its products.

In the operational risk quadrant, New Company would have risks from employee turnover or the inability to find skilled employees. It would also have business process risk related to how it manages its supply chain and information technology risk related to its automated manufacturing process.

In the financial risk quadrant, New Company would have exchange rate risk related to its European sales. It would also have price risk for raw materials and supplies.

Strategic risks include competition, economic factors that could affect consumer demand, and the political risk arising from countries in which the company's component suppliers are located.

ENTERPRISE RISK MANAGEMENT

The concept of enterprise risk management (ERM) emerged in the 1990s.[13] Since the failure of large corporations such as Enron and WorldCom and the financial crisis of 2008, financial regulators in the United States and Europe adopted the ERM concept, and it is now an integral part of various regulations.

Traditional risk management is concerned with an organization's pure risk, primarily hazard risk. The concept of ERM was developed in recent years as a way to manage all of an organization's risks, including operational, financial, and strategic risk. In practice, there is no clear dividing line between risk management and ERM, with the terms often used interchangeably.

ERM Definitions

The evolving similarity of the concepts of risk management and ERM is demonstrated in the International Organization for Standardization (ISO) 2009 definition of risk management in ERM terms: "coordinated activities to direct and control an organization with regard to risk."[14] The ISO definition of risk as "the effect of uncertainty on objectives" also reflects an ERM approach to risk and risk management. There are many definitions of ERM, and the exhibit highlights a few that are widely used. See the exhibit "Definitions of ERM."

The various definitions of ERM all include the concept of managing all of an organization's risks to help an organization meet its objectives. This link between the management of an organization's risks and its objectives is a key driver in deciding how to assess and treat risks.

Theoretical Pillars of ERM

Whether the source of a risk is financial, hazardous, operational, or strategic, risks managed separately are not the same as they are when managed together. Three main theoretical concepts explain how ERM works:

- Interdependency
- Correlation
- Portfolio theory

The silo type of management that is typical of traditional risk management ignores any interdependencies and assumes that a financial risk is unrelated to a hazard risk. Events are statistically independent if the probability of one event occurring does not affect the probability of a second event occurring. However, the traditional assumption of independence may not always be valid. When it isn't valid, the assumption may result in an inefficient treatment of an organization's portfolio of risks. For example, mortgage loans in different geographical regions may seem independent. However, the 2008 financial crisis revealed that there was actually a significant interdependency.

Definitions of ERM

Definition of ERM	Source
A strategic business discipline that supports the achievement of an organization's objectives by addressing the full spectrum of its risks and managing the combined impact of those risks as an interrelated risk portfolio.*	Risk and Insurance Management Society (RIMS)
The discipline by which an organization in any industry assesses, controls, exploits, finances, and monitors risks from all sources for the purpose of increasing the organization's short- and long-term value to its stakeholders.**	Casualty Actuarial Society (CAS)
Enterprise risk management is a process, affected by an entity's board of directors, management, and other personnel, applied in a strategy setting and across the enterprise, designed to identify potential events that may affect the entity, and manage risk to be within its risk appetite, to provide reasonable assurance regarding the achievement of entity objectives.***	Committee of Sponsoring Organizations of the Treadway Commission (COSO)

*Risk and Insurance Management Society, Inc. (RIMS), "ERM: An Overview of Widely Used Risk Management Standards and Guidelines," www.rims.org/resources/ERM/Documents/RIMS%20Executive%20Report%20on%20Widely%20Used%20Standards%20and%20Guidelines%20March%202010.pdf (accessed February 27, 2012).

**Casualty Actuarial Society: Enterprise Risk Management Committee, Overview of Enterprise Risk Management (Arlington, Va.: Casualty Actuarial Society: Enterprise Risk Management Committee, 2003), p. 8.

***Committee of Sponsoring Organizations of the Treadway Commission, "Enterprise Risk Management—Integrated Framework," September 2004, www.coso.org/documents/coso_erm_executivesummary.pdf (accessed February 28, 2012).

[DA08646]

Correlation increases risk, while uncorrelated risks can reduce risk to the extent that they provide a balance or hedge. For example, if all of an organization's suppliers are located in an earthquake-prone region in Asia, there is a significant correlation among suppliers in the organization's supply-chain risk.

The third concept that makes ERM work well is the portfolio theory. In an ERM context, a portfolio is a combination of risks. The portfolio theory assumes that risk includes both individual risks and their interactions. For example, an airline may experience an increased portfolio risk from increased fuel prices. This increase may affect not only the airline's costs but also consumer demand. The effect of rising gas prices on consumers' available disposable income could reduce the demand for air travel and constrict the airline's ability to offset its higher costs with higher prices. An airline that successfully hedged against rising oil prices may be able to take advantage of these circumstances to increase its market share.

Organizational Relationships

Under the traditional risk management organizational model, there is a risk manager and a risk management department to manage hazard risk. This traditional function mainly provides risk transfer, such as insurance, for the organization. Larger organizations typically include a claims management function. Many organizations include safety and loss prevention in the risk management department. See the exhibit "Example of a Traditional Risk Management Department."

In ERM, the responsibility of the risk management function is broader and includes all of an organization's risks, not just hazard risk. Additionally, the entire organization at all levels becomes responsible for risk management as the ERM framework encompasses all stakeholders.

The board of a public company has the ultimate responsibility for oversight of the organization's risks. The Dodd-Frank Act, which became U.S. law in 2010, requires that certain types of financial companies appoint board risk committees. A board risk committee may consist of the full board, the audit committee, or a dedicated risk committee. In addition, some public companies have formed an executive-level risk committee to assist the board in its risk oversight function. The executive-level committee might be chaired by a chief risk officer (CRO), who reports to both the chief executive officer (CEO) and the board risk committee. See the exhibit "Example of an ERM Governance Model."

As facilitator, the CRO engages the organization's management in a continuous conversation that establishes risk strategic goals in relationship to the organization's strengths, weaknesses, opportunities, and threats (SWOT). The stakeholders in the organization include employees, management, the board of directors, and shareholders. External stakeholders include customers, regulators, and the community.

The CRO's responsibility includes helping the enterprise to create a risk culture in which managers of the organization's divisions and units, and eventually individual employees, become risk owners. In the fully integrated ERM organization, identifying and managing risk become part of every job description and every project. Successful risk management of strategic objectives becomes a measure on all evaluations.

Example of a Traditional Risk Management Department

```
                    Risk Management
                        Director
                           |
        _____|_____
       |                   |                   |
  Insurance           Safety and            Claim
   Manager         Loss Prevention         Manager
       |              Manager                 |
       |          _____|_____            |
       |         |                 |           |
  Insurance    Safety         Industrial     Claim
 Administrator Engineer        Hygienist   Administrator
```

[DA01662]

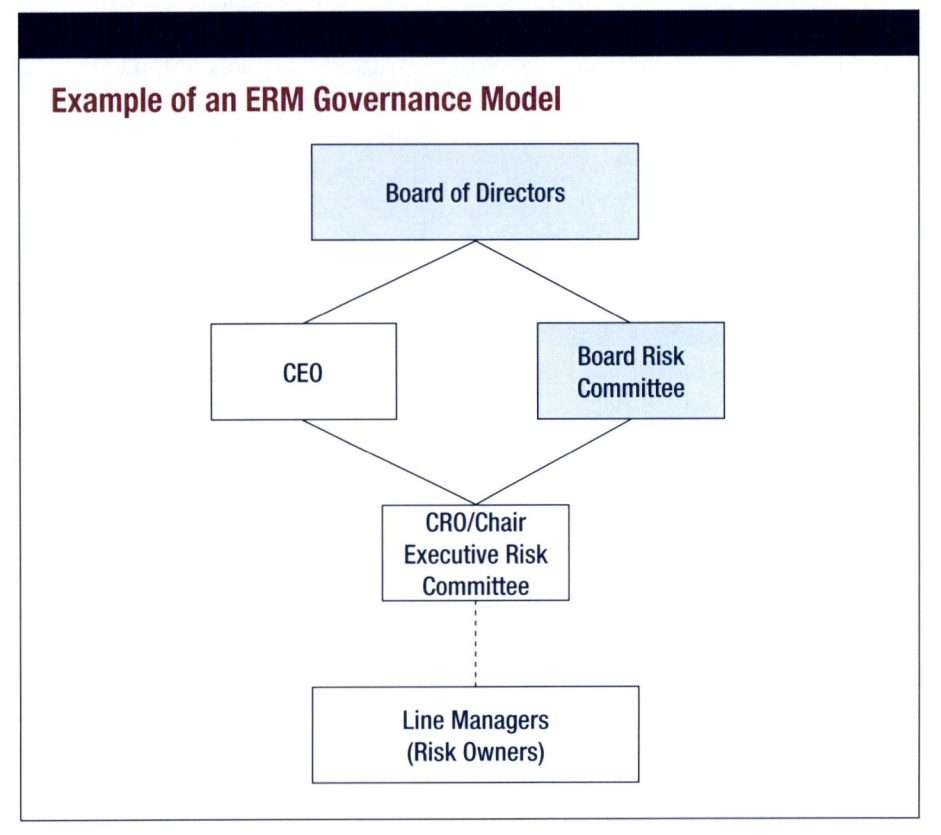

Example of an ERM Governance Model

```
              Board of Directors
                 /         \
              CEO        Board Risk
                         Committee
                 \         /
               CRO/Chair
              Executive Risk
                Committee
                    :
              Line Managers
              (Risk Owners)
```

[DA08658]

Implementing ERM

It is essential to have senior management's commitment in a mid-size to large organization to successfully implement an ERM program. The risk management professionals must have access to data from all organizational areas and levels to identify and assess the organization's risks. The risk management process to manage those risks must be integrated throughout the organization. To accomplish this, risk managers must have authority to make and enforce necessary changes, often against significant resistance.

Effective communication is essential to a successful ERM program. The CEO should meet with the senior managers of each organizational function to discuss the purpose and goals of ERM and the importance of management support. A task force comprised of representatives from each function to work with the CRO and/or risk professionals can help achieve buy-in from key stakeholders. It is important for risk professionals to provide communication to the various functions in addition to receiving communication from them. For example, operations managers may want more information about various types of risks, including hazard risks such as employee injuries or opportunity risks such as communities with high growth rates. It is also essential to find out the type of information the CEO and other senior managers need to understand the organization's risk portfolio.

An organization with a fully integrated ERM program develops a communication matrix that moves information throughout the organization. Communications include dialogue and discussions among the different units and levels within the organization. The establishment of valid metrics and the continuous flow of cogent data are a critical aspect to this communication process. The metrics are carefully woven into reporting structures that engage the entire organization, including both internal and external stakeholders.

Impediments to ERM

An impediment to successfully adopting ERM is technological deficiency. For ERM to succeed, people have to receive relevant information. Management needs information on all organizational risks in a timely and concise manner, for example, a "dashboard" look at the critical risks affecting the organization's ability to meet its objectives. Some risk management functions are able to use existing internet technology systems to produce this information, while others require new systems. The risk management information system (RMIS) of a broker or insurer could provide a starting point for a system to be tailored to the organization's ERM program.

Perhaps the single largest impediment to successful implementation of ERM is the traditional organizational culture with its entrenched silos. The risk management function traditionally purchased insurance and had claim oversight. The human resource function typically managed employee benefits and absence. The financial function managed prices; credit; investments, including hedges; and exchange rates. The operations function managed the core business operations, such as manufacturing or distribution. The safety function was separate or part of either risk management or operations. Information technology was a separate function or part of finance. Each of these functions typically had its own management structure.

In the new ERM culture, risk management is integrated throughout the organization. In many organizations, this involves operations managers taking responsibility for risk management within their areas of responsibility. For example, a bank branch manager would assume responsibility for speculative risk involved in growing the business and for financial risk, such as credit risk associated with the loans written by the branch. In large organizations, there may be a risk committee or task force headed by the CRO that includes representatives of each major function within the organization. To achieve accountability, many organizations charge back the gains and costs associated with risk management to the responsible function. For example, an operating division would be charged for the cost of hazard insurance and claims and also receive credit for new business or production improvements.

Apply Your Knowledge

An organization, with locations throughout the U.S., provides oxygen and related supplies to customers who need the oxygen for medical reasons. Oxygen is a flammable gas, and there is a risk of fire and explosion at these locations. Describe a traditional risk management approach to this risk versus an ERM approach.

Feedback: A traditional risk management approach would be to procure property, liability, and workers compensation insurance for this risk. Additionally, risk management might include the safety function to help prevent the occurrence and to provide an analysis of the cause if the event occurs. An ERM approach, in addition to risk transfer and safety, would assess additional risks such as those associated with the ability to provide a necessary medical product to customers, the organization's reputational risks in communities, the effect of demographics on the future of the business, and the ability to continue operations after a disaster.

SUMMARY

The understanding of risk and risk management has evolved beyond the traditional concepts dealing with risks of accidental loss. Although this type of risk remains a component of risk and risk management, it is only one aspect and is often interconnected with other risks in an organization's risk portfolio. The risk management environment is more global, complex, and interconnected than ever before. An organization's risk managers must develop risk management programs that reflect the evolving nature of risk, risk management, and the risk management environment.

An effective risk-management program provides benefits to an organization in meeting its goals and complying with regulations. Such programs also benefit the economy as a whole by helping to prevent business failures. Additionally, regulators who apply risk-management principles in their functions can help address systemic risk to ensure that risk provides economic benefits rather than negative consequences.

A risk management program provides a framework for planning, organizing, leading, and controlling the resources and activities of an organization to achieve the organization's objectives. The risk management program's goals should be aligned with those objectives. Because there may be inconsistency at times between an organization's objectives and risk management goals, trade-offs may be necessary to achieve the desired results.

Effective risk management should quantify risks and the results of risk management efforts to the extent possible. The basic measures that are applied to risk management include exposure, volatility, likelihood, consequences, time horizon, and correlation.

Classifying the various types of risk can help organizations manage risk. Some of the most commonly used classifications are pure and speculative risk, subjective and objective risk, and diversifiable and nondiversifiable risk. An organization's risks can also be categorized into quadrants as hazard risk, operational risk, financial risk, and strategic risk.

Traditional risk management took responsibility for hazard risk, typically arranging for risk transfer. ERM identifies operational, financial, and strategic risks in addition to hazard risks; develops an understanding of their relationships; and evaluates the potential effect of the risk portfolio on an organization's ability to achieve its objectives. ERM seeks to optimize a risk management strategy that is integrated into the entire organization.

ASSIGNMENT NOTES

1. Merriam-Webster's Collegiate Dictionary, 11th ed. (Springfield, Mass.: Merriam-Webster, Inc.), 2004.
2. Peter L. Bernstein, Against the Gods: The Remarkable Story of Risk (New York: John Wiley & Sons, Inc., 1998), p. 8.
3. www.businessdictionary.com (accessed February 13, 2012).
4. Casualty Actuarial Society, Enterprise Risk Management Committee, Overview of Enterprise Risk Management, 2003, www.casact.org/pubs/forum/03sforum/03sf099.pdf (accessed February 15, 2012).
5. World Economic Forum, Global Risks, 2011, Sixth Edition: An Initiative of the Risk Response Network (Geneva, Switzerland: World Economic Forum, January 2011), p. 41.
6. Bernstein, pp. 335-336.
7. Ben S. Bernanke, Speech At the Federal Reserve Bank of Chicago's Annual Conference on Bank Structure and Competition, Chicago, Illinois, May 15,

2008, www.federalreserve.gov/newsevents/speech/bernanke20080515a.htm (accessed February 15, 2012).

8. James Lam, Enterprise Risk Management: From Incentives to Controls, John Wiley & Sons, Inc., Hoboken, New Jersey, 2003, pp. 38-39.

9. "Exploring Risk Appetite and Risk Tolerance," RIMS Executive Report, Risk and Insurance Management Society, 2012, www.rims.org/resources/ERM/Documents/RIMS_Exploring_Risk_Appetite_Risk_Tolerance_0412.pdf (accessed June 1, 2012).

10. "Exploring Risk Appetite and Risk Tolerance," RIMS Executive Report, Risk and Insurance Management Society, 2012, www.rims.org/resources/ERM/Documents/RIMS_Exploring_Risk_Appetite_Risk_Tolerance_0412.pdf (accessed June 1, 2012).

11. Peter L. Bernstein, Against the Gods: The Remarkable Story of Risk (New York: John Wiley & Sons, Inc., 1998), p. 3.

12. James Lam, Enterprise Risk Management: From Incentives to Controls (Hoboken, N.J.: John Wiley & Sons, Inc., 2003), p. 26.

13. Gerry Dickinson, "Enterprise Risk Management: Its Origins and Conceptual Foundation," The Geneva Papers on Risk and Insurance, vol. 26, no. 3 (Oxford, England: Blackwell Publishers, 2001), p. 360.

14. International Organization for Standardization (ISO), ISO Guide 73 (Geneva, Switzerland: International Organization for Standardization (ISO), 2009), p. 2.

Direct Your Learning

Risk Management Standards and Guidelines

Educational Objectives

After learning the content of this assignment, you should be able to:

- Describe the general characteristics and elements of risk management standards and guidelines.
- Explain how ISO 31000 provides a framework and a process for an organization to manage its risks.
- Explain how the Committee of Sponsoring Organizations' Enterprise Risk Management—Integrated Framework provides a standard by which an organization can manage its risks.
- Explain how the Solvency II and Basel II and III regulatory standards apply to the insurance and banking industries, respectively.

Outline

Introduction to Risk Management Standards and Guidelines

ISO 31000 Risk Management—Principles and Guidelines

COSO Enterprise Risk Management—Integrated Framework

Solvency II and Basel II and III Regulatory Standards

Summary

Risk Management Standards and Guidelines

INTRODUCTION TO RISK MANAGEMENT STANDARDS AND GUIDELINES

To achieve its objectives, an organization should select a risk management standard that will align with its mission, goals, and structure.

An organization's risk management process should be designed, implemented, and maintained within the context of a recognized standard with a framework that will enable the organization to integrate risk management into its objectives, operations, and outcomes. Risk management professionals should understand the purpose, processes, and frameworks of the various accepted standards in the international risk community to provide guidance on the appropriate standard for an organization.

The Nature of Standards and Guidelines

A standard is a means of determining what something should be. It applies to rules, principles, or measures established by an authority.[1] To determine whether a product or process is effective, it is necessary to have a standard for comparison. Standards can be formal or informal. For example, an organization can develop its own standards over time, which may be communicated informally through the corporate culture. Formal standards are developed by recognized authorities or experts and apply to multiple organizations within an industry or within many different industries. For example, Six Sigma is a standard for manufacturing processes that can be applied to different types of organizations in various industries.

Although standards are developed by recognized authorities, they are voluntary for organizations. When a standard becomes a mandatory requirement of a governmental agency, it becomes a regulation. The use of a voluntary standard provides an organization with a method to evaluate a product or process as well as a common language to use in external discussions.

A **risk management standard** can be understood as defining the risk management process together with the framework that will be applied to the process. The **framework** is the structure that supports the organization's objectives and strategies. It provides the scaffold that an organization uses to construct and maintain its risk management process.

Various international organizations have developed risk management standards through working-group discussions and compilation of best practices.

Risk management standard
A document published by a recognized authority that includes principles, criteria, and best practices for risk management.

Framework
A structure, including elements such as concepts, methods, procedures, and metrics, that supports the risk management process.

Many of these standards provide a process for both risk management and internal financial controls. Most auditors of an organization's financial statements evaluate the organization's internal financial control throughout all areas and functions. Some standards—such as the Criteria of Control (CoCo), produced by the Canadian Institute of Chartered Accountants—apply only to audit controls for public and private companies in Canada. See the exhibit "Generic Risk Management Framework."

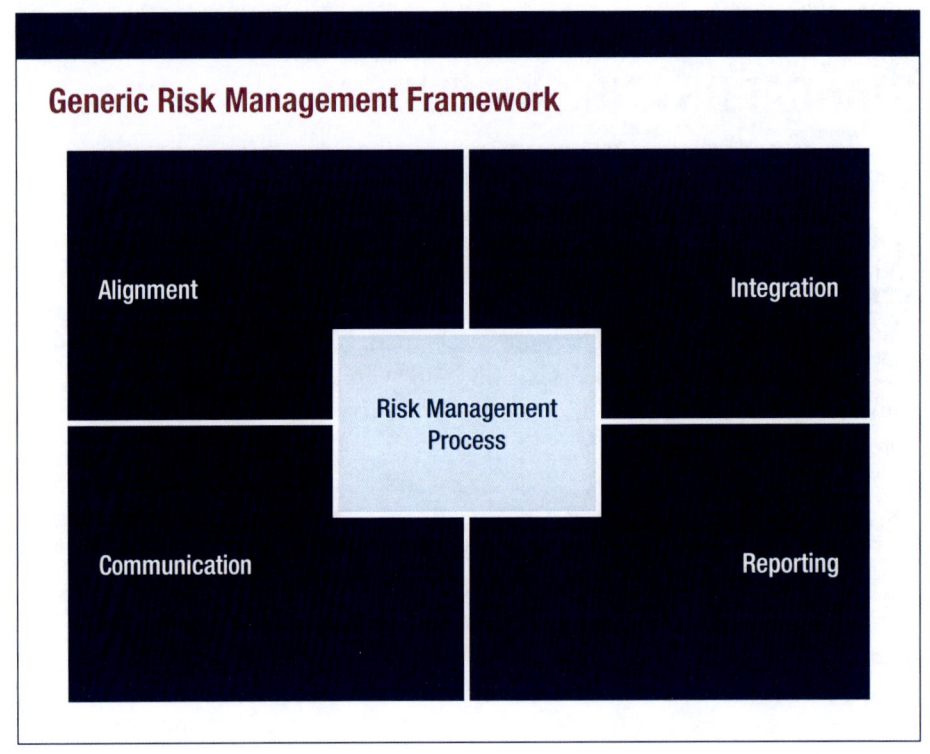

Generic Risk Management Framework

- Alignment
- Integration
- Risk Management Process
- Communication
- Reporting

[DA08626]

Common Elements of Risk Management Standards

To implement a successful risk management program, an organization must select the standard that will align with the organization's mission, values, objectives, and corporate structure. To make this selection, the responsible stakeholders in the organization should understand the different standards that are widely accepted and practiced.

All of the standards share a common purpose of helping organizations assess and manage risk. However, the differences among them can be profound. For example, the definition of risk varies between two major standards.

The major distinction between the International Standards Organization's ISO 31000 and the Committee of Sponsoring Organizations' (COSO) enterprise risk management (ERM) definitions of risk is significant. The COSO definition is "the possibility that an event will occur and adversely affect the achievement of objectives."[2] This definition reflects the traditional meaning of risk—namely, that it represents the potential only for adverse results. The ISO 31000 definition of risk is "the effect of uncertainty on objectives."[3] This definition reflects more recent thinking about risk, which encompasses the potential for positive as well as adverse results.

All of the standards and frameworks have these similarities:[4]

- Adoption of an enterprise approach
- Structured process steps
- Understanding of and accountability for defining risk appetite
- Formal documentation of risks in risk assessment activities
- Establishment and communication of risk management process goals and activities
- Monitored treatment plans

An organization may select one standard with a framework that can be adapted throughout its various functions. Alternatively, an organization may want to select different standards or guidelines for different functions. For example, a standard that focuses on internal controls may be best suited for an organization's financial function, while a broader standard may be the right choice for manufacturing operations.

For the risk management process to be implemented successfully, the standard(s) should be selected based on these criteria:[5]

- Alignment with organizational objectives
- Adherence to controls
- Need to meet regulatory requirements (compliance)
- **Risk governance**

Summary of the Major Standards and Guidelines

When an organization complies with a risk management standard, including a process and framework, it demonstrates that the organization is following best practices. This voluntary compliance helps prepare for aspects of risk management that are or may become compulsory. The risk management processes that organizations apply have received increasing regulatory and private scrutiny because of many well-publicized corporate risk events during the first decade of the twenty-first century. An increased magnitude and complexity of risk exists because of the interconnectedness of organizations and economies resulting from technology and globalization.

Frameworks and standards provide an organization with approaches for identifying, analyzing, responding to, and monitoring risks (threats and opportunities) within the internal and external contexts in which it operates. Compliance with the assumed best practices represented by the standards, including the frameworks, demonstrates that an organization is properly man-

Risk governance
Integration of the management principles governing the organization with the risk management process.

aging risk. An organization may use several risk management standards. See the exhibit "Risk Management Standards."

Risk management is an ongoing process of identifying and monitoring all of an organization's risk. For this process to be effective, an organization should conduct periodic self-assessments using an objective and consistent measurement tool with best practices elements and standards. The Risk and Insurance Management Society (RIMS) has developed a Risk Maturity Model (RMM) to provide such a tool. The RMM is not a standard, a prescribed process, or a framework. It focuses on seven essential attributes:[6]

- ERM-based approach
- ERM process management
- Risk appetite management
- Root cause discipline
- Uncovering risks
- Performance management
- Business resiliency and sustainability

Key drivers of each attribute are analyzed and measured to establish the maturity level. The organization bases its self-assessment on its performance in these attributes along a maturity continuum ranging from nonexistent at level zero to leadership at level five.

Apply Your Knowledge

The definition of risk as the effect of uncertainty on objectives is used in which of the following standards?

a. Six Sigma
b. ISO 31000
c. COSO ERM

Feedback: b. ISO 31000 defines risk as the effect of uncertainty on objectives.

A risk management standard includes which of the following? Select all that apply.

a. Process
b. Framework
c. Regulations

Feedback: a. and b. A risk management standard includes the risk management process and framework.

Risk Management Standards

Risk Management Standard	Description
ISO 31000: 2009	Provides an international standard for risk management as well as a generic approach to risk management applicable within any industry sector. Consists of three major parts: Principles—Rooted in risk management and designed to generate value and continuously scan and react to the environment Framework—Elements based on program design, implementation, and monitoring Processes—Emphasis on deliberative communication, context, risk assessment and treatment, and follow-up
COSO ERM	Defines risk management as a process, driven from an organization's board of directors, that establishes an organization-wide strategy to manage risk within its risk appetite. Focuses on threats to the organization and application of controls. Does not delve into details of risk management approaches and processes.
BS 31100	Published by British Standards Institution (BSI) as a code of practice for risk management. Provides recommendations for the model, framework, process, and implementation of risk management. Four primary goals: • Ensuring that an organization achieves its objectives • Ensuring that risks are managed in specific areas or activities • Overseeing risk management in an organization • Providing "reasonable assurance" on an organization's risk management

FERMA 2002	Adopted by Federation of European Risk Management Associations (FERMA).
	Recognizes that risk has both an upside and a downside.
	Standard has these elements:
	• Establishment of consistent terminology
	• Process by which risk management can be executed
	• Organized risk management structure
	• Risk management goals
OCEG Red Book	The Open Compliance and Ethics Group approach includes integration of governance, risk, and compliance processes.
	Relies on an integrated technology platform to identify and assess risk.
Basel II	Issued by the Basel Committee on Banking Supervision to provide recommendations on banking laws and regulations.
	Basel II is a regulation rather than a standard.
	Establishes risk and capital management rules.
Solvency II	Developed by the European Commission to provide regulatory requirements for insurance firms that operate in the European Union.
	Solvency II is a regulation rather than a standard.

[DA08627]

ISO 31000 RISK MANAGEMENT—PRINCIPLES AND GUIDELINES

An organization should reference a recognized standard when developing a risk management program. The International Organization for Standardization (ISO) provides an international standard, ISO 31000, that any organization can adapt to manage its operational, financial, strategic, and hazard risks.

For example, an electronics manufacturer with factories and suppliers in Asia and the United States would like to develop a risk management program for its supply-chain risks. As a recognized international standard, ISO 31000 could provide the framework and process for the organization's risk management program.

Background

ISO is a nongovernmental group. Its membership consists of the national standards institutes of 163 countries, some of which are government entities, while others are in the private sector. In 2009, ISO published ISO 31000:2009, Risk Management—Principles and Guidelines, an international risk management standard.

ISO 31000:2009, or ISO 31000, was developed largely from the Australian and New Zealand Risk Management Standard, AS/NZS 4360:1995.[7] ISO 31000 contains principles, a framework, and a process to manage risk; it can be tailored to meet the objectives of any organization. See the exhibit "ISO 31000 Standard: Risk Management Principles, Framework, and Process."

Scope

The ISO 31000 standard can be applied to all operations and most activities of the organization and to any type of risk, including hazard, operational, financial, and strategic risks. It also applies regardless of whether the risk has positive and/or negative consequences.

Although the standard is universally applicable, it is not intended to produce uniformity. On the contrary, its emphasis is on tailoring its process and framework to each organization.

Principles

ISO 31000 lists eleven principles of risk management. In general, these principles relate to uses, qualities, and application of effective risk management. Uses include protecting the organization's value, informing decision making, and dealing with uncertainty. The qualities of effective risk management include structure, timeliness, transparency, inclusiveness, dynamism, and responsiveness to change. Effectively applied, risk management is integrated into all of an organization's processes, is based on the best available information (and an understanding of the limitations of such information), and considers human and cultural factors.[8]

Framework

ISO 31000 includes a generic **risk management framework** that organizations can use to integrate the risk management process into their management and operational systems. The framework can be adapted to an organization's specific operations and objectives. A strong mandate and commitment from managers must be in place to implement a successful, company-specific risk management framework.

Designing a tailored framework begins with an evaluation of an organization's risk contexts, including all major factors both inside and outside the organiza-

> **Risk management framework**
> A foundation for applying the risk management process throughout the organization.

2.10 Risk Management Principles and Practices

ISO 31000 Standard: Risk Management Principles, Framework, and Process

Principles (Clause 3)

a. Creates value
b. Integral part of organizational processes
c. Part of decision making
d. Explicitly addresses uncertainty
e. Systematic, structured, and timely
f. Based on the best available information
g. Tailored
h. Takes human and cultural factors into account
i. Transparent and inclusive
j. Dynamic, iterative and responsive to change
k. Facilitates continual improvement and enhancement of the organization

Framework (Clause 4)

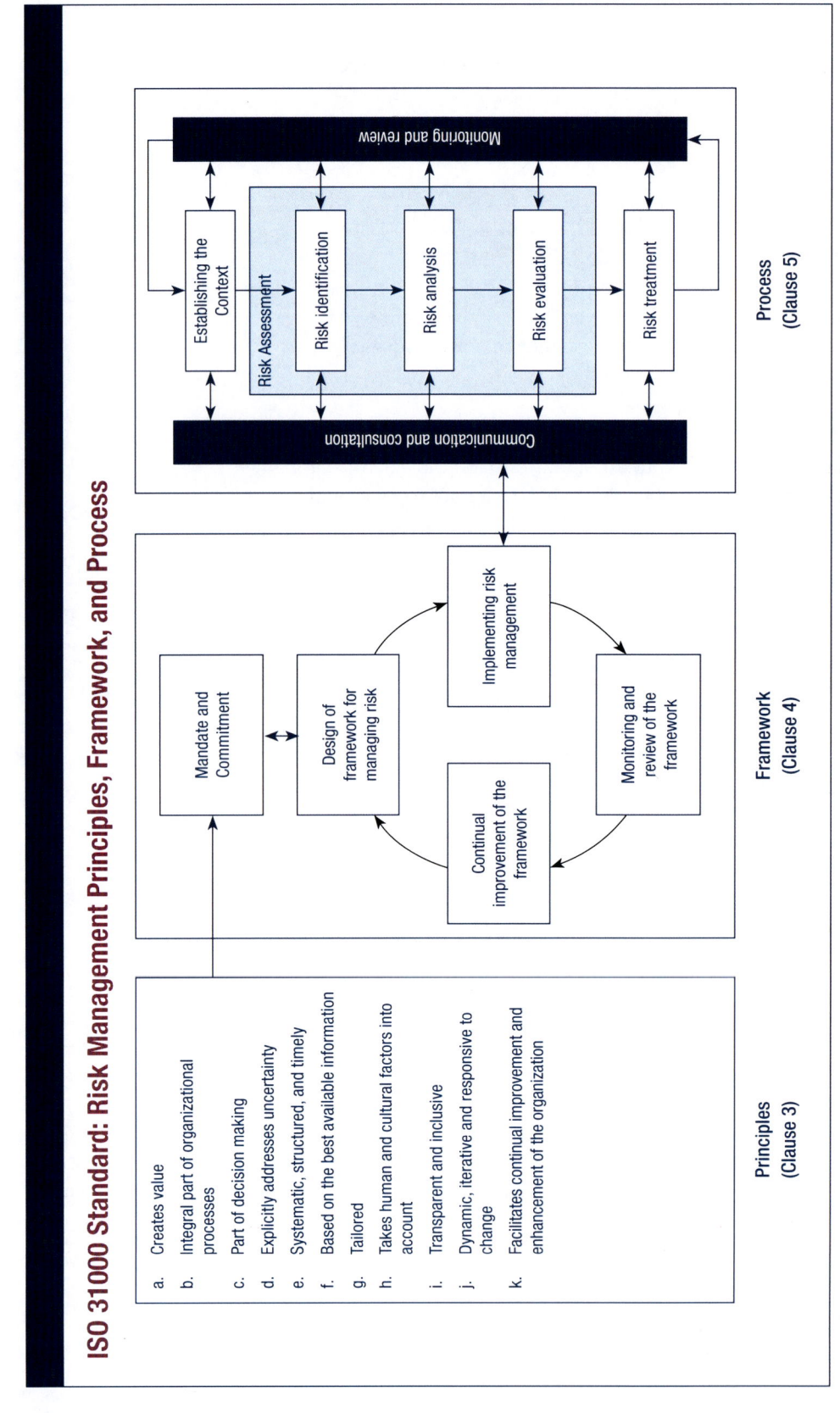

- Mandate and Commitment
- Design of framework for managing risk
- Implementing risk management
- Monitoring and review of the framework
- Continual improvement of the framework

Process (Clause 5)

Communication and consultation ↔ [Establishing the Context → Risk Assessment (Risk identification → Risk analysis → Risk evaluation) → Risk treatment] ↔ Monitoring and review

ISO 31000:2009, p. vii. Reproduced with permission from SAI Global Ltd under License 1207-c095. The standard is available for purchase at www.Saiglobal.com. [DA08629]

tion that affect its objectives and operations. For example, in January 2012, Apple's supply chain was disrupted by a fire at the factory of one of its major suppliers in China that caused injury and death to several skilled workers and required the plant, and the supply chain, to be shut down for a period of time.[9] An ISO 31000 framework would have assisted in identifying and addressing the related risks.

Based on a thorough understanding of its contexts, an organization can establish its risk management policy. This policy should address how the organization will identify risks and how it will measure, review, and communicate its risk management efforts. The framework also must incorporate accountability procedures for meeting risk management goals and must integrate risk management throughout the entire organization.

Appropriate resources should be available for designing and implementing the risk management framework. These resources should include staff with the necessary skills and any necessary equipment, such as that used for training or data management. Finally, the framework must establish internal communication and reporting methods and external communication with relevant stakeholders.[10]

Process

The ISO 31000 risk management process consists of several activities besides establishing the internal and external contexts of the organization and communicating: specifically, assessing risks, treating risks, and monitoring and reviewing the changes resulting from application of the process. Because the process is applied to different risks and functions of the organization, the specific context for each risk management process should be defined, in addition to the overall organizational context.

For example, an electronics manufacturer will have financial, marketing, manufacturing, distribution, and information technology functions. The manufacturing operations may have multiple plants in different countries with different suppliers. Therefore, particular risk management processes, such as the one for managing supply-chain risks, will need to be established in detail within the context of each country in which the organization does business, as well as within the overall context of the organization.

As part of establishing the internal and external contexts, an organization should define **risk criteria**. Risk criteria are based on measures used to evaluate the significance of the organization's various risks in relation to the organization's values and objectives as well as the legal and regulatory requirements to which it is subject. In establishing risk criteria, an organization considers factors such as possible consequences resulting from each risk, their likelihood of occurring, how they will be measured, and the organization's tolerance to the risk. An organization could use multiple measures for a single risk, such as its effect on both net income and reputation.

Risk criteria
Reference standards, measures, or expectations used in judging the significance of a given risk in context with strategic goals.

Risk Assessment

The ISO 31000 definition of risk assessment includes risk identification, risk analysis, and risk evaluation.

An organization should develop a comprehensive list of risks that can have either a positive or negative effect on objectives. From a traditional risk management viewpoint, this assessment has focused on hazard risks, which can result only in negative consequences. However, the risk management process has evolved for most standards, regulators, and organizations to include risks that have the possibility of negative or positive consequences. For example, an organization that chooses a plant location or supplier in a catastrophe-prone region, where labor costs are lower than in other areas and where currency exchange rates are favorable, is accepting risk with an expected positive outcome resulting from lower costs as well as risk with an expected negative outcome associated with supply-chain interruptions.

It is important to identify as many risks as possible, prioritizing key risks in terms of their effect on the organization's objectives. It is also essential that both line management and executive management are involved in identifying risks, as unidentified, or missed, risks will not be analyzed or addressed in the risk management process and, therefore, pose a greater threat of damage.

After risks are identified, the next step is analysis—quantitative, qualitative, or a combination of the two. This analysis includes determining the level of risk and its potential effects on the organization. Both the tangible and intangible effects of consequences should be considered.

The third step in risk assessment is evaluating the organization's risks. This step involves applying the selected risk criteria to the levels of risk determined during the analysis. The subsequent evaluation will allow decisions to be made regarding risk treatment.

Risk Treatment

Risk treatment is the ongoing process of deciding on an option for modifying risk and whether the residual level of risk is acceptable, selecting a new risk treatment if the current one is not effective, and then repeating this assessment.

In treating risks, an organization may choose to avoid, retain, or transfer all or part of a risk. Risks may also be treated by eliminating their sources, altering the likelihood that an event will result from a risk, or changing the consequences of events resulting from risk. For risks that present the possibility of positive outcomes, an organization may choose to assume a risk or even increase it. Selection of the risk treatment should include determining those within and outside the organization who are accountable, as well as performance measures that will be used in ongoing assessments of the risk treatment.

Risk treatment options can be applied individually or in combination following a deliberate sequence. For example, an organization may find it economical to alter the likelihood of an event and its consequences before transferring the risk.

Many organizations experienced severe supply-chain disruptions when they could not receive parts manufactured in Japan after the devastating earthquake and tsunami in 2011. As a result, an electronics manufacturer might now choose suppliers that are not located in earthquake-prone regions to eliminate the source of this risk.

Risk Monitoring and Review

Monitoring and reviewing both internal and external changes and how these changes affect risks and their treatment should be a planned part of the risk management process. Monitoring should also include recording the assessments and reporting them internally and externally, as needed; determining the frequency, distribution, and method of reporting is an integral part of developing the risk management process.

COSO ENTERPRISE RISK MANAGEMENT—INTEGRATED FRAMEWORK

The Committee of Sponsoring Organizations (COSO) is a voluntary organization in the private sector. COSO includes the Institute of Internal Auditors (IIA), the American Accounting Association (AAA), the American Institute of Certified Public Accountants (AICPA), Financial Executives International (FEI), and the Association of Accountants and Financial Professionals in Business (IMA).

In 2004, COSO issued a risk management standard. There are many similarities between COSO 2004 and other risk management standards, such as ISO 31000. A major difference, however, between COSO 2004 and other standards is that the COSO framework's components do not address root cause analysis. Although the framework can be applied to all the risks of an organization, the origin of the COSO standards is in financial risk.

Additionally, COSO defines the term "risk" somewhat differently than does ISO 31000. COSO defines risk as the possibility that an event will occur and adversely affect an organization's objectives, whereas ISO 31000 defines risk as "the effect of uncertainty on objectives." However, COSO does reflect in its framework for risk management that an event can have a positive as well as a negative effect.

An organization decides on the risk management standard(s) to use for all or part of the organization's risks. A bank, for example, might select COSO 2004 as its risk management standard because of this standard's historical focus on financial controls and its robust emphasis on control activities in the COSO

Enterprise Risk Management—Integrated Framework and risk management process.

Additionally, internal auditors, primarily in the United States, frequently use COSO 2004 as a standard when evaluating an organization's risk management. Internal auditors do not select or implement an organization's risk management standard. However, auditors have an important role in monitoring, reviewing, and evaluating the risk management process. Auditors can advise an organization on how well controls are working in different areas of operations and recommend improvements.

Background

COSO was organized in 1985 to sponsor the National Commission on Fraudulent Financial Reporting. This was an independent private-sector initiative to study the factors that lead to fraudulent financial reporting. The initiative developed recommendations for public companies and their independent auditors, the U.S. Securities and Exchange Commission and other regulators, and educational institutions.[11]

In 1992, COSO published a framework for the evaluation of internal control systems titled "Internal Control—Integrated Framework." This was updated in 2004 to be the Enterprise Risk Management—Integrated Framework, expanding beyond internal controls to include strategic objectives. A major reason for the development of this framework was to meet the requirements of the U.S.'s Sarbanes-Oxley Act.

Framework

The COSO Enterprise Risk Management—Integrated Framework is designed to help an organization achieve its objectives in four categories:

- Strategic—high-level goals, aligned with and supporting its mission
- Operations—effective and efficient use of its resources
- Reporting—reliability of reporting
- Compliance—compliance with applicable laws and regulations

There are eight interrelated components of the COSO framework that should be integrated within an organization's risk management process:

- Internal environment—Determine risk management philosophy and risk appetite, integrity and ethical values, and the operating environment. A board of directors is an important part of the internal environment with influence on the other aspects of the environment. In this component of the risk management process, senior management aligns the people, pro-

cesses, and infrastructure to make it possible for the organization to stay within its risk appetite.
- Objective setting—Align risk management objectives with the organization's mission and risk appetite. Objectives must be determined before management can identify the events that might affect their achievement.
- Event identification—Identify internal and external events that affect achievement of objectives, and distinguish between negative risk and opportunity risk. External events include economic, political, social, and technological elements. Internal factors include management decisions, people, infrastructure, processes, and technology.
- Risk assessment—Analyze risks, considering likelihood and impact. Likelihood is the possibility that a given event will occur. Impact is the effect of an event if it does occur. Risk assessment is first applied to **inherent risk**. After the development of risk responses, **residual risk** is determined.
- Risk response—Select how to respond to the risks identified, for example, by avoidance, reduction, or transfer.
- Control activities—Establish policies and procedures to carry out effective risk responses. Control activities are the policies and procedures to determine that risk responses are performed correctly.
- Information and communication—Use effective communication that flows down, across, and up the organization. An organization should use both historical and current data to have an effective risk management program.
- Monitoring—Make modifications through ongoing monitoring of the risk management process. An organization may use both internal and independent evaluations to monitor its risk management.

Inherent risk
Risk to an entity apart from any action to alter either the likelihood or impact of the risk.

Residual risk
Risk remaining after actions to alter the risk's likelihood or impact.

COSO states that "risk management is not strictly a serial process, where one component affects only the next. It is a multidirectional…process in which almost any component can and does influence another."[12] The process should be applied across all four levels of an organization: entity, division, business unit, and subsidiary. See the exhibit "COSO Risk Management: Relationship of Objectives and Components."

In the example of a bank, the organization would identify its strategic objectives to include return on capital, profit, and growth. The bank's operational objectives would support its strategic objectives in areas such as loan activity, customer growth, acquisitions, and expansion. The reporting and compliance objectives would focus on meeting regulatory requirements. The bank's managers would then apply the eight components of the COSO risk management framework across all of the organization's levels to align the bank's operations with its risk appetite and strategic objectives.

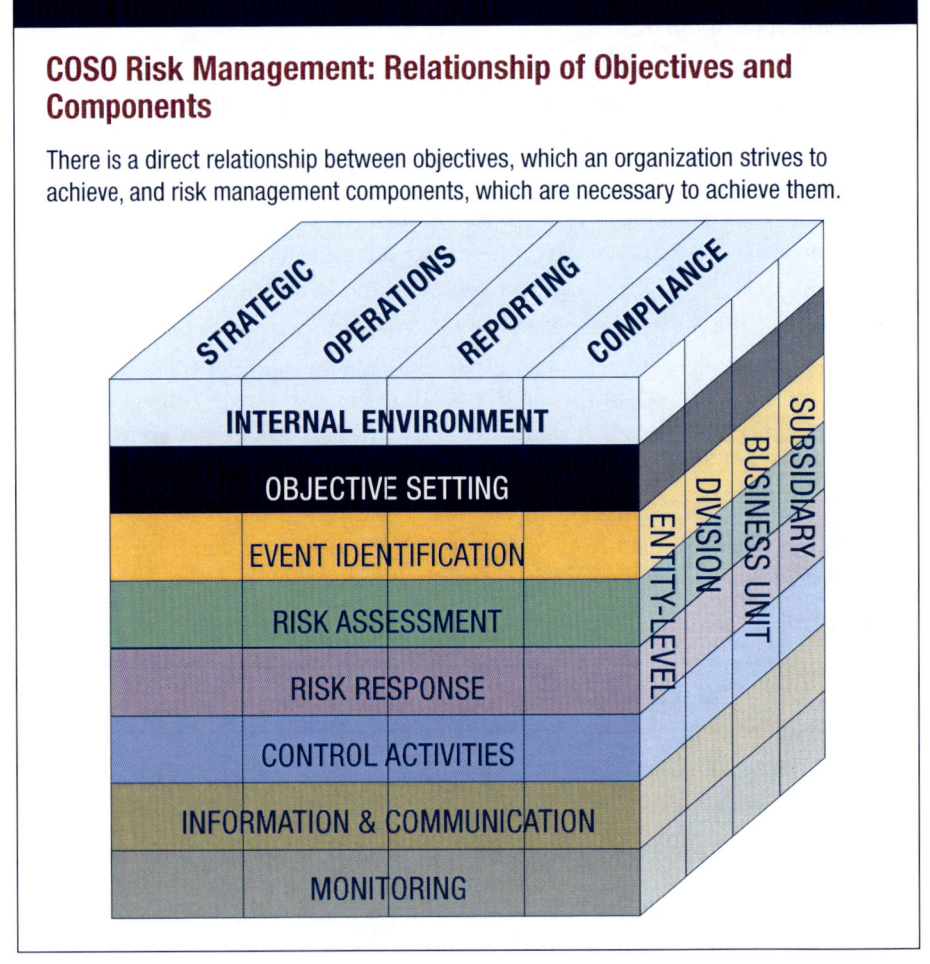

COSO Risk Management: Relationship of Objectives and Components

There is a direct relationship between objectives, which an organization strives to achieve, and risk management components, which are necessary to achieve them.

Copyright, 2004, Committee of Sponsoring Organizations of the Treadway Commission. All rights reserved. Reprinted with permission. [DA07300]

Control Activities

Section 404 of the Sarbanes-Oxley Act states that public companies are required to publish information in their annual reports regarding the scope and adequacy of their internal control structure and procedures for financial reporting. Additionally, the companies are required to assess the effectiveness of these internal controls and procedures. The registered accounting firm that provides an audit of the financial statement is required to attest to and report on the assessment of the effectiveness of the internal control structure and procedures for financial reporting.

Because COSO 2004 historically focused on financial controls and developed its risk management framework in the context of internal audits related to compliance with Sarbanes-Oxley, control activities are a key feature of this standard in comparison with other risk management standards.

Control activities are policies and procedures applied to each of the four categories of objectives—strategic, operations, reporting, and compliance. Overlap may exist in how controls relate to objectives and areas of operation. The most important function of a control is its role in achieving its objective. For example, a control activity may have the objective of ensuring that all bank loans conform to the bank's guidelines. The organization may apply this control activity across regional divisions and branch offices.

Control activities typically have two parts. The first part is the policy that states what should be done, and the second part is the procedure to accomplish the policy. For example, a policy states that all bank loans should conform to guidelines. The procedure is to enter all loan information into the bank's computer system and produce daily reports for branch managers, weekly reports for regional managers, and monthly reports for the risk manager.

The risk management process should be monitored to determine the effectiveness of control activities in meeting objectives. There are two types of monitoring. The first type is ongoing regular monitoring by an organization's management. For example, the percentage of nonconforming loans is compared to the guidelines on a daily basis. The second type is periodic evaluation, often by internal auditors. Internal auditors can identify areas where control activities are deficient and make recommendations to improve them.

Apply Your Knowledge

An internal auditor discovers that 17 percent of a bank's loans do not conform to the bank's guidelines. The control objective is that all loans conform to guidelines. The procedure includes entering information regarding each loan into the computer and producing reports for managers. Which one of the following is the auditor likely to recommend?

a. Review the objective
b. Review the procedure
c. Review both the objective and the procedure

Feedback: c. The auditor is likely to recommend a review of both the objective and the procedure. Has the bank changed its risk appetite? If so, the objective and loan guidelines may need to be revised. The bank's managers may want to do further review of the nonconforming loans and evaluate the effect on the bank's performance objectives. Additionally, the procedures regarding the quality of the information entered into the computer and how the reports are prepared and analyzed should be reviewed.

SOLVENCY II AND BASEL II AND III REGULATORY STANDARDS

Many risk management standards, such as ISO 31000, are voluntary. Solvency II and Basel II and III are regulatory standards that many countries' governments have adopted as required standards for financial organizations.

Solvency II is a new regulatory standard for insurers in the European Union (EU) to establish principles for risk management and consistency in regulation. Basel III is the new regulatory standard for the global banking industry that sets out risk management principles designed to prevent systemic risk from creating another financial crisis similar to the one that occurred in 2007.

Solvency II

Solvency I, adopted by the member countries of the European Union and the United Kingdom in the early 1970s, provided some harmonization of insurance regulation across Europe. It focused on capital adequacy and did not include any standards for risk management or governance within individual firms.

Solvency II will be adopted by all twenty-seven EU member states, plus three of the European Economic Area (EEA) countries. As a consistent European standard, Solvency II should reduce the likelihood of an insurer's insolvency, market disruption, and consumer loss. It should also make it easier for firms to do business across the EU, as the current patchwork of varying local standards (established to supplement Solvency I) will be replaced by more consistent requirements.

Solvency II aims to achieve consistency across Europe in these areas:

- Market-consistent balance sheets
- **Risk-based capital**
- Own risk and solvency assessment (ORSA)
- Senior management accountability
- Supervisory assessment

Solvency II contains three supporting pillars:

- Pillar 1—This pillar covers all the financial requirements and aims to ensure firms are adequately capitalized with risk-based capital. It includes the use of internal models that, subject to stringent standards and prior supervisory approval, enable a firm to calculate its regulatory capital requirements using its own internal **modeling**.
- Pillar 2—This pillar imposes higher standards of risk management and governance within an organization and gives supervisors greater powers to challenge their firms on risk management issues. The ORSA requires a

---

Risk-based capital (RBC)
Amount of capital an insurer needs to support its operations, given the insurer's risk characteristics.

Modeling
In data analysis, a system of calculating known outcomes based on current data and then applying these calculations to new data to predict future outcomes.

firm to undertake its own forward-looking self-assessment of its risks, corresponding capital requirements, and adequacy of capital resources.
- Pillar 3—This pillar aims for greater levels of transparency for supervisors and the public. There is a private annual report by insurers to supervisors and a public solvency and financial condition report that increases the required level of disclosure.

European insurers are required to have an effective risk management system, conduct their own risk and solvency assessment, have an effective internal control system in place, and provide for an effective internal audit function and an effective actuarial function.

Solvency II presents a dramatic change in an insurer's risk culture and management. It requires a strong link between decision-making and quantitative risk measurement. Insurers that can demonstrate a strong risk management standard, including framework, process, and monitoring, may have an opportunity to reduce capital requirements.[13]

The most immediate effect is on United States insurers that have subsidiaries in European countries that will be subject to Solvency II. It is expected that U.S. insurers with no European subsidiaries will be granted regulatory equivalency status under Solvency II.

Longer-term effects, however, are expected to be felt across the entire U.S. insurance industry. The National Association of Insurance Commissioners (NAIC) has a working group devoted to modernization and harmonization of U.S. and European regulation. The NAIC group is considering, for example, adopting guidelines from Pillar 1 of Solvency II, such as methods for regulators to review insurers' internal models. The NAIC is also discussing ORSA requirements for U.S. insurers.[14]

Basel II and III

The Basel Committee was established by the central-bank Governors of the Group of Ten countries in 1974. The Committee's members come from Argentina, Australia, Belgium, Brazil, Canada, China, France, Germany, Hong Kong SAR, India, Indonesia, Italy, Japan, Korea, Luxembourg, Mexico, the Netherlands, Russia, Saudi Arabia, Singapore, South Africa, Spain, Sweden, Switzerland, Turkey, the United Kingdom, and the U.S. Countries are represented by their central bank and/or the authority with formal responsibility for banking supervision. The Committee formulates standards that member and other nations may adopt as regulation.

In 1999, the Committee issued a proposal for a revised Capital Adequacy Framework, which consists of three pillars:
- Minimum capital requirements—Refinement of the standardized rules in the 1988 Accord that set out specific weights for different types of credit risk, such as government bonds and mortgages. Basel II offered more

sophisticated alternatives for evaluating credit risk, such as evaluations of a borrower's credit rating. The minimum capital standard, however, remained at 8 percent.

- Supervisory—Review of an institution's internal assessment process and capital adequacy.
- Disclosure—Effective use of disclosure to strengthen market discipline and complement supervisory efforts. The Basel Committee states that "Market discipline imposes strong incentives on banks to conduct their business in a safe, sound and efficient manner, including an incentive to maintain a strong capital base as a cushion against potential future losses arising from risk exposures."[15]

Following extensive interaction with banks, industry groups, and supervisory authorities that are not members of the Committee, the revised framework was issued on June 26, 2004, as Basel II.

Basel III is a revised standard in response to the financial crisis that began in 2007. The Basel Committee on Banking Supervision developed this standard to address both the risk of individual organizations and systemic risk. Basel III is a comprehensive set of reform measures to strengthen the regulation, supervision, and risk management of the banking sector. These are the goals of the reform measures:

- Improve the banking sector's ability to absorb shocks arising from financial and economic stress, whatever the source
- Improve risk management and governance
- Strengthen banks' transparency and disclosures

In 2011, the Basel Committee published *Principles for the Sound Management of Operational Risk*. This paper discusses the evolution of risk management standards, including the types of frameworks implemented since Basel II.

The Basel Committee states that risk management encompasses these processes:

- Identifying risks to a bank
- Measuring exposures to those risks where possible
- Ensuring that an effective capital planning and monitoring program is in place
- Monitoring risk exposures and corresponding capital needs on an ongoing basis
- Taking steps to control or mitigate risk exposures, and reporting to senior management and the board on the bank's risk exposures and capital positions.

Internal controls are typically embedded in a bank's day-to-day business and are designed to ensure, to the extent possible, that bank activities are efficient and effective; information is reliable, timely, and complete; and the bank is compliant with applicable laws and regulations.

The Basel III risk management standard consists of eleven principles:[16]

- Principle 1—The board of directors should take the lead in establishing a strong risk management culture. The board of directors and senior management should establish a corporate culture that is guided by strong risk management and that supports and provides appropriate standards and incentives for professional and responsible behavior.
- Principle 2—Banks should develop, implement, and maintain a framework that is fully integrated into the bank's overall risk management processes. The framework for operational risk management chosen by an individual bank will depend on a range of factors, including its nature, size, complexity, and risk profile.
- Principle 3—The board of directors should establish, approve, and periodically review the framework. The board of directors should oversee senior management to ensure that the policies, processes, and systems are implemented effectively at all decision levels.
- Principle 4—The board of directors should approve and review a risk appetite and tolerance statement for operational risk that articulates the nature, types, and levels of operational risk that the bank is willing to assume.
- Principle 5—Senior management should develop—for approval by the board of directors—a clear, effective, and robust governance structure with well-defined, transparent, and consistent lines of responsibility. Senior management is responsible for consistently implementing and maintaining throughout the organization policies, processes and systems for managing operational risk in all of the bank's material products, activities, processes, and systems consistent with the bank's risk appetite and tolerance.
- Principle 6—Senior management should ensure the identification and assessment of the operational risk inherent in all material products, activities, processes and systems to make sure the inherent risks and incentives are well understood.
- Principle 7—Senior management should ensure that there is an approval process for all new products, activities, processes and systems that fully assess operational risk.
- Principle 8—Senior management should implement a process to regularly monitor operational risk profiles and material exposures to losses. Appropriate reporting mechanisms should be in place at the board, senior management, and business line levels that support proactive management of operational risk.
- Principle 9—Banks should have a strong control environment that utilizes policies, processes and systems; appropriate internal controls; and appropriate risk mitigation and/or transfer strategies.

- Principle 10—Banks should have business resiliency and continuity plans in place to ensure an ability to operate on an ongoing basis and limit losses in the event of severe business disruption.
- Principle 11—A bank's public disclosures should allow stakeholders to assess its approach to operational risk management.

The Basel Committee members are working toward implementing Basel III. The U.S. is working to integrate Basel III with the requirements of the Dodd-Frank Wall Street Reform and Consumer Protection Act.

SUMMARY

Although the major international standards for risk management share common elements, they also contain significant differences in both purpose and process. While regulatory approaches such as Basel II and Solvency II are not standards, an organization should address compliance with these and other regulations when establishing its risk management process and framework. Each organization should align one or more risk management standards with its objectives, operations, and outcomes.

ISO 31000 provides an internationally recognized standard that any organization can use to manage all of its risks. This standard includes guiding principles and provides a generic framework that organizations can tailor to support their own risk management processes.

Similar to other risk management standards, the COSO Enterprise Risk Management—Integrated Framework assists organizations in meeting their objectives. COSO was originally developed to provide a framework for financial controls. Although its standard was expanded in 2004 to provide strategic risk management, it continues to emphasize control activities.

Solvency II and Basel III provide risk management standards for financial organizations, in addition to regulatory requirements for capital adequacy and other measurements of financial performance. The goal of both of these regulatory standards is a global financial system that is sustainable, resilient, and transparent.

ASSIGNMENT NOTES

1. Merriam-Webster's Collegiate Dictionary, 11th ed. (Springfield, Mass.: Merriam-Webster, Inc., 2004).
2. Committee of Sponsoring Organizations of the Treadway Commission, Enterprise Risk Management—Integrated Framework, 2004, p. 124
3. International Organization for Standardization, "Risk Management—Principles and Guidelines," ISO 2009 (Geneva, Switzerland: International Organization for Standardization, 2009), p. 1.

4. Risk and Insurance Management Society (RIMS), An Overview of Widely Used Risk Management Standards and Guidelines, 2011, www.rims.org (accessed January 27, 2012), p. 3.
5. An Overview of Widely Used Risk Management Standards and Guidelines, 2011, www.rims.org (accessed January 27, 2012), p. 3.
6. An Overview of Widely Used Risk Management Standards and Guidelines, 2011, www.rims.org (accessed January 27, 2012), p. 5.
7. AS/NZS-ISO 31000:2009: Risk Management—Principles and Guidelines, Standards Australia/Standards New Zealand, SAI Global, http://sherq.org/31000.pdf (accessed July 13, 2012).
8. "Risk Management—Principles and Guidelines," pp. 7-8.
9. Charles Duhigg and David Barboza, "In China, Human Costs Are Built Into an iPad," The New York Times, January 25, 2012, www.nytimes.com/2012/01/26/business/ieconomy-apples-ipad-and-the-human-costs-for-workers-in-china.html?_r=1&ref=todayspaper (accessed July 13, 2012).
10. "Risk Management—Principles and Guidelines," pp. 8-12.
11. Committee of Sponsoring Organizations of the Treadway Commission, "About Us," www.coso.org/aboutus.htm (accessed February 7, 2012).
12. Committee of Sponsoring Organizations of the Treadway Commission, "Enterprise Risk Management—Integrated Framework: Executive Summary," September 2004, pp. 3-4, www.coso.org/documents/coso_erm_executivesummary.pdf (accessed February 8, 2012).
13. Howard Mills, "Forward Focus: Solvency II from a U.S. Perspective," Deloitte, Winter 2011, www.deloitte.com/assets/Dcom-UnitedStates/Local%20Assets/Documents/FSI/US_FSI_ForwardFocus_011811.pdf (accessed February 7, 2012).
14. Therese M. Vaughan, "The Implications of Solvency II for U.S. Insurance Regulation," www.naic.org/Releases/2009_docs/090305_vaughan_presentation.pdf (accessed February 8, 2012).
15. Bank for International Settlements, "Working Paper on Pillar 3—Market Discipline," www.bis.org/publ/bcbs_wp7.htm (accessed February 8, 2012).
16. Bank for International Settlements, Basel Committee on Banking Supervision, "Principles for the Sound Management of Operational Risk," June 2011, www.bis.org/publ/bcbs195.pdf (accessed February 2, 2012).

Direct Your Learning

3

Hazard Risk

Educational Objectives

After learning the content of this assignment, you should be able to:

- Describe hazard risk and its treatment.
- Describe the following elements for property, liability, personnel, and net income loss exposures:
    - Assets exposed to loss
    - Causes of loss, including associated hazards
    - Financial consequences of loss
- Summarize the loss exposures addressed by each of the various commercial insurance policies.

Outline

The Nature of Hazard Risk

Loss Exposures

Commercial Insurance Policies

Summary

Hazard Risk

THE NATURE OF HAZARD RISK

Although four major categories of risk affect an organization's objectives (hazard, operational, financial, and strategic), insurance deals primarily with hazard risk.

Hazard risk is a pure risk. Traditionally, hazard risk was the main risk category that risk management professionals addressed. While the definition of risk and the scope of risk management have broadened, hazard risk remains an important focus of organizations' risk management programs.

Definition of Hazard Risk

There is no universal definition of hazard risk. Beyond the understanding of hazard risk as a type of risk that provides the potential for only a negative outcome, no precise meaning exists for hazard risk.

In this discussion, the actuarial approach to hazard risk will be used. In *Overview of Enterprise Risk Management*, the Casualty Actuarial Society describes hazard risk as these risks:[1]

- Fire and other property damage
- Windstorm and other natural perils
- Theft and other crime, personal injury
- Business interruption
- Disease and disability (including work-related injuries and diseases)
- Liability claims

Hazard risk is generally insurable.

Some theories of risk management include hazard risk in the operational risk category. This classification follows the Basel concept of operational risk used in determination of a financial institution's regulatory capital requirements. The Basel Committee defines operational risks as "the risk of loss resulting from inadequate or failed internal processes, people and systems or from external events."[2]

Hazard risk can be categorized in this manner:

- Personnel risk—Uncertainty related to the loss to a firm due to death, incapacity, loss of health, or prospect of harm to or unexpected departure of key employees. For example, the serious illness or death of the chief executive officer (CEO), such as Steve Jobs at Apple, is a major risk for most organizations.

- Property risk—Uncertainty related to loss of wealth due to damage or destruction of property. For example, the loss of a plant by fire can negatively affect an organization's productivity.
- Liability risk—Uncertainty related to financial responsibility arising from bodily injury (including death) or loss of wealth that a person or an entity causes to others.[3] For example, liability related to a product, such as Merck's Vioxx, can result in extensive financial loss and reputational damage.

Organizations face net income losses associated with property and liability loss exposures. Net income losses stemming from property losses result from physical damage to property (either property the organization owns or property of others on which the organization depends) that either prevents the organization from operating or that reduces its capacity to operate. Net income losses may not be independent of each other and can be catastrophic if the property losses they are associated with were caused by catastrophes such as windstorm. For example, a substantial portion of insured losses following Hurricane Katrina in 2005 were business income losses stemming from the property damage to businesses in the affected area.

Unlike the net income losses associated with property losses, no definite time period is associated with liability losses. For example, the Taco Bell restaurant chain suffered a loss of business and revenue after publicity regarding its alleged liability for salmonella related to some of its ingredients. There is no way to set a reasonable time period to restore a business's reputation and its related income after such a liability loss in a similar manner to the restoration of a business's property.

Measuring and Managing Hazard Risk

The hazard risks that an organization faces must be identified and classified correctly. After the exposures have been properly classified, they can be measured and managed.

Frequency
Number of losses.

Severity
The size of a loss.

The two measures that are traditionally used for hazard risk exposures are **frequency** and **severity**. An organization's risk managers should measure frequency and severity by line of insurance on an aggregate basis. Typically, several years of measurement are used, such as three to five years before the current year, to determine the average exposures for each line. The extent of the exposure usually determines the approach used in managing the risk.

Risk managers use various techniques to prevent losses or to reduce their frequency and/or severity. These techniques can be used separately or in combination:

- **Avoidance** eliminates any possibility of loss. The probability of loss from an avoided loss exposure is zero because the organization decides not to assume it (proactive avoidance) or to eliminate it (abandonment).
- **Separation** involves dispersing a particular activity over several locations.
- **Duplication** involves relying on backups that can be used if primary assets or activities suffer loss.
- **Diversification** involves providing a range of products and services used by a variety of customers.
- Prevention involves techniques to reduce the frequency of losses.
- Reduction involves techniques to reduce the severity of losses.

Avoidance, although it provides assurance that a loss will not occur, is only practical in certain instances. For example, an organization that is contemplating purchasing a particular property may decide against the purchase if it learns that the property was previously contaminated by a pollutant. An organization cannot avoid most of the risks associated with its business operations.

Similarly, the techniques of separation, duplication, and diversification can be used only by certain organizations in a narrow range of specific circumstances. A large organization may be able to manufacture components of products in separate locations and assemble them in another location. Such a large organization may also be able to rely on plants to back each other up and offer a range of products to its customers. However, these techniques are impractical for many organizations.

The most common techniques used by risk managers are prevention and reduction, often in combination. For example, an organization may use the prevention technique of fire-resistant materials to construct a new plant. It may also include an automatic fire sprinkler system in the plant to reduce the severity of any fire that occurs despite the preventive technique.

The Role of Insurance

Because losses cannot be eliminated, an organization must decide whether to retain or transfer its loss exposures. The loss measurement will assist the risk manager in recommending which losses should be retained and which should be transferred. Typically, losses with low frequency and severity are retained. Some losses with high frequency but low severity may also be retained, because the aggregate results are usually fairly predictable. Losses with high severity but low frequency are often transferred. Most organizations would avoid losses with high frequency and severity.

The most common method of risk transfer is **insurance**. The principal advantage of risk transfer is that it provides an offset to an organization's exposure

---

Avoidance
A technique that involves ceasing or never undertaking an activity so that the possibility of future gains or losses occurring from that activity is eliminated.

Separation
A risk control technique that isolates loss exposures from one another to minimize the adverse effect of a single loss.

Duplication
A risk control technique that uses backups, spares, or copies of critical property, information, or capabilities and keeps them in reserve.

Diversification
A risk control technique that spreads loss exposures over numerous projects, products, markets, or regions.

Insurance
A risk management technique that transfers the potential financial consequences of certain specified loss exposures from the insured to the insurer.

to large losses. Additionally, risk transfer can lessen the variability of the cash flows of an organization. Most organizations, especially mid-size and large ones, use a combination of retention and transfer. A large deductible or a high self-insured retention would likely be used for the vehicle liability coverage of the organization in the previous example with a fleet of delivery vehicles.

Insurance has its own terminology, and policy language may be unfamiliar to those outside the insurance industry. Risk professionals should be familiar with basic insurance terms. Some common terms are outlined in the exhibit. See the exhibit "Basic Terminology of Hazard Risk Insurance."

Basic Terminology of Hazard Risk Insurance

Term	Meaning
Peril	The cause of a loss
Wrongful act	Any actual or alleged error, misstatement, misleading statement, act or omission, or neglect or breach of duty
Legal liability	The legally enforceable obligation of a person or an organization to pay a sum of money (called damages) to another person or organization
Errors and omissions (E&O)	Negligent acts (errors) committed by a person conducting insurance business that give rise to legal liability for damages; a failure to act (omission) that creates legal liability
Exclusion	A policy provision that eliminates coverage for specified exposures
Policy limits	The maximum that can be paid on the claim, regardless of the actual value of the property damaged
Business income insurance	Insurance that covers the reduction in an organization's income when operations are interrupted by damage to property caused by a covered peril
Directors and officers (D&O) liability insurance	Insurance that covers a corporation's directors and officers against liability for their wrongful acts covered by the policy and also covers the sums that the insured corporation is required or permitted by law to pay to the directors and officers as indemnification
Environmental hazard	Any hazardous condition beyond the control of the property owner that might give rise to a covered loss

[DA08678]

There are several significant limitations to the risk transfer provided by insurance. In addition to deductibles and self-insured retentions, there are also policy limits for most lines of insurance that may not provide sufficient coverage in the event of a large loss. Additionally, most policies exclude certain types of exposures. For example, standard commercial general liability (CGL) policies exclude liability for most pollution and many cyber risks. Business income insurance provides coverage for loss of business income due to property damage resulting from covered perils, but there is no insurance available to provide coverage for loss of business income resulting from liability losses. Directors and officers (D&O) and errors and omissions (E&O) policies typically do not provide coverage for fines or penalties. Most policies in any line of insurance do not provide coverage for punitive damages.

Some estimates indicate that insurance provides coverage for only 20 to 30 percent of operational risk losses.[4] This is based on the assumption that operational risks include hazard risks. Although operational risk encompasses losses other than hazard risk losses, 80 percent of uninsured loss still represents a significant financial loss for any organization. A risk study at Microsoft found that risk financing covered only approximately 30 percent of Microsoft's risk.[5] An option that Microsoft is exploring as a result of this study is holistic insurance coverage to match its holistic risk management approach. Some insurers, such as Lloyd's, are also beginning to explore holistic coverage for operational risk rather than merely offering the traditional types of hazard insurance.[6]

A thorough risk management analysis should include all of the coverage gaps that result from the organization's traditional insurance. Risk managers should then explore whether specialty or alternative forms of insurance or risk transfer are necessary or available to meet those gaps. For example, cyber risk insurance should be considered by any organization that handles consumer information, such as credit cards. Most standard CGL policies do not provide sufficient coverage for data breaches, and these losses can be significant. For example, the 2007 criminal hacking of the T.J. Maxx customer database cost its parent company, TJX, more than $50 million.

Apply Your Knowledge

A chemical manufacturing company has a commercial package policy that includes property, general liability, and business income and expense insurance. The company also has a workers compensation and employers liability policy and a business auto policy. One of the company's trucks is involved in an accident that results in a spill of 1,000 gallons of a corrosive chemical onto a highway. Both the truck driver and the driver of the other vehicle were injured. It is determined that the company's driver was at fault. There was extensive media coverage of this accident. Which of the following claims would be covered under the company's insurance policies? Select all that apply.

a. Chemical spill cleanup
b. Company driver's injury
c. Injury of other vehicle's driver
d. Damage to the company's reputation

Feedback: b. and c. The company driver's injury would be covered under the company's workers compensation policy. The injury sustained by the other vehicle's driver would be covered under the auto liability policy because the company's driver was at fault. The chemical spill would be excluded from coverage. None of the policies would provide coverage for reputational damage.

LOSS EXPOSURES

Individuals and organizations incur losses when assets they own decrease in value. Situations or conditions that expose assets to loss are called loss exposures. In order to effectively manage risk, individuals and organizations must identify all the loss exposures they face.

Every **loss exposure** has three elements:

- An asset exposed to loss
- Cause of loss (also called a peril)
- Financial consequences of that loss

These three elements can be described for each of these four basic types of loss exposures: property loss exposures, liability loss exposures, personnel loss exposures, and net income loss exposures.

Because hazard risk is a pure risk, risk analysis focuses solely on exposure to loss. This type of risk is generally insurable; therefore, the elements of a hazard loss exposure are based on assets, causes of loss, and financial consequences—all of which are the subjects of insurance policies.

Elements of Loss Exposures

The three elements are necessary to completely describe a loss exposure. For example, identifying a building (an asset exposed to loss) is not sufficient for describing that building as a loss exposure. It is also necessary to identify the causes of loss associated with that building (such as fire, flood, or hurricane) and the financial consequences of that loss (such as a decline in the market value of the building or in the income produced by the use of the building).

Asset Exposed to Loss

The first element of a loss exposure is an asset exposed to loss. This asset can be anything of value an individual or organization has that is exposed to loss. Assets owned by organizations can include property (such as buildings, automobiles, and office furniture), investments, money that is owed to them, and cash. In addition to these are assets that are often overlooked, including intangible assets (such as patents, copyrights, and trademarks) and human resources.

Loss exposure

Any condition or situation that presents a possibility of loss, whether or not an actual loss occurs.

Individuals may have many of the same assets as organizations (property, money, investments, and so on). In addition, individuals may have intangible assets such as professional qualifications, a unique skill set, or valuable experience.

Cause of Loss

The second element of a loss exposure is cause of loss. Fire, windstorm, explosion, and theft are examples of causes of loss that present a possibility of loss to property.

Loss exposures and causes of loss that affect them can be influenced by **hazards**. For example, a fire hazard, such as storing oily rags next to a furnace, increases the frequency and/or severity of loss caused by fire. Insurers typically define hazards according to these four classifications:

- Moral hazard
- Morale hazard
- Physical hazard
- Legal hazard

Hazard
A condition that increases the frequency or severity of a loss.

Regardless of whether they are moral, morale, physical, or legal, hazards can have a compounding effect. For example, the loss frequency associated with a safe driver in a safe car is increased by either the physical hazard of an unsafe car or the moral hazard of an unsafe driver. The frequency is further increased by the compound effect of an unsafe driver in an unsafe car. Therefore, risk management and insurance professionals need to carefully monitor any situation that may involve multiple hazards.

Examples of a **moral hazard** include intentionally causing, fabricating, or exaggerating a loss. For example, one moral hazard incentive is financial difficulty. Someone who is facing overwhelming debt might be tempted to intentionally cause a loss in an attempt to profit from the situation and thereby reduce or eliminate the debt.

Moral hazard
A condition that increases the likelihood that a person will intentionally cause or exaggerate a loss.

Purchasing an insurance policy is another moral hazard incentive—some people might be inclined to behave differently once they enter into a contract that shifts the financial consequences of risk to another party. In insurance, this behavior can include filing false claims, inflating a claim on a loss that did occur, or intentionally causing a loss.

Driving carelessly, failing to lock an unattended building, or failing to clear an icy sidewalk to protect pedestrians are examples of **morale hazard**.

Both moral and morale hazards are behavior problems that can increase the frequency and/or severity of losses. The fundamental difference between these two types of hazard is intent. A moral hazard results from a deliberate act; a morale hazard results from carelessness or indifference.

Morale hazard (attitudinal hazard)
A condition of carelessness or indifference that increases the frequency or severity of loss.

Physical hazard
A tangible characteristic of property, persons, or operations that tends to increase the frequency or severity of loss.

A **physical hazard** is a condition of property, persons, or operations that increases the frequency and/or severity of loss. For example, a slip-and-fall accident is more likely to occur on an icy sidewalk, a fire is more likely to start in a building with defective wiring, and an explosion is more likely to occur in a painting area that has inadequate ventilation. Inadequate ventilation may also create environmental problems for workers and therefore increase the frequency and/or severity of workers compensation claims.

Legal hazard
A condition of the legal environment that increases loss frequency or severity.

A **legal hazard** is a condition of the legal environment that increases the frequency and/or severity of loss. For example, courts in some geographic areas are much more likely to find in favor of the plaintiff or to grant large damages awards in liability cases than are courts in other areas. Various trends can also be legal hazards. For example, an increasing number of decisions against tobacco manufacturers would present a legal hazard for companies participating in the tobacco industry.

Financial Consequences of Loss

The third element of loss exposures is the financial consequences of the loss. The financial consequences of a loss depend on the type of loss exposure, the cause of loss, and the loss frequency and severity. Some financial consequences can be established with a high degree of certainty; for example, the value of a building that has been damaged by fire.

Other financial consequences may be more difficult to determine, such as the value of business lost while the building damaged by fire is being restored. In addition, although some financial consequences are known as soon as a loss occurs, such as the value of property lost in a robbery, others may take months or years to determine, such as the ultimate value of liability claims regarding a defective product.

Types of Loss Exposures

For insurance and traditional risk management purposes, loss exposures are typically divided into these four types:

- Property loss exposures
- Liability loss exposures
- Personnel loss exposures
- Net income loss exposures

The three elements of loss exposures apply to each of these four types. However, each type is distinguished in relation to how it affects the first element of a loss exposure, that is, the asset exposed to loss.

Property Loss Exposures

Property loss exposure
A condition that presents the possibility that a person or an organization will sustain a loss resulting from damage (including destruction, taking, or loss of use) to property in which that person or organization has a financial interest.

A **property loss exposure** is a condition that presents the possibility that a person or an organization will sustain a loss resulting from damage (including destruction, taking, or loss of use) to property in which that person or organization has a financial interest. Property can be categorized as either tangible property or intangible property.

Tangible property is property that has a physical form, such as a piece of equipment. Tangible property can be further subdivided into **real property** and **personal property**. **Intangible property** is property that has no physical form, such as a patent or copyright. See the exhibit "Elements of Property Loss Exposures."

> **Tangible property**
> Property that has a physical form.
>
> **Real property (realty)**
> Tangible property consisting of land, all structures permanently attached to the land, and whatever is growing on the land.
>
> **Personal property**
> All tangible or intangible property that is not real property.
>
> **Intangible property**
> Property that has no physical form.

Elements of Property Loss Exposures

1. **Asset Exposed to Loss**
   - Tangible property
   - Real property, such as offices and warehouses
   - Personal property, such as office furniture and office equipment
   - Intangible property, such as patents, copyrights, trademarks, trade secrets, and customer goodwill

2. **Cause of Loss**

   Some of the more frequent causes of loss include the following:
   - Lightning or hail
   - Tornadoes or high wind
   - Water from failure of indoor appliances; heavy rain or flooding; or sewers or drains
   - Theft
   - Snow or ice
   - Fire
   - Mold

3. **Financial Consequences of Loss**

   The maximum financial consequence of a property loss is limited by the value of the property. However, a property loss may also have an effect on the financial consequences of liability, personnel, or net income losses.

[DA02384]

Damage to property can cause a reduction in that property's value, sometimes to zero. For example, when property is stolen, the owner suffers a total loss of that property because the owner no longer has use of it. In addition to these losses, property damage can result in a loss of income (net income loss exposure) because the property cannot be used to generate income or because extra expenses are incurred to continue operations.

Liability Loss Exposures

Liability loss exposure
Any condition or situation that presents the possibility of a claim alleging legal responsibility of a person or business for injury or damage suffered by another party.

A **liability loss exposure** results from the claim itself, not necessarily the payment of damages. See the exhibit "Industry Language—Property and Liability Loss Exposures."

Industry Language—Property and Liability Loss Exposures

Property

A property loss occurs when a person or an organization sustains a loss as the result of damage (including destruction, taking, or loss of use) to property in which that person or organization has a financial interest. The possibility that such a situation could occur is a property loss exposure.

Insurance professionals often use the term "loss" to mean the event itself. In addition, they often refer to the loss in terms of the applicable property, the cause of loss, the consequences, or the applicable policy.

- When focusing on the type of property, they often refer to a "building loss" or a "personal property loss," regardless of the peril involved.
- When focusing on causes of loss, they often refer to a "fire loss," a "smoke loss," or a "theft loss."
- When focusing on consequences, they often refer to a "business income loss," an "extra expense loss," or an "additional living expense loss," regardless of the type of property or causes of loss involved.
- When focusing on the applicable policy, they often use the policy name or type, such as a "homeowners loss," an "auto loss," or a "business interruption loss."

Similar language is used for loss exposures. Insurance practitioners often refer to a building loss exposure, a fire loss exposure, a homeowners loss exposure, or a business interruption loss exposure.

Liability

Insurance and risk management professionals often refer to specific types of liability losses in terms of the applicable coverage or the activity leading to the loss. For example, a claim for damages arising out of a product defect might be referred to as a "products liability loss," and the possibility of such a claim might be referred to as a "products liability loss exposure." Similarly, owning, operating, maintaining, or using an automobile might be referred to as "auto liability" or "auto liability loss exposures."

[DA02385]

Even if a claim is successfully defended, and therefore does not result in payment of damages, the party against whom the claim was made nonetheless incurs defense costs, other claim-related expenses, and potentially adverse publicity, all of which produce a financial loss. See the exhibit "Elements of Liability Loss Exposures."

Elements of Liability Loss Exposures

1. **Asset Exposed to Loss**

The asset exposed to loss for a liability loss exposure is money. Payments that may be required include the following:

- Damages to the plaintiff if the claim is not successfully defended
- Settlement costs if the claim settles out of court
- Legal fees
- Court costs

2. **Cause of Loss**

The cause of a liability loss is the making of a claim or suit against the particular organization by another party seeking damages or some other legal remedy. Even the threat of another party to make such a claim or suit can cause a liability loss in the form of costs the organization incurs to investigate and settle the threatened liability claim or suit.

3. **Financial Consequences of Loss**

In theory, the financial consequences of a liability loss exposure are limitless. In practice, financial consequences are limited to the total wealth of the person or organization. Although some jurisdictions limit the amounts that can be taken in a claim, liability claims can result in the loss of most or all of a person's or an organization's assets, as well as in a claim on future income.

[DA02386]

Personnel Loss Exposures

A **personnel loss exposure** is a condition that presents the possibility of loss caused by a key person's death, disability, retirement, or resignation that deprives an organization of that person's special skill or knowledge that the organization cannot readily replace. A key person can be an individual employee, an owner, an officer or manager of the organization, or a group of employees who possess special skills or knowledge that is valuable to the organization. See the exhibit "Elements of Personnel Loss Exposures."

For example, the possibility that the CEO of an organization can resign to take a position in a more prestigious organization is a personnel loss exposure. The exhibit reviews the three elements of a personnel loss exposure.

If the key person is viewed in terms of his or her family, the loss exposure associated with the loss of that key person is often called a **personal loss exposure** or human loss exposure. Although the terminology is slightly different, the definition is almost the same. For example, a family would face a personal loss exposure with the possibility of the primary wage earner dying.

Personnel loss exposure

A condition that presents the possibility of loss caused by a person's death, disability, retirement, or resignation that deprives an organization of the person's special skill or knowledge that the organization cannot readily replace.

Personal loss exposure

Any condition or situation that presents the possibility of a financial loss to an individual or a family by such causes as death, sickness, injury, or unemployment.

3.14 Risk Management Principles and Practices

> ### Elements of Personnel Loss Exposures
>
> 1. **Asset Exposed to Loss**
>
> The asset exposed to loss for a personnel loss exposure is the value that the key person adds to the organization.
>
> 2. **Cause of Loss**
>
> Circumstances that can lead to a personnel loss exposure include the following:
>
> - Death
> - Disability
> - Retirement
> - Voluntary separation, such as resignation
> - Involuntary separation, such as layoff or firing
>
> 3. **Financial Consequences of Loss**
>
> The financial consequences of a personnel loss vary based on the cause of loss and can be partial or total as well as temporary or permanent. For example, the death of a key employee is a total, permanent loss. If the personnel loss is caused by a disability, the loss of value to the organization may only be a partial loss if the employee is able to continue to add some value to the organization. It may also only be temporary, if a full recovery from the disability is expected.

[DA02387]

Net Income Loss Exposures

Net income loss exposure
A condition that presents the possibility of loss caused by a reduction in net income.

A **net income loss exposure** is a condition that presents the possibility of loss caused by a reduction in net income. Net income equals revenues minus expenses and income taxes in a given time period. If you consider income taxes to be part of an organization's expenses, a net income loss is a reduction in revenue, an increase in expenses, or a combination of the two. Both individuals and organizations have net income loss exposures. See the exhibit "Elements of Net Income Loss Exposures."

For example, a fire at an organization's production facilities could not only destroy the facilities (a property loss exposure) but also force the organization to stop operations for a few weeks, resulting in a loss of sales revenue (a net income loss exposure). Similarly, if a tornado damages the retail store of a self-employed business owner, the inability to earn income while the store is being repaired represents a net income loss exposure. The exhibit reviews the three elements of a net income loss exposure.

Net income losses are often the result of a property, liability, or personnel loss (all of which are direct losses). Therefore, net income losses are considered to be indirect losses. A direct loss is a loss that occurs immediately as the result

> ### Elements of Net Income Loss Exposures
>
> 1. **Asset Exposed to Loss**
>
> The asset exposed to loss for a net income loss exposure is the future stream of net income cash flows of the individual or organization.
>
> 2. **Cause of Loss**
>
> Circumstances that can lead to a net income loss exposure include the following:
> - Property loss
> - Liability loss
> - Personnel loss
> - Losses stemming from business risks; for example, losses resulting from poor strategic planning
>
> 3. **Financial Consequences of Loss**
>
> The financial consequences of a net income loss vary based on the cause of loss. A reduction in revenues, an increase in expenses, or a combination of the two can have financial consequences. The worst case scenario for a net income loss is a decrease in revenues to zero and a significant increase in expenses for a prolonged period.

[DA02388]

of a particular cause of loss, such as the reduction in the value of a building that has been damaged by fire.

An indirect loss is a loss that results from, but is not directly caused by, a particular cause of loss. For example, the reduction in revenue an organization suffers as a result of fire damage to one of its buildings is an indirect loss. Estimating indirect losses is often challenging because of the difficulty in projecting the effects that a direct loss will have on revenues or expenses. For example, a risk management professional working at a restaurant chain may be able to project the amount needed to settle a lawsuit brought by a customer accusing the restaurant of food poisoning (direct liability loss) with some certainty. However, projecting the effect that any negative publicity relating to the lawsuit would have on future restaurant sales (indirect loss) would be more difficult.

In the insurance industry, the term "net income losses" is usually associated with property losses, and some insurance policies provide coverage for net income losses related to property losses. However, there are many other causes of net income losses.

Some net income losses are associated with the liability or personnel loss exposures that have traditionally been the focus of risk management. Other net income losses are associated with organizational activities that have not traditionally been the focus of risk management, such as strategic marketing or branding decisions. Besides these, other potential net income losses that may affect individuals or organizations include these:

- Loss of goodwill—Organizations are concerned with maintaining goodwill among customers and other stakeholders. Goodwill can be lost in many ways, including providing poor service, offering obsolete products, or mismanaging operations. For a not-for-profit organization, goodwill is equivalent to reputation. Goodwill has broader implications than just reputation in for-profit organizations, because goodwill may have a monetary value. To maintain goodwill, many organizations choose to pay for certain accidents for which they are not legally responsible. For example, if a guest sustains an injury on an organization's premises, and the organization did not cause or contribute to the injury, that organization might still choose to pay any medical bills in order to maintain goodwill and avoid adverse publicity.

- Failure to perform—Net income losses may occur as a result of some type of failure to perform, including a product's failure to perform as promised, a contractor's failure to complete a construction project as scheduled, or a debtor's failure to make scheduled payments.

- Missed opportunities—An organization may suffer a net income loss as a result of a missed opportunity for profit. For example, an organization that delays a decision to modify its product in response to changes in market demand might lose market share and profit that it could have made on that updated product.

COMMERCIAL INSURANCE POLICIES

Insurers provide insurance coverage for many different types of commercial loss exposures. Risk management professionals need to understand the types of insurance available and the coverage provided by each so that they can evaluate whether it would be possible to effectively transfer their organization's risk through insurance.

Insurance policies have developed through regulation, common usage, and standardization. The publication and use of common forms, such as a public liability or commercial auto policy, makes it easier for risk managers to understand the coverage provided for typical exposures. It is then simpler to compare different insurers' products and to address gaps in coverage.

Classifying Commercial Insurance Policies

In the United States, nonlife insurance is referred to as **property-casualty insurance**. In some markets outside the U.S., it is referred to as general insurance. There are two major categories of property-casualty insurance: **property** and **liability**.

Property-casualty, or general, insurance is further categorized by **line of business**. See the exhibit "Classification of Commercial Lines of Insurance."

Property-casualty insurance
One of the two main sectors of the insurance industry, encompassing numerous types of insurance, most of which cover the financial consequences of damage to one's own property or legal liability to others.

Property
The real estate, buildings, objects or articles, intangible assets, or rights with exchangeable value of which someone may claim legal ownership.

Liability
A legal responsibility for the consequences of an act or omission.

Line of business
A general classification of insurance, such as commercial property, commercial general liability, commercial crime, or commercial auto.

Classification of Commercial Lines of Insurance

Commercial Line	Product	Loss Exposures Addressed	U.S./Outside U.S.
Property			
• Commercial Property	Building and Personal Property (BPP)	Fire, explosion, windstorm, and other natural and miscellaneous perils	U.S.
	Fire and Natural Forces	Fire, explosion, storm, and other natural perils	Outside U.S.
	Other Damage to Property	Perils other than natural perils except to property in transport	Outside U.S.
• Business Income	Business Income and Extra Expense	Loss of business income and extra expenses incurred during repair of property damaged by a covered peril	U.S.
	Consequential Loss Insurance	Business interruption	Outside U.S.
Liability	General Liability	Typically covers an organization's liability except for motor vehicle, aircraft, and specific exclusions	U.S.—Commercial General Liability Public Liability (Outside U.S.)
Motor Vehicle	Business Auto	Covers property and/or liability for an organization's autos	U.S.
	Land Vehicles	Covers damage to an organization's land vehicles	Outside U.S.
	Motor vehicle liability	Covers liability for use of motor vehicles on land	Outside U.S.
Marine, Aviation, and Transportation (MAT)	Various policies provide coverage for vessels, aircraft, and railroads	Policies may cover property damage/and or liability	U.S./Outside U.S. Large policies may be underwritten by P&I clubs or specialty international insurers
Pecuniary Loss	Credit policies	Insolvency, export credit, mortgages	U.S./Outside U.S.
	Miscellaneous Financial Loss (Fidelity, Crime, Surety)	Employee dishonesty, surety bonds, other forms of financial loss	U.S./Outside U.S.
Occupational Injury and Disease	Workers Compensation and Employers Liability	Employee injuries and occupational diseases	U.S.
	Accident & Sickness	Employee injuries and occupational diseases	Outside U.S.

[DA08698]

Property Insurance

Commercial property insurance encompasses various types of coverage.

Monoline and **package policies** are available in the U.S. and most developed countries. For example, fire insurance policies are monoline policies that provide coverage only for fire and related causes of loss. In contrast, commercial package policies typically include coverage for business property, business income, and liability.

Publishers, such as Insurance Services Office, Inc. (ISO), provide standard commercial policy forms in the U.S. and international markets that can be used by brokers and underwriters who do not develop their own policy forms.

A policy will provide **named perils** coverage or **direct physical loss** coverage, which was once referred to as **all-risks** coverage. Named-perils policies provide coverage only for perils that are specifically named in the policy, while direct physical loss policies provide coverage for all perils that are not specifically excluded.

In the U.S., the ISO Building and Personal Property coverage form can be written to provide either named perils or direct physical loss coverage for a wide variety of businesses. Similar policies are available in non-U.S. markets. There is limited coverage under this policy for the personal property of others. Businesses that commonly have customers' personal property on their premises can add an endorsement to cover this type of property or use a separate **bailees' customers policy**. In the United Kingdom, for example, a form such as the Car Park and Cloakroom policy can be used to provide this type of coverage.

Another classification of property coverage is **replacement cost** value versus **actual cash value**. In the U.S. market, many commercial property policies contain an **insurance-to-value provision**, where a **coinsurance clause** applies a penalty if the insured purchases coverage for less than 80 percent of the market value of the property.

For most organizations, a significant loss exposure related to property damage or loss is the possible loss of business that can result. For example, if a store or restaurant is severely damaged by fire, business will not be able to resume until the damaged property is repaired or replaced. A serious property loss can result in a loss of business for many months.

Business Income Insurance

Business income insurance, also called consequential loss insurance, is designed to provide coverage for the loss of business income and, if necessary, extra expenses incurred while repairs are made after a covered loss. These losses are sometimes referred to as "time element losses" or "business interruption losses." In the U.S. and other markets, this coverage can be written as a separate policy or combined into a commercial package policy.

Commercial property insurance
Insurance that covers commercial buildings and their contents against various types of property loss.

Monoline policy
Policy that covers only one line of business.

Package policy
Policy that covers two or more lines of business.

Named peril
A specific cause of loss listed and described in an insurance policy. Also used to describe policies containing named perils.

Direct physical loss
A loss that is physical (not just financial) and results immediately from the occurrence.

All-risks policy
An insurance policy that covers any risk of physical loss unless the policy specifically excludes it.

Bailees' customers policy
A policy that covers damage to customers' goods while in the possession of the insured, regardless of whether the insured is legally liable for the damage.

Replacement cost
The cost to repair or replace property using new materials of like kind and quality with no deduction for depreciation.

Two adverse financial consequences of a business interruption are extra expenses and a decrease in revenues, both of which reduce net income.

$$\text{Net income} = \text{Revenues} - \text{Expenses}$$

Some insurers offer endorsements that provide coverage for business interruption resulting from a **dependent property exposure** loss or a loss in utility services resulting from a covered peril. Dependent property loss exposures are increasingly significant because of the increase in global trade and supply chains.

Industrial All-Risk (Special Risk) Insurance

Large enterprises, some of which are international organizations, have many different types of property and exposures. Industrial all-risk policies are tailored to the individual needs of such organizations.

For example, Raheja QBE in India offers an all-risks policy that contains coverage in Part I for fire and special perils, burglary, earthquake, and machinery breakdown; and, in Part II, coverage for business interruption.[7] This coverage is broader than that in most property policies, which typically exclude earthquake and machinery breakdown.

Builders' All-Risk Insurance

Builders' risk coverage forms are designed to address several risks or characteristics that are not faced by most organizations. One risk builders have is that the value of a building under construction increases as the construction progresses. This requires coverage limits that increase as their project progresses. Another characteristic that requires special consideration is that there are typically several different insured interests involved in a building under construction, such as the building owner, the contractor, and any subcontractors hired. The third characteristic is the additional exposure to a building under construction, such as increased susceptibility to theft because construction materials are left in the open and vulnerability to windstorm or fire in the early stages of construction.

Equipment Breakdown (Boiler & Machinery) Insurance

Equipment breakdown coverage is a specialized area of insurance underwritten only by certain insurers. Coverage typically applies to these types of property:

- Boilers and pressure vessels
- Electrical equipment
- Mechanical equipment
- Air conditioning and refrigeration equipment
- Business equipment and systems

Actual cash value

A method in valuing property which is calculated as the cost to replace or repair property minus depreciation, the fair market value, or a valuation determined by the broad evidence rule.

Insurance-to-value provision

A provision in property insurance policies that encourages insureds to purchase an amount of insurance that is equal to, or close to, the value of the covered property.

Coinsurance clause

A clause that requires the insured to carry insurance equal to at least a specified percentage of the insured property's value.

Business income insurance

Insurance that covers the reduction in an organization's income when operations are interrupted by damage to property caused by a covered peril.

Dependent property exposure

The possibility of incurring business income loss because of physical loss occurring on the premises of an organization that the insured depends on for materials, products, or sales.

Although loss caused by a resulting fire is usually covered, most standard commercial property policies exclude coverage for loss caused by the explosion of steam boilers, steam pipes, steam engines, and steam turbines that are owned or leased by the insured or operated under the insured's control. Also, most commercial property policies exclude damage caused by artificially generated electric current to electrical devices, appliances, or wires, which is a common cause of loss to electrical equipment, including computers.

Most equipment breakdown policies, in addition to providing coverage for property damage to the covered equipment, also provide coverage for the business income and extra expense exposures. This provides coverage for lost business income or incurred expenses that would not be covered under standard business interruption policies because the causes of loss are not covered by those policies.

Fidelity and Crime Insurance

Commercial crime insurance covers money, securities, and other property against a wide range of criminal acts committed by persons other than the insured. Although other types of commercial policies cover loss caused by some criminal acts, those policies do not cover all the crime loss exposures of most organizations.

These are examples of fidelity and crime insurance coverages:

- Employee dishonesty—An employee, either alone or with others, taking money or other property from his or her employer without authorization.
- Computer fraud—Using a computer to steal money or other property.
- Extortion—Using a threat to extract property, such as money.
- Forgery or alteration—Forgery includes a false signature or document; alteration is the unauthorized change to a document.
- Theft and robbery—Theft is the unlawful stealing of property; robbery is theft committed by force or the threat of force.

Surety Bonds

Although surety bonds are usually considered a type of property-casualty insurance, there are important differences. Surety bonds, unlike most insurance contracts, are three-party agreements involving the **principal**, the **surety**, and the **obligee**. The surety is answerable to the obligee if the principal defaults, unlike an insurer that is primarily responsible to its insured. The surety theoretically does not expect losses, while the insurer should.

There are various types of surety bonds issued for different purposes. Among the most common are surety bonds issued for construction operations. These bonds are widely used to guarantee that a contractor (the principal) will complete a building project according to specifications and within a stated time

---

Principal
The party to a surety bond whose obligation or performance the surety guarantees.

Surety
The party (usually an insurer) to a surety bond that guarantees to the obligee that the principal will fulfill an obligation or perform as required by the underlying contract, permit, or law.

Obligee
The party to a surety bond that receives the surety's guarantee that the principal will fulfill an obligation or perform as promised.

frame; that the contractor will pay certain bills for labor and materials; and that the contractor's work will be free from defects for a specified period.

General Liability Insurance

The concept of legal liability is what distinguishes liability loss exposures from other types of loss exposures. Organizations of all types in the U.S. and other markets purchase general liability insurance, sometimes called public liability insurance, to provide coverage for their liability loss exposures.

General liability insurance provides coverage when the insured becomes legally obligated to pay damages. An insured may become legally obligated to pay damages as the result of a legal wrong for which the applicable civil law provides a remedy in the form of damages. Such wrongs typically include a **tort** or **breach of contract**.

A general liability policy does not cover all legal obligations to pay damages. It only covers those obligations that are within the scope of the **insuring agreement** and are not excluded under the policy provisions. A typical insuring agreement provides coverage for personal injury or property damage caused by an **occurrence** during the policy period for which the insured is liable.

Many general liability policies provide additional coverage to defend the insured against an allegation of liability. The duty to defend is typically broader than the duty to **indemnify**. There are policies available to provide coverage for defense and related expenses in the non-U.S. market when this coverage is not provided under the general liability policy.

Unlike most commercial property policies, coverage is not provided under general liability policies for indirect expenses incurred as a result of an actual or alleged liability. For example, if a product is found to be defective, the insured would be covered for injuries or property damage sustained by customers. However, the insured would not be covered for the expenses associated with product recall, loss of business income, or any other indirect loss associated with the product liability.

General liability policies exclude liability that is the subject of motor vehicle, workers compensation (employee accident and sickness), and other exposures that are typically covered under other policy types. General liability policies also contain exclusions for most types of environmental liability and many types of cyber risk.

Auto Insurance

In many nations, liability coverage is required for individuals or organizations that operate motor vehicles on public roads. Some organizations also choose to purchase property coverage for their vehicles. Policies are available to

Breach of contract
The failure, without legal excuse, to fulfill a contractual promise.

Tort
A wrongful act or an omission, other than a crime or a breach of contract, that invades a legally protected right.

Insuring agreement
A statement in an insurance policy that the insurer will, under described circumstances, make a loss payment or provide a service.

Occurrence
An accident, including continuous or repeated exposure to substantially the same general harmful conditions.

Indemnify
To restore a party who has sustained a loss to the same financial position that party held before the loss occurred.

provide combined property and liability coverage for various types of motor vehicles.

Commercial auto policies typically exclude coverage for vehicles that are used solely to perform off-road functions, such as excavators or forklifts. Coverage for this type of equipment is usually provided under the general property and liability policies. Auto policies also typically exclude environmental liability related to materials being hauled by insured vehicles, such as oil or other chemicals.

Specialized policies are available for auto dealers and other types of organizations that have unusual auto exposures.

Workers Compensation and Employers Liability Insurance

In the U.S., most states require the majority of employers to provide workers compensation coverage for their employees. In some other countries, a similar type of insurance called "accident and sickness coverage" is required.

Workers compensation provides medical and wage replacement benefits as specified in the applicable law to employees who are injured on the job. In exchange for these benefits, employees in the U.S. and some other countries usually do not have the right to sue the employer.

Employers liability insurance provides coverage for the rare instances when employees are permitted to sue their employers. For example, if the employer acted in a dual capacity, such as the manufacturer of the product that injured the employee as well as the employer, the employee may be permitted to sue. Because employee injuries are excluded from coverage under most general liability policies, the employers liability section of a workers compensation policy provides coverage for this exposure.

Professional Liability or Errors and Omissions Insurance

Professional liability insurance is often referred to as errors and omissions (E&O) or malpractice insurance, and the terms are used interchangeably in the insurance industry. Professional liability is based on the concept that professionals have a duty to perform the services for which they were hired, and they also have a duty to perform those services in accordance with the appropriate standards of conduct for their profession. Coverage for failure to perform a professional duty or to conform to appropriate standards is usually excluded from general liability policies.

Professional liability policies are usually written on forms developed by individual insurers rather than on standard policy forms. A limited number of insurers may specialize in a certain area of professional liability coverage, such as medical malpractice. In contrast to the majority of liability policies, professional liability policies may provide a **claims-made coverage form** rather than the typical **occurrence coverage form**. The reason for use of the claims-made form is that allegations of professional liability are often made years after the actual occurrence that is the basis for the allegations. The claims-made form provides more certainty for the insurer because it eliminates the late reporting of claims, which is common with the occurrence form.

Management Liability Insurance

There are three major types of management liability loss exposures:

- Directors and officers (D&O) liability
- Employment practices liability
- Fiduciary liability

Directors and Officers Liability Insurance

In the U.S. and other countries, directors and officers (D&O) liability exposure increased for many organizations after the Enron collapse followed by the 2008 financial crisis. One of the most common D&O lawsuits is a securities class action lawsuit. This type of suit usually alleges that the corporation's directors and officers made material misrepresentations in public communications that artificially inflated the value of the stock, insiders profited by selling the stock, and then the corporation's stock price sharply dropped, resulting in a severe financial loss to investors.

D&O coverage is provided on forms developed by the insurers who write this coverage rather than by a policy form publisher, such as ISO. Coverage A, sometimes called "Side A," insures the individual directors and officers. Coverage B, often called "Side B," insures the corporation for the amounts that it is lawfully permitted or required to pay to defend or to settle claims against the directors or officers. These legal costs represent a significant exposure. Some policies also provide **entity coverage** for the organization in addition to its directors and officers. Almost all D&O policies have a **claims-made coverage trigger**.

Employment Practices Liability

Employment practices liability (EPL) loss exposures arise from laws that protect employees against discrimination, sexual harassment, unfair wage practices, and other prohibited employer practices. Until recently this was primarily a U.S. exposure. However, many countries now have laws prohibiting discrimination and harassment, and litigation of these issues has become a global issue.

Insurance is available globally to provide coverage for employment practices liability. For example, Liberty International Underwriters offers a European

---

Claims-made coverage form
A coverage form that provides coverage for bodily injury or property damage that is claimed during the policy period.

Occurrence coverage form
A coverage form that covers bodily injury or property damage occurring during the policy period.

Entity coverage
Coverage extension of D&O liability policies for claims made directly against a corporation (the "entity") for wrongful acts covered by the policy.

Claims-made coverage trigger
The event that triggers coverage under a claims-made coverage form; the first making of a claim against any insured during either the policy period or an extended reporting period.

Employment Practice Liability Insurance Policy that provides coverage for discrimination, harassment, retaliation, breach of employment contract, libel, defamation, or slander. Most EPL policies, similar to D&O policies, are written on a claims-made basis.

Fiduciary Liability

Fiduciary liability insurance policies are similar to D&O and EPL policies. The standard for a fiduciary is high. Any person involved in the design, administration, funding, or management of a benefit plan or of its assets has a duty to act solely in the best interests of the plan and all of its participants and beneficiaries. Additionally, a fiduciary must ensure that the plan's investments are sufficiently diversified to minimize the risk of large losses and to act according to plan documents and applicable law. A fiduciary who invests plan assets will be held to the same standard of care as professionals who perform investment activities. An employee plan administrator has vicarious liability for breaches of fiduciary duty by an employee or agent as well as liability for his or her own actions.

Aircraft Insurance

Three common elements of aviation loss exposures distinguish them from other types of loss exposures:

- The potential for catastrophic loss
- A limited spread of risk
- Diversifying factors that distinguish the loss exposures of each individual aircraft and pilot

Because of the nature of aviation loss exposures, they are not only excluded from general liability policies, but there are few insurers with the capacity and expertise to provide this type of coverage. Most aviation coverage is provided by aviation pools or by Lloyds correspondents. In the U.S., two pools, the United States Aircraft Insurance Group and the Associated Aviation Underwriters, have the largest share of the aviation insurance market. A typical aircraft insurance policy provides both physical damage and liability coverage.

Ocean Marine Insurance

There are three general categories of coverage in marine insurance:

- The vessel
- Liability
- Cargo

Hull insurance provides coverage on the vessel plus collision liability coverage for property damage to property not on board the vessel. Hull insurance

---

Fiduciary liability insurance
Insurance that covers the fiduciaries of an employee benefit plan against liability claims alleging breach of their fiduciary duties involving discretionary judgment.

is usually written on a named-perils basis for **perils of the seas** and several additional perils.

Protection and indemnity (P&I) insurance provides coverage for vessel liability loss exposures as well as several other incidental expenses. The main providers of P&I for vessels used in international trade are P&I clubs, which are mutual insurers controlled by the vessel owners they insure. In the U.S., conventional insurers are a common source of P&I for commercial vessels that navigate inland or coastal waters.

P&I coverage can be written to provide coverage for cargo on vessels, but not all coverage forms provide this coverage. Ocean cargo insurance can also be purchased separately by the owner or shipper of the cargo. Additional marine insurance is available for special purposes, such as marinas, shipbuilders and repairers, and offshore oil and gas facilities. The energy market typically provides offshore oil and gas coverage on a subscription basis with multiple insurers providing coverage for an insured because of the size of the exposures.

> **Perils of the sea**
> Accidental causes of loss that are peculiar to the sea and other bodies of water.

Environmental Insurance

Environmental liability is excluded from most general liability and auto policies. In the U.S., there are a number of federal laws, such as the Clean Water Act, the Clean Air Act, and the Motor Carrier Act of 1980, that seek to improve the quality of the environment by prohibiting and regulating the discharge of pollutants. There are various environmental insurance policies that provide coverage for these exposures. The policies are categorized as site-specific, operations-specific, or professional liability. These policies are developed by individual insurers, and coverage provisions vary widely.

In the European Union, the Environmental Liability Directive (ELD) introduces remediation costs for polluters along with strict liability. However, environmental liability insurance is not compulsory under the ELD, and there is not yet a widespread demand for this coverage.

SUMMARY

Risk management professionals should classify the types of hazard risks in their organizations. After the risks are classified, they should be measured according to their frequency and severity. The risks can then be managed through risk control, risk transfer (typically insurance), or a combination of the two.

Individuals and organizations incur losses when assets they own decrease in value. Situations or conditions that expose assets to loss are called loss exposures. The elements of any loss exposure are an asset exposed to loss, the cause of loss (or peril), and the financial consequences of the loss. Property loss exposures, liability loss exposures, personnel loss exposures, and net income loss exposures each contain the three elements.

Commercial insurance is divided into two major categories, property and liability. It is then further categorized into different lines of business. Risk management professionals should understand the coverage provided—and excluded—in the typical policy forms for each line of coverage in order to cost-effectively transfer their organizations' risks.

ASSIGNMENT NOTES

1. "Overview of Enterprise Risk Management," Casualty Actuarial Society: Enterprise Risk Management Committee, www.casact.org/research/erm/overview.pdf, 2003 (accessed March 7, 2012).
2. The Basel Committee on Banking Supervision, Consultative Document: Operational Risk (Geneva, Switzerland: Bank for International Settlements, 2001), p. 2.
3. Harold D. Skipper and W. Jean Kwon, Risk Management and Insurance: Perspectives in a Global Economy (Victoria, Australia: Blackwell Publishing, 2007), p. 22.
4. Douglas G. Hoffman, Managing Operational Risk (New York: John Wiley & Sons, Inc., 2002), p. 11.
5. James Lam, Enterprise Risk Management: From Incentives to Controls (Hoboken, N.J.: John Wiley & Sons, Inc., 2003), p. 288.
6. Hoffman, Managing Operational Risk, p. 11.
7. Industrial All Risks Policy, www.rahejaqbe.com/Corporate/Commercial-Property/IndustrialAllRisksPolicy/Insurance.html (accessed March 12, 2012).

Direct Your Learning

Operational, Financial, and Strategic Risk

Educational Objectives

After learning the content of this assignment, you should be able to:

- Describe operational risk and its subcategories.
- Explain how risk indicators are used to track the level of operational risk.
- Describe financial risk and its subcategories.
- Apply the concepts of value at risk and earnings at risk to financial risk.
- Explain how regulatory capital provides protection from the downside of financial and operational risks.
- Apply the concept of economic capital to insurers.
- Describe strategic risk and its major subcategories.

Outline

Operational Risk

Operational Risk Indicators

Financial Risk

Value at Risk and Earnings at Risk

Regulatory Capital

Economic Capital

Strategic Risk

Summary

Operational, Financial, and Strategic Risk

OPERATIONAL RISK

Operational risk is an integral part of each organization's functions. Successful organizations define, understand, and manage their operational risks.

It is essential that organizations understand how operational risk has evolved. Traditional informal methods of managing operational risk are no longer effective. To successfully manage operational risk, an organization must have a framework that classifies it. A typical framework includes these risk categories:

- People
- Process
- Systems
- External events

Operational Risk in General

Traditionally, operational risk was managed during the course of business by an organization's front-line managers. However, large operational losses in recent years, regulatory interest, and risk management trends resulted in a new focus on operational risk.

In 2008, a rogue trader at the French bank Société Générale lost 4.9 billion euros for the bank. This scandal and other headline examples of large operational losses, including those during the financial crisis of 2008, led to an understanding of the potential impact of operational risk on financial institutions. However, this risk applies to any organization. The publicity and lawsuits related to acceleration problems in Toyota vehicles in 2009 are examples of the consequences of operational risk in a manufacturing organization. The collapse of Enron in 2001 illustrates the result of inappropriate risk taking, while the bankruptcy of Kodak in 2012 illustrates the result of failing to take risk by embracing new technology. See the exhibit "Factors Underlying the Emphasis on Operational Risk."

Operational Risk Definitions

There are various definitions of operational risk. Financial institutions and their regulators typically define operational risk as any risk that is not market risk or credit risk. Therefore, financial institutions include hazard risk in their definition of operational risk. Basel II states that "operational risk is the risk of

Factors Underlying the Emphasis on Operational Risk

Headline financial services losses/recognition of risk costs	For example, J. P. Morgan reported a $2 billion trading loss in May 2012.
Regulatory developments	In response to the increase in business complexity and headline financial losses, there is an increase in regulatory focus on operational risk.
Trends in risk management	The interest in enterprise risk management and other risk management trends has increased the focus on operational risk.
Advances in technology	An increase in the speed of transactions also increases the risks in executing those transactions. The increasing use of e-commerce increases risks of hacking and data breaches.
Business complexity	Global competition and an increasingly mobile workforce increase operational risk.
Global litigiousness	The global increase in litigation increases the financial and reputational cost of operational risk.
Increased competition/ squeezed margins	The pressure to compete can result in cost-cutting and a corresponding risk to quality. Additionally, compressed margins lead to increased significance of any size operational loss.
Insurance environment	There are few traditional insurance products available to provide transfer of operational risk.
Frequency of natural disasters	The frequency of catastrophic natural disasters such as windstorm and earthquake has increased in recent years. Global supply chains increase the impact of these disasters for many international organizations.

Adapted from Douglas G. Hoffman, Managing Operational Risk (New York: John Wiley & Sons, Inc., 2002), pp. 31-34. [DA08703]

loss resulting from inadequate or failed internal processes, people and systems, or from external events." Under this definition, the portion of operational risk that comprises hazard risk is insurable.

Many organizations other than financial institutions view hazard risk and operational risk as separate categories. Definitions of operational risk used by these organizations may include positive, or opportunity, risk in addition to negative risk. It is essential for each organization to define operational risk based on its own assessment of its objectives and risks.

The ISO 31000 definition of risk—an event that would affect an organization's objectives if it occurs—is critical to an organization in understanding and managing its operational risk. Operational risk is integrated in every activity of an organization, from undertaking a major new venture to executing core business transactions. An organization should decide at the senior management level its strategic objectives, along with its risk appetite and risk tolerance. Operations managers should align their activities with the organization's objectives and risk management philosophy. They should be responsible and accountable for effective risk management. Accountability can include incentives, such as bonuses, increases in compensation, promotions, and recognition.

People, Process, Systems, and External Events

After defining operational risk, an organization should categorize its specific operational risks to develop a framework for managing them. Four commonly used categories of operational risk are people, process, systems, and external events. An organization can adapt these categories or use other classifications that match its operating structure and risks.

People

The category of people typically includes all of the employees of an organization. It can also include an organization's contractors, vendors, clients, and other people that the organization chooses to classify in this category. Selecting the right people provides an organization with the opportunity to grow. People can also present downside risk.

Many of the risks associated with people are hazard risks or other types of insurable risk. For example, discrimination or harassment by managers can be insured under employment practices liability coverage. However, not all of the consequences of these risks are insurable. For instance, a publicized case of discrimination can cause reputational damage or discourage highly qualified candidates from applying for employment.

Although employee theft and dishonesty may be insurable, rogue trading and other types of risky conduct that employees engage in are often not insurable. Additionally, opportunity risks that employees, especially managers, do not take are not insurable. For example, an employee who refuses to customize a product or service for a key customer because the customization does not strictly conform to an organization's standard procedure could cost the organization a significant customer and corresponding revenue.

Errors made during the course of business can lead to significant cost, either in aggregate or as a result of one particularly costly error. Errors and omissions (E&O) insurance and liability insurance can provide coverage for some of these errors but will rarely provide coverage for errors that do not affect a third party. For example, if a bank employee incorrectly keys in the amount of a payment so that a customer's account is credited more than it should have been, this type of error would not be covered by insurance. If the customer notices and reports this error, the bank could also suffer reputational loss. See the exhibit "Strategies to Mitigate People Risk."

> ### Strategies to Mitigate People Risk
>
> **Recruitment**
>
> Recruitment methods can be used to identify appropriate candidates for hire. For example, recruitment on college campuses, recruitment of military veterans, or the use of employment consultants to recruit and screen candidates can assist in identifying the right people for an organization.
>
> **Selection**
>
> Various selection procedures can mitigate people risk. Checking of references and criminal backgrounds, when legally permitted, can identify people who pose risks. Interviews and pre-employment tests conducted within legal guidelines can identify people with risk profiles that match an organization's risk philosophy.
>
> **Training and Development**
>
> Training should be designed to address the risks relevant to a particular employee. Managers responsible for employment decisions should be trained regarding legally acceptable behavior with employees. Employees should be trained regarding desirable and undesirable risk taking. Thorough training and continuing education can help employees perform effectively and reduce the risks associated with suboptimal performance.
>
> **Performance Management**
>
> Employee performance should be addressed at periodic reviews as well as in connection with questionable behavior. Employees who are meeting expectations should know that, because it will reinforce their behavior and can influence the behavior of others. Management of employees who exhibit questionable behavior should be handled according to written and well-understood guidelines.
>
> **Incentives**
>
> Incentives can be used to manage risky behaviors, encouraging appropriate risk taking and discouraging inappropriate risk taking. There have been reports, for example, that rogue trading at some financial organizations was encouraged through incentives when the trading was profitable and was discouraged only when a loss occurred. This type of incentive program will inevitably result in a large loss at some point.
>
> Rewards, including recognition and financial compensation, can be used to draw the attention of other employees to desirable behavior as well as to applaud a successful employee. Studies have indicated that employees desire recognition from their managers for jobs well done as much as they desire salary increases and bonuses.
>
> **Succession Planning**
>
> Organizations should have a plan for succession for key executive positions. Positions such as CEO and CFO are critical to an organization. It is also important to have processes to replace other employees who perform the essential functions of an organization. For example, an online job application process can provide a bank of resumes to a manager when a position becomes available.

[DA08704]

Each organization should be aware of the significance of its culture in managing its people risk. Some cultures encourage risk taking, while others encourage risk avoidance. Cultures are mainly informal and therefore can be difficult to change. In addition to observation and informal employee feedback, techniques such as employee surveys can be effective in determining important facets of an organization's culture and provide a basis for making changes when necessary.

Process

Process risk typically includes the procedures and practices organizations use to conduct their business activities. Managing these risks includes a framework of procedures and a mechanism to identify practices that deviate from the procedures. A risk often occurs at the point at which a practice departs from procedure. Occasionally, such departures are creative and present a new and potentially more effective method. However, much of the time, these departures create a negative risk. For example, failure to follow product inspection procedures in an effort to speed production can result in unacceptable product failures, with severe consequences.

An organization's procedures should represent best practices and be designed for quality and for the safety of products and employees. Analysis of losses and close calls can provide a continuous feedback loop to help monitor the effectiveness of procedures and redesign them when necessary. For example, hospitals typically track rates of infection to determine whether a potential source of infection exists at the facility and needs to be addressed.

Systems

Systems risk includes risks associated with technology and equipment. Technology risks include both the equipment used and the software. The risks concern the function of the technology, the risks of intentional or accidental failure, and security risks. The evolution of technology is one of the factors that led to greater recognition of operational risk. A data breach at a financial organization in which customer records are stolen can cause a loss that might threaten the organization's existence.

Equipment failure may present hazard risk as well as risk for an organization's continuing operations. Some of this risk is insurable; however, other aspects, such as the potential loss of customers and market opportunity, are not.

External Events

For organizations that include hazard risk in their definition of operational risk, external events include natural disasters such as windstorm or earthquake. Operational risks from disasters include business interruption in addition to loss of property.

The loss of a key supplier, either temporarily or permanently, can create operational risk. The organization may not be able to meet production goals until another source for the supplies can be found.

Similarly, a utility failure or inadequacy can cause operational risk. Although some utility failures may result from a hazard that is insurable, many failures or inadequate supplies of power result from the overload of an electrical system. Such interruptions can cause production delays and other problems.

Changes in external systems an organization uses, such as software changes, can create the need for additional employee training, taking time away from production.

OPERATIONAL RISK INDICATORS

A risk management best practice is the development and use of key risk indicators (KRIs) to determine operational risk.

Risk management professionals should identify operational KRIs by operational risk class. Additionally, they should identify exposure and control indicators. Trend analysis and benchmarks can help identify how risk indicators affect outcomes.

Introduction to Risk Indicators

Risk management is most effective when the issues that may lead to losses are identified and managed before a loss occurs. Analysis of historical losses can identify **root causes** and target issues for management. However, retrospective analysis may be too late to prevent a catastrophic loss.

A more successful approach is to analyze near misses, or incidents, before a loss occurs. This approach involves recording and tracking incidents in addition to losses. For example, any incident of a trader at a bank trading outside his or her authority level would be reported and addressed, whether or not the trade resulted in a loss.

The most successful risk management approach is to identify issues before incidents occur and eventually result in losses. This approach requires developing leading indicators of risk: **key risk indicators (KRIs)**. See the exhibit "Progression of Issues to Losses."

If risky issues can be identified before they lead to incidents, and before the incidents lead to losses, then those issues can be either removed or managed. To that end, KRIs must be leading, rather than lagging, to be effective. If a bank learns of rogue trading after a billion-dollar loss, the bank may not survive long enough to use this lagging indicator to prevent future occurrences.

Root cause
The event or circumstance that directly leads to an occurrence.

Key risk indicator (KRI)
A financial or nonfinancial metric used to help define and measure potential losses.

Progression of Issues to Losses

Losses

Incidents

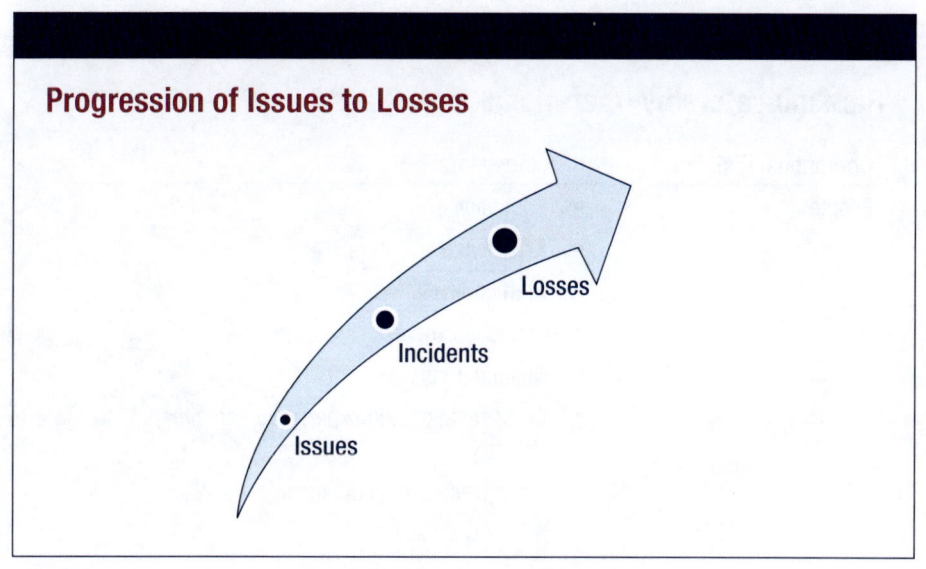

Issues

[DA08720]

Indicators by Operational Risk Class

Although each organization will have risk indicators that apply exclusively to its type of business or operations, generic risk indicators also exist and can be identified by three operational risk classes: people, processes, and systems. See the exhibit "Risk Indicators by Operational Risk Class."

For example, Jerome Kerviel, the rogue trader who caused a multibillion-dollar loss for Societe Generale, had little experience in the type of trading he was involved in. A mismatch between an employee's experience and responsibility is a KRI that can be applied to any organization.

If a KRI to determine whether traders are exceeding authority levels had been used, the loss that Kerviel caused for his bank could have been prevented. A review of daily reports of trading activities could have provided this KRI for internal auditors.

A bank's computer system can be programmed with red flags to provide KRIs for irregular financial transactions. Unauthorized attempts to access a computer can also provide KRIs of potential hacking or fraud.

Exposure Indicators

Exposure indicators are indicators that are integral to an organization's operations. For example, an insurer's risk of loss in a line of business is integral to the insurer's operations. Exposure indicators are also referred to as inherent indicators.

Most organizations have data available regarding their exposures, and this data can be used to identify key exposure indicators. Typically, organizations will already be using such indicators. An insurer tracks losses for regulatory

Exposure indicator
A metric used to identify risk inherent to an organization's operations.

Risk Indicators by Operational Risk Class

Operational Risk Class	Risk Indicators
People	• Education
	• Experience
	• Staffing levels
	• Employee surveys
	• Customer surveys
	• Compensation and experience benchmarked to industry
	• Incentives such as bonuses
	• Authority levels
	• Management experience
Processes	• Quality scorecards
	• Analysis of errors
	• Areas of increased activity or volume
	• Review of outcomes
	• Internal and external review
	• Identification of areas of highest risk
	• Quality of internal audit procedures
Systems	• Benchmarks against industry standards
	• Internal and external review
	• Analysis to determine stress points and weaknesses
	• Identification of areas of highest risk
	• Testing
	• Monitoring

[DA08721]

Loss ratio
A ratio that measures losses and loss adjustment expenses against earned premiums and that reflects the percentage of premiums being consumed by losses.

Control indicator
A metric used to identify an organization's management of risk.

and financial reporting purposes as well as for its own information. Details about these losses are readily available from various functions within the organization. The insurer can benchmark its **loss ratio** to industry results for this line of business.[1]

Control Indicators

Control indicators usually provide information about management. An insurer can, for example, develop key control indicators regarding claim handling of reported losses. Indicators such as claim representative, claim volume, and skill level can provide people with risk indicators regarding the management of claim offices. Claim closure rates and average claim costs can provide process indicators. System training requirements and data completion can provide indicators of the effectiveness of the claim system. Benchmarking between different claim offices of the insurer can be useful in identifying issues that need to be managed.[2]

Relating Indicators and Outcomes

Risk management professionals may want to evaluate how a control indicator affects outcomes. For example, a temporary staffing organization may want to analyze how the experience of its employees in their fields relates to complaints received from the company's clients.

The first level of analysis may be to chart the number of complaints received from clients and the experience level of employees assigned to those clients. See the exhibit "Risk Indicator: Client Complaints Versus Years of Employee Experience."

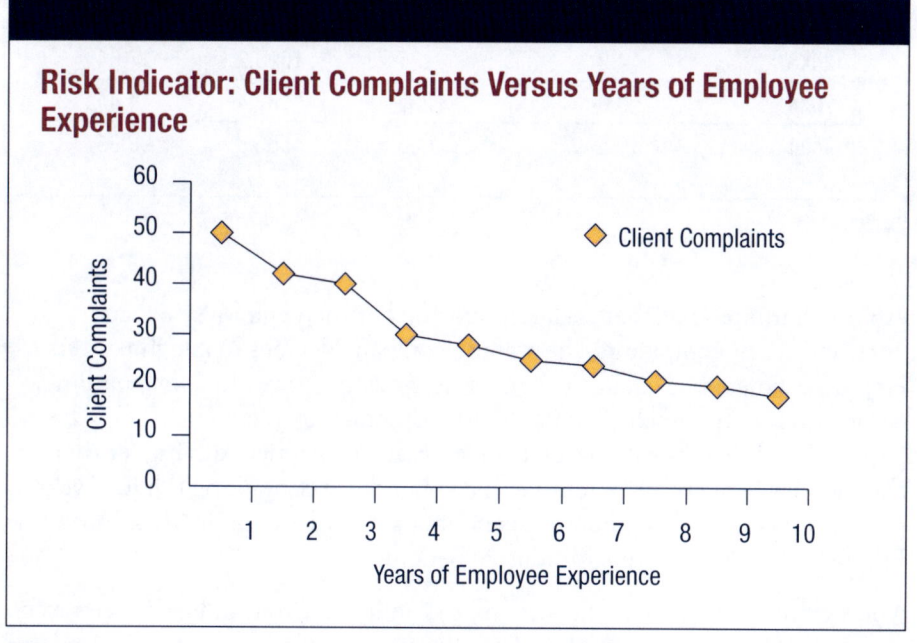

Risk Indicator: Client Complaints Versus Years of Employee Experience

[DA08722]

The staffing company sees a correlation between the experience level of its employees and its client complaints and decides to analyze the trend. To perform this analysis, the company's risk manager can use a regression to evaluate the relationship between average employee experience (x) and client complaints (y) over a four-year period. An equation is used to provide a model of the variables:

$$y = a + bx$$

where:

$$a = (\Sigma y)(\Sigma x^2) - (\Sigma x)(\Sigma xy) \div n(\Sigma x^2) - (\Sigma x)^2$$

$$b = n(\Sigma xy) - (\Sigma x)(\Sigma y) \div n(\Sigma x^2) - (\Sigma x)^2$$

Through such an equation, a regression analyzes the relationship between variables and can be used to indicate a trend in the relationship over time. See the exhibit "Regression of Annual Client Complaints Against Annual Average Employee Experience."

Regression of Annual Client Complaints Against Annual Average Employee Experience

Year	x: Average Experience (Years)	y: Complaints	xy	x²
20X1	6.0	197	1182.0	36.00
20X2	5.5	210	1155.0	30.25
20X3	4.2	261	1096.2	17.64
20X4	3.8	298	1132.4	14.44
Total	19.5	966	4565.6	98.33

[DA08724]

After confirming that there is a relationship between employee experience and client complaints, the staffing company decides to benchmark its employee experience against others in its industry; however, data regarding complaints are not readily available from other companies. The staffing company did find that its employees' average years of experience is higher than the industry benchmark of four years ago but decreased during the four-year period and is now lower than the benchmark. See the exhibit "Risk Indicator: Employee Experience Versus Industry Benchmark."

The staffing company now has several risk indicators that indicate issues to be managed. The company learned that client complaints appear to be correlated to employee experience. It also learned that the average experience of its employees is decreasing and is currently lower than the industry benchmark. Finally, the company learned that the number of client complaints is increasing. The company already knows that inexperienced workers tend to have more occupational injuries.

Through these KRIs, the company has identified an issue of decreasing experience level in its employees and can now manage this issue. It can change its advertising and recruitment strategies to attract employees with more experience. It can also consider benchmarking its compensation to the industry to

Risk Indicator: Employee Experience Versus Industry Benchmark

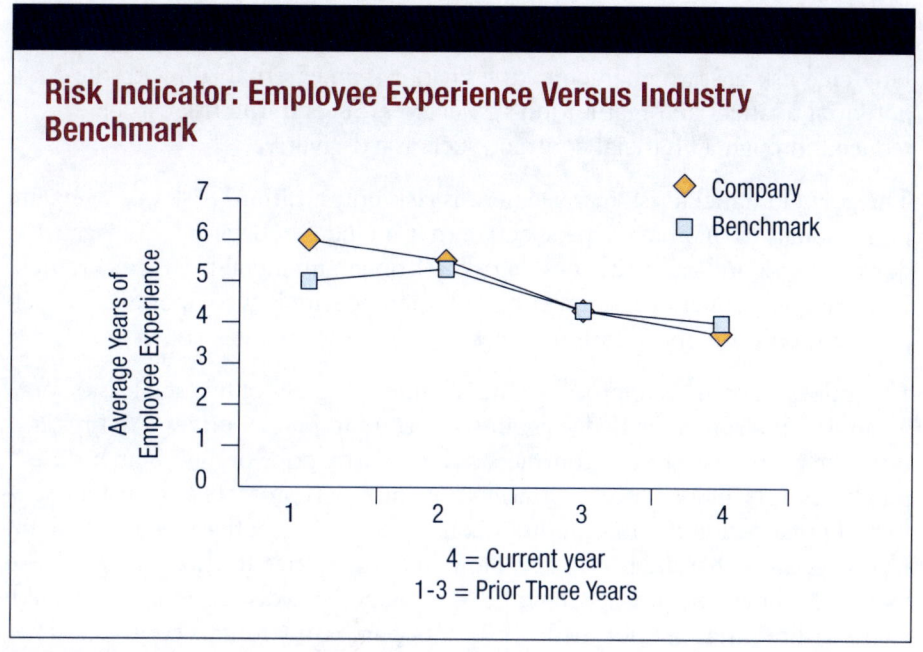

(Chart: Average Years of Employee Experience, showing Company vs. Benchmark across years 1-4, where 4 = Current year and 1-3 = Prior Three Years)

[DA08725]

be sure that it is paying experienced employees appropriately. The company can further take steps to conduct basic customer service training for all of its employees to improve client satisfaction.

FINANCIAL RISK

Financial risk was central to the financial crisis of 2008. Ironically, derivatives that were designed to manage this risk were major factors in the global crisis. As a result, there is a new focus on financial risk management by organizations and regulators.

Most organizations face some financial risks. These are the three major types of financial risk:

- Market risk
- Credit risk
- Price risk

There are various techniques used to manage financial risk. Hedging, including the use of derivatives, is a useful risk management technique. However, for this technique to be effective, it should be used in the context of a risk management framework and process that comprehensively addresses an organization's risks and their interrelationships.

Financial Risk in General

Financial risk has two characteristics. First, it is an external risk with the potential to affect an organization's objectives. Second, the risk can be reduced through a financial contract, such as a derivative.[3]

The goal of financial risk management is **risk optimization**. Risk management professionals should have a perspective that includes both protecting against downside risk and capturing upside risk. Although financial risks are external, internal management's risk appetite and tolerance are key components of each organization's risk optimization process.

Hedging is a common approach to many different types of financial risk. For example, an airline may hedge against volatility in jet fuel prices. An organization may purchase future contracts to lock in the price of fuel. If an airline purchases a six-month futures contract, the airline is protected against a rise in fuel price during the intervening six months and may offer lower fares than its competitors that did not hedge. However, if the price in this highly volatile market declines, the airline would be at a competitive disadvantage compared to the airlines that did not incur the cost of purchasing futures contracts. The airline could instead purchase both call and put positions, called a collar, to provide a price range. These options provide the opportunity to buy and sell the commodity at specified prices which determine the range, limiting the airline's price risk in either direction. A financial institution may purchase derivative contracts to hedge some of its credit risk. For example, a bank may purchase a credit default swap (CDS) that will pay the bank if a corporate debtor defaults on a bond payment.

There is a transaction cost associated with the use of financial contracts to reduce financial risk. In addition to the fee or premium charged by the firm that issues the contract, there is also the risk of allocating capital to a hedge that may or may not be useful to an organization. Mathematical models and simulations can assist with these decisions and help achieve risk optimization. However, models must be used with caution because they may not adequately reflect reality. For example, the models used to develop collateralized debt obligations (CDOs) derived from mortgages prior to the financial crisis did not account for the possibility that housing prices could fall.

Market Risk

Market risk arises from changes in the value of financial instruments. Some of these risks are **systematic risk**, while others are nonsystematic. Many of these types of instruments are traded on exchanges, while others are customized contracts. These are the major categories of market risk:

- Currency price risk
- Interest rate risk
- Commodity price risk

Risk optimization
A state whereby risk and return are balanced so that a maximum return is achieved for the level of risk accepted by an organization.

Hedging
A financial transaction in which one asset is held to offset the risk associated with another asset.

Systematic risk
Risk that is common to all securities of the same general class and that therefore cannot be eliminated by diversification.

- Equity price risk
- Liquidity risk

Market risk has both downside and upside potential. For example, the risk associated with the price of a stock includes the potential for the stock to rise or fall.

Currency Price Risk

Organizations that operate in more than one country have risks related to changes in the currency exchange rates of those countries. Large multinational organizations have risks related to the currency rates of the countries in which they manufacture products as well as those in which they sell products.

For example, Volkswagen AG stated in its *2010 Annual Report* that it hedges principal foreign currency risks against the euro in these currencies: United States dollars, sterling, Czech koruna, Swedish krona, Russian rubles, Australian dollars, Polish zloty, Swiss francs, Mexican pesos, and Japanese yen. Volkswagen also stated that it primarily uses "natural" hedging by adapting production capacity around the world and procuring many components locally.

Interest Rate Risk

Interest rate risk is a systematic risk that affects all organizations. The U.S. Federal Reserve's federal funds interest rate influences the interest rates on U.S. treasury bonds, bank interest rates, and a wide range of macroeconomic factors. There are several risk management techniques that can be applied to interest rate risk. Variable interest rates can be negotiated. **Swaps** can be used to hedge against interest rate volatility.

Insurers are vulnerable to interest rate risk for two reasons. First, insurers have investments, typically bonds, with durations linked to expected claim payments from different lines of business. Second, insurers earn much of their income from investment returns on reserves before they are needed to pay claims. **Cash matching** provides a means of eliminating interest rate risk because it provides a predictable stream of income until losses are due. An insurer only needs to hold an investment until it matures. Changes in interest rates will not matter if the insurer does not plan to sell the investment in the market before it matures.

However, the cash matching strategy has significant limitations. It only works when the insurer can purchase **zero-coupon bonds** with maturity dates and maturity values that precisely match the expected cash outflows from the underwriting portfolio. A zero-coupon bond is a corporate bond that is sold at a discount to par value, with the difference between the discounted sale price and the par value redemption price providing a compounded fixed return amount over the life of the bond. Second, even if such bonds are available, the insurer would need to purchase enough of each type of security to match

---

Interest rate risk
The risk that a security's future value will decline because of changes in interest rates.

Swap
An agreement between two organizations to exchange payments based on changes in the value of an asset, yield, or index over a specific period.

Cash matching
The process of matching an investment's maturity value with the amount of expected loss payments.

Zero-coupon bond
A corporate bond that does not pay periodic interest income.

its expected claim payments. In practice, neither condition can be expected to be met, especially for insurers with large underwriting portfolios in different lines of business.

Most bonds are not zero-coupon bonds, but instead pay interest. The insurer must decide how to reinvest the interest payments until the loss payments are due, creating a second type of interest-related risk called **reinvestment risk**. The insurer must not only be concerned about the interest rates available at the time the original investment is made, but also about the prevailing interest rates when each interest payment is received and reinvested.

Commodity Price Risk

Commodity price risk affects many different types of organizations. Airlines, trucking companies, and utilities use fuel produced from oil. Manufacturers of food products use agricultural products. Changes in commodity prices can have a significant effect on an organization's **cash flow**.

Organizations can manage their commodity price risk through purchase of **commodity futures contracts**. Hedging through the use of derivatives linked to the price of a commodity is a technique that some organizations use successfully to manage commodity price risk.

Equity Price Risk

Equity price risk can have various effects on organizations. These effects can be classified as such:

- Risks related to an organization's own share price
- Risks related to an organization's investments in external stocks and other securities
- Risks related to the average share price in a market or market sector

An organization's share price can rise or fall for many different reasons. A fall in share price can constrict the organization's ability to raise capital. Financial organizations typically have significant investments in the securities of other organizations. A change in the price of a major investment can affect a financial institution's profit. Change in the price of a market index, such as the Standard & Poor's (S&P) stock index, can have a broad effect on a financial organization's investment portfolio.

Risk management techniques for equity price risks associated with investments include hedging with derivatives and options. **Call options** and **put options** allow an investor to narrow the range of price risk for a security. Organizations may use stock repurchase or dividends to manage equity price risk of their own shares. Investors typically value stocks that provide dividends, and issuing a dividend or increasing the amount of a dividend may make an organization's stock more attractive to potential investors. When an organization repurchases shares of stock, there are fewer outstanding shares.

Reinvestment risk
The risk that the rate at which periodic interest payments can be reinvested over the life of the investment will be unfavorable.

Commodity price risk
The risk associated with a change in the prices of commodities that are necessary to an organization's operations.

Cash flow
Cash inflow minus cash outflow.

Commodity futures contract
A contract either to make or to accept delivery of a specified quantity of a commodity on a given date.

Equity price risk
The risk that changes in the price of a stock or another security will increase or decrease.

Call option
An option to buy a set amount of the underlying security at any time within a specified period.

Put option
An option giving the holder the right to sell a set amount of the underlying security at any time within a specified period.

Therefore, the earnings per share increase and may make the stock more attractive to investors.

Liquidity Risk

An organization's liquidity is related to its cash or its ability to raise cash. It is closely related to an organization's solvency, which is its ability to meet its financial obligations. Financial institutions have two distinct types of liquidity risk that are inherent to the nature of these organizations:

- The possibility that large numbers of clients could withdraw funds (a run on the bank)
- The possibility of off-balance sheet commitments, such as a line of credit, being exercised

Either one of these types of liquidity risk requires significant amounts of cash (liquidity) that can prevent a financial institution from meeting its objectives or possibly cause the institution's insolvency.

Financial organizations use either stored liquidity or purchased liquidity to manage their liquidity risks. Stored liquidity is the cash reserve of the bank or insurer. Purchased liquidity is cash raised in credit markets. The U.S. Federal Reserve may lend emergency funds to a bank that requires liquidity.[4]

Credit Risk

Unlike market risk, credit risk has only negative potential. If a borrower pays as agreed, there is no realized risk. If a borrower defaults, the downside of risk is realized. All organizations have some exposure to credit risk. However, for financial organizations, credit risk is an inherent exposure.

Banks are in the business of lending money to individuals and organizations. During the past twenty-five years, banks have also entered into the business of packaging loans, often made by other institutions, and selling pieces of the packaged loans to investors. There are two types of credit risk: firm-specific risk and systemic credit risk.

Firm-specific credit risk is specific to a particular financial institution and is associated with its portfolios of credit transactions. Depending on the size of the institution, these may include home mortgages, secured and unsecured personal loans, commercial loans, credit cards, and lines of credit. Risk management techniques for firm-specific risk include diversification of both the types and durations of credit issued, evaluation of the creditworthiness of borrowers, and transfer of some risk by selling loans to other organizations.

The latter risk management technique of many financial institutions—selling loans to other organizations—was one of the practices that led to systemic credit risk. When a borrower defaults on a loan originated and held by one financial institution, the risk is borne entirely by that financial institution. If enough of that institution's loans default, it may become insolvent. However, when many loans are sold to financial institutions that then repackage the loans and sell portions of the packages to a wide variety of institutions, default by a sufficient number of borrowers can create a systemic credit crisis. This began to occur in 2007 with securities backed by subprime mortgage loans and was one of the factors that led to the financial crisis of 2008. Management of systemic credit risk because of its nature involves regulatory oversight.

Price Risk

> **Price risk**
> The potential for a change in revenue or cost because of an increase or a decrease in the price of a product or an input.

Unlike credit risk and similar to market risk, **price risk** has both positive and negative potential. Price risk has two aspects for most organizations:

- The price charged for the organization's products or services
- The price of assets purchased or sold by an organization

An organization usually tries to set prices for its products or services to be competitive and to earn a profit. If the organization's prices are too high relative to its competitors, it may lose customers and market share. If its prices are too low, its profit margins will be squeezed.

If an organization owns assets, increases in the market price of those assets will increase their value on the organization's balance sheet.

Apply Your Knowledge

A bank is considering whether to purchase the auto loan portfolio of another bank. What are the financial risk(s) associated with this purchase?

a. Equity price risk
b. Commodity price risk
c. Credit risk

Feedback: c. The bank would pay for a portfolio of credit products where borrowers might default, creating credit risk.

VALUE AT RISK AND EARNINGS AT RISK

To evaluate financial risk, a risk management professional should understand the range of potential financial outcomes.

Risk management professionals can use metrics such as value at risk (VaR) or **earnings at risk (EaR)** to determine the probability of various financial outcomes.

> **Earnings at risk**
> The maximum expected loss of earnings within a specific degree of confidence.

VaR is a method of determining the probability of loss on an investment portfolio over a certain, usually short, time horizon. VaR is primarily used by financial institutions that have extensive investments in securities. Similar to VaR, EaR is a measure that can be used for nonfinancial organizations.

Value at Risk

VaR measures the probability of the loss in an investment's value exceeding a threshold level. In addition to working within a short time horizon, VaR is typically characterized by low probability. For example, a one-day, 5 percent VaR of $300,000 means there is a 5 percent probability of losing $300,000 or more over the next day.

VaR provides three key benefits as a risk measure:

- The potential loss associated with an investment decision can be quantified.
- Complex positions are expressed as a single figure.
- Loss is expressed in easily understood monetary terms.

However, VaR also has a limitation. It does not accurately measure the extent to which a loss might exceed the VaR threshold. This limitation can be addressed with **conditional value at risk (CVaR)**. CVaR provides the same benefits as VaR and also takes into account the extremely large losses that may occur, usually with low probabilities, in the tail of a value distribution. See the exhibit "VaR Distribution."

Conditional value at risk
A model to determine the likelihood of a loss given that the loss is greater than or equal to the VaR.

Apply Your Knowledge

A one-day VaR of $20,000 is determined from the VaR exhibit by:

a. Adding all the probabilities to the right of $20,000.
b. Adding all the probabilities to the left of $20,000.
c. Adding all the probabilities to the right of -$20,000.
d. Adding all the probabilities to the left of -$20,000.

Feedback: d. A one-day VaR of $20,000 is determined from the exhibit by adding all the probabilities to the left of –$20,000.

Earnings at Risk

Determining EaR entails modeling the influence of factors such as changes in the prices of products, sales, prices of commodities and components used in production, and production costs on an organization's earnings. Models are developed using **Monte Carlo simulation**, and the distribution is usually presented in a histogram. The EaR represents the lower end of projected earnings within a specific confidence, such as 95 percent. The probability that an organization's earnings will be greater than its EaR is represented under the distribution curve to the right of the EaR value. The area to the left of the EaR in the exhibit represents the risk that earnings will be below the EaR. For example, if earnings at risk are $100,000 with 95 percent confidence, then

Monte Carlo simulation
A computerized statistical model that simulates the effects of various types of uncertainty

VaR Distribution

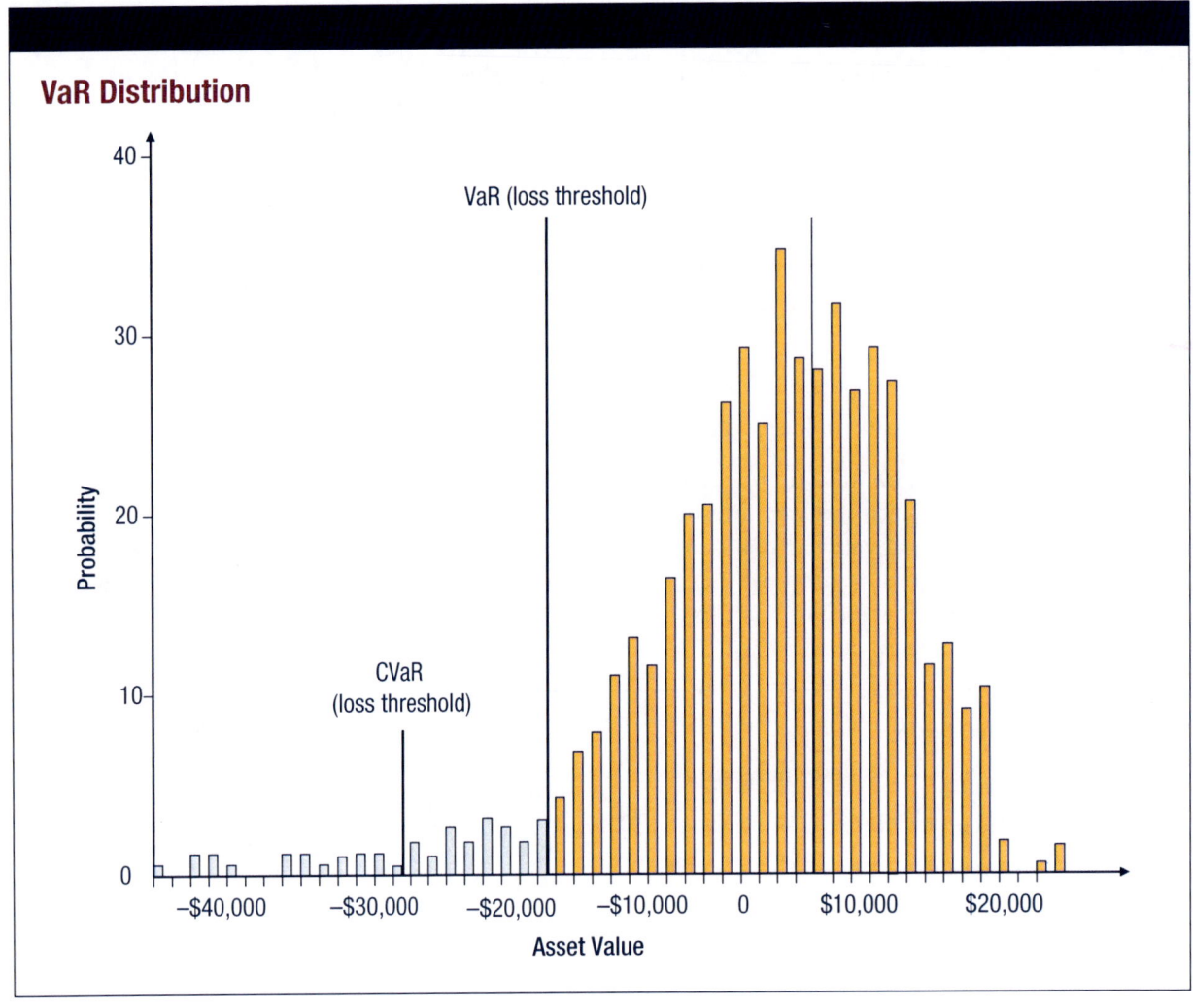

(Chart: histogram showing Probability vs. Asset Value from −$40,000 to over $20,000, with vertical lines marking "VaR (loss threshold)" near −$20,000 and "CVaR (loss threshold)" near −$32,000.)

[DA03927]

earnings at risk are projected to be $100,000 or greater 95 percent of the time and less than $100,000 5 percent of the time. See the exhibit "Histogram of EaR."

EaR is helpful in comparing the likely effects of different risk management strategies on earnings. However, there are limitations, including the complexity of the calculations and a need to understand the relationship of different variables on an organization's results.[5]

REGULATORY CAPITAL

Financial organizations are essential to national and increasingly global economies. Therefore, these organizations must be able to weather adverse events and function effectively.

Histogram of EaR

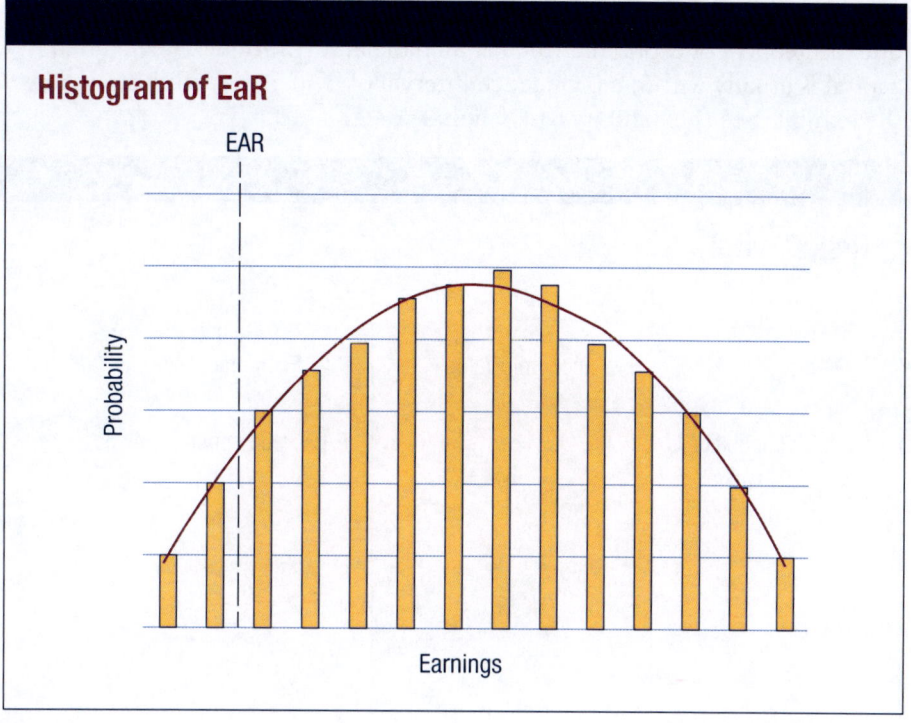

(Chart: Probability vs. Earnings, with EAR marked as a dashed vertical line on the left side of a bell-shaped distribution)

[DA08747]

The financial crisis of 2008 highlighted the leverage of many global financial institutions. At the height of the crisis, some of these highly leveraged institutions required injections of capital from their governments to survive. Regulators have since focused on risk-based capital adequacy. Basel II prescribes capital requirements to protect banks and the economy from the effects of downside risks.

Introduction to Regulatory Capital

Governments (state, national, or multinational) generally prescribe **capital** requirements for financial institutions. Financial institutions differ from other types of organizations in several respects. In addition to their key economic role, these institutions hold funds on behalf of individuals and public and private organizations. The business model of financial institutions involves the investment of these funds to earn profits. These investments entail varying levels of risk.

Because governments do not view the loss of other people's money as an acceptable risk for depository banks or insurers, there are regulations regarding the capital that these institutions must hold to protect against this type of loss. The primary risk for financial organizations is financial (market, credit, and liquidity), but they also have exposures in the other three risk quadrants (operational, hazard, and strategic).

> **Capital**
> The accumulated assets of a business or an owner's equity in a business.

Risk capital is the level of capital required to provide a cushion against unexpected loss of economic value at a financial institution. The required risk capital is usually within a confidence interval of 95 percent, as illustrated in the exhibit. See the exhibit "Risk Capital."

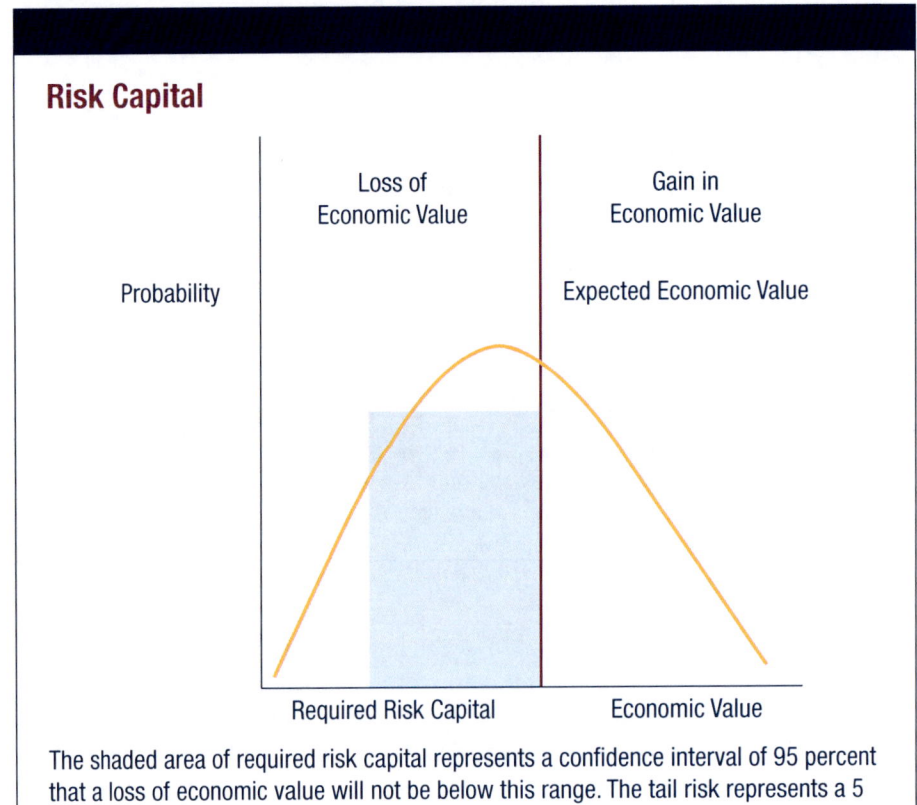

Risk Capital

The shaded area of required risk capital represents a confidence interval of 95 percent that a loss of economic value will not be below this range. The tail risk represents a 5 percent risk of loss beyond the level of required risk capital.

[DA08732]

In 1988, the United States joined with the other member nations of the Bank for International Settlements (BIS) to implement two risk-based capital ratios for the banks in their jurisdictions. This agreement is known as Basel I and was fully implemented in 2003. It followed a period of international bank failures, including the U.S. savings and loan crisis.

Basel I defined bank capital based on two tiers:

- Tier 1—Also referred to as core capital, it is essentially the same as the bank's **equity capital**.
- Tier 2—Also referred to as supplementary capital, it includes all capital other than core capital, such as gains on investment assets, long-term debt with maturity more than five years, and excess reserves for loan losses. Short-term unsecured debts are not included in the definition of capital.

Equity capital
Preferred stock, surplus, common stock, undivided profits and capital reserves, and net unrealized holding gains (or losses) on securities that are not available for sale.

Basel I prescribed a total risk-based capital ratio and a Tier I (core) capital ratio as the level of capital adequacy for banks.

Total risk-based capital ratio = Total capital (Tier 1 plus Tier 2)/Risk-adjusted assets ≥ 8 %

Tier 1 (core) capital ratio = Core capital (Tier 1)/Risk-adjusted assets ≥ 4%

The Basel I capital adequacy ratios included assets' credit risk in capital requirement determinations. These ratios replaced the simpler and weaker ratio of capital-to-assets, which did not take into account the relative risk of various assets.[6]

Although the Basel I capital requirements provided a more sophisticated measurement of banks' capital adequacy by evaluating the comparative risk of assets, this methodology had weaknesses. The calculations of risk-adjusted assets did not sufficiently take into account changes in the risk of assets or systemic risk.

Leverage was a major factor in the 2008 financial crisis. Most post-crisis regulatory approaches to capital requirements, as illustrated in the Bank of England's graph, involve risk-adjusted capital requirements for each financial institution that would vary according to leverage and other risk factors in each institution. The Bank of England also proposes adjusting capital requirements according to macroeconomic cycles. See the exhibit "Future Regulatory Capital Framework Proposed by the Bank of England."

> **Leverage**
> The practice of using borrowed money to invest.

The proposal of the Bank of England to vary capital requirements according to phases of the business cycle is similar to Section 616 of the Dodd-Frank Act in the U.S., which states, "In establishing capital regulations…the appropriate Federal banking agency shall seek to make such requirements countercyclical so that the amount of capital required to be maintained by a company increases in times of economic expansion and decreases in times of economic contraction, consistent with the safety and soundness of the insured depository institution." [7]

Regulatory Risk Capital Under Basel II

The BIS proposed changes to determinations of capital adequacy, which were published in 2004. These are the three pillars of Basel II:

- Minimum capital requirements that address risk
- Supervisory review
- Market discipline

The first pillar contains regulatory requirements for capital to address three categories of risk: credit risk, market risk, and operational risk. A significant difference from Basel I is the inclusion of a capital requirement for operational risk.

> **Future Regulatory Capital Framework Proposed by the Bank of England**
>
> The Bank of England proposes a regime for regulatory capital at financial institutions that includes capital buffers that vary over the credit cycle along with a hard minimum capital requirement. The hard minimum would be a backstop measure to capture uncertainty over the value of a bank's assets and therefore its solvency. This minimum capital would not be a usable source of capital for banks. An additional capital buffer would be needed to absorb unexpected losses while maintaining lending to the real economy, which would vary over time.
>
> Capital requirements (percent of risk-weighted assets)
>
> Time-varying overall level
>
> Time-varying buffer
>
> "Cycle-neutral" buffer
>
> Minimum requirement (hard floor)
>
> Time
>
> The y-axis represents the percentage of risk-weighted assets required as capital. The x-axis represents time corresponding to the business cycle.

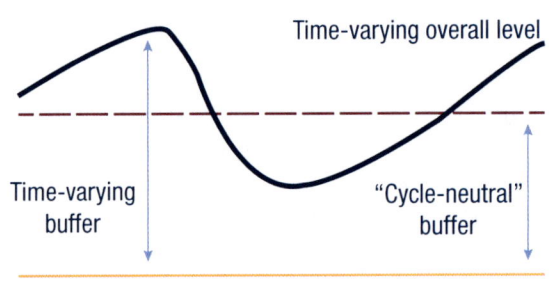

Bank of England, "Preserving Financial Stability," p. 57, www.bankofengland.co.uk/publications/Documents/fsr/2010/fsr27sec5.pdf (accessed April 5, 2012). [DA08734]

The Basel II capital framework allows two approaches to measuring a financial institution's credit risk: the standardized approach and the Internal Ratings Based (IRB) approach. The standardized approach uses ratings from international rating agencies to determine an institution's creditworthiness. The Internal Ratings Based Approach (IRBA) allows banks to use their advanced internal risk management systems for calculating regulatory capital.[8]

Under Basel II, market risk is usually measured by a bank's value at risk (VaR) models. See the exhibit "Methods Used to Determine Basel II Risk Capital Requirements."

Also under Basel II, operational risk includes risk other than financial risk and, in a significant departure from Basel I, prescribes operational risk capital requirements. There are three approaches under Basel II for determining the capital charge for a financial institution's operational risk:

- The basic indicator approach applies a capital charge of 15 percent of average annual gross income over the previous three years.
- The standardized approach applies factors ranging from 12 to 18 percent of annual revenue on each of eight business lines at the financial institu-

Methods Used to Determine Basel II Risk Capital Requirements

Basel II requires banks to maintain capital to address three categories of risk: credit risk, market risk, and operational risk. This chart outlines the methods to determine the capital required for each risk category.

Credit Risk Capital
- Standardized
- Internal Measurement

Market Risk Capital
- VaR

Operational Risk Capital
- Basic Indicator
- Standardized Approach
- Advanced Approach

[DA08735]

tion. The eight business lines are corporate finance, trading and sales, retail banking, commercial banking, payment and settlement, agency services, asset management, and retail brokerage.

- The advanced approach allows authorized financial institutions to use their own models.[9] These models must conform to a regulatory framework. A key aspect of this framework is the Basel definition of operational risk as "the risk of loss resulting from inadequate or failed internal processes, people and systems or from external events."[10] Banks will also be required to include four major factors in quantifying operational risk: internal loss data, external loss data, scenario analysis, and business environment and internal control factors.[11]

The banking supervisor will evaluate which method is appropriate for individual financial institutions to use in determining operational risk capital. The standardized approach requires an individual bank to have loss data by business line and risk type. Banks that do not have sufficient data will have to use the basic indicator approach. Banks must apply to their regulator to use the advanced approach to determine operational risk capital. This approach requires a comprehensive risk management program and extensive effort for the financial institution.

The second pillar of Basel II provides for regulatory review of the capital adequacy measures outlined in Pillar I and provides a mechanism for regulators to address systemic risks. The third pillar requires improved disclosure of capital and risk by financial institutions.

Basel II was not adopted by most member nations before the financial crisis of 2008. Since then, Basel III has been proposed by the BIS. Because of the Dodd-Frank Act and other concerns, the U.S. has not fully implemented Basel II. There has been criticism in the U.S. and elsewhere about allowing the use of banks' own measurements to determine capital adequacy under Basel II. Critics believe that this methodology continues to keep leverage at too high a level in many large international financial institutions. Basel III imposes additional capital requirements, and the BIS goal is for full implementation by 2013.

ECONOMIC CAPITAL

Economic capital is becoming an accepted, if not required, global standard for capital requirements of insurers.

Economic capital, a form of regulatory capital, is an estimate of the amount of capital a firm needs to remain solvent at a given risk tolerance level. It differs from other types of regulatory capital because rather than being based on a formula, it is based on the fair (market) values of the firm's assets and liabilities as well as their variability.

Economic capital is developed by modeling the potential variability in market value of a firm's assets and liabilities, taking into consideration all of the firm's risks (market, credit, liquidity, underwriting, operational). These risks are considered together to estimate at the firm level the probabilities of various amounts by which the market value of the firm's liabilities may exceed the market value of its assets over a one-year period. This probability measure is based on the value at risk (VaR) concept, which uses variability in market values of an asset to estimate the probability of a loss in market value exceeding a threshold level over a given time period. For example, the firm overall may be expected to incur a $50 million or greater loss of "capital" (based on the market value of its assets minus the market value of its liabilities) 0.5 percent of the time (1 out of every 200 years). Looked at another way, the firm may be expected to incur a capital loss of no more than $50 million 99.5 percent of the time (199 out of every 200 years). Using this standard, the firm's economic capital level should be set at $50 million.

The concept of economic capital underlies new European regulatory standards for insurers ("Solvency II"), which will affect not only European-based insurers but also United States insurers with European subsidiaries or parents.

Fair Value Accounting

The determination of an organization's economic capital starts with the fair value accounting of its assets and liabilities. Fair value is a market-based measurement based on the price the asset owner would receive by selling the asset, or that a liability holder would pay to transfer the liability. The latter is sometimes called an exit price.

As defined in Statement of Financial Accounting Standards No. 157 (SFAS 157), "Fair Value Measurements," the fair value of an asset or liability is the price a knowledgeable and independent entity would pay in an active market, excluding any transaction costs. For example, the fair value of an actively traded bond is its trading price at the time of valuation.

The fair value market price of an asset or a liability incorporates several factors. The most important are the future cash flows and the risk attached to those cash flows. For example, the present value of a bond issued by an organization in financial difficulty would reflect the possibility of default on interest or principal payments. The valuation of assets or liabilities that are not traded on active markets is based on a hypothetical transaction on the valuation date. The valuation can be based on an estimate of the value of similar items or the present value of expected future cash flows.

Fair value accounting differs from **generally accepted accounting principles (GAAP)** or **statutory accounting principles (SAP)** used by insurers in the U.S., both of which at times use nonmarket values. For example, under GAAP, assets such as machinery and buildings are valued at depreciated cost. Under GAAP and SAP, bonds that will be held to maturity may be valued at amortized cost. SAP excludes furniture and equipment from its calculation of assets. In some instances, use of a particular accounting practice can result in misleading indications of an organization's financial status. For example, basing the value of real estate on cost rather than on a market value that is lower can lead to financial difficulty for a financial organization.

Under GAAP, an organization's net worth (assets less liabilities) is often called equity. Under SAP, an insurer's net worth is called policyholders' surplus. Fair value accounting, which uses actual or estimated market values, calls net worth **market value surplus (MVS)**.

Fair Value of Insurers

The calculation of an insurer's fair value is complicated because no readily available market exists for trading insurers' largest liabilities: loss reserves (including loss adjustment expenses) and unearned premium reserves. These liabilities are generally carried on an insurer's balance sheet at the undiscounted estimate of future payments or earned amounts. However, these reserve estimates are uncertain, particularly for future loss payments. Therefore, it is unlikely that an insurer would be able to transfer these reserves to a reinsurer or another party at their present value. The assuming entity would require additional payment for the potential that the reserves prove to be inadequate. This additional payment is called a risk premium, risk margin, or market value margin. Therefore, to calculate the fair value of an insurer's

Generally accepted accounting principles (GAAP)
A common set of accounting standards and procedures used in the preparation of financial statements to ensure consistency of presentation and reported results.

Statutory accounting principles (SAP)
The accounting principles and practices that are prescribed or permitted by an insurer's domiciliary state and that insurers must follow.

Market value surplus
The fair value of assets minus the fair value of liabilities.

reserves, estimated future amounts are discounted to present value and a market value margin is added.

An insurer's MVS can therefore be calculated in this manner:

Market value surplus (MVS) of insurer = Fair value of assets − Fair value of liabilities
= Fair value of assets − (Present value of liabilities + Market value margin)

MVS can be considered a risk-adjusted form of policyholders' surplus. MVS is already adjusted for risk because fair value takes into account the risk inherent in the cash flows arising from assets and liabilities and because a market value margin is added to the present value of the liabilities.

Economic Capital for Insurers

An insurer's economic capital is the amount of capital required to maintain solvency (that is, an MVS greater than zero) at a given risk tolerance level.

The underlying paradigm of economic capital is similar to an insurer's risk-based capital (RBC) calculation. Both attempt to quantify the various risks faced by an insurer, such as these:

- Market risk (for example, changes in bond or stock prices)
- Credit risk (for example, defaults by those owing money)
- Liquidity risk (losses due to improper matching of asset and liability cash flows)
- Insurance risk (potential for adverse loss experience or catastrophe losses)
- Operational risk (for example, failed internal processes due to data system problems)

A major difference between the calculation of RBC and economic capital is that RBC uses factors to calculate a risk margin for the underlying risks. In contrast, economic capital is calculated using probability models of the various factors affecting results.

Probability models estimate the likelihood of potential outcomes by allowing for variation over time of inputs such as loss ratios, interest rates, and the effect of regulation changes. The variations are usually based on historical experience. For example, a model using interest rates as an input would include the probabilities of a 1 percent increase in a year, a 2 percent decrease, and so on. Probability models are used to estimate the effect of various stresses on the market value of an organization's assets, liabilities, and MVS. Insurers are particularly concerned about the variability of insured losses, both from current policies and in the loss reserves for prior claims. Numerous models are needed to simulate the potential risks to an organization across all aspects of its operation.

The results of the various models are combined, taking into account any overlapping effects or correlation between risks. The output is a distribution of possible fair value profits and losses (gains and losses in market value surplus), which is unique for each organization. Economic capital is equal to the value of a loss in MVS that is expected to be exceeded at the selected level of probability (threshold)—for example, only 1 percent of the time if the standard is to have sufficient capital 99 percent of the time. See the exhibit "Graphical View of Economic Capital."

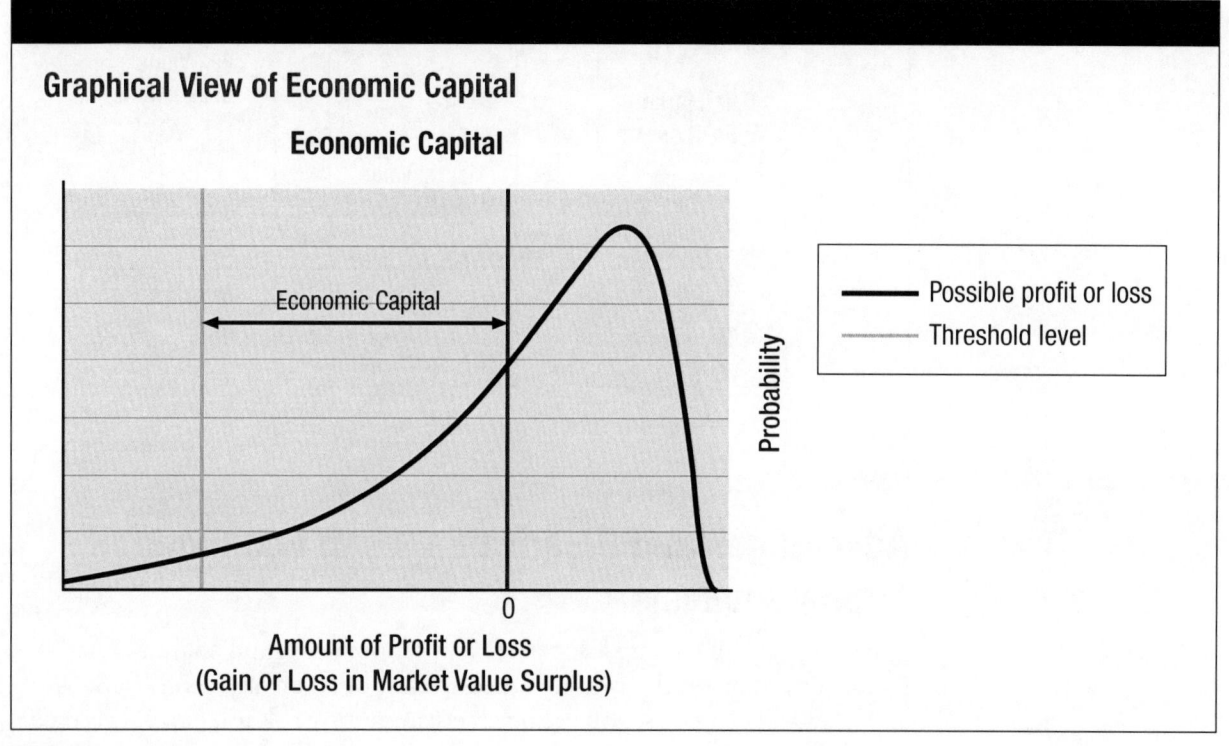

Graphical View of Economic Capital

Economic Capital

- Possible profit or loss
- Threshold level

Amount of Profit or Loss
(Gain or Loss in Market Value Surplus)

[DA06544]

The economic capital is defined using the concept of value at risk, the maximum loss at a selected probability or threshold level. The threshold level used is based on the organization's risk tolerance, market expectations, and regulatory requirements. For example, ING Group uses a 99.95 percent (1 in 2000) threshold level for its economic capital in order to achieve an AA financial rating from outside rating agencies.[12]

If an organization's MVS is larger than its economic capital, then it has excess capital. If its MVS is less than its economic capital, a deficiency exists. This deficiency could require management or regulators to take action, such as some combination of increasing its available capital and reducing its risk level and economic capital requirement. See the exhibit "Property-Casualty Insurer Market-Consistent Balance Sheet."

Property-Casualty Insurer Market-Consistent Balance Sheet

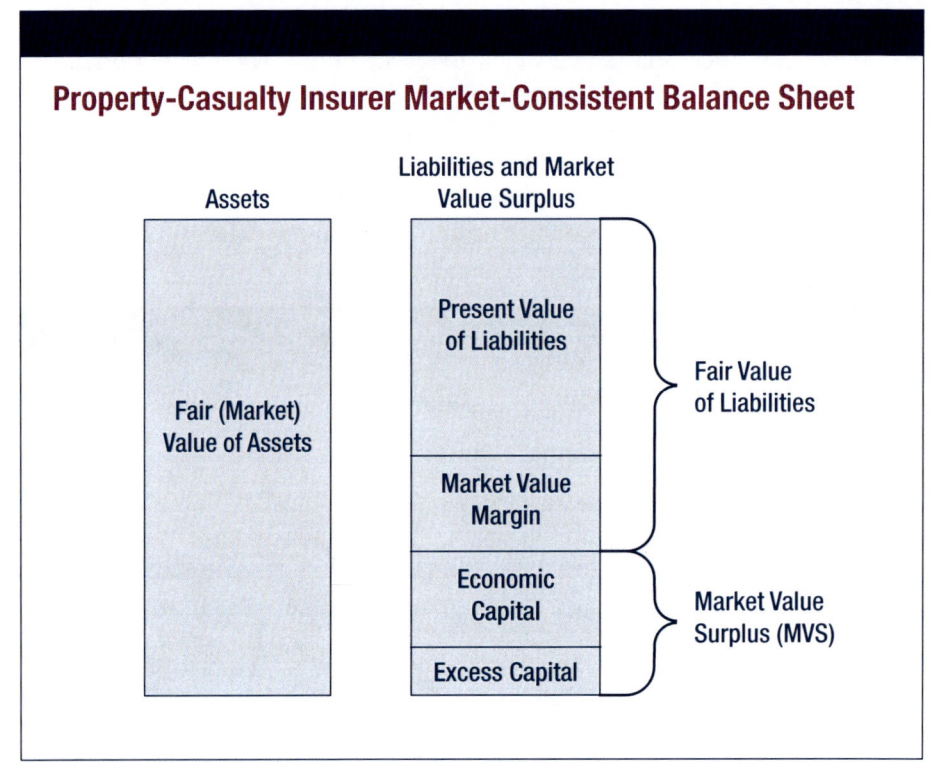

Assets: Fair (Market) Value of Assets

Liabilities and Market Value Surplus:
- Present Value of Liabilities ⎫
- Market Value Margin ⎬ Fair Value of Liabilities
- Economic Capital ⎫
- Excess Capital ⎬ Market Value Surplus (MVS)

[DA06543]

Advantages and Disadvantages of Economic Capital Analysis

Numerous advantages are associated with economic capital analysis. First, it focuses attention on the risks attached to each of an organization's various activities and can be used to define an organization's risk tolerance. It is used to put a value on an organization's overall level of risk. An organization can use economic capital analysis to establish the amount of capital it needs, or the risks that can be taken with a given amount of capital. It can reveal capital requirements for different operations and improve capital allocation. In addition, it can help an organization understand its economic capital position in order to deal with investors, rating agencies, and regulators, all of whom are increasingly using economic capital as a standard of financial adequacy. Overall, economic capital analysis provides a quantitative measure for a company's **enterprise risk management** program.

However, economic capital analysis is complex and sophisticated. Its reliance on the underlying assumptions and probability estimates of various outcomes is another disadvantage. Also, the use of fair value to assess all assets and liabilities at market value may produce changes in MVS unrelated to the company's ability to operate on an ongoing basis (for example, a change in the value of an organization's owned headquarters building is unrelated to the results of its day-to-day operations).

Enterprise risk management
An approach to managing all of an organization's key business risks and opportunities with the intent of maximizing shareholder value.

Solvency II

Solvency II is a fundamental review of the capitalization of insurers in the European Union (EU). It aims to "establish a revised set of EU-wide capital requirements and risk management standards…"[13]

Solvency II has three "pillars." The first deals with quantitative requirements of capital based on each insurer's specific circumstances. This includes a solvency capital requirement akin to economic capital that would ensure a 99.5 percent probability that the insurer would meet its obligations over the next year. The second pillar sets requirements for insurers' internal risk management process and for the supervision of insurers. The third focuses on reporting, disclosure, and transparency of the risk assessment to the public and regulators.

Solvency II applies to insurers in the EU, including the European operations and subsidiaries of insurers based outside the EU. As a consequence, many parent companies are adopting Solvency II standards corporate-wide.

STRATEGIC RISK

A strategic risk, such as a financial crisis or recession, can threaten an organization or provide an opportunity.

Strategic risks are external to an organization. They are systemic risks and therefore are outside the control of any individual organization. They are also speculative risks, which have both positive and negative potential. Ironically, strategic risk management, a discipline to achieve an organization's strategic objectives, cannot be applied to strategic risk. However, risk management professionals can understand strategic risks and develop plans to respond to threats or opportunities.

Strategic risks exist in national and global contexts. The same risks are present in differing degrees for all organizations that operate within those contexts. As in other types of risk, the first step is to identify and evaluate strategic risks and their potential effects on each organization's objectives.

Although there are many different global and national strategic risks confronting organizations, this discussion will focus on three major risks:

- Economic environment
- Demographics
- Political environment

Economic Environment

The macroeconomic environment in which an organization operates produces many different effects on the organization's results. These are examples of key economic risk factors:

- Gross Domestic Product (GDP)
- Inflation
- Financial crises, including sovereign debt crises
- International trade flows and restrictions

GDP

During periods of economic expansion, there is significant positive GDP growth. In contrast, recessions are characterized by negative GDP growth. Most organizations benefit from economic expansions when demand for most goods and services increases. However, organizations can also position themselves to succeed during recessions or periods of slow GDP growth.

Many organizations, for example, may trim costs and profit margins to compete successfully. Organizations offering new or different products often succeed even in difficult environments. Television and magnetic records first appeared for consumer use during the Great Depression of the 1930s. Apple introduced the iPod during the recession of 2001, and launched new versions of its iPhone and iPad during the economic downturn following the financial crisis of 2008. Advertising, especially radio advertising, increased during the Great Depression as organizations competed to attract consumers to their products.

Inflation

Mild inflation, such as that within a central bank's target rate, is typically beneficial for most organizations in an expanding economy. Organizations can then pass any increase in costs along to consumers and not feel compelled to squeeze margins. Mild inflation in a growing economy is also typically accompanied by reasonable wage increases, allowing consumers to spend more and fueling further economic growth. However, large increases in the rate of inflation or deflation are difficult for both organizations and consumers. In a deflationary environment, which has characterized much of the period since the financial crisis of 2008, organizations must cut prices to compete. Price-cutting places great demands on these organizations, especially when commodity inflation (not included in the rate of core inflation addressed by the United States Federal Reserve and other central banks) increases production costs.

Financial Crises

Financial crises, including sovereign debt crises, place various strains on many organizations. The most serious problem for many is restricted access to credit. Most organizations fund their daily operations through short-term credit. During serious financial crises, credit markets may seize up, including short-term credit facilities. Credit for business expansions or investments may not be available. There is typically a contagion effect from sovereign debt crises where financial organizations become unable or unwilling to conduct normal lending operations.

Organizations with large cash reserves may be able to compete effectively during financial crises because they are not as dependent on the availability of credit. However, even those organizations will likely experience some negative effects because customers and suppliers are likely to have difficulties due to reduced access to credit.

International Trade Flows and Restrictions

The global economy is based on various free trade agreements between governments that allow products from other nations to enter their respective markets with few barriers or restrictions. The relatively free flow of trade across the globe often characterizes an expanding global economy. However, the benefits are not always equally distributed. For example, U.S. manufacturing output has been eclipsed by Chinese manufacturing. This has resulted in a decline in manufacturing regions of the U.S., now referred to as "rust belts," with negative effects on many individuals and organizations. However, opportunities resulted for those U.S. manufacturing organizations which were able to succeed due to lower production costs in China.

Especially during times of global economic downturns, some governments may impose **tariffs** or other trade restrictions. When one government imposes restrictions, others typically follow, and the result is often a slowdown in global economic activity. The effects can be widespread as the impacts ripple through the global economy. Diversification in products and markets can help organizations succeed in a global environment characterized by trade restrictions.

Tariff
A tax that shields domestic producers from foreign competition.

Demographics

The **demographics** of developed nations are rapidly changing. The transformation is population aging resulting from increasing life expectancy for older members and declining fertility for younger members. The effects of this demographic trend for many organizations is likely to include a smaller pool of workers, strains on pension funds and retiree healthcare obligations, and shrinking markets for some products. The increased governmental burden for healthcare is likely to result in increased taxation and reductions in government funding in other areas, such as research and technology.[14] However, organizations that manufacture products or provide services that target the

Demographics
The statistical characteristics of human populations.

older population may be successful. For example, by the second quarter of 2011, 30 percent of e-reader users were over the age of 55.[15]

Political Environment

Political risk is a result of governmental actions. These risks can affect foreign organizations operating in another country or domestic organizations with foreign operations.

Governmental actions range from minor requirements to seizure of all of an organization's assets within a country. For example, in 2006 and 2007, Venezuela confiscated the assets of foreign firms. War and rebellions produce various political risks, such as difficult operating conditions or a change of government that could result in drastic actions against foreign firms.

Multinational organizations should identify as many political risks as possible that could affect the organization as well as risks specific to the countries in which the organization operates. Organizational risks include its financial capacity and expertise to operate internationally. Those that apply to its countries of operations include regulations, competitive environment, taxes, and the potential for loss of assets from governmental actions.[16]

> **Political risk**
> Any action by a government that favors domestic over foreign organizations or poses a threat to foreign organizations.

SUMMARY

Risk management professionals should assist organizations in understanding and defining their operational risk. A system that effectively categorizes an organization's operational risk provides a framework to manage it.

KRIs provide leading information regarding issues that risk management professionals should manage before the issues lead to incidents and then losses. KRIs can be categorized by exposure and control indicators in each operational risk class. Trend analysis and benchmarks assist in determining how KRIs affect outcomes.

Financial risk can be categorized as market risk, credit risk, and price risk. The goal of financial risk management is risk optimization. Market and price risk should be managed to increase upside potential while reducing downside potential. Various risk management techniques can be applied to reduce firm-specific credit risk.

VaR and EaR are metrics used in evaluating financial risk. VaR is used primarily by financial organizations to determine the probability of investments falling below a threshold value. EaR is used primarily by nonfinancial organizations to model the effects of changes in various factors on an organization's earnings.

Regulators require financial organizations to have minimum capital levels to protect depositors and the economy. Basel II prescribes methods to determine the capital required for financial (liquidity, credit, and market) risk and operational risk.

Economic capital is an estimate of the amount of capital a firm needs to stay solvent at a given risk tolerance level. Fair value of assets and liabilities uses market prices (actual or hypothetical), which are based on future cash flows and the risks attached to those cash flows. Insurer reserves for unpaid claims and unearned premiums generally have no readily available market, and therefore there is considerable uncertainty in estimating their fair value. An organization's economic capital is calculated using probability models of the various risks it faces. Economic capital is increasingly being used as a standard of financial adequacy.

Strategic risks are systemic risks that affect all organizations and include economic, demographic, and political risks. Although organizations cannot control these risks because they are external, risk management professionals can identify and understand these risks to help their organizations minimize negative risks while maximizing opportunity risks.

ASSIGNMENT NOTES

1. Douglas G. Hoffman, Managing Operational Risk (New York: John Wiley & Sons, Inc., 2002), pp. 242-243.
2. Hoffman, Managing Operational Risk, pp. 243-245.
3. Daniel A. Rogers, "Managing Financial Risk and Its Interaction with Enterprise Risk Management," in Enterprise Risk Management, ed. John Fraser and Betty J. Simkins, (Hoboken, N.J.: John Wiley & Sons, Inc., 2010), p. 322.
4. Anthony Saunders and Marcia Millon Cornett, Financial Markets and Institutions: A Modern Perspective, (New York: The McGraw-Hill Companies, Inc.,) 2004, pp. 573-577.
5. Rick Nason, "Market Risk Management and Common Elements With Credit Risk Management," Enterprise Risk Management, ed. John Fraser and Betty J. Simkins (Hoboken, N.J.: John Wiley & Sons, Inc., 2010), pp. 249-250.
6. Anthony Saunders and Marcia Millon Cornett, Financial Markets and Institutions (New York: McGraw-Hill, 2004), pp. 419-422.
7. Bank of England, "Preserving Financial Stability," p. 57, www.bankofengland.co.uk/publications/Documents/fsr/2010/fsr27sec5.pdf (accessed April 5, 2012).
8. Stijn Claessens and Geert Embrechts, "Basel II, Sovereign Ratings and Transfer Risk: External versus Internal Ratings," Bank of International Settlements, May 7, 2002, www.bis.org/bcbs/events/b2eacla.pdf (accessed April 5, 2012).
9. "Implementation of the Basel II Capital Framework; 2. Standardised approach to operational risk," Australian Prudential Regulation Authority, July 28, 2005, www.apra.gov.au/adi/Documents/cfdocs/dp0022.pdf (accessed April 5, 2012).
10. "Definition of operational risk," www.basel-ii-accord.com/Basel_ii_644_to_682_Operational_Risk.htm (accessed April 10, 2012).
11. Patrick de Fountnouvelle, Victoria Garrity, Scott Chu, and Eric Rosengren, "The Potential Impact of Explicit Basel II Operational Risk Capital Charges on the

Competitive Environment of Processing Banks in the United States," Federal Reserve Bank of Boston, January 12, 2005, www.federalreserve.gov/generalinfo/basel2/docs2005/opriskjan05.pdf (accessed April 10, 2012).

12. ING Group, *2008 Annual Report*, page 203, http://annualreports.ing.com/2008/cons_annual_accounts/risk_mgmt/model_disclosures/ (accessed March 3, 2010).

13. www.fsa.gov.uk/pages/About/What/International/solvency/index.shtml (accessed August 30, 2010).

14. Harold D. Skipper and W. Jean Kwon, Risk Management and Insurance: Perspectives in a Global Economy, Blackwell Publishing, 2007, pp. 154-155.

15. LowEndMac, http://lowendmac.com/inews/11ios/0902.html (accessed April 10, 2012).

16. Harold D. Skipper and W. Jean Kwon, Risk Management and Insurance: Perspectives in a Global Economy, Blackwell Publishing, 2007, pp. 431-435.

Segment B

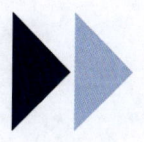

Assignment 5
Risk Management Framework and Process

Assignment 6
Risk Identification

Assignment 7
Risk Analysis

Assignment 8
Risk Treatment

Direct Your Learning

Risk Management Framework and Process

Educational Objectives

After learning the content of this assignment, you should be able to:

- Describe the purpose and component parts of an enterprise-wide risk management framework.
- Explain how to design and implement an enterprise-wide risk management framework and process.
- Compare the enterprise-wide risk management process with the traditional risk management process.
- Apply the enterprise-wide risk management framework and process to an organization's hazard risk.

Outline

Modeling an Enterprise-Wide Risk Management Framework and Process

Designing and Implementing an Enterprise-Wide Risk Management Framework and Process

Comparing the Enterprise-Wide Risk Management Process With the Traditional Risk Management Process

Applying the Enterprise-Wide Risk Management Framework and Process

Summary

Risk Management Framework and Process

MODELING AN ENTERPRISE-WIDE RISK MANAGEMENT FRAMEWORK AND PROCESS

All recognized risk management standards contain frameworks for organizations to use as they design their risk management programs. Some also specify a risk management process, while others do not. Just as a building is constructed on a frame, a risk management program should be built on a framework.

A risk management framework designed according to best practices will include several major components. These components apply on an enterprise-wide basis across all of the organization's risks. Adapting these components to an organization's objectives and operations will provide a good start toward developing a successful risk management program.

Purpose of a Risk Management Framework

The fundamental purpose of a risk management framework is to integrate risk management throughout the organization. The framework is intended to support a risk management process. A risk management framework from an international risk management standard, such as the ISO 31000 framework or the COSO ERM framework, can be applied to any type of organization and can be customized to the needs of a particular one. The principle that underlies a risk management framework is that risk management should add value to the organization. It should not only reduce negative risk but also contribute to profit, reputation, and health and safety.

Enterprise-Wide Risk Management Framework and Process Model

The enterprise-wide risk management framework and process model illustrates the components of a framework and the steps of a process. This model encapsulates key concepts from various international risk management standards and is just one of many forms an ERM framework and process can take. Each organization should adopt an ERM framework and process that best meets its needs.

These are the four components of the framework model:

- Lead and establish accountability
- Align and integrate
- Allocate resources
- Communicate and report

These are the five steps of the process model:

- Scan environment
- Identify risks
- Analyze risks
- Treat risks
- Monitor and assure

An organization's framework and process should be reviewed periodically to make sure they continue to meet the organization's needs. See the exhibit "Enterprise-Wide Risk Management Framework and Process Model."

The model also illustrates that the risk management process occurs within and is supported by the risk management framework. The risk management process occurs at various levels and applies to various functions throughout the organization. Typically, the framework will be established by an organization's senior management and chief risk officer, while the process may be established by just the chief risk officer or another risk management professional.

Components of a Risk Management Framework

The four components of the risk management framework model demonstrate the organization's commitment to risk management and help drive the integration of risk management throughout the organization. The framework components also support the risk management process. They are not meant to be carried out in any particular order, and an organization should adapt the components to suit its specific circumstances.

Lead and Establish Accountability

The first component of a risk management framework involves an organization's senior management, usually the chief executive officer (CEO), leading and establishing accountability for risk management. Leadership includes development of the organization's risk management philosophy and mission. It also includes commitment to risk management at the highest levels of an organization. The tone for major projects and initiatives is set at the top of the organization, and a tone of sincere commitment to and support for risk management is essential for the process to be successful. Senior management's commitment also involves holding everyone in the organization

Enterprise-Wide Risk Management Framework and Process Model

Framework (black circles): Lead and Establish Accountability; Align and Integrate; Communicate and Report; Allocate Resources

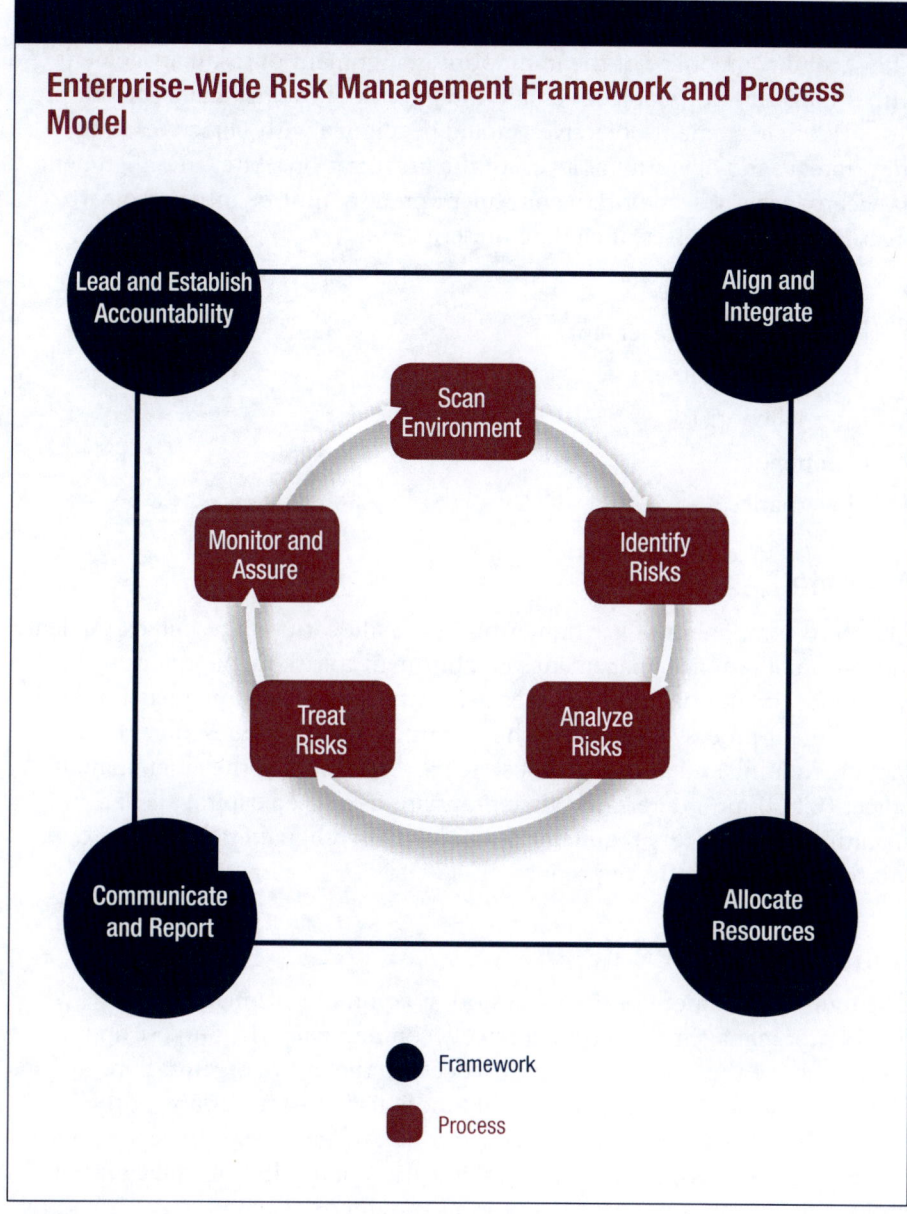

Process (red boxes, cyclical): Scan Environment → Identify Risks → Analyze Risks → Treat Risks → Monitor and Assure

[DA08717_1]

accountable for risk management. These techniques can be used to establish accountability:

- Identify **risk owners** and their roles in the organization
- Establish **key performance indicators (KPI)**
- Establish key risk indicators (KRI) and use them to evaluate performance
- Develop risk criteria to evaluate the significance of risks

Risk owner
An individual accountable for the identification, assessment, treatment, and monitoring of risks in a specific environment.

Key performance indicator (KPI)
Financial or nonfinancial measurement that defines how successfully an organization is progressing toward its long-term goals.

Align and Integrate

The second component of the framework is alignment of risk management with an organization's objectives and integration of the risk management process. Risk management objectives should be aligned with objectives at both the strategic and operational levels of the organization. After this alignment has been developed, the risk management process must be integrated with organizational processes, including these:

- Strategic planning
- Performance management
- Process management
- Internal control
- Compliance
- Governance

Allocate Resources

The third component of the framework is the allocation of resources. A clear indication of senior management's commitment to risk management is the willingness to allocate the resources necessary to effectively implement a risk management process throughout the organization. Typical resource needs include training and adaptation of systems. Additionally, the chief financial officer (CFO) must determine an appropriate risk-based capital allocation according to regulatory requirements and the risk characteristics of the organization's business units or products.

Communicate and Report

The fourth component of the framework is communication and reporting. Senior management must effectively communicate the purpose and importance of the risk management process to the entire organization. Communication across organizational functions is also necessary for the design and implementation of an effective risk management process. After the process is integrated, proficient communication of results must take place to provide the basis for ongoing monitoring and improvement.

The risk management framework should include procedures to report information about risks and the results of risk management to appropriate stakeholders. Senior management should receive executive summary reports at regular intervals. More detailed reports should be prepared and reviewed by managers regarding risks in their areas of responsibility. For the risk management process to be optimally effective, information about emerging risks should be included in risk reports.

Risk Management Policy

To obtain buy-in from managers and employees throughout the organization, a clear statement of the risk management policy should be present. The policy should support the risk management framework and be communicated throughout the organization and to appropriate external stakeholders. See the exhibit "Example of Risk Management Policy Statement."

The risk management policy statement shown in the exhibit touches on several aspects of components in the risk management framework model. It mentions establishing senior management commitment and support, applying processes, maintaining effective communication, and training.

Example of Risk Management Policy Statement

Policy Statement on Risk Management

Mission Statement

Canterbury City Council's Risk Management Policy is to adopt best practice in the identification, evaluation and cost-effective control of risks, to ensure that they are either eliminated or reduced to an acceptable level.

Risk is a factor of everyday life and can never be eliminated completely. All employees must understand the nature of risk and accept responsibility for risks associated with their area of authority. The necessary support, assistance and commitment of senior management will be provided.

Our Risk Management objectives are to:

1. Integrate Risk Management into the culture of the organisation.
2. Manage risk in accordance with best practice.
3. Consider legal compliance as an absolute minimum.
4. Anticipate and respond quickly to social, environmental and legislative change.
5. Prevent injury and damage and reduce the cost of risk.
6. Raise awareness of the need for risk management.

These objectives will be achieved by:

1. Establishing a Corporate Governance/Risk Management organisational structure to act in an advisory and guiding capacity and which is accessible to all employees.
2. Include Corporate Governance/Risk Management as one of the implications to be considered in every committee report.
3. Adopt processes, which demonstrate that Corporate Governance/Risk Management principles are being applied across the whole organisation.
4. Provide training in risk awareness and Corporate Governance.
5. Maintain documented procedures for the control of risk and provision of suitable information, training and supervision.
6. Maintain an appropriate system for recording incidents and carrying out post event checks to ascertain causes and identify preventive measures against re-occurrence.
7. Devise and maintain contingency plans in key risk areas to secure business continuity where there is a potential for an event having a major impact upon the council's ability to function.
8. Maintain effective communication and involvement of all staff and members.
9. Monitor arrangements on an ongoing basis.

Canterbury City Council Online, "Policy Statement on Risk Management," www.canterbury.gov.uk/main.cfm?objectid=938 (accessed April 10, 2012). [DA08834]

DESIGNING AND IMPLEMENTING AN ENTERPRISE-WIDE RISK MANAGEMENT FRAMEWORK AND PROCESS

Risk management professionals should use a recognized international standard as a model for the framework and process that will integrate risk management practices throughout their organizations. A recognized standard is more likely both to meet any regulatory risk management guidelines and to provide effective methods for organizations.

Before designing a risk management framework and process, risk management professionals should understand the major international risk management standards and consider which one best reflects the needs of the organization. After a standard is selected, risk management professionals should use the standard as broad guidance as they design and develop an appropriate framework and process for their organizations.

As a risk management professional, how would you design and implement a risk management framework and process for your organization, based on a recognized international standard?

Risk management professionals can adapt a risk management framework and process to their organizations' needs. Best practices in risk management involve continuously reviewing the framework and process as results are obtained and analyzed. Any major change within the organization should also prompt a reevaluation of the framework and process. These are the stages in designing and implementing a risk management framework and process:

- Gap analysis
- Evaluation of internal and external environments
- Integration into existing processes
- Commitment of resources
- Communication and reporting
- Monitoring and improvement

Gap Analysis

A risk management professional should first compare an organization's existing risk management framework and process against that of an internationally recognized standard, such as ISO 31000 or COSO ERM. Each component of the selected risk management framework and process should be matched with a similar aspect of the current risk management program and the responsible organizational function.

Any component or subcomponent of the framework and process that does not have a match in the organization's current risk management program represents a gap. Identifying these gaps allows the organization to better use resources. Additionally, matched components can form key supports of the framework and process because they are already integrated within the organization's procedures and culture.

Evaluation of Internal and External Environments

After performing a gap analysis, risk management professionals should evaluate the internal and external environments in which the organization operates.

Internal Environment

Evaluating the internal environment begins by understanding the organization's overall objectives and risk appetite—the amount of uncertainty an organization is prepared to accept in total or, more narrowly, within a certain business unit or risk category, or for a specific initiative.[1] Then the evaluation proceeds to the organization's key strategies. For example, applying a risk management framework to an organization that is pursuing an organic growth strategy will be different from applying one to a company with a mergers-and-acquisitions strategy.

Risk management professionals, usually with a team representing key organizational functions, should next evaluate the organizational structure and the major categories of risk within each area. Results of the gap analysis can be used to identify areas in which application of the risk management framework and process needs to be modified. For example, the gap analysis may indicate that risk management is not explicitly included in an organization's procurement process. Procurement could then become a focus in the design of the risk management framework and process.

After mapping the organizational structure and its key risk categories, the risk management team should evaluate the resources necessary to implement and maintain the risk management framework and process. These resources may include equipment, systems, and people. For example, integrating risk management into procurement may involve training employees and acquiring computer software.

The internal context evaluation should also provide an overview of the formal and informal communication channels within the organization. This should include perspectives on the corporate culture. Is the overall culture risk taking or risk averse? What are the general attitudes and viewpoints of subgroups on risk management? Surveys and discussion groups can be used to gather this information.

External Environment

The external environment of an organization includes these factors:

- Economic
- Political
- Legal and regulatory
- Technology
- Natural
- Competitive landscape

Risk management professionals should evaluate the external environment for all of the organization's operations. The key risk categories for each factor should be included in this evaluation. For example, risks associated with the natural environment will have different effects on energy providers, insurers, farming organizations, and electronic manufacturers.

Integration Into Existing Processes

There are two major keys to successful integration of the risk management framework and process. The first is to align risk management objectives and policy with the organization's overall objectives and risk appetite. The second is to use existing processes.

The gap analysis will identify existing risk management policies and procedures. Using existing processes as components of the risk management framework and process serves two purposes. First, any long-existing process is likely embedded into the organization's culture; therefore, the organization will not experience the usual resistance to change from introducing new procedures. Second, resources will not have to be allocated to designing and implementing pieces of the framework and process that already exist.

Traditionally, most organizations have risk management procedures to address human resources practices, employee safety, product safety, credit risk, financial processes, and regulatory requirements. Although a risk management framework and process can be designed with existing components, risk management professionals should consider how well the current procedures meet the organization's needs and how these processes should be adapted to comply with a recognized standard. Additionally, this consideration should address how well the current procedures meet the organization's needs.

As the framework is being designed, those involved in its planning and implementation should consider where new paradigms might better achieve objectives. For example, in many organizations, different functions purchase supplies and services. In a manufacturing organization, a central purchasing division may procure the components and materials used in production. However, a risk management department may purchase property and casualty insurance, a human resources department may purchase health and disability insurance, and an information technology department may purchase computers and related services. The organization may want to consider adding cross-functional risk management to coordinate these various processes.

A critical component of the integration is assigning responsibility and accountability for risk management within each of the organization's functions. Ideally, everyone in the organization would embrace the risk management vision, but specific persons would be designated as responsible for risk management. Typically, managers of divisions and business units are responsible for managing the risks in their areas of operations: for example, the chief financial officer (CFO) has regulatory responsibility for most financial risk, and managers reporting to the CFO have responsibility for their functions.

Commitment of Resources

Plans for the risk management framework and process should include the additional resources required and a commitment from senior management to provide those resources. These are categories of necessary resources:

- Technology, including equipment and systems
- Administrative persons
- Specialists, either internal or external
- Analysts
- Training

The nature and extent of these resources vary widely in different organizations. The size of the organization, how many locations it has, the geographical dispersion of its business units, the nature of its operations, and the extent of existing risk management all determine what resources are necessary.

For many organizations, implementing a risk management framework and process takes several years. A large quantity of information needs to be assembled and evaluated to design an effective framework and process, determine the necessary resources, and integrate the framework and process throughout the organization. A lengthy time frame allows organizations to allocate the necessary funds in stages.

Communication and Reporting

Communication is a key aspect of the risk management framework and process. A framework should establish the types and channels of communication within the organization. This is a complex process, and key stakeholders within the organization should be involved during the planning of risk management communication. These stakeholders should also be included in designing metrics for both evaluating risk management and reporting results.

Communication

Communicating the risk management policy is a key step in integrating the risk management framework and process throughout the organization. The way the policy is communicated sets the tone. For example, a chief executive officer who visits a manufacturing organization's factories to deliver the policy and discuss it with employees sends a powerful message that the policy is important to the organization's objectives.

Many other types of communication besides policy dissemination must occur before, during, and following implementation of the risk management framework and process. Successful integration of the framework and process will depend on the quality of these communications.

During design of the framework and process, detailed and thoughtful communication should occur among all key areas of the organization. A task force comprised of representatives of these areas who can commit significant amounts of time to the risk management framework and process can be an effective resource. Often, organizations will use an external risk management consultant to facilitate the process of developing the communication plan.

The implementation phase requires communication of both the policy and procedures that will be integrated throughout the organization. Training may be required, especially for those responsible and accountable for results.

Communication after the framework and policy are in place should focus not only on metrics and analysis of results, but also on how well the organizational culture is adapting to the policies and procedures. Any areas of resistance to the integration of the framework and process should be identified and addressed through both formal and informal communication, training, surveys, and other methods.

Reporting

Those who are responsible and accountable for risk management results in an organization must receive timely and relevant information regarding key metrics for their areas of responsibility. Many organizations use a scorecard approach and distribute results quarterly. If an organization reports financial results quarterly, tying risk metrics to the quarterly financial results can be a valuable way of determining and reporting on the effect of risk management on the organization's overall objectives. For example, improvements in customers' credit quality could be tied to its effect on the organization's balance sheet.

In addition to internal reports, most organizations must produce reports to external stakeholders to meet regulatory or other requirements. These mandated reports should be included in the design of the risk management framework with defined reporting responsibilities.

Monitoring and Improvement

An effective risk management program should lead to improvements in results. As objectives are met, new objectives are set to encourage continual improvement. The risk management framework and process should provide mechanisms to encourage continuous improvement, such as regular review of objectives, team discussion of results, and benchmarking to other organizations in the same industry.

The plan-do-check-act cycle (**P-D-C-A Cycle**) can be used in many different settings as an improvement model. The "act" step of the cycle simultaneously restarts it, with evaluation of the implemented improvement reinitiating the "plan" phase.

Additionally, risk management professionals and other key stakeholders should participate in educational programs and professional associations, read professional journals, and stay current on broad business trends. The risk management framework and process should be able to adapt and respond to changing circumstances. For example, if a new regulation will change capital or reporting requirements, risk and financial managers should be aware of the potential change and how it will affect the organization. Plans should be made to address it within the risk management framework.

> **P-D-C-A Cycle**
> The P-D-C-A Cycle, also known as the Shewhart cycle and the Deming cycle, is an expansion of an approach to process improvement. The steps include Plan, Do, Check, and Act.

Apply Your Knowledge

After studying the methods to design and implement a risk management framework and process based on an internationally recognized standard, explain a risk management professional's first step in designing and implementing a risk management framework and process for an organization.

Feedback: The risk management professional should first conduct a gap analysis of the organization. This step involves determining the existing risk management program, including procedures in different areas of the organization. The structure of the entire organization should be charted, indicating which functions have explicit risk management processes. Additionally, key risk categories for each area should be mapped. Next, those functions that do not have explicit risk management procedures, as well as key risks that are not currently addressed, should be identified. The risk management framework and process can be designed using the risk management components that are already in place.

COMPARING THE ENTERPRISE-WIDE RISK MANAGEMENT PROCESS WITH THE TRADITIONAL RISK MANAGEMENT PROCESS

The enterprise-wide risk management process provides a broader approach to risk than the traditional risk management process, which applies primarily to hazard risk.

Enterprise-wide and traditional risk management processes provide cycles of continuous improvement to address an organization's risk. These processes also include similar steps of risk identification, analysis, and treatment. However, the enterprise-wide risk management process applies to all of an organization's risks (hazard, operational, financial, and strategic), while the traditional risk management process focuses mainly on hazard risk.

Enterprise-Wide Risk Management Process

The enterprise-wide risk management process addresses risks with both positive and negative potential effects on an organization.

Five major steps are included in the enterprise-wide risk management process:

- Scan environment
- Identify risks
- Analyze risks
- Treat risks
- Monitor and assure

These activities may take place concurrently as well as sequentially. The exhibit indicates the cyclical nature of the process. See the exhibit "Enterprise-Wide Risk Management Process Model."

Scan the Environment

Risk management professionals should conduct a specific and detailed review of both the internal and external environments of an organization. For example, the risk management processes related to employee safety in the United States would include the legal and regulatory requirements of the Occupational Safety and Health Administration (OSHA) and state or federal workers compensation statutes, the procedures of external stakeholders (such as insurers), and the organization's internal procedures for health and safety.

Scanning the environment includes an evaluation of how each of an organization's risk management processes aligns with its overall objectives. For example, the organization's objectives may be to achieve profitable growth and to promote the health, safety, and well-being of its employees. The risk management process related to employee safety should therefore be aligned

Enterprise-Wide Risk Management Process Model

- Scan Environment
- Identify Risks
- Analyze Risks
- Treat Risks
- Monitor and Assure

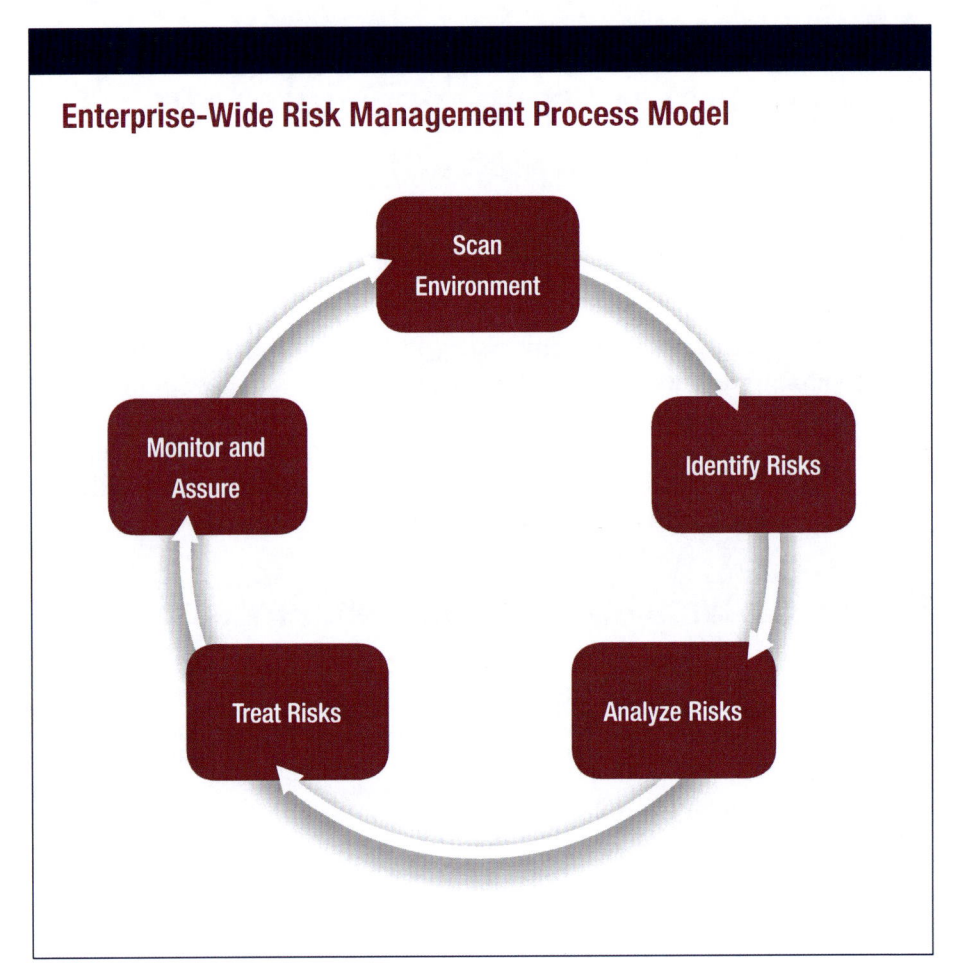

[DA08717_2]

both with the objective of employee health, safety, and well-being and also with the organization's profit goals. A risk management objective to reduce the number of employee injuries would align with organizational objectives. Reducing injuries would improve employee safety and reduce the expenses associated with employee injuries (and thereby increase profits).

Additionally, risk management professionals should engage with others in the organization to define risk criteria. These criteria should be aligned with the organization's objectives, resources, and risk management policy. These factors should be considered in defining risk criteria:

- Causes of risk
- Effects of risk
- Metrics used to measure effects of risk
- Timeframe of potential effects
- Methods to determine level of risk
- Approach to combinations of risk

Identify Risks

The purpose of risk identification is to develop a comprehensive list of risks that could affect the organization's objectives. Although it is not feasible or practical to identify all risks, it is essential to identify key and emerging risks that could significantly affect an organization's meeting its objectives. It is also important to identify multidimensional aspects of risk that may traditionally have been categorized into only one risk quadrant. For example, the risk of a customer being injured by an organization's product may traditionally have been viewed as a hazard risk. However, in an enterprise-wide process, related risks in other quadrants can be identified. There could be reputational risk from publicity about the injury, which could have both strategic and financial effects. If a product recall becomes necessary, it would result in operational as well as financial risks.

Analyze Risks

Risk analysis involves applying the defined risk criteria to determine the source, cause, likelihood, and potential consequences of each of the identified risks. Depending on the circumstances, the analysis can be quantitative, qualitative, or both. If a risk of a customer being injured by an organization's product is identified, the potential cost of litigation by the customer or class action litigation can be quantified from the organization's prior experience or by benchmarking with other cases. The effect on the organization's reputation, however, would be more difficult to quantify and would probably be expressed qualitatively.

Treat Risks

After risk analysis, decisions are made regarding risk treatment. When there are no regulatory requirements, an organization should compare the total level of risk determined during the risk analysis with the risk criteria established in the first step of the process. This comparison will guide decisions regarding risk treatment. For example, if the total level of risk exceeds the organization's average annual profit, the organization may decide to employ risk treatment in order to reduce the level of risk to a range that would not threaten profit objectives.

After this comparison, risk management professionals—along with appropriate stakeholders in the organization—decide where and how to apply risk treatment. These are the major options available for risks:

- Avoid the risk
- Modify the likelihood and/or impact of the risk
- Transfer the risk
- Retain the risk
- Exploit the risk

Risk management professionals should understand that risk treatment can present risks. For example, the use of derivatives to hedge against financial risk caused severe consequences for many organizations during the 2008 financial crisis. Avoiding risk by not pursuing an opportunity may ultimately have negative consequences for an organization.

Monitor and Assure

Effective risk management processes include ongoing monitoring with periodic review of results. These are the key purposes of monitoring:

- Determine the effectiveness of controls
- Obtain information to improve risk assessment
- Analyze events and their consequences to understand trends, successes, and failures
- Observe changes in internal and external environments
- Identify emerging risks

Traditional Risk Management Process

The traditional risk management process consists of six steps that can be applied to actual or potential accidental losses. It provides organizations and their risk management professionals with a systematic approach to assess and treat accidental loss (hazard risk) exposures. Applying the risk management process on an ongoing basis enables an organization to meet its pre-loss and post-loss risk management goals. The exhibit illustrates the continuous, cyclical nature of the traditional risk management process. See the exhibit "The Risk Management Process."

Identifying Loss Exposures

The traditional risk management approach focuses primarily on one quadrant of risk: hazard risk. Some attention is given to operational risks that have negative potential for the organization. The first step in this process is to identify an organization's risks. Risk management professionals identify many loss exposures by reviewing historical losses. Techniques to identify hazard risk before a loss occurs include inspections, compliance reviews, and risk assessment checklists. Techniques to identify operational risks include internal control audits and review of organizational policies and procedures. Risk management professionals may use expertise outside the organization to assist with risk identification. Typical sources of outside expertise include an insurer's or a producer's risk control consultant and an organization's outside auditor and accountant.

The Risk Management Process

- Step 1: Identifying loss exposures
- Step 2: Analyzing loss exposures
- Step 3: Examining feasibility of risk management techniques
- Step 4: Selecting the appropriate risk management techniques
- Step 5: Implementing selected risk management techniques
- Step 6: Monitoring results and revising the risk management program

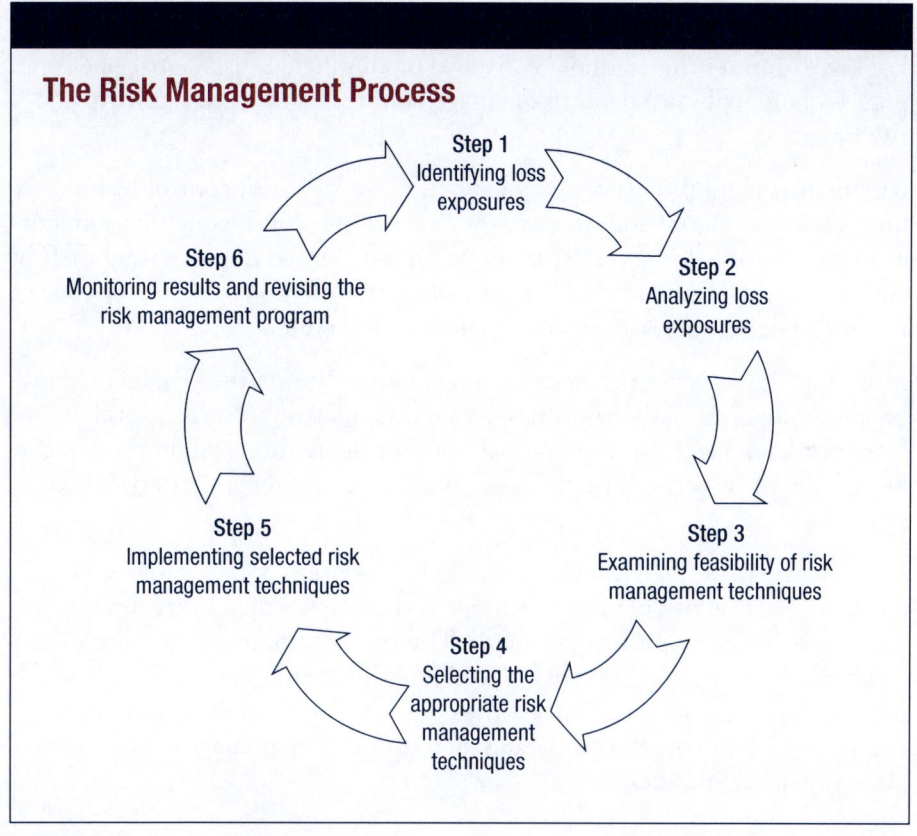

[DA02595]

Analyzing Loss Exposures

Risk management professionals analyze the likely significance of the loss exposures identified in step one of the risk management process. Loss exposures are analyzed along these four dimensions:

- Loss frequency—the number of losses (such as property damage, liability claims, bad debt charge-offs, or employee thefts) within a specific time period
- Loss severity—the amount, in dollars, of a loss for a specific occurrence
- Total dollar losses—the total dollar amount of losses for all occurrences during a specific time period
- Timing—when losses occur and when loss payments are made

After analyzing these dimensions, risk management professionals can develop loss projections and prioritize risk management efforts toward the most significant loss exposures.

Examining the Feasibility of Risk Management Techniques

For loss exposures that cannot be avoided or eliminated, risk management professionals apply two main risk management techniques: **risk control** and risk financing.

Risk management professionals evaluate the available risk control techniques for each loss exposure and whether they are suitable for the organization. For example, continual supervisory observation is a method of preventing theft by employees who handle cash. However, while this method may be cost-effective for a large casino, it may not be effective for a retail store.

Most organizations use **risk financing techniques**, primarily insurance. Many organizations, especially large ones, retain a significant percentage of their losses. Risk management professionals must evaluate those exposures that can be covered by insurance and the level of retention the organization should assume.

Risk management techniques are not used in isolation. Organizations typically apply at least one risk control technique and one risk financing technique to each of their significant loss exposures. The risk control technique alters the estimated frequency and severity of loss, and the financing technique pays a portion of losses that occur despite the controls. For example, organizations use a combination of safety programs and insurance to manage workers compensation loss exposures.

Selecting the Appropriate Risk Management Techniques

Financial considerations are important in evaluating and selecting risk management techniques. For all organizations, the potential costs of loss exposures being completely untreated must be compared with the costs of risk management techniques. A financial analysis of a risk management technique may be based on three different forecasts:

- A forecast of the dimensions of expected losses (frequency, severity, timing of payment, and total dollar losses)
- A forecast, for each feasible combination of risk management techniques, of the effect of the combined techniques on the frequency, severity, and timing of these expected losses
- A forecast of the after-tax costs involved in applying the various risk management techniques, such as insurance premiums or the installation of risk control equipment

Nonfinancial considerations include the ability of the organization to continue operations, concerns for the safety and welfare of people (such as consumers or employees), and the organization's reputation.

Risk control
A conscious act or decision not to act that reduces the frequency and/or severity of losses or makes losses more predictable.

Risk financing techniques
Risk management techniques, such as retention or transfer, that generate funds to finance losses that risk control techniques cannot entirely prevent or reduce.

Implementing the Selected Risk Management Techniques

After risk management techniques are selected, they must be implemented. Risk financing techniques are typically implemented by a risk management professional. Risk control techniques are usually implemented by operations managers.

How successfully risk management techniques are implemented will determine whether the risk management process is successful. For example, risk financing involves selecting appropriate programs and partners; however, the implementation of risk financing, such as insurance, involves much more than merely paying a premium or allocating funds. A risk financing program also typically includes claim administration and other services. Risk control implementation includes communicating techniques to the appropriate operations managers along with any necessary training or resources.

Monitoring Results and Revising the Risk Management Program

After a risk management program is established, the ongoing activities and results require constant attention. Circumstances may develop that require revision to a risk management program, such as these:

- New loss exposures, for example from a new merger or acquisition
- New developments in existing loss exposures, such as a product defect resulting in liability
- Different risk management techniques, such as the feasibility of a captive insurance program

Similarities

There are several similarities between the enterprise-wide risk management process and the traditional risk management process. Both of these processes are cyclical and provide for continuous improvement. Both processes use similar steps of identifying, analyzing, and treating risk.

Differences

The most significant difference between the enterprise-wide risk management process and the traditional risk management process is the type of risk addressed.

The traditional risk management process primarily addresses hazard risk along with some operational risk. The traditional approach views risk as having only negative potential for the organization, and the purpose of the risk management process is to minimize the effect of risk.

The enterprise-wide approach addresses all four quadrants of risk—strategic, financial, operational, and hazard risk. This approach views risk as having both negative and positive potential. The purpose of an enterprise-wide approach is to optimize the effects of risk on the organization.

Another key difference between the enterprise-wide risk management process and the traditional risk management process is the development of an understanding of an organizational environment. To some extent, this understanding is implicit in the evaluation of risk in the traditional risk management approach. However, it is the first step in the enterprise-wide risk management process and therefore frames the process as part of a holistic approach to risk.

APPLYING THE ENTERPRISE-WIDE RISK MANAGEMENT FRAMEWORK AND PROCESS

Applying the enterprise-wide risk management framework and process to the facts of a case can help risk management professionals understand how their organizations' risks can be managed. Although this process can be applied to all of an organization's risks, this case focuses on hazard risk.

Case Facts

Power, Inc., is a regional energy provider located in the northeastern United States. Power owns and operates natural gas plants in seven states. Its operations include installing and maintaining gas pipelines and customer hookups. Power has a fleet of service trucks used to connect and disconnect customer gas service and a fleet of maintenance vehicles used to perform repairs to main gas pipes. Additionally, Power has an office building where fifty employees perform accounting, administrative, legal, and human resources functions.

Power had an increasing frequency of vehicle accidents over the past three years, although the severity of those accidents remained essentially the same. Service technicians, however, have experienced less frequent but more severe injuries during the same time period. Two minor injuries involving Power's clerical employees occurred at the company's office building. Nationally, one tropical storm during the previous three years caused major damage to a key pipeline and resulted in injury to employees who repaired damage during the storm.

During the three-year period, three ruptures to pipelines necessitated evacuating the immediate area because of a release of gas. No injuries resulted. There has been an increase in the number of property damage claims from customers alleging damage to appliances and homes resulting from Power's installations and maintenance. One lawsuit filed involved the deaths of a family from a gas explosion, and several lawsuits were filed related to nonfatal injuries in similar incidents.

Power's senior management includes a chief executive officer (CEO), a chief financial officer (CFO), and a chief operating officer (COO). A vice president is in charge of each of its plants and each corporate division (legal, human resources, and procurement). Line managers are responsible for direct management of areas of operation and for employees at each of the plants, such as energy generation and service.

This case provides an opportunity for you to apply the enterprise-wide risk management framework and process to Power's hazard risks.

Overview of Steps

These are the four components of the enterprise-wide risk management framework:

- Lead and establish accountability
- Align and integrate
- Allocate resources
- Communicate and report

These are the steps in the enterprise-wide risk management process:

- Scan environment
- Identify risks
- Analyze risks
- Treat risks
- Monitor and assure

Applying the Risk Management Framework

When an organization adapts an enterprise-wide risk management approach, it must develop a framework. The main purpose of the framework is to integrate risk management throughout the organization; however, it also supports the risk management process.

Lead and Establish Accountability

Senior management must provide the leadership to develop and integrate enterprise-wide risk management. The commitment of the organization's leaders is necessary, and they must also establish accountability for results among the organization's risk owners.

Knowledge to Action

What performance standards can Power's senior management use to establish accountability from line managers for hazard risk? Select all that apply.

a. Key performance indicators (KPIs)
b. Severity of employee injuries
c. Key risk indicators (KRIs)
d. Storm response time

Feedback: a. and c. Power's senior management should design KPIs and KRIs that align with Power's risk management and strategic objectives. The organization's managers have little direct control over the severity of employee injuries (b.). Although storm response time (d.) could be included as a KPI, an evaluation would need to be performed of the storm's severity and other factors that are beyond the managers' control.

Align and Integrate

The risk management framework must align the organization's risk management approach with its strategic objectives and integrate risk management throughout the organization.

Knowledge to Action

Explain which levels in Power's organizational structure need to be involved in the integration of an enterprise-wide risk management process.

Feedback: All levels of Power's organizational structure need to be involved in the integration of the risk management process. Each level must take ownership of risk and be accountable for results. Senior management is responsible for the risk management policy and commitment. Plant and division managers are responsible for results in their areas of operation. Line managers are responsible for their functions. Additionally, employees must be risk owners and accountable for results.

Allocate Resources

Senior management demonstrates its commitment to risk management by allocating resources, such as training, systems, equipment, and consultants.

Knowledge to Action

What type(s) of resources would best assist Power's risk management process? Select all that apply.

a. Technician training in installation and maintenance procedures
b. Driver training
c. New computer system
d. Lightning rods

Feedback: a. and b. Property damage claims have increased in frequency as a result of installations and maintenance. Vehicle accident frequency has also experienced an increase. Training service technicians in safe driving techniques and proper installation and maintenance procedures would be an appropriate allocation of resources to assist the risk management process. Power has identified its hazard risks and found no need for a new computer system at this time (c.). Lightning rods (d.) could not be effectively deployed along all of Power's pipelines.

Communicate and Report

Communication and reporting is an essential component of the risk management framework.

Knowledge to Action

Who would be the best person(s) in the organization to communicate Power's commitment to risk management?

a. CEO
b. Vice president of human resources
c. Plant managers
d. Line managers

Feedback: a. Communication from the top is important to emphasize an organization's commitment to risk management. However, communication at all levels is also important as the risk management process is integrated.

Applying the Risk Management Process

Once the risk management framework is in place, the risk management process can be designed and integrated throughout the organization.

Scan Environment

The first step in the process involves scanning the internal and external environments and defining the criteria that will be used in the assessment of risk.

Knowledge to Action

Which factors would you include in the external environment for Power's hazard risk management?

Feedback: Factors in the external environment for Power's hazard risk management include the regulatory, legal, and natural environments. Regulations affect many aspects of Power's hazard risk management process—for example, there are federal regulations regarding employee safety and state regulations regarding utilities, vehicles, and employee injuries. The legal environment affects the likelihood and potential outcome of litigation, and the natural environment affects risks such as storms or wildfires.

Identify Risks

The next step in the risk management process is risk identification.

Knowledge to Action

Identify Power's key hazard risks. Categorize these risks according to whether they arise from external causes (such as weather) or internal causes (such as employee operations).

Feedback: These are Power's key hazard risks arising from external causes:

- Weather-related damage to property or injury to employees
- Explosion of gas pipelines related to fire or other external causes
- Damage to pipelines that causes release of gas

These are Power's key hazard risks arising from internal causes:

- Vehicle accidents with vehicle or other property damage
- Vehicle accidents with personal injury
- Various risks of employee injury while working on gas pipes or installing equipment
- Risk of injury to clerical employees
- Damage to customers' property from interruption to gas supply, gas leakage, or explosion
- Injury to customers from interruption to gas supply, gas leakage, or explosion

Analyze Risks

Risk analysis focuses on the causes of risks, their likelihood, and their consequences.

Knowledge to Action

Place each of Power's risks into one of these categories:

- High potential impact/high likelihood
- High potential impact/low likelihood
- Low potential impact/high likelihood
- Low potential impact/low likelihood

Feedback: These are the risks in the high potential impact/high likelihood category:

- Vehicle accidents with personal injury
- Various risks of employee injury while working on gas pipes or installing equipment

These are the risks in the high potential impact/low likelihood category:

- Weather-related damage to property or injury to employees
- Explosion of gas pipelines related to fire or other external causes
- Damage to pipelines that causes release of gas
- Injury to customers from interruption to gas supply, gas leakage, or explosion

These are the risks in the low potential impact/high likelihood category:

- Vehicle accidents with property damage
- Damage to customers' property from interruption to gas supply, gas leakage, or explosion

This is the risk in the low potential impact/low likelihood category: risk of injury to clerical employees.

Treat Risks

The first step in treating risk is to decide which risks qualify for risk treatment and to prioritize them.

Knowledge to Action

Select and prioritize Power's risks for risk treatment.

Feedback: These are the risks Power faces that are suited for risk treatment:

- Explosion of gas pipelines
- Weather-related damage to property or injury to employees
- Damage to pipelines that causes release of gas
- Injury to customers from interruption to gas supply, gas leakage, or explosion
- Vehicle accidents with personal injury
- Employee injuries

Risks with high potential impacts and low likelihood are most suitable for risk treatment. Risks with high potential impact and high likelihood are also suitable for risk treatment options. Also, various regulations, determined during the first step of scanning the environment, necessitate risk treatment for vehicle and employee injuries.

Risks with low potential impact and high likelihood should be addressed through operational procedures. Finally, risks with low impact and low likelihood are the lowest priority for risk treatment.

After risks have been evaluated and prioritized, treatment options can be selected. These risk treatment options can be used in various combinations:

- Avoiding the risk
- Changing the likelihood/impact
- Financing the risk
- Retaining the risk

Knowledge to Action

Which risk treatment approach(es) would you recommend for risk of damage to pipelines from weather or other external causes? Select all that apply.

a. Avoiding the risk
b. Changing the likelihood/impact
c. Financing the risk
d. Retaining the risk

Feedback: c. and d. It is impossible for Power to avoid the risk from external events to pipelines (a.). Although an engineering evaluation may determine methods to change the potential impact (b.), such as more-resistant piping material, the best combination of risk treatment for Power is to retain a portion of the risk and to finance the remainder through insurance.

Which risk treatment approach(es) would you recommend for risks to employees from severe weather? Select all that apply.

a. Avoiding the risk
b. Changing the likelihood/impact
c. Financing the risk
d. Retaining the risk

Feedback: b., c., and d. Power cannot completely avoid the risk to its employees from severe weather. Damage to gas pipelines must often be dealt with immediately to avoid additional hazards. Power can change the likelihood of employee injury by carefully selecting employees for its crisis response teams, training them, and providing protective equipment. Power should also use a combination of retention and financing to treat this risk.

Which risk treatment approach(es) would you recommend for the risk of injury to customers? Select all that apply.

a. Avoiding the risk
b. Changing the likelihood/impact
c. Financing the risk
d. Retaining the risk

Feedback: b., c., and d. Power cannot avoid the risk associated with its gas pipes and service without losing its customers. It can, however, change the likelihood of injury to its customers by training and supervising its employees, and it should also use a combination of retention and financing to treat this risk.

Which risk treatment approach(es) would you recommend for Power's risk of vehicle accidents with injuries? Select all that apply.

a. Avoiding the risk
b. Changing the likelihood/impact
c. Financing the risk
d. Retaining the risk

Feedback: b., c., and d. The severity of Power's vehicle accidents has remained level, while the frequency has increased. This risk cannot be avoided because vehicles must be used to perform essential business functions. Power can change the likelihood of vehicle accidents by hiring drivers with safe driving histories and training the drivers it employs. A combination of financing and retaining this risk is also recommended. In addition to meeting state requirements for auto liability insurance, Power would benefit from limiting the potential impact of this risk within its ability to do so, such as through electronic monitoring of its drivers.

Which risk treatment approach(es) would you recommend for Power's risk of injury to its service technicians? Select all that apply.

a. Avoiding the risk
b. Changing the likelihood/impact
c. Financing the risk
d. Retaining the risk

Feedback: b., c., and d. Although the frequency of Power's employee injuries has been decreasing, an ongoing focus on safety and injury prevention will probably lower both likelihood and impact. A review of Power's return-to-work and claims programs can also help improve the impact of employee injuries. Workers compensation insurance is required in almost every state, and Power should use a combination of retention and financing for this risk.

Although the risk of damage to customers' property has low potential consequences because of the lower cost compared with the risk of injury, this risk—in combination with increasing frequency of vehicle accidents—indicates a need for better risk management of service technicians' work performance. Hiring, training, and supervising service technicians should be important risk management priorities for Power.

Monitor and Assure

To be effective over time, a risk management process should be monitored to provide assurance that risks are being managed appropriately.

Knowledge to Action

Which activity or activities of the risk manager can assist with monitoring and assurance of hazard risk management? Select all that apply.

a. Reporting results, such as accident statistics
b. Meeting with managers to review results
c. Writing warnings to employees who have accidents
d. Conducting employee training

Feedback: a. and b. The risk manager's activities should include reporting results and meeting with managers to review results. Performance management (c.) and training of employees (d.) should be conducted by employees' managers or by trainers with subject-matter expertise, such as in safe driving techniques.

SUMMARY

The primary purposes of a risk management framework are to integrate risk management throughout an organization and to support the risk management process. These are the four components of the risk management framework:

- Lead and establish accountability
- Align and integrate
- Allocate resources
- Communicate and report

An established risk management policy statement should clearly communicate the policy to everyone in an organization.

A gap analysis of an organization's current risk management program compared with an internationally recognized standard is the first step in designing and implementing a risk management framework and process. After completing the gap analysis and a study of the organization's internal and external environments, an organization can design a framework and process and integrate them throughout all areas.

An enterprise-wide risk management process provides a broad approach to all of an organization's risks. Its focus includes opportunity risks as well as risks with potentially negative consequences. Its approach includes a review of the internal and external environments, such as regulatory requirements and organizational structure. The traditional risk management process focuses mainly on hazard risk. The six steps of the traditional process focus on loss exposures and do not view risk as providing any opportunities.

You should be able to apply the enterprise-wide risk management framework and process to an organization's risks. The components of the framework will allow you to integrate and support the risk management process in the organization. The process begins with scanning the environment, including the relevant laws and regulations. The next steps in the process enable you to identify and analyze risks. After risks have been identified and analyzed, the most appropriate risk treatment options can be selected. Monitoring the process assures an organization's managers that optimal risk management is in place. Although this case focused on hazard risk, you should be able to apply this process to all of an organization's risks.

ASSIGNMENT NOTE

1. Risk and Insurance Management Society, "Exploring Risk Appetite and Risk Tolerance," RIMS Executive Report, 2012, www.rims.org/resources/ERM/Documents/RIMS_Exploring_Risk_Appetite_Risk_Tolerance_0412.pdf (accessed June 1, 2012).

Direct Your Learning

Risk Identification

Educational Objectives

After learning the content of this assignment, you should be able to:

▸ Describe risk identification and its purpose.

▸ Explain how an organization can use each of the following team-oriented techniques to identify its risks:
- Facilitated workshops
- Delphi technique
- Scenario analysis
- HAZOP (hazard and operability study)
- SWOT (strengths, weaknesses, opportunities, and threats)

▸ Describe the purpose and the composition of a risk register.

▸ Describe the purpose and the composition of a risk map.

▸ Describe the following methods of loss exposure identification:
- Document analysis
- Compliance review
- Personal inspections
- Expertise within and beyond the organization

▸ Given a description of a business operation, recommend techniques for identifying and mapping risk.

Outline

Introduction to Risk Identification

Team Approaches to Risk Identification

Risk Registers

Risk Maps

Identifying Loss Exposures

Identifying Risk

Summary

Risk Identification

INTRODUCTION TO RISK IDENTIFICATION

Risks must be identified before they can be managed. To optimize risk management, organizations need to identify emerging risks in addition to existing risks.

Risk identification is one of the initial steps in the risk management process. Each organization, in tailoring a standard risk management process to its needs, should define how it will identify risk and the tools it will use in the process. A best practice for risk management professionals is a holistic approach to risk identification. See the exhibit "Enterprise-Wide Risk Management Process Model."

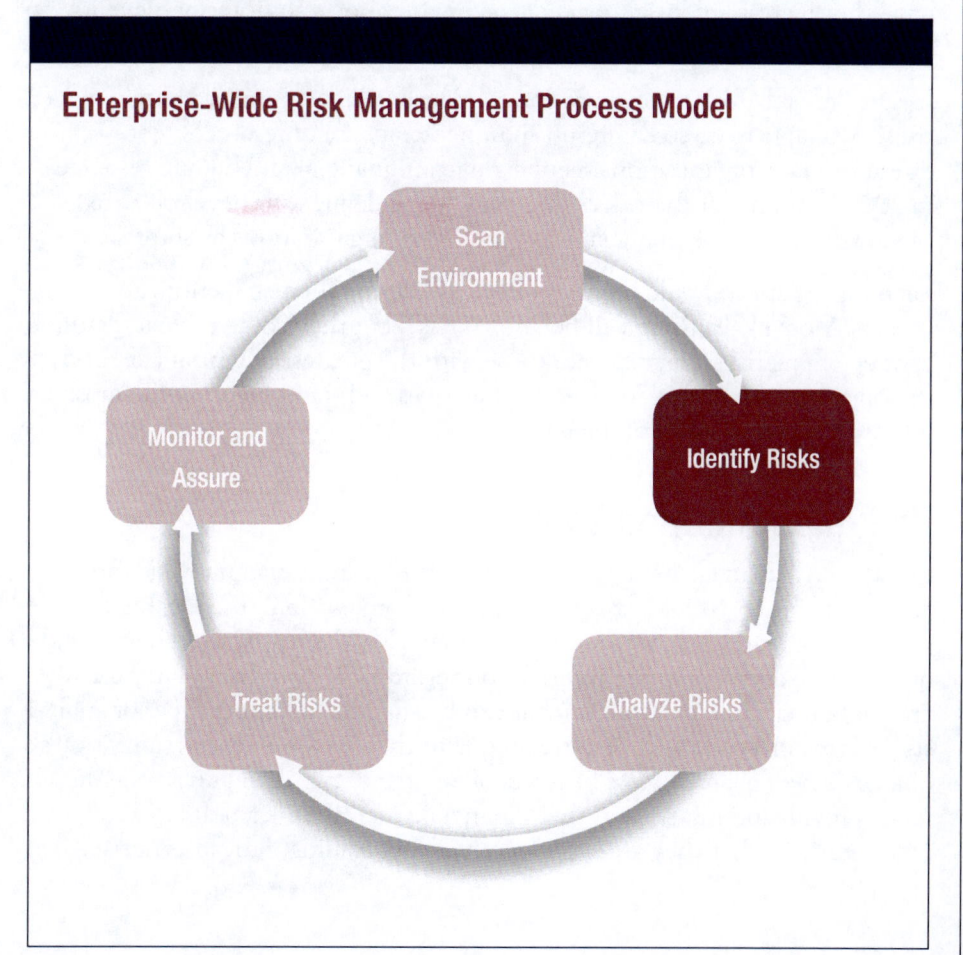

Enterprise-Wide Risk Management Process Model

A circular process diagram showing five stages connected by arrows: Scan Environment → Identify Risks → Analyze Risks → Treat Risks → Monitor and Assure, returning to Scan Environment. "Identify Risks" is highlighted.

Definition of Risk Identification

International risk management standards such as ISO 31000 and COSO ERM, as well as traditional risk management processes, include risk identification as an initial step in the process. COSO ERM uses the term "event identification," which it defines as management identifying "potential events affecting an entity's ability to successfully implement strategy and achieve objectives."[1] The traditional definition of risk identification is to employ methods of identifying specific loss exposures that could interfere with achieving an organization's primary goals.

The traditional risk identification process involves identifying loss exposures, which are negative risks. Standards such as ISO 31000 and COSO ERM use a broader approach in identifying risks with positive as well as negative potential for the organization. Each organization must decide which definition aligns with its objectives.

Organizations should identify all known risks, which are typically those that have previously affected them. Organizations should also attempt to identify emerging risks. Each organization should define the types of emerging risk that have the greatest potential to affect the organization's ability to achieve its objectives.

It is not feasible for any organization to identify all emerging or unknown risks. Attempts to do so can result in unnecessary use of resources. For example, many organizations spent significant financial and human resources in 2005 planning for the risk of an avian flu pandemic that never occurred. Meanwhile, the 2008 financial crisis took most organizations by surprise.

Each organization should highlight key risks during the risk identification process. Most likely, these will be known risks, but they could include significant emerging risks. Key risks are those with the greatest potential effect on the organization's ability to meet its objectives and should receive the most intensive risk management focus.

Risk Identification Tools

Standard risk management processes provide tools that organizations can adapt to identify risks. Most risk management professionals use loss histories as part of risk identification. Loss histories offer several advantages. They provide quantitative and qualitative information regarding known risks. They usually are contained within a database that can be adapted to various types of analysis. Loss histories can also be correlated with their effect on the organization's objectives. For example, loss histories of an organization's liability or credit losses provide information on their financial cost. However, a disadvantage of loss histories is that they are lagging rather than leading indicators of risk.

Various techniques are available to identify current and future risks:

- Checklists—An advantage of checklists is their ease of use by non-risk-management professionals. They can be divided into the four quadrants of risk (financial, strategic, operational, and hazard) and completed by managers in each area of an organization. For example, the manager of each branch of a bank could use a checklist to identify risks. The results for all of the branches could then be compiled and analyzed by a risk management professional. Questionnaires can be sent to customers to identify risks in providing products and services. Disadvantages of checklists include the possibility of failing to identify key risks or not identifying the effects of risks on other areas of the organization.

- Interviews and workshops—Risk management professionals or consultants can interview various people either internally or externally to identify risks. Managers and other employees can identify risks in their work activities, sometimes before an event occurs. For example, an employee could identify a lapse in the product inspection process.

- Escalation or threshold triggers—These can identify risk by comparing current transactions or events to prescribed criteria. For example, if the number of bank loans that do not conform to standards exceeds a threshold, this may indicate an escalation of risky lending practices.

- Process flow analysis—This technique analyzes processes within the organization from input to output. For example, a pharmaceutical company may analyze quality checks of ingredients used to make drugs, quality controls during the manufacturing process, and inspection of final products.

- Audits—Internal and external audits can identify areas of negative risk as well as opportunity risks. For example, audits of an organization's customer service telecommunications can identify opportunity risks where representatives offered or failed to offer products or services to customers. Safety audits can identify hazard and operational risks.

- Computer software—Various software can assist with risk identification. Examples include RISKMASTER™, RiskTrak™, and the Microsoft Excel-based Vulnerability Assessment Workbook. Advantages of software include its ability to identify risks as an integral part of business processes and to produce reports. For example, software systems can analyze financial transactions to determine whether they followed protocols and generate reports on questionable transactions. However, software applications may have limitations on the type of risk that can be identified and the methods used in identification.

- Team approaches to risk identification—Various team approaches can be used to identify risks. Teams that include key organizational stakeholders can use brainstorming and scenario analysis. The team approach identifies risks and the interconnectedness of risk across organizational functions. For example, a weather catastrophe may result in property damage or injury as well as production problems and supply chain interruption. The Delphi method provides input from a select group of experts. HAZOP and SWOT analyses are often used to identify the risks associated with a new product or procedure.

Holistic Approach to Risk Identification

The concept of a holistic approach to risk identification is easier for organizations to embrace conceptually than to put into practice. For most organizations, different types of risks are concentrated in specific areas. Financial risk exists in the accounting and financial areas of the organization, while products liability risk exists in the manufacturing areas. This silo nature of risk can prevent or delay risk identification and an understanding of how risk may ripple through an organization. For example, failure to recognize problems with a supplier could result in delayed or inferior product inputs that, in turn, could result in production difficulties that later result in employee injuries and product defects.

The use of risk quadrants to identify and categorize risk can provide a framework for holistic risk identification. Within the quadrants of strategic, financial, operational, and hazard risk, risks should be identified as internal or external. After the risks have been identified in each quadrant, a scenario analysis can be performed to assign event likelihoods and consequences. Developed scenarios can represent different levels of severity. For example, tornado risk can be developed in scenarios ranging from a tornado warning that stops production for two hours to a tornado that destroys a building and injures workers.[2]

The exhibit illustrates that risk is identified for each quadrant, and then the effects of each quadrant's risk on the other quadrants are also identified. In the previous example, the tornado represents a hazard risk that can cause damage or injury. However, related operational risks are also present, such as the loss of production capability. Depending on the tornado's severity, there could also be strategic and financial risks to the organization. See the exhibit "Holistic Risk Identification Using Risk Quadrants."

There are other methods of holistic risk identification. The COSO ERM standard also recommends categorizing risks, but in addition to doing so by type of risk, it suggests using a cascading hierarchy, beginning with high-level objectives and cascading down to risks related to the objectives of business units or functions. The University of California uses a computerized information system dashboard to identify risks across the organization.[3] Risk management professionals should develop a customized holistic approach that will work well within their organizations.

Some organizations use a top-down approach for holistic risk identification. With this approach, senior management decides which risks pose a significant threat or opportunity for the organization. The advantage of the top-down approach is that it provides a high-level view of the entire organization and the risks that are central to meeting the organization's objectives. Two disadvantages are its dependence on reports from middle management to senior management and its limited view of risks that may be percolating in various areas of the organization.

Holistic Risk Identification Using Risk Quadrants

- Hazard Risk — Hazard Risk Identification
- Operational Risk — Operational Risk Identification
- Financial Risk — Financial Risk Identification
- Strategic Risk — Strategic Risk Identification

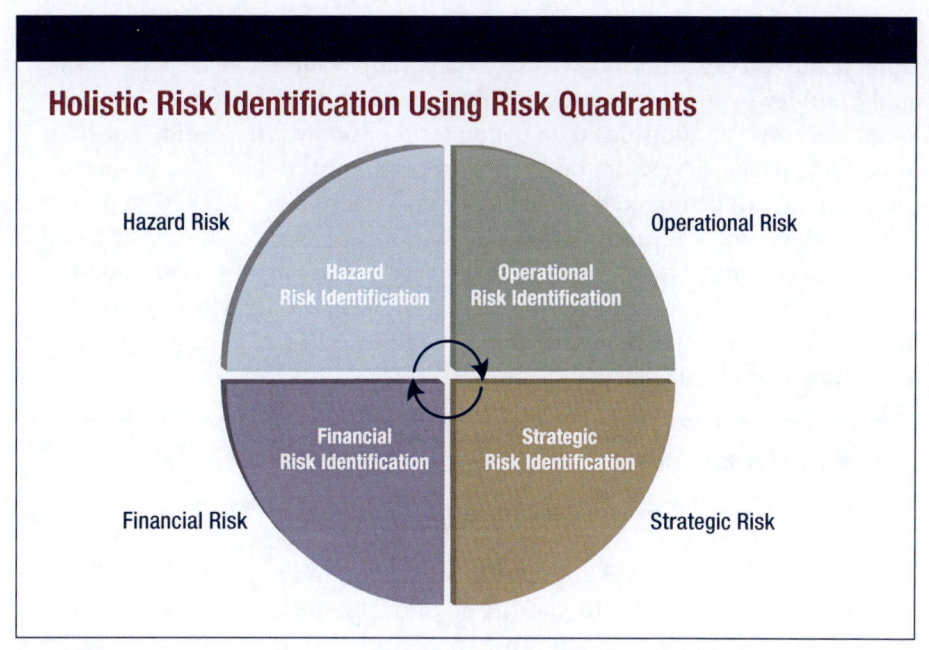

[DA08799]

Another approach to holistic risk identification is the bottom-up approach. One of the advantages of this approach is that the views of employees are included, which contributes to a realistic observation of the organization's operations and operating environments. Disadvantages are the time it takes to compile and analyze risk indicators and the possibility of details obscuring the desired holistic view. See the exhibit "Top-Down and Bottom-Up Approaches."

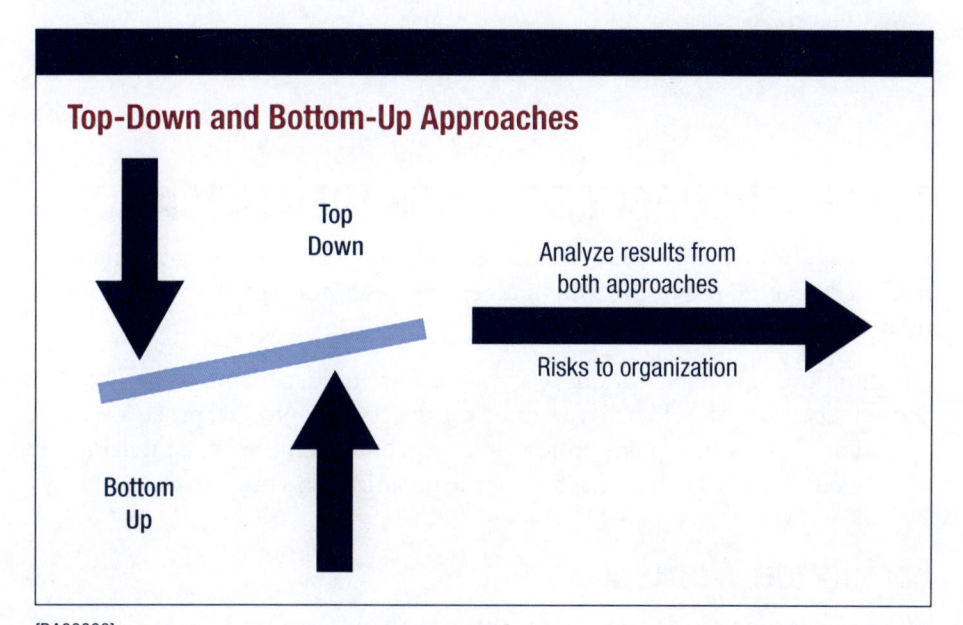

Top-Down and Bottom-Up Approaches

Top Down

Bottom Up

Analyze results from both approaches

Risks to organization

[DA08800]

Top-down and bottom-up approaches can be combined to develop a global approach to an organization's risks.[4] Computerized surveys or selected visits and interviews can be used to streamline the bottom-up approach. Having employees answer questions on a computerized survey is more efficient than processing paper surveys or conducting in-person interviews. Key production centers can be targeted for site visits and interviews with key employees, which is less time-consuming than interviewing all employees or visiting all locations in a large organization. The results of these surveys, visits, and interviews can be analyzed along with information from the top-down perspective to provide a more realistic identification of risks than would be possible using either approach by itself.

Apply Your Knowledge

John is a new risk manager at a medium-size manufacturing organization. The chief financial officer (CFO) would like John to develop a holistic approach to the organization's risk. Although an insurance program is in place, there has never been an attempt to identify all of the organization's risks. Describe one or more techniques John may use to identify this organization's risks.

Feedback: Because John is a new risk manager, it would be helpful for him to have checklists prepared by managers of different areas of the organization. Each of the manufacturing, shipping, procurement, legal, human resources, and other key managers could prepare checklists outlining the risks in their areas. Because these checklists may omit key risks and would not evaluate how risks can combine or affect other areas, John could then have a team workshop to discuss these risks. He could also use a combined top-down and bottom-up approach by receiving the CFO's perspective on risk, along with an employee survey.

TEAM APPROACHES TO RISK IDENTIFICATION

A team approach to risk identification can identify the interconnectedness of risk in addition to providing a comprehensive description of an organization's risks.

Organizations can adapt various team approaches to identifying risks. The chosen technique should be customized for the specific project, process, or operation. Risk management professionals can use several team approaches when identifying risks that affect all of the organization's objectives.

Facilitated Workshops

When risk management professionals meet with an organization's leaders, key employees, and other stakeholders, the group discussion identifies risks in a dynamic way. The groups can brainstorm to initiate discussion and allow a free flow of ideas. A skilled facilitator can design workshops to encourage brainstorming and follow-up discussion.

It is helpful to include representatives from diverse groups in the organization during these workshops because discussion of the combined and cascading effects of risks provides valuable information on level of risk and priority. Such discussion can identify opportunity risks as well as risks with potentially negative consequences. The facilitated workshops technique can be used for a specific project or process, and it can also be used to identify those risks that affect overall organizational objectives.

If facilitated workshops are used to identify all organizational risks, the facilitator must be skilled in risk identification and management as well as in group communication. Such action would typically be a long-term project. If the facilitator is a consultant, he or she could meet with the team at defined intervals after the team has worked independently on identifying the risks in each of the risk quadrants.

Delphi Technique

The Delphi technique—which originates from the myth of the all-knowing Oracle at Delphi—uses the opinions of a select group of experts to identify risks. Typically, these experts do not meet but respond to a survey or inquiry.

The standard Delphi technique involves submitting two rounds of queries to the selected experts. First, each expert is asked a question, and the combined answers, which remain anonymous, are presented to the group. The same question is then posed again to the individual experts, who are instructed to consider revising their responses based on the results that were reported to the group. This question-and-response cycle continues for a predetermined number of rounds or until consensus is achieved.

The Delphi technique was originally used to forecast new developments, such as innovations in technology. Now used for a range of different projects or processes, it is more cost-effective than assembling a facilitated workshop of experts and also eliminates some group bias by keeping responses anonymous. However, it has the possible disadvantage of obtaining current thinking on a particular project based on the group's consensus. If an organization is considering a novel product or project, the current expert opinion may not be as useful as the opinion of a group of potential product users or the community where a project is proposed.

Scenario Analysis

Scenario analysis identifies various risks and projects the potential consequences of those risks. For example, windstorm is identified as a risk. The outcomes associated with windstorm are not limited to the hazard risks of property damage and bodily injury. They also include business interruption, disruptions in customer relations, and possibly reputational risk based on how an organization responds during and after a windstorm. For example, after the 2011 earthquake and tsunami in Japan, in addition to coping with damage to its nuclear reactors at the Fukushima power plant, Tokyo Electric Power Company (TEPCO) had to deal with intense publicity of its pre- and post-crisis response to the earthquake and tsunami threat.

Scenario analysis is useful in identifying a range of potential consequences and in prioritizing risks. An organization should assemble an internal cross-functional team to obtain a multidimensional view of the potential consequences of a risk. For example, an operations manager may be primarily concerned with damage to a facility and employees in the event of windstorm. A member of the legal team may be concerned with liability if flammable materials are stored at the facility. A financial representative may be concerned about the effect on input prices if there are supply chain disruptions.

Disadvantages to scenario analysis include the possibility of missing key risks and limits in the imagination of the team conducting the analysis. Although cross-functional teams reduce these disadvantages, they do not eliminate them, especially if all of the team members are members of the organization who have never experienced a particular risk.

HAZOP

The term "HAZOP" is derived from hazard and operability study, which is a comprehensive review of a process or system. A team of appropriate experts and stakeholders identifies the risks associated with a given process and recommends a solution.

HAZOP is primarily used to design complex, scientific systems such as those used in engineering, chemical, mechanical, electronic, and computer operations. It can be adapted to analyze certain organizational strategies and initiatives.

A study team assembles in a facilitated workshop and follows these steps:

- Subdivides the project or system design into small components
- Reviews each component to identify risks
- Identifies cause and potential outcome for each risk
- Develops a solution for each risk

The level of expertise and time involved in this process make it appropriate for projects and systems where virtually all risks must be eliminated. For example, aircraft and biomedical engineering projects require risks to be identified and eliminated during the project design.

SWOT

The term "SWOT" is an acronym for strengths, weaknesses, opportunities, and threats. This type of team approach is useful in analyzing a new project or product. The strengths and weaknesses are internal factors to be considered. The opportunities and threats are external factors.

Different team members, representing different organizational functions, may analyze specific quadrants. For example, the marketing and legal functions may analyze the opportunities and threats. The research, operations, and financial functions may analyze the internal strengths and weaknesses. See the exhibit "SWOT Analysis."

SWOT Analysis

Environmental Factors		Strengths (S)	Weaknesses (W)
	Internal	Technology	High cost structure
		Distribution channels	Absence of key skills
		Customer loyalty	Staff turnover
		Product quality	Brand recognition
		Opportunities (O)	**Threats (T)**
	External	New technology	Shift in customer tastes
		New distribution channels	Emergence of competitors
		Unmet customer needs	New regulations
		Change in demographics	Tax increases

[DA08766]

A SWOT analysis is useful when there is a specific goal, such as determining whether engaging in a new product or project is feasible. It is less useful in analyzing current processes and procedures to identify risks unless there is a specific objective, such as whether a procedure conforms to new regulations or customer specifications. A goal is necessary to keep the SWOT analysis from becoming too general or from failing to provide actionable information.

The SWOT analysis should ideally conclude with a "Go" or "No Go" recommendation for a specific project and should include discussion on whether weaknesses or threats can be converted into strengths or opportunities. For example, if competitors have emerged in the organization's space, can the proposed project or product differentiate the organization and help it gain market share? If high costs are an obstacle to undertaking the project, can solutions be found that will not only help the project succeed but also help the organization gain a competitive advantage?

Apply Your Knowledge

You are a risk management professional for a computer software organization. The new products division has just developed a design for software to be used in a biomedical research project. Several key pharmaceutical organizations have expressed a need for this type of product. With previous projects, the organization spent a great deal of time working out problems after software was designed. The chief executive officer would like to eliminate that time and better meet customers' needs. Which team approach would you recommend to provide a solution?

a. Facilitated workshops
b. Delphi technique
c. HAZOP
d. SWOT

Feedback: c. A HAZOP technique will subdivide the design process into components and identify the risks associated with each. The HAZOP team can develop risk solutions for each component during the design and before the product's final development.

RISK REGISTERS

Risk management professionals can use a risk register to identify and prioritize the risks associated with a project, a process, a department, or an entire organization.

Scenario models capture the risks associated with events to provide a realistic view of what could happen to an organization under various circumstances. A **risk register** provides a matrix to record the likelihood of a scenario and its associated risks along with their probability, consequences, and impacts for the organization.

Risk register
A tool developed at the risk owner level that links specific activities, processes, projects, or plans to a list of identified risks and results of risk analysis and evaluation and that is ultimately consolidated at the enterprise level.

Purpose of Risk Registers

Risk registers can be used for specific projects, departments, business units, and processes. Risk management professionals can use these individual risk registers as the basis for an organizational risk register that displays key risks in order of priority. To be effective, the organizational risk register must be a dynamic matrix rather than a compilation of documents. A best practice is to use an interactive computer system in which risk owners, such as department managers and project managers, continually update risk information, and risk management professionals continually evaluate the information.

Each organization should design its risk register with parameters that adequately reflect its risks. A best practice is for the organizational risk register to provide a platform for managing risks after they have been identified.

Use of Risk Registers With Scenario Models

A risk register can be developed to depict the risks associated with a scenario model. For example, Airygen, an organization in the United States, supplies oxygen for medical use. Airygen's risk manager worked with each branch of the organization to complete a risk register for a windstorm scenario. The scenario presented for each branch manager to identify in the risk register is the occurrence of a windstorm, ranging from a severe thunderstorm to a major hurricane or tornado. See the exhibit "Airygen's Windstorm Risk Register—Miami Branch."

The likelihood of the windstorm scenario will vary significantly according to the location of Airygen's branches. The Miami branch has a high likelihood of experiencing the severe windstorm scenario because, in south Florida, severe thunderstorms are frequent and hurricanes are relatively common. Similarly, the branches in the Midwestern plains will have a relatively high likelihood of windstorm because of tornado threats. In contrast, the Pennsylvania branches will have a relatively low likelihood for this scenario. After each branch completes the risk register, the risk manager can combine them into regional and organizational risk registers for the windstorm scenario.

The level of risk indicated in the risk register is determined by the significance to the organization, not merely by a formula multiplying likelihood by consequences and impacts. In the Airygen example, the disruption of medical supplies to customers has a high level of risk relative to its estimated likelihood and financial consequences. Because many medical supplies, particularly oxygen, are critical to hospitals and individuals with serious medical conditions, the risk of not being able to deliver them can potentially damage Airygen's reputation. This risk is not quantifiable.

In a location where a major windstorm, such as a hurricane, could affect transportation as well as the branch itself, Airygen needs a plan to address the transportation risk. The catastrophe plan could include discussion of emergency plans with customers before hurricane season and a computer record of customers' plans, such as a plan to evacuate if a hurricane watch is issued or a plan to order additional supplies. System backups of computer records would ensure that this information is available in the event of a power loss or damage to the branch's computers.

Airygen's Windstorm Risk Register—Miami Branch

Scenario	Risk Description	Risk Owner	Likelihood	Consequences	Level of Risk	Improvement Action	Review Date
Windstorm	Storm damage range: minimal to catastrophic	Risk management Regional and branch management	90	$0 – $100 M+	10	Develop catastrophe plan Review property insurance	3/1/20X3
Risk Quadrant							
Hazard Risks	Wind damage	Risk management	40	$0 – $10 M	5	Safety procedures	1/1/20X3
	Oxygen explosion	Regional and branch management	10	$0 – $100 M+	10	Safety plan for employees	
	Fire	Safety and human resources	20	$0 – $100 M+	8		
Operational Risks	Emergency disruption of medical supplies to customers	Operations management	50	$0 – $50 K	9	Develop backup plan with Ft. Lauderdale	2/1/20X3
	Loss of business records	Regional management	60	$0 – $25 K	2	Review system backup	4/1/20X3
	Period of repair/rebuilding	Information technology	40	$0 – $20 M	7	Review business interruption coverage	1/1/20X3
		Risk management				Plan with Ft. Lauderdale and Orlando	2/1/20X3
		Operations management					
Financial Risks	Credit risk—customers will be unable or delayed in ability to pay	Finance	5	$0 – $100 K	1	Develop emergency payment plans for customers	5/1/20X3
	Price risk—the cost of product will increase after a major storm	Procurement Finance	6	$0 – $50K	1	Backup supplies from other branches	3/1/20X3
Strategic Risks	Reputational damage if customers cannot receive critical medical oxygen	Legal Operations Management Marketing	25	Potentially major damage	10	Catastrophe plan	3/1/20X3

Measurement Scales:

Likelihood: 1 – 100, 1 = lowest

Level of Risk: 1 – 10, 1 = lowest

Consequences: Estimated dollar range for quantitative measures

Organizational Risk Register

In addition to their use with specific scenario models, risk registers can be used to depict all of the organization's risk scenarios. The specific-scenario risk registers can be combined into one risk register for the entire organization.

Airygen's organizational risk register would include many risks in addition to those arising from the windstorm scenario. The scenario method is only one approach to identifying risks for the risk register. Other methods include a list of known and potential risks by risk quadrant, business unit, or risk owner. See the exhibit "Airygen's Windstorm Risk Register—Organizational Roll-Up."

Color codes can be used in reports produced from the risk register to highlight the level of risk. Potentially severe risks and moderate risks could be highlighted in different colors, as indicated in the Airygen example. If a computer risk management information system (RMIS) is used, a dashboard can list the highest-priority risks. Another advantage of a computer system is that a diary feature can trigger follow-up actions, such as insurance-program or safety reviews.

However an organization chooses to design its risk register, risk management professionals should ensure the risk register has these characteristics:

- Adequately identifies the organization's risks
- Prioritizes risk according to the potential effect on the organization
- Provides interactive use for risk owners
- Forms a matrix to manage risks

Airygen's Windstorm Risk Register—Organizational Roll-Up

Scenario	Risk Description	Risk Owner	Risk Quadrant	Likelihood	Consequences	Level of Risk	Improvement Action
Windstorm	Cat 3 or > hurricane strikes Miami	Risk management Operations management Regional and branch management Legal Finance Information technology (IT) Human resources	**Hazard:** Loss of property Injury Liability **Operational:** Business interruption **Financial:** Customer credit Input price **Strategic:** Reputational risk	40	$0 – $100 M+	10	Develop catastrophe plan with all stakeholders Review property and liability insurance
Data Breach	Theft of customer information	IT Risk management Legal	**Hazard:** Liability **Operational:** Interruptions to business processes **Financial:** Possible decline in stock value **Strategic:** Reputational risk	30	$10K – $100M	8	Review IT security Review insurance coverage
Rail Strike	Rail strike prevents delivery of oxygen to regional centers	Operations management Procurement	**Operational:** Disruption in supply **Strategic:** Reputational risk if medical supply is interrupted	25	$10K – $100K	3	Backup distribution plan

Measurement Scales:

Likelihood: 1 – 100, 1 = lowest

Level of Risk: 1 – 10, 1 = lowest

Consequences: Estimated dollar range for quantitative measures

[DA08753]

RISK MAPS

Risk mapping is a technique that can be used to provide a visual perspective of an organization's risks and to prioritize those risks.

Basic risk maps provide a matrix of the likelihood and impact (consequences) of risks identified on an organization's risk register. Variations of these maps can add other dimensions or aspects of risk. These maps can also be used to categorize risk in relation to an organization's risk appetite, which is the "total exposed amount that an organization wishes to undertake on the basis of risk-return trade-offs for one or more desired and expected outcomes."[5] The categorization of risk relative to risk appetite will help determine the appropriate level of risk management.

Basic Risk Map

A basic **risk map** translates the risks identified in the risk register into a risk matrix. This matrix can be used to analyze the risks that are within or outside an organization's risk appetite. Risk management professionals can then use the risk map as a basis to prioritize risk management and treatment for the risks that are outside the organization's risk appetite.

The exhibit illustrates an example of a risk map for Airygen, a national organization supplying oxygen for medical use. The term "impact" is used to convey the concept that the outcome can be either positive or negative. For example, if Airygen assumes the risk of acquiring another company, the organization will anticipate a positive outcome. The different colors represent the different levels of impact and likelihood combined. The technique of using colors to indicate different levels is sometimes referred to as heat mapping. See the exhibit "Basic Risk Map—Airygen Risks."

Risk Map Variations

Risk management professionals can use variations of the risk map to bring in different dimensions, such as time.[6] The exhibit illustrates how Airygen's risk manager can use this type of risk map to identify the urgency in time for each of the risks. Because this risk map was prepared on April 1 (near the beginning of hurricane season), the Miami windstorm risk is an urgent time priority. The catastrophe plan should be reviewed along with the property insurance. The change in healthcare regulations is imminent, and this becomes a high priority. The major acquisition is in the early stages and, therefore, is less urgent.

Time dimension risk maps can be used with the basic risk map to set monthly, quarterly, or annual priorities. These maps can be used to assist in the design and implementation of the risk management process as well as for follow-up in existing programs. See the exhibit "Impact and Time Risk Map—Airygen: 4/1/20X2."

Risk map
A template depicting the likelihood and potential impact/consequences of risks.

Basic Risk Map—Airygen Risks

Impact/Consequences		1. Rare	2. Unlikely	3. Moderate	4. Likely	5. Almost Certain
5. Extreme		Volcano eruption; Terrorist attack; Pandemic	Earthquake	Data breach; Wildfire; Arson; Flood	Midwestern windstorm (tornado)	Florida windstorm (hurricane)
4. Very High		Sudden, unexpected loss of C-suite-level manager; Public incident damaging to reputation (for example, scandal involving senior-level manager)	Financial crisis (interruption in credit facilities); Major workforce disruption (strike)	Interruption in regional product supply (strike, supply chain interruption); New strategic opportunity (acquisition)	Vehicle accident with injury; Customer accident with injury	Fire/explosion
3. Medium		Repairs requiring branch closure for a period of time	Employee dishonesty; Robbery/burglary	Minor incidents with products (for example, stuck valve); Loss/gain of key customer	Moderate vehicle accidents (property damage); Competitor pricing; Human resources issues	Employee injury
2. Low		Travel problems cause delay in meeting with key customer	Interruption of communication with a branch office for more than one hour (for example, power outage); Sudden, unexpected loss of branch manager	Customer service problems; Branch closure due to inclement weather	Minor vehicle accidents (property damage)	Employee illness/time off; Customer credit issues
1. Negligible		New computer system requiring staff training	Interruptions in noncritical supply chain (for example, office supplies)	Computer system unavailable for more than one day; Traffic delays in major distribution routes	Property and equipment maintenance issues	Billing errors

Likelihood

■ = highest impact/likelihood   ■ = medium impact/likelihood   ■ = low impact/likelihood

[DA08764]

Impact and Time Risk Map—Airygen: 4/1/20X2

Impact/Consequences	Low	Moderate	High
Significant (>$10M)	Reputation risk	Miami windstorm	Major acquisition / Healthcare regulations
Moderate ($2-10M)	Labor issue in New York	Workers compensation injuries (review safety program) / Change in Department of Transportation regulations	Vehicle accidents (review insurance)
Low (<$2M)	Small acquisition	Increase in price of oxygen in Georgia	Increase in vehicle repair costs / Increase in executive health insurance plan
	Low	**Moderate**	**High**

Likelihood

■ = most urgent　■ = moderate　■ = least urgent

[DA08765]

Risk management professionals can also use risk mapping to identify inherent, residual (current), and optimum levels of risk. Inherent risk is important because the difference between inherent and residual risk provides a measure of the necessity and the effectiveness of the current risk treatment. If the difference between inherent and residual risk is small, either the risk does not need to be treated or the treatment is ineffective. The difference between the residual (current) level of risk and the **optimum risk** represents the risk treatment opportunity to further reduce the risk. A risk map can be used to depict the effects of the current risk treatment techniques on the likelihood and impact of risks. It can also show opportunities to improve risk treatment. See the exhibit "Inherent, Residual, and Optimum Risk Map—Airygen's Miami Windstorm Risk."

The difference between the inherent and residual risk for Airygen's Miami windstorm risk is $90 million; therefore, the current risk treatment, which focuses on risk transfer, is still necessary and effective. However, the current risk treatment does not address all of Airygen's risks associated with a severe Miami windstorm. Reputation risk is potentially significant for the organization if Airygen's customers, such as hospitals, do not have adequate supplies of oxygen after a major hurricane. Implementing a catastrophe plan to address these critical customer needs will help treat this risk. The catastrophe plan can also help reduce the likelihood as well as the consequences of risk.

Optimum risk
The level of risk that is within an organization's risk appetite.

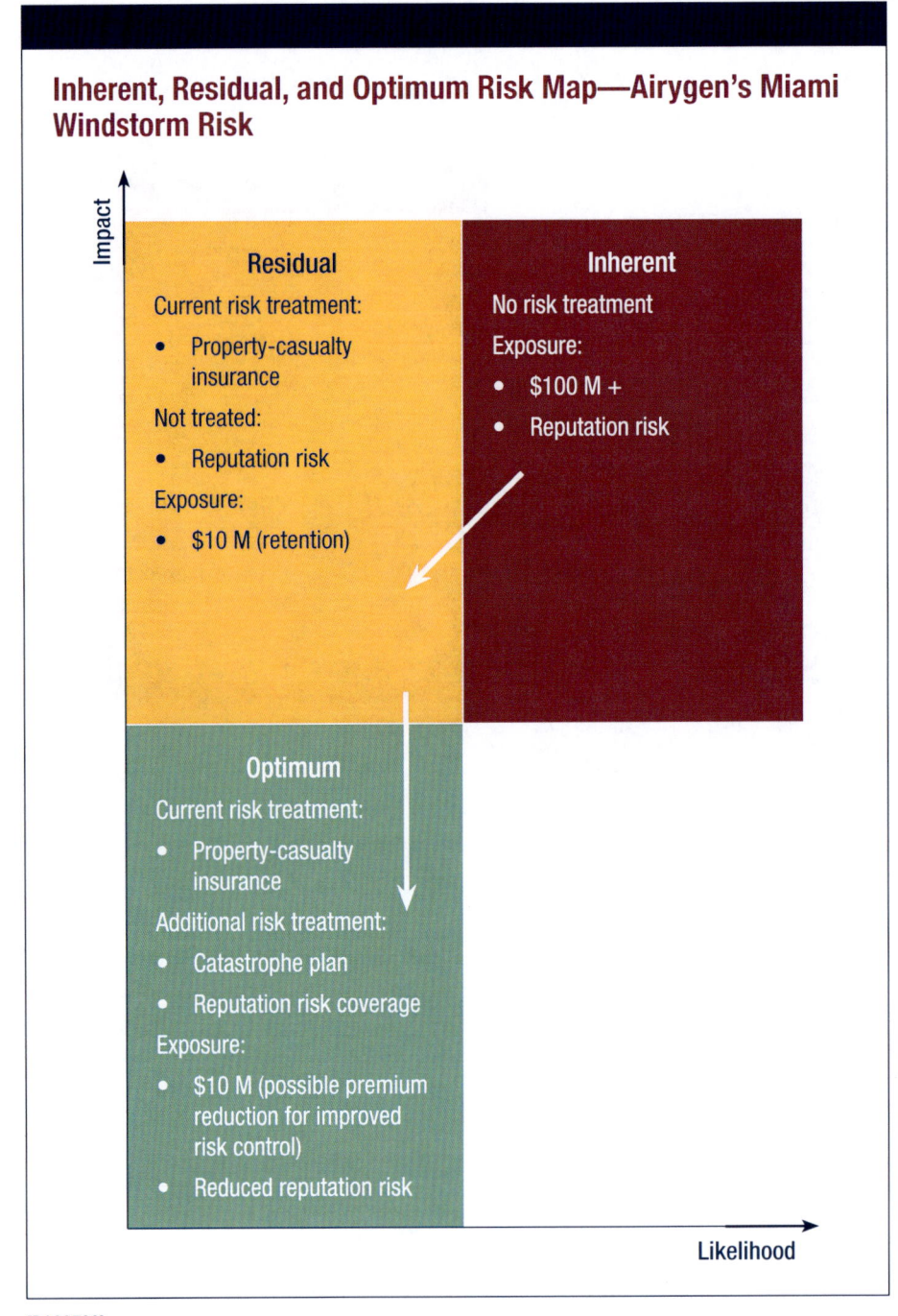

Inherent, Residual, and Optimum Risk Map—Airygen's Miami Windstorm Risk

Residual
Current risk treatment:
- Property-casualty insurance

Not treated:
- Reputation risk

Exposure:
- $10 M (retention)

Inherent
No risk treatment
Exposure:
- $100 M +
- Reputation risk

Optimum
Current risk treatment:
- Property-casualty insurance

Additional risk treatment:
- Catastrophe plan
- Reputation risk coverage

Exposure:
- $10 M (possible premium reduction for improved risk control)
- Reduced reputation risk

[DA08780]

Illustrating Risk Treatment Decisions

Risk management professionals can use a risk map to prioritize risks and select risk treatment options. Whenever practical, the organization may choose to avoid negative risks with the highest levels of likelihood and impact. For example, when considering several possible locations for expansion, Airygen may choose not to open a branch in an earthquake-prone area. Similarly, the organization may select the opportunity risks with the highest likelihood of producing the most significant impact. For example, Airygen may decide to make one major acquisition that will increase its national footprint rather than several smaller acquisitions at the same cost.

A map similar to Airygen's basic risk map can be used to identify the most appropriate risk treatment opportunities. Risks within the "red zone" should typically be exploited, controlled, or transferred according to the nature of the risk. Airygen will likely transfer a significant portion of the risks identified in the "red" area on its basic risk map. Risks within the yellow, or moderate, area should be evaluated according to the potential benefit or exposure and the cost of treating or pursuing the risk. For example, Airygen may decide it prefers to retain its vehicle property damage exposure. Risks that fall into the green, or low-risk, area are usually treated through normal operational processes and procedures. For example, Airygen should have customer service and accounting procedures to address billing errors.

IDENTIFYING LOSS EXPOSURES

For individuals, common property and liability exposures can be identified by a property-casualty insurance producer as part of an assessment of insurance needs. Similarly, individuals' net income loss exposures can be identified by life insurance producers as part of a needs assessment for life and health insurance products. For organizations, loss exposure identification is typically more complex, using a variety of methods and sources of information.

The methods of information that enable an organization to take a systematic approach to identifying loss exposures include these:

- Document analysis
- Compliance review
- Inspections
- Expertise within and beyond the organization

Document Analysis

The variety of documents used and produced by an organization can be a key source of information regarding loss exposures. Some of these documents are standardized and originate from outside the organization, such as questionnaires, checklists, and surveys. These standardized documents broadly categorize the loss exposures that most organizations typically face and are completed with information that is exclusive to the organization.

Other documents are organization-specific, such as financial statements and accounting records, contracts, insurance policies, policy and procedure manuals, flowcharts and organizational charts, and loss histories. Although the use and function of the various documents may overlap, causing possible duplication in loss exposure identification, reviewing multiple documents is necessary to avoid failing to identify important loss exposures.

In addition to the documents discussed in this section, virtually any document connected to an organization's operations also reveals something about its loss exposures. For example, Web sites, news releases, or reports from external organizations such as A.M. Best or D&B may indicate something about an organization's loss exposures. Although it is not feasible to review every document that refers to an organization, some of these additional sources may be useful.

Risk Assessment Questionnaires and Checklists

Standardized documents published outside an organization, such as insurance coverage checklists and risk assessment questionnaires, broadly categorize the loss exposures that most organizations typically face. A variety of checklists and questionnaires have been published by insurers, the American Management Association (AMA), the International Risk Management Institute (IRMI), the Risk and Insurance Management Society (RIMS), and others.

Although some organizations or trade associations have developed specialized checklists or questionnaires for their members, most are created by insurers and concentrate on identifying insurable hazard risks. Some focus on listing the organization's assets, whereas others focus on identifying potential causes of loss that could affect the organization.

Checklists typically capture less information than questionnaires. Although checklists can help an organization identify its loss exposures, they do not show how those loss exposures support or affect specific organizational goals. Linking loss exposures with the goals they support can be useful in analyzing the potential financial consequences of loss. Therefore, checklists are of limited benefit in the analysis step of the risk management process.

A questionnaire captures more descriptive information than a checklist. For example, as well as identifying a loss exposure, a questionnaire may capture information about the amounts or values exposed to loss. The questionnaire can be designed to include questions that address key property, liability, net income, and at least some personnel loss exposures.

Questionnaire responses can enable an insurance or a risk management professional to identify and analyze an organization's loss exposures regarding real property, equipment, products, key customers, neighboring properties, operations, and so on. Additionally, the logical sequencing of questions helps in developing a more detailed examination of the loss exposures an organization faces.

Both checklists and questionnaires may be produced by insurers (such questionnaires are known as insurance surveys). Most of the questions on these surveys relate to loss exposures for which commercial insurance is generally available.

Risk management or risk assessment questionnaires have a broader focus and address both insurable and uninsurable loss exposures. However, a disadvantage of risk assessment questionnaires is that they typically can be completed only with considerable expense, time, and effort and still may not identify all possible loss exposures.

Standardizing a survey or questionnaire has both advantages and disadvantages. Standardized questions are relevant for most organizations and can be answered by persons who have little risk management expertise.

However, no standardized questionnaire can be expected to uncover all the loss exposures particularly characteristic of a given industry, let alone those unique to a given organization. Additionally, the questionnaire's structure might not stimulate the respondent to do anything more than answer the questions asked; that is, it will elicit only the information that is specifically requested. Consequently, it may not reveal key information. Therefore, questionnaires should ideally be used in conjunction with other identification and analysis methods.

Because even a thoroughly completed checklist or questionnaire does not ensure that all loss exposures have been recognized, experienced insurance and risk management professionals often follow up with additional questions that are not on the standardized document.

Financial Statements and Underlying Accounting Records

Risk management professionals with accounting or finance expertise sometimes begin the loss exposure identification process by reviewing an organization's financial statements, including the balance sheet, income statement, statement of cash flows, and supporting statements. As well as identifying current loss exposures, financial statements and accounting records can be used to identify any future plans that could lead to new loss exposures.

An organization's **balance sheet** is the financial statement that reports the assets, liabilities, and owners' equity of the organization as of a specific date. Owners' equity, or net worth, is the amount by which assets exceed liabilities. Asset entries indicate property values that could be reduced by loss. Liability entries show what the organization owes and enable the risk management professional to explore two types of loss exposures: (1) liabilities that could be increased or created by a loss and (2) obligations (such as mortgage payments) that the organization must fulfill, even if it were to close temporarily as a result of a business interruption.

The **income statement** is particularly useful in identifying net income loss exposures; that is, those loss exposures that reduce revenue or increase expenses.

Balance sheet
The financial statement that reports the assets, liabilities, and owners' equity of an organization as of a specific date.

Income statement
The financial statement that reports an organization's profit or loss for a specific period by comparing the revenues generated with the expenses incurred to produce those revenues.

Statement of cash flows
The financial statement that summarizes the cash effects of an organization's operating, investing, and financing activities during a specific period.

The **statement of cash flows** (also called the statement of sources and uses of funds) is the financial statement that summarizes the cash effects of an organization's operating, investing, and financing activities during a specific period.

Funds-flow analysis on the statement of cash flows can identify the amounts of cash either subject to loss or available to meet continuing obligations. For example, the statement of cash flows would indicate the amount of cash that is typically on hand to pay for any losses resulting from loss exposures that have been retained by the organization.

Financial statements can reveal that an organization is subject to significant financial risks, such as fluctuations in the value of investments, interest rate volatility, foreign exchange rate changes, or commodity price swings. However, the primary advantage of financial statements from a risk management professional's perspective is that they help to identify major categories of loss exposures.

For example, property loss exposures can be seen in the asset section of the balance sheet. Some liability loss exposures, especially contractual obligations such as loans or mortgages, can be seen in the liabilities section of the balance sheet. The potential effects of net income loss exposures can be seen by comparing revenues with expenses on the income statement.

The major disadvantage of using financial statements for identifying loss exposures is that although they identify most of the major categories of loss exposures (property, liability and net income are identified but personnel loss exposures are not), they do not identify or quantify the individual loss exposures. For example, the balance sheet may show that there is $5 million in property exposed to loss, but it does not specify how many properties make up that $5 million, where those properties are located, or how much each individual property is worth. Moreover, the real and personal property values recorded in financial statements are based on accounting conventions and are not accurate for purposes of insurance or risk management.

Another disadvantage is that financial statements depict past activities—for example, revenue that has already been earned, expenses that have already been incurred, prior valuations of assets and liabilities, and business operations that have already taken place. They are of limited help in identifying projected values or future events. Therefore, even after using financial statements for loss exposure identification, insurance and risk management professionals still need to project what events might occur in the future, determine how these future events could change loss exposures, and analyze and quantify potential losses accordingly.

Contracts

A contract is an agreement entered into by two or more parties that specifies the parties' responsibilities to one another. Analyzing an organization's contracts may help identify its property and liability loss exposures and help determine who has assumed responsibility for which loss exposures. It is often necessary to consult with legal experts when interpreting contracts.

Contract analysis can both identify the loss exposures generated or reduced by an organization's contracts and ensure that the organization is not assuming liability that is disproportionate to its stake in the contract. Ongoing contract analysis is part of monitoring and maintaining a risk management program.

Entering into contracts can either increase or reduce an organization's property and liability loss exposures. For example, a contract to purchase property or equipment will increase the organization's property loss exposures, whereas a contract to sell property or equipment will reduce property loss exposures.

A contract can generate liability loss exposures in two ways. First, the organization can accept the loss exposures of another party through a contract, such as a **hold-harmless agreement** (sometimes referred to as an indemnity agreement). For example, an organization may enter into a hold-harmless agreement with its distributor under which the organization agrees to indemnify the distributor (pay the losses for which the distributor is liable) if the distributor is found liable for a products liability claim. **Indemnification** is the process of restoring an individual or organization to a pre-loss financial condition.

The second way a contract may generate a liability loss exposure is if the organization fails to fulfill a valid contract. For example, if an organization agrees to deliver manufactured goods to a distributor and then fails to deliver those goods, the distributor is entitled to bring a legal claim against the organization. The distributor's claim presents a liability loss exposure for the organization.

Alternatively, an organization can reduce or eliminate liability loss exposures by entering into a contract that transfers its liability to another organization. For example, an organization can enter into a hold-harmless agreement under which the second party agrees to indemnify the organization in the event of a liability claim.

Insurance Policies

Although insurance is a means of risk financing, reviewing insurance policies can also be helpful in risk assessment.

Analyzing insurance policies reveals many of the insurable loss exposures that an organization faces. However, this analysis may either indicate the organization is insured for more loss exposures than it really has, or, alternatively, may not show all the loss exposures the organization faces.

As insurance policies typically are standardized forms, an organization does not necessarily face every loss exposure covered by its policies. Furthermore, the organization may face many other loss exposures that either cannot be

---

Hold-harmless agreement (or indemnity agreement)
A contractual provision that obligates one of the parties to assume the legal liability of another party.

Indemnification
The process of restoring an individual or organization to a pre-loss financial condition.

covered by insurance policies or are covered by policies the organization has chosen not to purchase.

To identify insurance coverage that an organization has not purchased, and therefore potentially identify insurable loss exposures that have not been insured, a risk management professional can compare his or her organization's coverage against an industry checklist of insurance policies currently in effect.

Organizational Policies and Records

Loss exposures can also be identified using organizational policies and records, such as corporate by-laws, board minutes, employee manuals, procedure manuals, mission statements, and risk management policies. For example, policy and procedure manuals may identify some of the organization's property loss exposures by referencing equipment, or pinpoint liability loss exposures by referencing hazardous materials with which employees come into contact. See the exhibit "Internal Documents as Loss Exposures."

Internal Documents as Loss Exposures

Internal documents, in addition to identifying loss exposures, need to be analyzed to determine their appropriateness and consistency with external publications. An organization's internal documents are not typically written in anticipation that they will be viewed outside the organization. However, many internal documents are used during legal proceedings and therefore may present a potential liability loss exposure to the organization. This illustrates the need for internal documents to be consistent with external information the organization releases.

[DA02555]

As well as identifying existing loss exposures, some documents may indicate impending changes in loss exposures. For example, board minutes may indicate management's plans to sell or purchase property, thereby either reducing or increasing its property loss exposures.

One drawback to using policies and records to identify loss exposures is the sheer volume of documents that some organizations generate internally. It may be virtually impossible to have one employee or a group of employees examine every internal document. In these instances, insurance and risk management professionals would need to examine a representative sample of documents. This makes the task manageable, but increases the likelihood that not all loss exposures will be identified.

Flowcharts and Organizational Charts

A flowchart is a diagram that depicts the sequence of activities performed by a particular organization or process. An organization can use flowcharts to show the nature and use of the resources involved in its operations as well as the sequence of and relationships between those operations.

A manufacturer's flowchart might start with raw material acquisition and end with the finished product's delivery to the ultimate consumer. Individual entries on the flowchart, including the processes involved and the means by which products move from one process to the next, can help identify loss exposures—particularly critical loss exposures.

For example, the flowchart might illustrate that every item produced must be spray-painted during the production process. This activity presents a critical property loss exposure, because an explosion at the spray-painting location might disable the entire production line. The simplified flowchart in the exhibit reveals that difficulties with getting the furniture through customs at the Los Angeles Port could disrupt the entire furniture supply chain. See the exhibit "Furniture Manufacturer Flowchart."

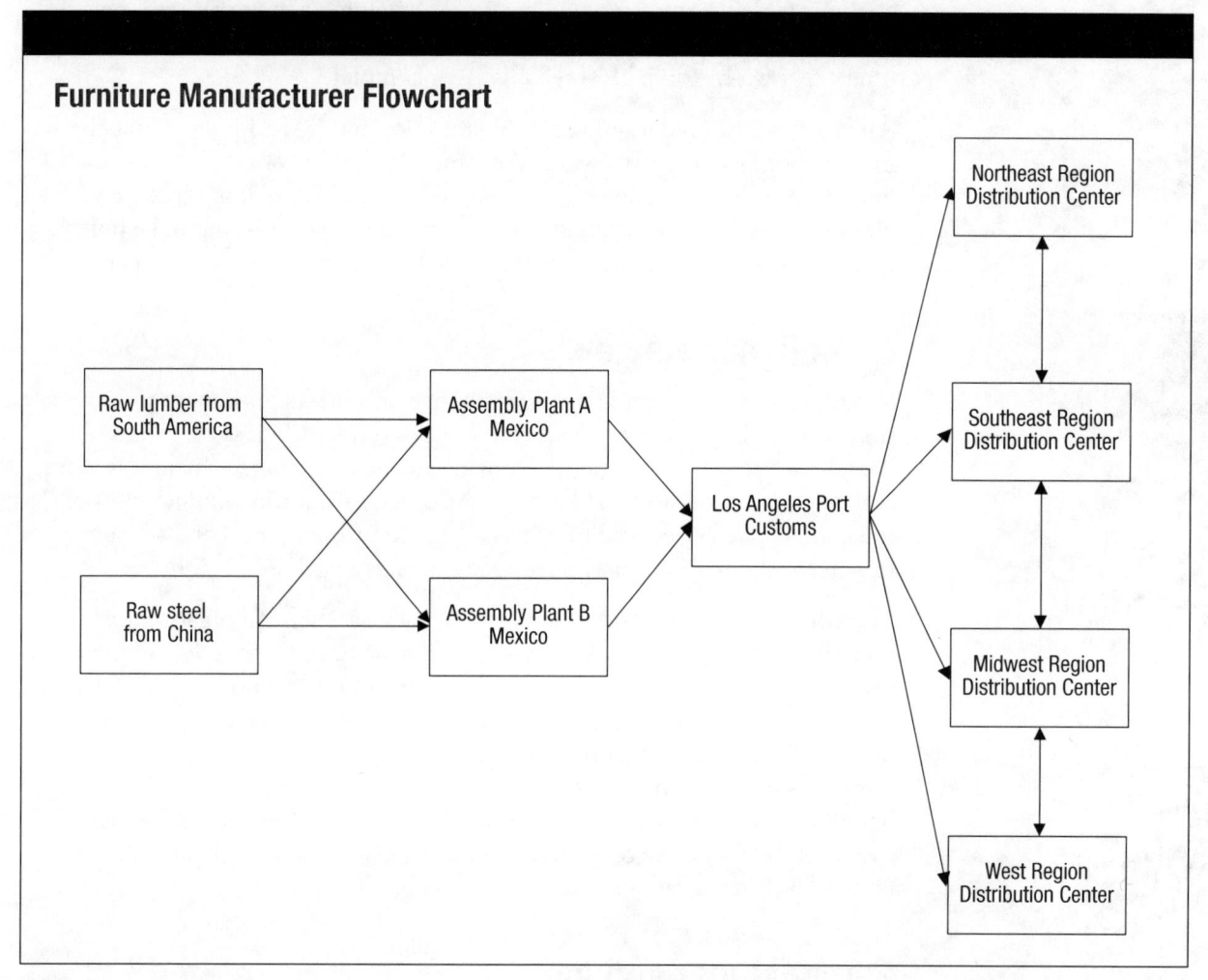

Furniture Manufacturer Flowchart

Raw lumber from South America and Raw steel from China → Assembly Plant A Mexico and Assembly Plant B Mexico → Los Angeles Port Customs → Northeast Region Distribution Center, Southeast Region Distribution Center, Midwest Region Distribution Center, West Region Distribution Center

[DA02556]

Information can also be obtained from organizational charts. An organizational chart depicts the hierarchy of an organization's personnel and can help to identify key personnel for whom the organization may have a personnel loss exposure. This chart can also help track the flow of information through an organization and identify any bottlenecks that may exist. Although organizational charts can be fundamental in properly identifying personnel loss exposures, an individual's place on an organizational chart does not guarantee that he or she is a key employee. The organizational chart does not necessarily reflect the importance of the individual to the continued operation or profitability of the organization.

Loss Histories

Loss history analysis, that is, reviewing an organization's own losses or those suffered by comparable organizations, can help a risk management or an insurance professional to both identify and analyze loss exposures. Loss histories of comparable organizations are particularly helpful if the organization is too small or too new to have a sizeable record of its own past losses, or if the organization's own historical loss records are incomplete.

Any past loss can recur unless the organization has had a fundamental change in operations or property owned. Accordingly, loss histories are often an important indicator of an organization's current or future loss exposures. However, loss histories will not identify any loss exposures that have not resulted in past losses. Therefore, use of loss histories alone is inadequate.

Compliance Review

In addition to document analysis, insurance and risk management professionals may also conduct compliance reviews to identify loss exposures. A compliance review determines an organization's compliance with local, state, and federal statutes and regulations. The organization can conduct most of the compliance review itself if it has adequate in-house legal and accounting resources. Otherwise, it may have to use outside expertise.

The benefit of compliance reviews is that they can help an organization minimize or avoid liability loss exposures. However, a drawback of compliance reviews is that they are expensive and time consuming. Furthermore, because regulations are often changing, remaining in compliance requires ongoing monitoring. As a result, conducting a compliance review simply to identify loss exposures is often impractical. However, because noncompliance is a liability loss exposure, loss exposure identification can be part of the justification of the cost of a compliance review and is an ancillary benefit once a review has been completed.

Personal Inspections

Some loss exposures are best identified by personal inspections, that is, information-gathering visits to critical sites both within and outside an organization. Such visits often reveal loss exposures that would not appear in written descriptions of the organization's operations and therefore should lead to a more complete list of loss exposures.

Personal inspections should ideally be conducted by individuals whose background and skills equip them to identify unexpected, but possible, loss exposures. Additionally, the person conducting the inspection should take the opportunity to discuss the particular operations with front-line personnel, who are often best placed to identify nonobvious loss exposures. Therefore, a personal inspection can overlap with consulting expertise within and beyond the organization.

Expertise Within and Beyond the Organization

Thorough loss exposure identification should include soliciting expertise both inside and outside the organization. Doing so renders a more complete and objective picture of the organization's loss exposures.

Interviews with employees can be conducted to gather information about their jobs and departments. Whereas an inspection can only reveal what is happening during the inspection, interviews can elicit information about what occurred before the inspection, what might be planned for the future, or what could go or has gone wrong that has not been properly addressed.

Interviews should include a range of employees from every level of the organization. Questionnaires can be designed for use in conjunction with these interviews to ensure that they are comprehensive and are eliciting as much information as possible.

To obtain an external perspective, practitioners in fields such as law, finance, statistics, accounting, auditing, and the technology of the organization's industry can be consulted. The special knowledge of experts in identifying particular loss exposures is an invaluable resource.

One area of specialization that often requires such expert services is **hazard analysis**. For example, a business consultant might identify conditions that cause the organization to overlook opportunities for growth. Alternatively, concerns about environmental hazards might require a specialist to take air or water samples and a specialized laboratory to analyze them. Although hazard analysis is focused on loss exposures that have already been identified, the results of the analysis often identify previously overlooked loss exposures.

Hazard analysis
A method of analysis that identifies conditions that increase the frequency or severity of loss.

IDENTIFYING RISK

It is important to know how to apply risk identification techniques to the facts of a case. By carefully considering the facts provided and answering the Knowledge to Action questions, this activity should help you make the transition from knowing about the methods of risk identification to knowing how to apply those methods in an actual risk management process.

Case Facts

Ann is the new risk manager at Finder, Inc., a global Internet search engine organization. Her predecessor developed a comprehensive insurance program for Finder, including cyber risk, directors and officers (D&O), and employment practices liability coverage in addition to their commercial property and general liability insurance.

Finder's chief executive officer (CEO), chief financial officer (CFO), and board of directors want Ann to develop a holistic risk management approach. After reviewing Finder's operating environment, Ann initiates the risk management process by identifying Finder's risks.

What techniques would Ann use in identifying Finder's risks?

Case Analysis Tools

There are various techniques Ann can use to assist with risk identification. There are several team approaches:

- Facilitated workshop
- Delphi technique
- Scenario analysis
- Hazard and operability (HAZOP)
- Strength, Weakness, Opportunity, and Threat (SWOT)

She can also use various types of risk registers and risk mapping in identifying Finder's risks.

Overview of Steps

Identifying Finder's risks involves a detailed analysis of the four quadrants of risk:

- Hazard
- Operational
- Financial
- Strategic

Identifying risks also involves prioritizing those risks by likelihood and potential impact on the organization's objectives.

Identifying Risks—Team Approach

Ann decides to use a team approach to identify Finder's risks. After considering the various team methods, she decides to use a facilitated workshop.

Knowledge to Action

Explain the advantages of the facilitated workshop in identifying Finder's risks.

Feedback: Ann is new to the organization and is also starting a new, holistic approach to risk management. She will need the collective expertise of the various functions of this global organization to identify Finder's risks. She can also benefit from the skilled leadership of a consultant to facilitate the workshop.

Which team approach would you recommend that Ann use along with the facilitated workshop?

a. Delphi
b. Scenario
c. HAZOP
d. SWOT

Feedback: b. Scenario analysis will allow the team to explore various risks and combinations of risks. The Delphi, HAZOP, and SWOT techniques are more appropriate for a specific project, product, or process.

After the initial workshop, the team is divided into subgroups to identify risks within their organizational functions. A follow-up workshop is then scheduled to present and discuss the risk scenarios identified in the subgroups and how those risks may be connected to other areas of the organization. These are six of the scenarios the team identifies:

- Finder is looking at the possible acquisition of a data mining organization, which presents a new business area for the organization.
- A competitor is the defendant in a large class action lawsuit alleging invasion of privacy. There are concerns that Finder could find itself a defendant in litigation of this type.
- There are uncertainties involving whether and to what extent computer programs can be protected by patent or copyright.
- There is an increase in competition among search engine organizations.
- Several of the countries in which Finder operates are considering restrictions to Internet content.
- Finder has several data operation and storage facilities around the world. One of the largest of these is located on the San Andreas Fault and is therefore at risk of earthquake.

Risk Register

The next step in the risk identification process is to develop a risk register of the scenario models presented by the subgroups. At the next team meeting, Ann has the group design the register's format. At subsequent meetings, they populate the register with their scenarios, the major risks associated with each scenario by risk quadrant, and the overall risk level. The team agrees to use risk levels ranging from one to ten, with ten being the highest level of risk for the organization.

Knowledge to Action

Design a risk register to include the six risk scenario models Ann's team identified. Your register should include each scenario's risk level and quadrant(s) of risk.

Feedback: See the exhibit "Finder's Risk Register."

Risk Mapping

Ann and her team decide to design a risk map to depict the impact and consequences of each risk identified. They also want to indicate the urgency of addressing each of the risks to assist with prioritization and decision making.

Knowledge to Action

Design a risk map for the six Finder risks identified in the risk register. The vertical axis should be designated as impact/consequences with these categories:

- Significant
- Moderate
- Minimal

The horizontal axis should be designated as likelihood with these categories:

- High
- Medium
- Low

Place each of the six risks in the area of the map that applies to its impact and likelihood. Use a color code or another technique to indicate each risk according to the urgency you assign it.

Feedback: See the exhibit "Finder's Risk Map."

Explain the reasons for your urgency designations. It is more important for risk management professionals to understand and be able to communicate the criteria they would use to determine urgency than to arrive at a specific answer.

Finder's Risk Register

Scenario	Hazard Risk	Operational Risk	Strategic Risk	Financial Risk	Risk Level	Action Plan
Acquisition of data mining organization	Risks associated with operations of acquisition	Integration of operating systems and corporate culture	Return on investment	Effect on Finder's capital and share price	6	Review report from Mergers & Acquisition Department and plan follow-up steps
Class action lawsuit related to privacy	Data privacy litigation	Procedures to safeguard privacy of system users Compliance with regulations	Reputation risk if there is a major privacy issue or litigation	Effect on Finder's share price in the event of negative publicity	7	Review operating systems for privacy safeguards Review applicable regulations and case law Review insurance coverage
Allegations of copyright/patent infringement	Intellectual property litigation	Checks on existing patents/copyrights before proceeding with technology innovations	Loss of competitive advantage Reputation risk	Effect on Finder's share price	4	Obtain legal opinion from outside counsel with intellectual property expertise Follow up based on legal opinion
Increase in competition	Increase in employee injuries because of production demands resulting from cost cutting Product liability resulting from decreased production time for new or upgraded products	Tighter production deadlines Decrease in production resources Quality control concerns	Market reputation as a result of reduced quality control Ability to meet price and product demands to stay competitive	Effect on revenue and share price	5	Market research and benchmark study
Government restrictions on Internet content	Litigation by government agencies	Adjust processes and procedures for different regulatory standards	Loss of customers Resource drain in challenging regulations	Effect on revenue and share price	4	Legal research Lobbying
San Andreas earthquake	Property loss or damage Employee injury	Disruption of operations	Inability to provide service to customers	Effect on revenue and share price	9	Review insurance Engineering/architecture review of data center for ability to withstand earthquake Develop data back-up program

[DA08769]

Finder's Risk Map

Impact/Consequences	Low	Medium	High
Significant		San Andreas earthquake	
			Privacy lawsuit
Moderate	Government restrictions on Internet content	Increase in competition	Acquisition of data mining organization
Minimal			Allegations of copyright/patent infringement

Likelihood

■ = High urgency   ■ = Moderate urgency   ■ = Low urgency

[DA08770]

The potential consequences of a San Andreas earthquake or a privacy lawsuit are significant. Because a competitor is already facing a privacy lawsuit, there is a greater likelihood of litigation than a San Andreas earthquake, which is a relatively rare event. However, because of the significance of the consequences of either of these events, they are both rated as having high urgency.

The proposed acquisition has a potential for positive impact for the organization, but is not likely to be of the highest level of significance. It represents a new business area for Finder rather than the acquisition of a key competitor. Because such deals usually have timelines, there is a significant level of urgency to complete the review and make a recommendation of whether to proceed with the potential acquisition.

Increase in competition is a moderate-level risk. However, because there will always be a competitive environment, the urgency to address this risk is low.

There are no immediate threats of government restrictions to Internet content listed in the team's risk identification. However, this is something that should be researched in the action plan. The potential consequences are moderate, although at this time there is no indication of significant likelihood. A moderate level of urgency should be directed toward this risk to clarify that there are no pending regulations in any of the countries where Finder operates. If any are discovered during the review, the risk level and urgency might increase.

The risk of alleged patent or copyright infringement is likely to be an ongoing risk for an Internet organization. Therefore this is designated as lower urgency. If there is a change in the litigation or regulatory environment, the significance of this risk could increase.

SUMMARY

Risk management professionals should be aware of how major international risk management standards define risk identification. They should then customize the definition for their organizations. Various tools can be adapted to assist in identifying existing and emerging risks. A holistic approach to risk identification is a best practice for organizations to recognize and understand their risks.

A team approach to identifying the risks associated with a project, product, or organization can provide diverse perspectives. In addition to identifying specific risks, it can illuminate interconnected risks that might not be apparent to an individual. To meet the particular needs of their organization, risk management professionals should adapt the various team approaches, such as facilitated workshops, the Delphi technique, scenario analysis, HAZOP, and SWOT. Some techniques work better for specific complex projects, while others can be used to identify organizational risks.

Risk management professionals can use a risk register when identifying the risks associated with a scenario. The scenario method provides a view of a possible event and its associated risks. The risk register is a matrix that helps to identify the likelihood, consequences, risk level, and action steps for the scenario as well as the risks in all four risk quadrants.

Risk mapping is a valuable technique for risk management professionals to use in analyzing their organizations' risks. These maps can prioritize risks and assist with risk management decisions.

Because identifying loss exposures is the beginning of the risk management process, it should be done thoroughly and systematically. Various methods can be used to identify loss exposures, including document analysis, compliance review, inspections, and expertise within and beyond the organization.

You should now be able to develop a team approach to risk identification and be able to design risk registers and risk maps to categorize and prioritize the risks identified. It is important for risk management professionals to be able to use various techniques to outline how risks can affect their organizations across all four of the risk quadrants and determine their potential significance in regard to their organizations' objectives.

ASSIGNMENT NOTES

1. Committee of Sponsoring Organizations of the Treadway Commission, "Enterprise Risk Management—Integrated Framework: Executive Summary," September 2004, p. 38, www.coso.org/documents/coso_erm_executivesummary.pdf (accessed February 8, 2012).
2. M. D. Abkowitz and J. S. Camp, "Identifying Risks and Scenarios Threatening the Organization as an Enterprise," pp. 6-7, www.memphis.edu/cait/pdfs/Risk___Scenario_Identificaton_-_CAIT.pdf (accessed April 26, 2012).

3. Joanne Wojcik, "Integrated RMIS Tool Aids Holistic Approach," Business Insurance, April 16, 2012, p. 22.
4. Puneet Kapoor, "Uncovering Risks: A Critical Precursor to Effective Risk Handling," presentation at the Risk and Insurance Management Society Conference on Enterprise Risk Management, November 3, 2011, San Diego, Calif.
5. RIMS, "Exploring Risk Appetite and Risk Tolerance," RIMS Executive Report: The Risk Perspective (New York: Risk and Insurance Management Society, Inc.), April 12, 2012, p. 3.
6. Harold D. Skipper and W. Jean Kwon, Risk Management and Insurance (Malden, Mass.: Blackwell Publishing, 2007), pp. 303-304.

Direct Your Learning

Risk Analysis

Educational Objectives

After learning the content of this assignment, you should be able to:

▸ Describe risk analysis and its importance.

▸ Explain how probability analysis can be used to estimate the likelihood and consequences of an event.

▸ Describe the following characteristics of probability distributions:
- Expected value
- Mean
- Standard deviation
- Coefficient of variation
- Normal distribution

▸ Explain how regression analysis can be used to forecast gains or losses.

▸ Compare decision tree analysis and event tree analysis in terms of the methods they use to evaluate event consequences.

▸ Explain how to analyze loss exposures considering the four dimensions of loss and data credibility.

Outline

Introduction to Risk Analysis

Probability Analysis

Characteristics of Probability Distributions

Trend Analysis

Analyzing Event Consequences

Analyzing Loss Exposures

Summary

Risk Analysis

INTRODUCTION TO RISK ANALYSIS

An organization must understand the risks it faces before it can decide how to treat them.

Risk analysis provides information for understanding risks and for making decisions regarding treatment of those risks. Sources and consequences of an identified risk are also considered during risk analysis. When considering consequences, an organization examines not only the range of potential consequences of a risk, but also the likelihood of each consequence and the effectiveness of any existing controls. With this information, an organization can determine its level of risk. See the exhibit "Enterprise-Wide Risk Management Process Model."

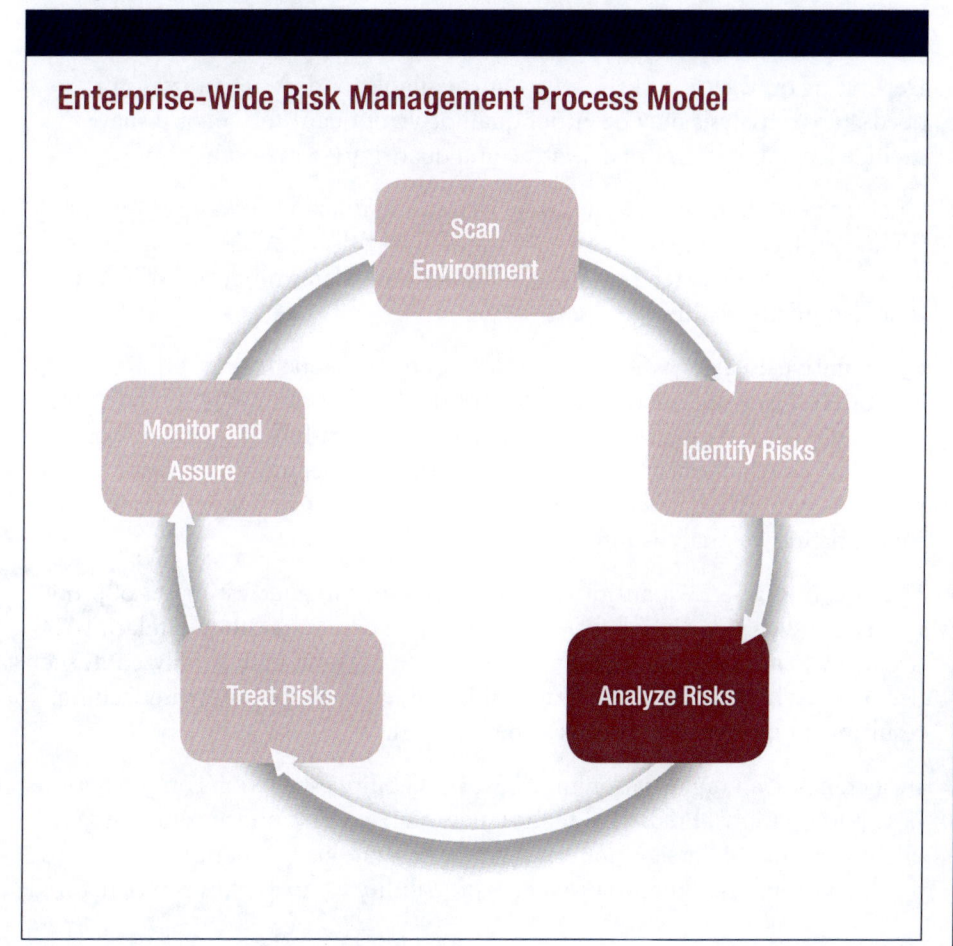

Enterprise-Wide Risk Management Process Model

Scan Environment → Identify Risks → Analyze Risks → Treat Risks → Monitor and Assure → (cycle continues)

[DA08717_5]

The Nature of Risk Analysis

As part of its overall risk analysis approach, an organization might analyze the risk related to a potential event, a product line, a project, or a process. For an identified risk, the organization would note the range of possible consequences and determine the probability of each. Consequences of a risk relate to how the risk might affect—either positively or negatively—the ability of the organization to accomplish its objectives.

An identified consequence may be so unlikely or insignificant that it requires little or no further analysis. In contrast, a single event may trigger multiple, far-reaching consequences that can potentially affect many of an organization's objectives. For more complex consequences, several methods of analysis may be required to determine the level of risk involved.

Some risk analyses focus on the consequences of a specific event, such as a hurricane or a power failure. Others may focus on a process (such as the manufacture of a product) or a system (such as automated inventory tracking) and examine the risks associated with each step of the process or each component of the system.

Qualitative Assessment and Quantitative Analysis

Depending on the type of risk, the data available, and the organization's needs, a risk analysis may be either qualitative or quantitative, or it may include a combination of qualitative and quantitative measures.

Qualitative assessment measures a risk by the significance of consequences; it may use such ratings as "high," "medium," and "low." A clear, written explanation of the agreed-on bases for qualitative determinations should be included in any qualitative assessment.

Quantitative analysis assigns specific values to consequences and their probabilities to reach a numeric indication of the level of risk. This approach may not be feasible, or even useful, for measuring every risk because of lack of historical information or data or because of other uncertainties related to the risks being analyzed. In such cases, an organization may choose to incorporate some qualitative analysis into the process.

Both qualitative and quantitative approaches may include estimates of probability to assess risk. Probabilities may be based on historical data relating to occurrences arising from the same types of risk as those being analyzed. If such occurrences have been infrequent or if historical data are otherwise lacking, resulting probability estimates will be uncertain.

In such cases, an organization may base probability estimations on predictions or expert opinions. Predictive techniques, such as decision tree analysis and event tree analysis, assign numerical values to various components related to a risk and combine them to produce a probability estimate. Several structured processes have been developed to incorporate expert opinions into probability estimations involving risk.

Assessing Controls

To accurately determine its level of risk, an organization must examine the effectiveness of its current risk control measures. All current measures designed to prevent or control a specific risk should be identified. The organization should verify whether each measure is capable of achieving the intended level of treatment or control and whether its effectiveness can be demonstrated when required. Verification depends on the existence of records and documentation of the control's performance in relation to the risk.

Control assessment can be quantitative, qualitative, or both. Although such information need not be detailed, it is useful in helping an organization decide whether to retain a control, improve it, or replace it with a different control method.

PROBABILITY ANALYSIS

The use of probability analysis to estimate the likelihood and consequences of an event or a series of events is an important aspect of risk analysis.

The probability of an event is the relative likelihood (frequency) with which the event can be expected to occur in the long run in a stable environment. Similarly, an event has a range of consequences (severities), each of which has a probability of occurring. Probability-related concepts include theoretical probability, empirical probability, and the law of large numbers.

Probability distributions can be constructed for empirical or theoretical probabilities. The information provided by probability distributions can be instrumental in analyzing loss exposures, estimating both the positive and negative consequences of risk, and making risk management decisions.

The Nature of Probability

Any probability can be expressed as a fraction, percentage, or decimal. For example, the probability of the heads side landing on a coin toss can be expressed as 1/2, 50 percent, or .50. The probability of an event that is impossible is zero, and the probability of a certain event is 1.0. Therefore, the probabilities of all events that are neither totally impossible nor absolutely certain are greater than zero but less than 1.0.

Theoretical and Empirical Probabilities

Probabilities can be developed either from theoretical data distributions or from historical data. **Theoretical probability** is associated with events such as coin tosses or dice throws and is unchanging. For example, from a description

Theoretical probability
Probability that is based on theoretical principles rather than on actual experience.

of a regular coin or die, a person who has never seen either a coin or a die can calculate the probability of flipping a head or rolling a four.

Empirical probability (a posteriori probability)
A probability measure that is based on actual experience through historical data or from the observation of facts.

An example of **empirical probability** is the probability that a male will die at age sixty-two. That probability cannot be theoretically determined but must be estimated by studying the loss experience of a sample of men age sixty-two. The empirical probabilities deduced solely from historical data may change as new data are discovered or as the environment that produces those events changes.

Empirical probabilities are only estimates. Their accuracy depends on the size and representative nature of the samples being studied. In contrast, theoretical probabilities are constant as long as the physical conditions that generate them remain unchanged.

Although it may be preferable to use theoretical probabilities because of their unchanging nature, they are not applicable or available in most of the situations that insurance and risk management professionals are likely to analyze, such as automobile accidents or workers compensation claims. As a result, empirical probabilities must be used.

Law of Large Numbers

Probability analysis
A technique for forecasting events, such as accidental and business losses, on the assumption that they are governed by an unchanging probability distribution.

Probability analysis is particularly effective for projecting the likelihood and consequences of losses or gains in organizations that have both a substantial volume of data on past losses or gains and fairly stable operations so that (except for price level changes) loss and gain patterns presumably will continue. In organizations with this type of unchanging environment, past losses or gains can be viewed as a sample of all possible losses or gains the organization might sustain.

The larger the number of past losses an organization has experienced, the larger the sample of losses that can be used in the analysis. Consequently, the forecasts of future losses are more reliable (consistent over time) because the forecast is based on a larger sample of the environment that produced the losses. This is an application of the law of large numbers, which also applies to gains and other outcomes.

As an example, suppose an urn holds four marbles. One of the marbles is red and three are black. The task is to estimate the theoretical probability of choosing a red marble on one draw (sample) from the urn by repeatedly sampling the marbles and replacing each in the urn after the sampling. Assume that after twenty samples, a red marble has been chosen eight times, yielding an empirical frequency of 40 percent (8/20). However, this estimate is inaccurate because the theoretical probability is 25 percent (1/4), given that only one of the four marbles is red.

According to the law of large numbers, the relative inaccuracy between the empirical frequency (40 percent in this case) and the theoretical probability (25 percent) will decline, on average, as the sample size increases. That is, as the number of samples increases from 20 to 200, or 2,000, the empirical frequency of choosing a red marble will move closer and closer to 25 percent.

The law of large numbers has some limitations. It can be used to more accurately forecast future events only when the events being forecast meet all three of these criteria:

- The events have occurred in the past under substantially identical conditions and have resulted from unchanging, basic causal forces.
- The events can be expected to occur in the future under the same, unchanging conditions.
- The events have been, and will continue to be, both independent of one another and sufficiently numerous.

Probability Distributions

Although insurance and risk management professionals work with theoretical distributions on occasion, relatively few of the loss exposures or other outcomes they analyze involve theoretical probabilities. Therefore, most of the work they do involves empirical **probability distributions**.

A properly constructed probability distribution always contains outcomes that are both mutually exclusive and collectively exhaustive. For example, on a particular flip of a coin, only one outcome is possible: heads or tails. Therefore, these outcomes are mutually exclusive. Similarly, these two outcomes are the only possible outcomes and, therefore, are collectively exhaustive. For example, the exhibit shows the hypothetical probability distribution of the number of hurricanes making landfall in Florida during any given hurricane season. Each outcome (number of hurricanes) is mutually exclusive, and the sum of the outcomes is 1.0, so they are collectively exhaustive. See the exhibit "Number of Hurricanes Making Landfall in Florida During One Hurricane Season."

Probability distribution
A presentation (table, chart, or graph) of probability estimates of a particular set of circumstances and of the probability of each possible outcome.

Number of Hurricanes Making Landfall in Florida During One Hurricane Season

Number of Hurricanes Making Landfall	Probability
0	.300
1	.350
2	.200
3	.147
4	.002
5+	.001
Total Probability	1.000

Those results can also be shown in a pie chart. See the exhibit "Probability of Hurricanes Making Landfall in Florida During One Hurricane Season."

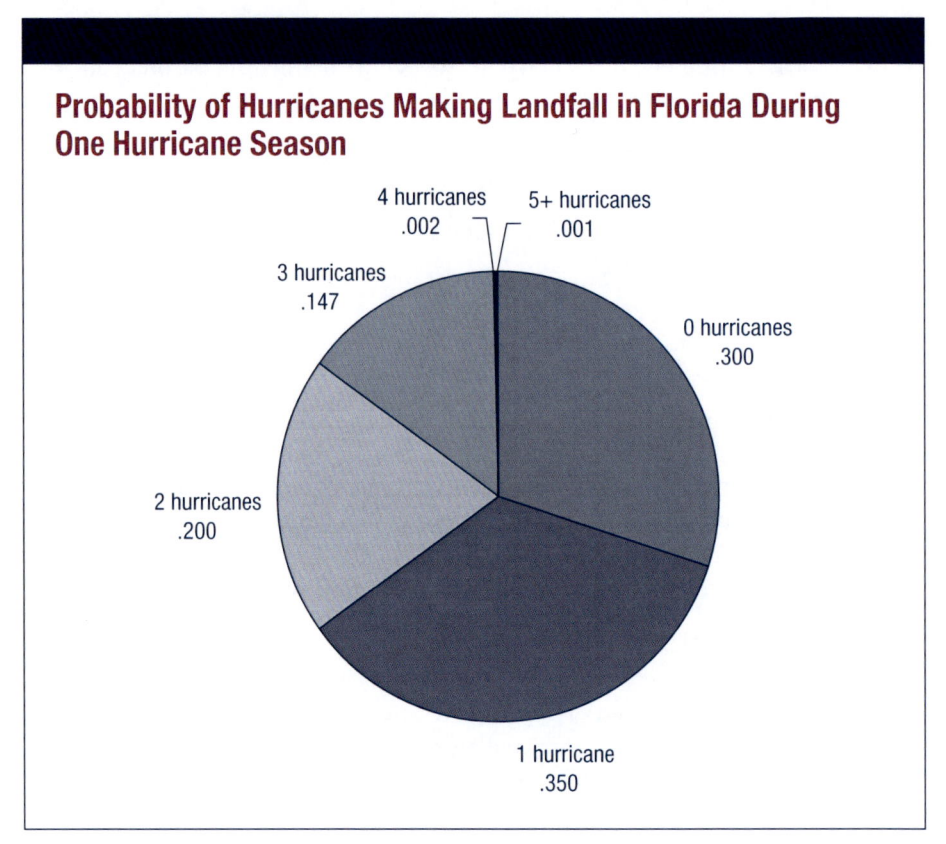

Probability of Hurricanes Making Landfall in Florida During One Hurricane Season

- 0 hurricanes: .300
- 1 hurricane: .350
- 2 hurricanes: .200
- 3 hurricanes: .147
- 4 hurricanes: .002
- 5+ hurricanes: .001

[DA02573]

To provide a mutually exclusive, collectively exhaustive list of outcomes, a distribution's categories (bins) must be designed so that all outcomes can be included. One method is to divide the bins into equal sizes, with each bin size being a standard size. The probability distribution then defines the set of probabilities associated with the possible outcomes for each bin. The exhibit shows an empirical probability distribution with bins of $10,000 each. Note that the probabilities in the second column total 100 percent. See the exhibit "Estimated Probability Distribution of an Investment's Gains or Losses."

Probability distributions come in two forms: discrete probability distributions and continuous probability distributions. Discrete probability distributions have a finite number of possible outcomes, whereas continuous probability distributions have an infinite number of possible outcomes.

Discrete probability distributions are usually displayed in a table that lists all possible outcomes and the probability of each outcome. These distributions are typically used to analyze how often something will occur; that is, they are shown as frequency distributions. The number of hurricanes making landfall in Florida is an example of a frequency distribution.

Estimated Probability Distribution of an Investment's Gains or Losses

Size Category of Gains/Losses	Probability (Percentage of Total Gains/Losses)
$40,001 – $50,000	7
$30,001 – $40,000	12
$20,001 – $30,000	15
$10,001 – $20,000	20
$1 – $10,000	27
–$10,001 – $0	18
–$20,001 – –$10,000	14
–$30,001 – –$20,000	4
–$40,001 – –$30,000	2
–$50,000 – –$40,000	1

[DA08726]

Discrete probability distributions have a countable number of outcomes. For example, it is impossible to have 2.5 outcomes. In contrast, continuous probability distributions have an infinite number of possible outcome values and are generally represented by a line graph.

The "Continuous Probability Distributions" exhibit illustrates two representations of continuous probability distributions. The possible outcomes are presented on the horizontal axes, and the likelihood of those outcomes is shown in the vertical axes—specifically represented by the height of the line or curve above the outcomes. The outcomes in a continuous probability distribution are called probability density functions. Continuous probability distributions are typically used for the consequences of an event—they depict the value of the loss or gain rather than the number of outcomes. See the exhibit "Continuous Probability Distributions."

Continuous Probability Distributions

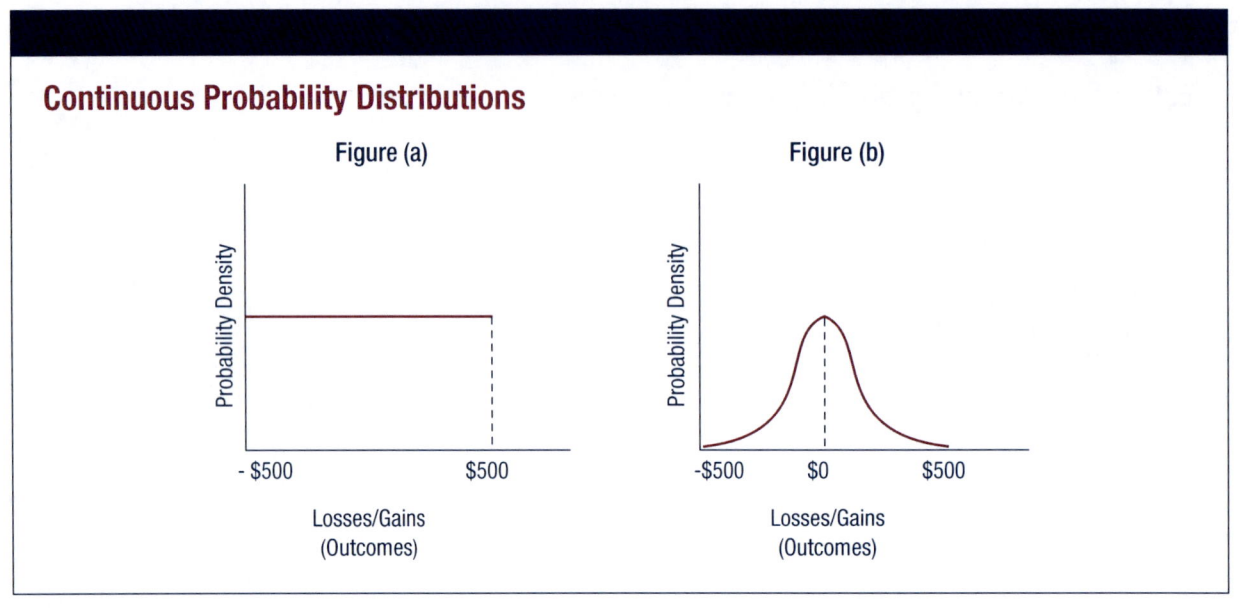

Figure (a) — Probability Density vs Losses/Gains (Outcomes), flat line from −$500 to $500.

Figure (b) — Probability Density vs Losses/Gains (Outcomes), bell curve peaked at $0, ranging from −$500 to $500.

[DA08715]

Figure (a) in the "Continuous Probability Distributions" exhibit, which has a flat line above the interval –$500 to $500, illustrates that all of the outcomes between –$500 to $500 are equally likely. Figure (b), which has a curve that starts at near zero probability and –$500 and increases until it reaches a peak at $0 before declining to near zero probability again at $500, illustrates that the high losses (–$500) and high gains ($500) are very unlikely and that losses and gains around $0 are much more likely.

By definition, continuous probability distributions have an infinite number of possible outcomes; therefore, the probability of any given outcome is zero, as an uncountable number of other outcomes exist. By dividing the continuous distribution into a finite number of bins, an insurance or risk management professional can calculate the probability of an outcome falling within a certain range.

For example, in a discrete frequency distribution, the probability of a high-rise office building not having a fire (zero fires) may be .50; of having one fire, .35; and of having two fires, .15. If a fire occurs, the damage may be anywhere between $0 and $100 million, which is a continuous severity distribution. Assigning a probability to the likelihood of having a loss amount of $35,456.32 would be nearly impossible. However, if the severity distribution is divided into a finite number of bins, $0–$1,000,000, $1,000,001–$2,000,000, and so on, a probability can be assigned to each bin.

Apply Your Knowledge

Westview Manufacturing, which has six factories located in the north central United States, plans to open a seventh factory on the Gulf Coast. Westview's risk manager is basing loss probability estimates for the new plant exclusively on historical loss data from its existing six factories. The risk manager believes the combined loss experience from the six plants provides sufficient data to ensure accurate loss predictions and that the law of large numbers applies because the new plant will use the same manufacturing processes and employ similar numbers of workers as existing plants. Do you agree with the risk manager's approach? Explain why or why not.

Feedback: Disagree. Although the new plant's operations and employee numbers may indicate substantially identical conditions, the risk manager has failed to consider conditions on the Gulf Coast that may substantially differ from conditions at the other plants. The most obvious example is the threat of hurricane loss on the Gulf Coast. The law of large numbers can be used to forecast future events based on past events only if the future events can be expected to occur under the same, unchanging conditions as those on which the predictions are based.

CHARACTERISTICS OF PROBABILITY DISTRIBUTIONS

When analyzing probability distributions, insurance and risk management professionals consider expected values, means, standard deviations, coefficients of variation, and normal distributions.

After determining empirical probabilities and constructing probability distributions, the insurance or risk management professional can use **central tendency** and **dispersion** to compare the characteristics of those probability distributions.

Central tendency represents the best guess as to what the outcome will be. For example, if a manager asked an underwriter to estimate the expected losses from fire at an insured's business, the underwriter would multiply the central tendency of the frequency distribution by the central tendency of the severity distribution; both central tendencies should be determined with the same measure. If the expected number of fires was two, and each fire had an expected severity of $5,000, the underwriter would expect $10,000 in losses.

Many probability distributions cluster around a particular value, which may or may not be in the exact center of the distribution's range of values. Two such specific values measuring central tendency are the expected value and the mean.

Dispersion describes the extent to which a distribution is spread out rather than concentrated around the expected value. Two widely used statistical measures of dispersion are standard deviation and coefficient of variation.

Some distributions have the characteristics of a normal probability distribution, which is useful in predicting future losses.

Central tendency
The single outcome that is the most representative of all possible outcomes included within a probability distribution.

Dispersion
The variation among values in a distribution.

Expected Value

Expected value
The weighted average of all of the possible outcomes of a probability distribution.

The **expected value** measures central tendency by weighting and averaging outcomes. The weights are the probabilities of the outcomes. The outcomes of a probability distribution are symbolized as $x_1, x_2, x_3, \ldots x_n$ (x_n represents the last outcome in the series), having respective probabilities of $p_1, p_2, p_3, \ldots p_n$. The distribution's expected value is the sum of $(p_1 \times x_1) + (p_2 \times x_2) + (p_3 \times x_3) + \ldots (p_n \times x_n)$.

In the example of a probability distribution of total points on one roll of a pair of dice, the distribution's expected value of 7.0 is shown in the exhibit as the sum of the values in Column 3. See the exhibit "Calculating the Expected Value of a Probability Distribution—The Two Dice Example."

Calculating the Expected Value of a Probability Distribution—The Two Dice Example

(1) Total Points—Both Dice (x)	(2) Probability (p)	(3) p × x	(4) Cumulative Probability (sum of p's)
2	1/36	2/36	1/36
3	2/36	6/36	3/36
4	3/36	12/36	6/36
5	4/36	20/36	10/36
6	5/36	30/36	15/36
7	6/36	42/36	21/36
8	5/36	40/36	26/36
9	4/36	36/36	30/36
10	3/36	30/36	33/36
11	2/36	22/36	35/36
12	1/36	12/36	36/36, or 100%
Total	36/36 = 1	252/36 = 7.0	

Expected Value = 252/36 = 7.0
Median = 7 (There is an equal number of outcomes (15) above and below 7.)
Mode = 7 (The most frequent outcome.)

[DA02577]

The procedure for calculating the expected value applies to all theoretical discrete probability distributions, regardless of their shape or dispersion. For continuous distributions, the expected value is also a weighted average of the possible outcomes. However, calculating the expected value for a continuous distribution is much more complex and therefore is not discussed here.

Mean

Probabilities are needed to calculate a theoretical distribution's expected value. However, in an empirical distribution constructed from historical data, the expected value is estimated using the **mean**. Just as the expected value is calculated by weighting each possible outcome by its probability, the mean is calculated by weighting each observed outcome by the relative frequency with which it occurs.

For example, if the observed outcome values are 2, 3, 4, 4, 5, 5, 5, 6, 6, and 8, then the mean equals 4.8, which is the sum of the values, 48, divided by the number of values, 10. The mean is a good estimate of the expected outcome only if the underlying conditions determining those outcomes remain constant over time.

Unlike the expected value, which is derived from theory, the mean is derived from experience. If the conditions that generated that experience have changed, the mean that was calculated may no longer be an accurate estimate of central tendency. Nonetheless, insurance or risk management professionals often use the mean as the single best guess to forecast future events.

For example, the best guess as to the number of workers compensation claims an organization will suffer in the next year is often the mean of the frequency distribution of workers compensation claims from previous years.

> **Mean**
> The sum of the values in a data set divided by the number of values.

Standard Deviation

Insurance and risk management professionals use measurements of dispersion of the distributions of potential outcomes to gain a better understanding of the loss exposures being analyzed. One measure of dispersion is the **standard deviation**. The standard deviation indicates how widely dispersed the values in a distribution are. The higher the standard deviation, the more dispersed the values.

For example, the expected number of workers compensation claims in a given year is important, but it is only one element of the information that can be gleaned from a distribution. The standard deviation can be calculated to provide a measure of how sure an insurance or risk management professional can be in his or her estimate of the number of workers compensation claims.

> **Standard deviation**
> A measure of dispersion between the values in a distribution and the expected value (or mean) of that distribution, calculated by taking the square root of the variance.

Coefficient of Variation

The **coefficient of variation** is another measure of the dispersion of a distribution. For example, the coefficient of variation for the distribution of total points in rolling two dice equals 2.4 points (the standard deviation of the distribution) divided by 7.0 points (the mean or expected value), which is 0.34.

If two distributions have the same mean (or expected value), the distribution with the larger standard deviation has the greater variability. If the two distri-

> **Coefficient of variation**
> A measure of dispersion calculated by dividing a distribution's standard deviation by its mean.

butions have different means (or expected values), the coefficient of variation can be used to determine which of the two distributions has the greater variability relative to its mean (or expected value).

Insurance and risk management professionals can use the coefficient of variation to determine whether a particular loss control measure has made losses more predictable or less so (that is, whether the distribution is more variable or less so).

For example, a risk management professional may calculate that an organization's theft losses have a severity distribution with a mean of $3,590 and a standard deviation of $3,432, for a coefficient of variation of 0.96. If the organization installs a new security system, the theft losses may have a severity distribution with a mean of $2,150 and a standard deviation of $2,950, for a coefficient of variation of 1.37.

Although the security system has reduced the mean severity, it has actually made the losses less predictable because the new severity distribution is relatively more variable than the old distribution without the security system.

The coefficient of variation is useful in comparing the variability of distributions that have different shapes, means, or standard deviations. The distribution with the largest coefficient of variation has the greatest relative variability. The higher the variability within a distribution, the more difficult it is to accurately forecast an individual outcome.

Normal Distribution

Normal distribution
A probability distribution that, when graphed, generates a bell-shaped curve.

The **normal distribution** is a theoretical distribution often observed in practice that can help in the accurate forecasting of the variability around some central, average, or expected value.

The exhibit illustrates the typical bell-shaped curve of a normal distribution. Note that the normal curve never touches the horizontal line at the base of the diagram. In theory, the normal distribution assigns some probability greater than zero for every outcome, regardless of its distance from the mean. The exhibit also shows the percentage of outcomes that fall within a given number of standard deviations above or below the mean of a distribution. See the exhibit "The Normal Distribution—Percentages of Outcomes Within Specified Standard Deviations of the Mean."

For example, for all normal distributions, 34.13 percent of all outcomes are within one standard deviation above the mean and, because every normal distribution is symmetrical, another 34.13 percent of all outcomes fall within one standard deviation below the mean. By addition, 68.26 percent of all outcomes are within one standard deviation above or below the mean. The portion of a normal distribution that is between one and two standard deviations above the mean contains 13.59 percent of all outcomes, as does the portion between one and two standard deviations below the mean. Hence, the area between the mean and two standard deviations above the mean

The Normal Distribution—Percentages of Outcomes Within Specified Standard Deviations of the Mean

```
              5,000
              hours
       4,700         5,300
       hours         hours
   4,400                 5,600
   hours                 hours
4,100                        5,900
hours                        hours
  -3    -2    -1    x̄    +1    +2    +3

0.13% | 2.15% | 13.59% | 34.13% | 34.13% | 13.59% | 2.15% | 0.13%
              |          68.26%          |
        |            95.44%              |
  |                  99.74%                   |
```

x̄ = mean or expected value of the distribution

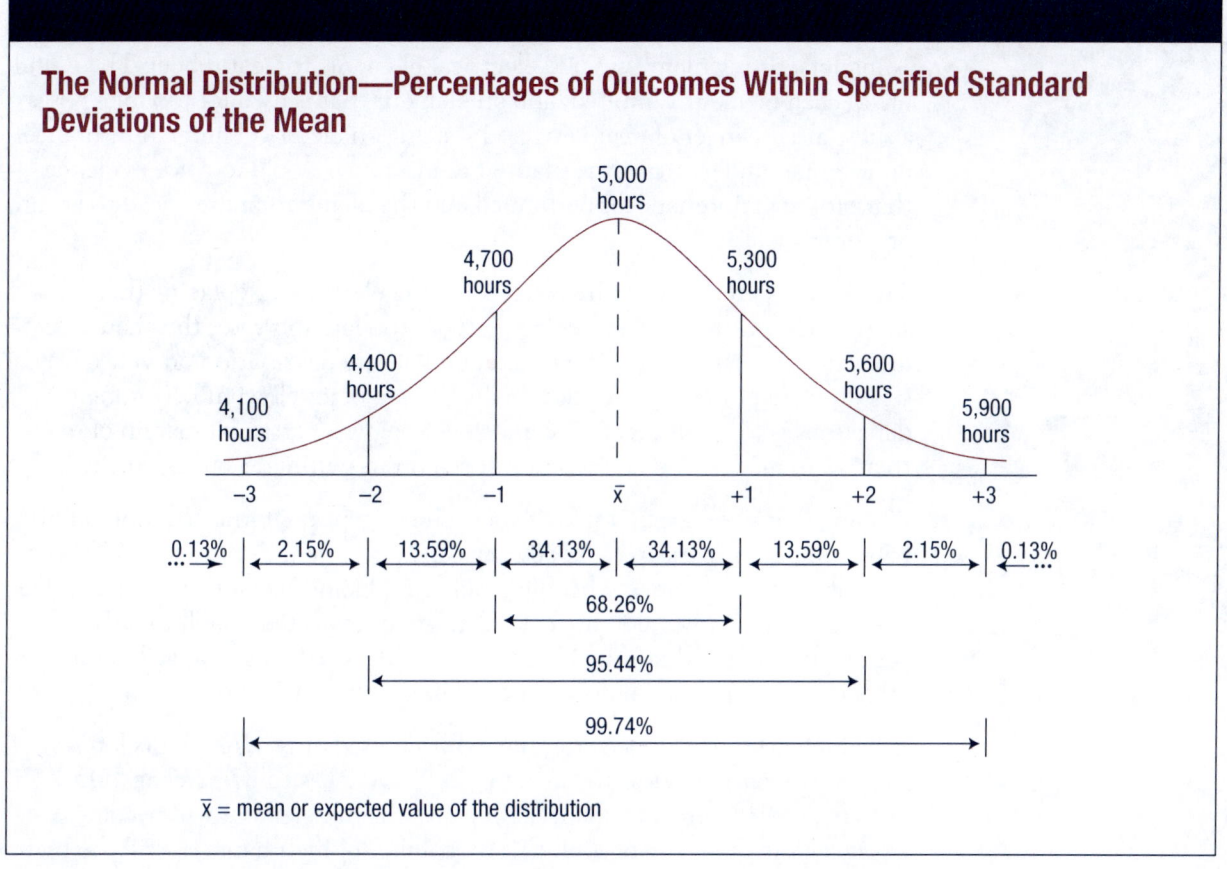

[DA02585]

contains 47.72 percent (34.13 percent + 13.59 percent) of the outcomes, and another 47.72 percent are two standard deviations or less below the mean.

Consequently, 95.44 percent of all outcomes are within two standard deviations above or below the mean, and fewer than 5 percent of outcomes are outside two standard deviations above or below the mean. Taking this a step further, 2.15 percent of all outcomes are between two and three standard deviations above the mean, and another 2.15 percent are between two and three standard deviations below the mean. Therefore, 49.87 percent (34.13 percent + 13.59 percent + 2.15 percent) of all outcomes are three standard deviations or less above the mean, and an equal percentage are three standard deviations or less below the mean.

The portion of the distribution between three standard deviations above the mean and three standard deviations below it contains 99.74 percent (49.87 percent × 2) of all outcomes. Therefore, only 0.26 percent (100 percent − 99.74 percent) of all outcomes lie beyond three standard deviations from the mean. Half of these outcomes (0.13 percent) are more than three standard deviations below the mean, and the other half (0.13 percent) are more than three standard deviations above the mean.

Practical Application: Normal Distribution

A manufacturing plant uses 600 electrical elements to heat rubber. The useful life of each element is limited, and an element that is used for too long poses a substantial danger of exploding and starting an electrical fire. An insurance professional underwriting the plant's fire insurance would look for evidence that proper maintenance is performed and the elements are replaced to ensure proper fire safety.

The issue is determining when to replace the elements. Replacing them too soon can be costly, whereas replacing them too late increases the chance of fire. The characteristics of the normal probability distribution provide a way of scheduling maintenance so that the likelihood of an element becoming very dangerous before it is replaced can be kept below a particular margin of safety that is specified by the organization based on its willingness to assume risk.

Assume that the expected safe life of each element conforms to a normal distribution having a mean of 5,000 hours and a standard deviation of 300 hours. Even if the maintenance schedule requires replacing each element after it has been in service only 5,000 hours (the mean, or expected, safe life), a 50 percent chance exists that it will become unsafe before being changed, because 50 percent of the normal distribution is below this 5,000-hour mean.

If each element is changed after having been used only 4,700 hours [one standard deviation below the mean (5,000 – 300)], a 15.87 percent (50 percent – 34.13 percent) chance still exists that an element will become unsafe before being changed. If this probability of high hazard is still too high, changing each element after 4,400 hours [two standard deviations below the mean (5,000 – (2 × 300))] reduces the probability of high hazard to only 2.28 percent, the portion of a normal distribution that is more than two standard deviations below the mean.

A still more cautious practice would be to change elements routinely after only 4,100 hours [three standard deviations below the mean (5,000 – (3 × 300))], so that the probability of an element becoming highly hazardous before replacement would be only 0.13 percent, slightly more than one chance in 1,000.

Using this analysis, management can select an acceptable probability that an element will become unsafe before being replaced and can schedule maintenance accordingly.

Apply Your Knowledge

An insurer is beginning to write policies in a new state. The insurer's claim manager wants to know how many new claim representatives to hire. The insurer's marketing department has provided an estimate of additional premium volume from the new state. Based on that estimate and industry data, the manager has determined the mean number of new claims to be 8,000, with a standard deviation of 2,000 in a normal distribution. If a claim representative can adjust 600 claims per year and the manager wants to be approximately 98 percent certain that she has enough representatives, how many will she need to hire?

Feedback: As shown in the exhibit titled "The Normal Distribution—Percentages of Outcomes Within Specified Standard Deviations of the Mean," 2.28 percent of all outcomes (2.15 percent + 0.13 percent) are more than two standard deviations above the mean, and 97.72 percent (100 percent – 2.28 percent) of all outcomes fall under the normal distribution below two standard deviations above the mean. Therefore, by rounding up the 97.72 percent, the claim manager can be approximately 98 percent certain that the actual number of claims will fall at or below two standard deviations above the mean.

In the claim manager's distribution, two standard deviations above the mean is 12,000 claims (calculated as 8,000 + 2,000 + 2,000). Because each claim representative can adjust 600 claims per year, the manager will need to hire 12,000/600, or 20, new representatives.

TREND ANALYSIS

Risk management uses trend analysis to forecast losses or gains. Such forecasts help an organization's management make cost-effective risk management decisions.

Organizations use **trend analysis** to identify predictable patterns of change in dynamic environments and, from those patterns, develop forecasts. **Regression analysis**, a type of statistical trend analysis, can increase the accuracy of forecasting by examining variables that affect trends. For example, changes in hazard loss frequency or severity might coincide with changes in some other variable, such as production, in such a way that loss frequency or severity can be forecast more accurately. Trend analysis and regression analysis can also be used to detect and forecast patterns of gains.

Organizations must develop sound forecasts of their property, liability, personnel, and net income losses, as well as any gains associated with risk exposures. To develop these forecasts, risk management professionals examine data on past losses and gains and subject these data to probability analysis and/or trend analysis to project the expected value of future losses and gains. Resulting projections help management determine the costs and benefits of each alternative and choose the one(s) with the greatest benefits over costs.

Trend analysis is commonly used to adjust forecasted future dollar amounts of losses or gains using an anticipated inflation rate. For example, projected inflationary trends would increase the cost of future physical damage losses;

Trend analysis
An analysis that identifies patterns in past data and then projects these patterns into the future.

Regression analysis
A statistical technique that is used to estimate relationships between variables.

therefore, inflation must be considered in an estimate of the property losses an organization will finance through retention if it adopts a particular deductible.

Regression Analysis

Regression analysis assumes that the variable being forecast varies predictably with another variable. The variable being forecast is the dependent variable. The variable that determines the value of the variable being forecast is the independent variable. **Linear regression analysis** deals with a constant rate of change. For example, if the independent variable is time measured in years, then a linear regression analysis assumes that the change in the dependent variable is the same from year to year. In this case, the regression line is straight (or linear), not curved. See the exhibit "Diagram of Linear Time Series Analysis Trend Line."

Linear regression analysis
A form of regression analysis that assumes that the change in the dependent variable is constant for each unit of change in the independent variable.

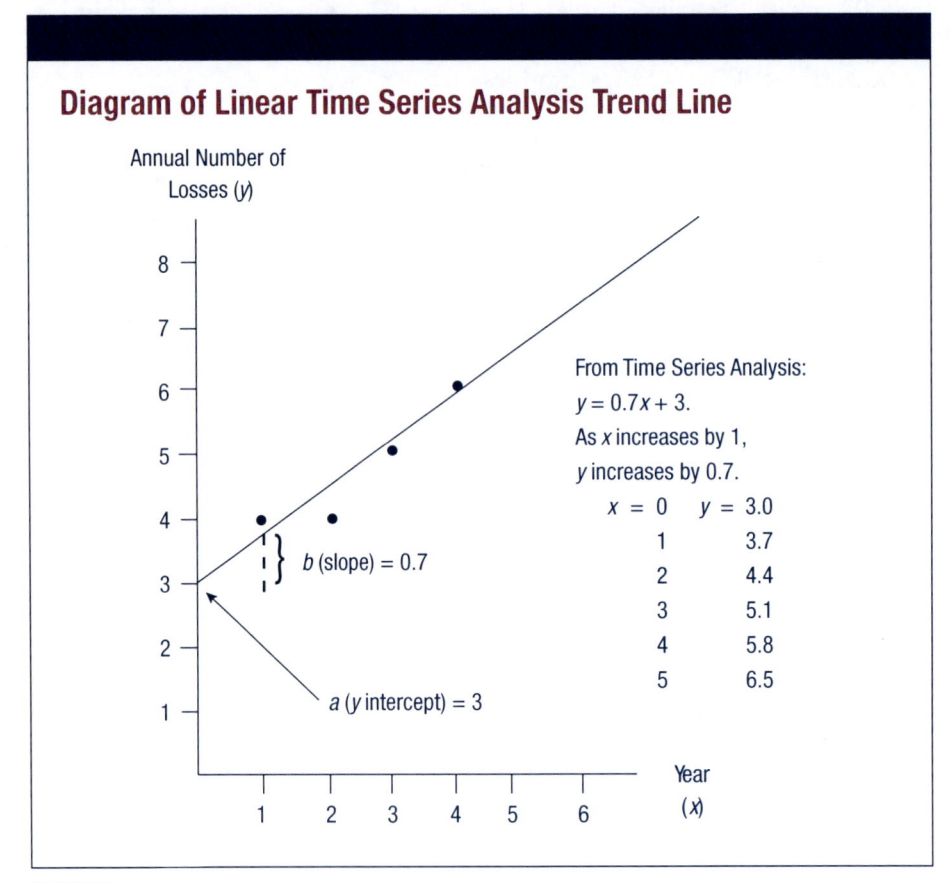

Diagram of Linear Time Series Analysis Trend Line

From Time Series Analysis:
$y = 0.7x + 3$.
As x increases by 1, y increases by 0.7.

x	y
0	3.0
1	3.7
2	4.4
3	5.1
4	5.8
5	6.5

b (slope) = 0.7
a (y intercept) = 3

[DA02077]

The exhibit plots annual machinery losses on a graph. The dependent variable (annual number of losses) is charted on the vertical (y) axis; the independent variable (years) is charted on the horizontal (x) axis. The data points show that 4, 4, 5, and 6 losses occurred, respectively, in Year 1 through Year 4.

The goal of regression analysis is to find the equation for the line that best fits these four data points and to project this line to forecast the number of future losses.

A logical first step in calculating a linear regression line is to plot the data points and sketch an approximate line. Such a sketch helps to intuitively estimate the two determinants of any linear regression line. The first determinant is the point at which the line crosses the vertical y axis, labeled "*a*" in the diagram (*y*-intercept) or the value of *y* when *x* equals zero. The second determinant is the slope of the line, the amount by which *y* increases or decreases with a one-unit increase in *x*. The length of the dashed line labeled "*b*" signifies the slope. A line slanting upward from left to right has positive slope; a line slanting downward has negative slope. Therefore, the *y*-intercept and the slope determine a line.

This is the equation of a line:

$$y = bx + a,$$

Where

y is the dependent variable

x is the independent variable

a is the *y*-intercept

b is the slope of the line

In the machinery example, *y* is the number of machinery losses, and *x* is the number of years beyond year zero. Given the values for *x* and *y*, the values of *a* and *b* that provide the best fit for the data can be determined. This calculation is typically accomplished with computer software or a calculator.

Two aspects of interpreting linear regression lines need to be recognized. First, a linear regression line might not be accurate when it gets very far away from the actual data values used. For example, it may be suitable to use this linear trend line to forecast losses in Year 5 or Year 6, but it probably would not be accurate for forecasting losses in Year 25 or Year 26.

Second, for any past year, the dependent variable's value calculated by the linear regression line is not likely to exactly equal the historical value for that past year. Any regression line represents the "best fit" of a straight or smoothly curved line to actual historical data for all past years. For any given year, the projected trend value will probably differ from the actual outcome, both in the past and in the future. The size of this difference between actual and projected values will also vary. For example, in the preceding exhibit, the historical outcome for Year 2 is farther from the projected regression line than is the outcome for Year 1.

In the machinery loss example, the dependent variable (the annual number of losses) varies only with the passage of time (the independent variable). An alternative possibility is to assume that the annual number of machinery losses is affected by a variable such as the volume of items processed or the number of hours in operation. Therefore, one of these other variables (such as volume of output) could be substituted for time as the independent variable that projects the number of future machinery losses. Indeed, any reasonable causative variable that can be measured and projected with more accuracy than accidental losses can be an independent variable.

Regression Analysis Example

Assume a risk management professional wants to use a firm's annual output (in 100,000-ton units) to project the annual number of machinery losses. The professional compiles data that show the number of machinery losses sustained and the tons of output (in hundreds of thousands) in each year from Year 1 to Year 4. See the exhibit "Relationship of Losses to Exposure (Tons of Output)."

Relationship of Losses to Exposure (Tons of Output)

Year	Annual Number of Losses	Tons of Output (× 100,000)
1	4	35
2	4	60
3	5	72
4	6	95
	19	262

This information can be used to project trends that relate the number of machinery losses to time and to annual tons of rubber output.

[DA02079]

With this information, regression analysis can be used to project trends that relate the number of machinery losses to tons of output. The risk manager graphs the annual tons of output horizontally on the x axis as the independent variable and graphs the annual number of machinery losses vertically on the y axis as the dependent variable. See the exhibit "Diagram of Linear Regression Line."

The four data points in the graph correspond to the pairs of numbers of losses and tons of output shown in the preceding exhibit, and the solid portion of the linear regression line approximates the trend of the historical data. The dashed extension of the regression line projects annual numbers of machin-

Diagram of Linear Regression Line

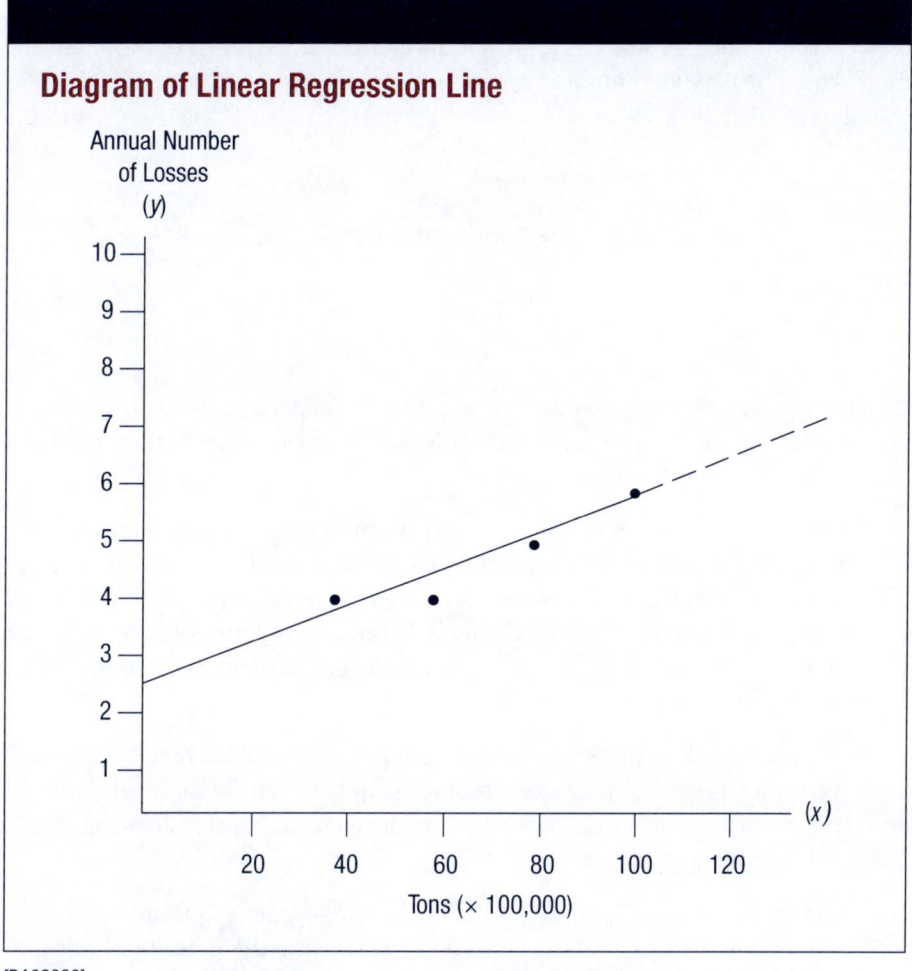

[Figure: Scatter plot with Annual Number of Losses (y) on vertical axis (0 to 10) and Tons (× 100,000) (x) on horizontal axis (0 to 120). Data points shown near (40, 4), (60, 4), (80, 5), (100, 6) with a fitted regression line extending as dashed line beyond the data.]

[DA02080]

ery losses for levels of output (in units of 100,000) beyond the range of these particular historical data. Developing such a diagram and approximating a regression line can help in visualizing this relationship.

A computer program or calculator can be used to determine the values of *a* and *b* for the actual linear regression line. In this example, the indicated value for *a* is 2.46 machinery losses, and the value for *b* is 0.035. If the number of losses is linearly related to output for all possible levels of output, the 2.46 value for *a* means that, even if annual output were zero, it would still sustain 2.46 (actually 2 or 3) machinery losses each year. The indicated value for *b* is 0.035, implying that, with each 100,000-ton increase in output, 0.035 additional machinery losses can be expected. Also, one more machinery loss can be expected with approximately each additional 2,900,000 tons of output (calculated as 100,000 tons × [1 ÷ 0.035]).

Although arithmetically correct, these values may not be valid for very low or very high volumes of output, as the regression extends the line too far beyond the bounds of past experience.

To forecast losses from these regression results, assume the organization expects to produce 10 million (or 100 hundred thousand) tons of products next year. The expected number of machinery losses for next year can then be calculated:

$$y = bx + a$$
$$= 2.46 + (0.035 \times 100)$$
$$= 2.46 + 3.50$$
$$= 5.96 \text{ losses}$$

Because fractional numbers of machine losses are impossible, a reasonable forecast would be for six machinery losses in a year when production is expected to be 10 million tons.

A risk management professional can apply more than one linear regression line by incorporating several independent variables simultaneously. An example is a series of equations that would forecast the total dollar amount of losses in a future year based on combined effects of forecast freight volumes, weather conditions, price levels, and perhaps other independent variables more easily forecast than the losses themselves.

In some cases, a risk manager may need to apply a curvilinear regression line. This technique is used to measure a relationship between the independent and dependent variables that changes at an accelerating or decelerating rate rather than at a constant rate.

Forecasts should be accepted only if the underlying assumptions are valid. Therefore, knowing these assumptions and recognizing the potential limitations in these forecasting techniques are important.

Trend analyses can be powerful tools for forecasting future losses and gains, but they must be used with care. Results must be interpreted with reason and not with automatic acceptance just because they are mathematically based. Furthermore, perhaps more for risk management than for some other uses of these forecasting techniques, the seeming scarcity of loss data, when compared with the apparent wealth of data in other management specialties, makes forecasts of accidental losses more difficult.

Apply Your Knowledge

Green Mountain Trucking (GMT) has a regular schedule of maintenance and service for each of its trucks. GMT's risk manager wants to know, for each truck, how each 10,000 miles of travel beyond 60,000 affects the cost of repairs.

The risk manager begins by creating a simple linear regression analysis. Identify the variables the risk manager will use for the x axis and the y axis.

Feedback: The risk manager designates as *x* (the independent variable) the trucks' odometer readings (in 10,000 mile increments), and as *y* (the dependent variable) the total road-trip repair costs.

The risk manager uses a calculator to determine the regression's value of *a* and *b* and has found a linear relation between truck mileage beyond 60,000 and road-trip repair costs. For purposes of this linear regression, describe what *b* represents.

Feedback: For purposes of this linear regression, *b* implies that, with each additional 10,000 miles a truck travels beyond 60,000 miles, repair costs would increase by *b*'s value.

ANALYZING EVENT CONSEQUENCES

The selection of a course of action or the occurrence of an event can generate multiple consequences and/or payoffs. Organizations use decision tree analysis and event tree analysis to predict the likelihood and severity of consequences or payoffs arising from decisions or events.

Decision tree analysis examines the consequences, including costs and gains, of decisions. An organization may use decision tree analysis to compare alternative decisions and select the most effective strategy to achieve a goal.

Event tree analysis examines all possible consequences of an accidental event, their probabilities, and existing measures to prevent or control them. An organization may use this approach to examine the effectiveness of systems, risk treatment, or risk control measures and to identify, recommend, and justify expenditures of money, time, or resources for improvements.

Decision Tree Analysis

A decision tree analyzes the uncertainties of decision outcomes. An organization might use a decision tree in selecting the best course of action from multiple options or to manage risks associated with a project. By analyzing various options and the events that may affect them, decision makers can reduce the uncertainty involved in decision making.

Decision trees can provide both qualitative and quantitative analysis. Qualitatively, they can help generate scenarios, progressions, and consequences that could potentially result from a decision. Quantitatively, they can estimate probabilities and frequencies of various scenarios resulting from a decision.

Constructing a decision tree begins with a statement of the initial decision under consideration, for example, which of two products to develop. From that point, various sequences of events ("pathways") are charted for each alternative; each pathway leads to an outcome. For a quantitative analysis, probabilities are assigned to each event on a pathway, and expected values (costs or gains) of each pathway can be estimated for the outcome. The product of the probabilities of each event in a pathway and the value of its outcome can be compared to determine the pathway that produces the highest expected value. See the exhibit "Example of a Decision Tree Diagram."

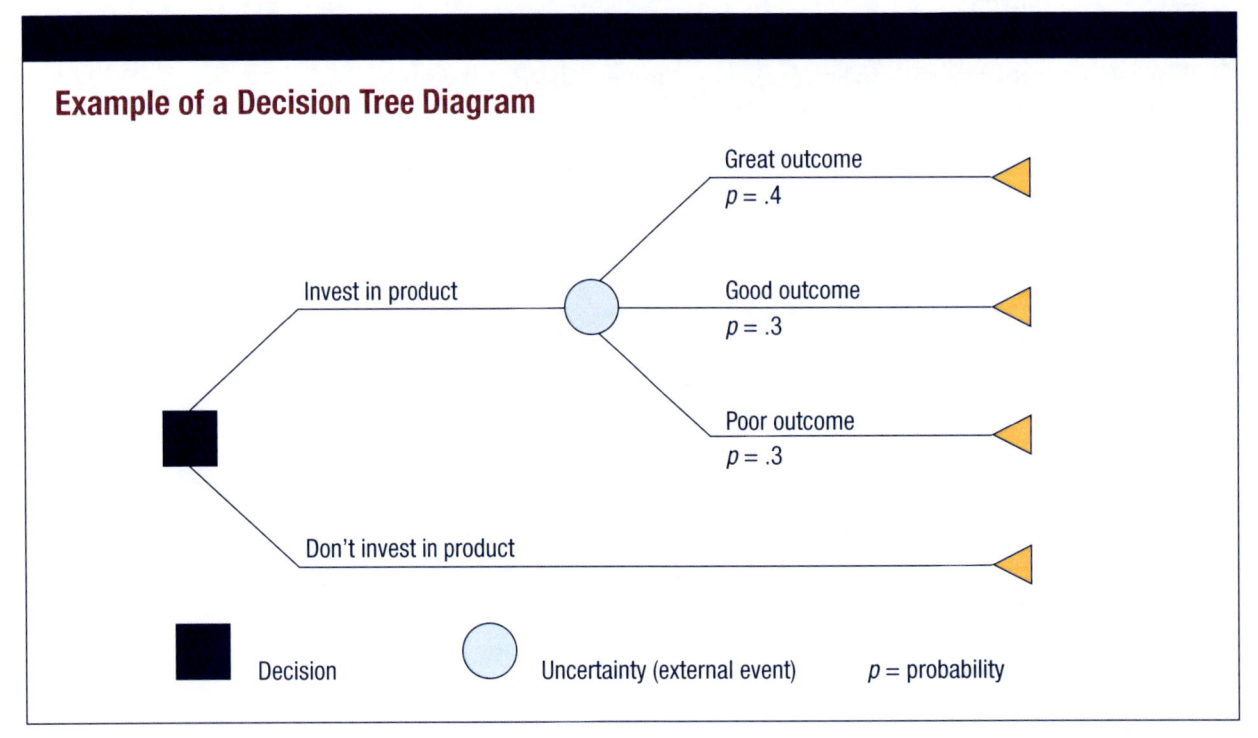

Example of a Decision Tree Diagram

Invest in product
- Great outcome, $p = .4$
- Good outcome, $p = .3$
- Poor outcome, $p = .3$

Don't invest in product

■ Decision ● Uncertainty (external event) p = probability

[DA08712]

Decision tree analysis offers the advantages of visual portrayal of event sequences and outcomes and a means to calculate the best pathway through a problem. However, decision tree diagrams of complicated or many-faceted problems may become so complex that they are ineffective in communicating the rationale for a decision to those not involved in the process. Conversely, a decision tree may oversimplify a problem, reducing the effectiveness of resulting decisions.

Event Tree Analysis

Event trees are similar to decision trees in their portrayal and analysis of various pathways and their outcomes; however, event trees analyze the consequences of accidental events rather than decisions. An accidental event is defined as the first significant deviation from a normal situation that may lead to unwanted consequences.[1]

Like a decision tree, an event tree can provide both qualitative and quantitative analysis. Qualitatively, it can help generate scenarios, progressions, and consequences that could potentially result from an accidental event. Quantitatively, it can estimate probabilities and frequencies of various scenarios and outcomes and help organizations determine the effectiveness of or need for controls and safeguards. Event trees are often used to determine the need for and to examine the effectiveness of risk treatment methods.

The starting point of an event tree is identification of an accidental event. The various progressions of events that could follow the accidental event are then determined. Progressions may vary because of factors such as other systems, human responses, and even the weather (for example, wind direction during an outdoor fire) or because of the performance or failure of "barriers" to consequences (for example, alarm or detection systems, emergency procedures, or other loss control measures).

This analysis of progressions results in a list of potential consequences of the initial event and identification of any existing barriers for each consequence. From that information, an event tree diagram is constructed. See the exhibit "Example of an Event Tree Analysis."

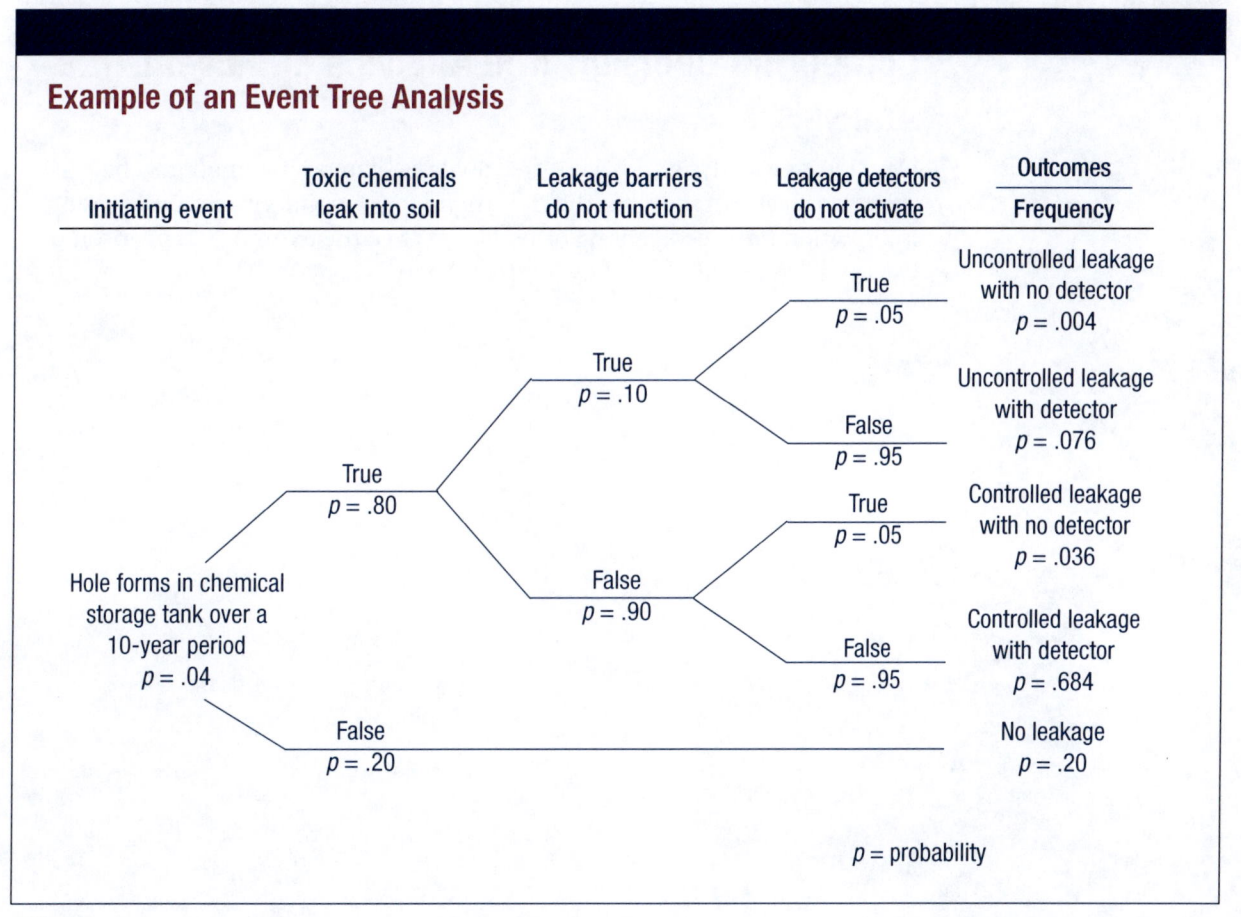

Example of an Event Tree Analysis

Initiating event	Toxic chemicals leak into soil	Leakage barriers do not function	Leakage detectors do not activate	Outcomes	Frequency
Hole forms in chemical storage tank over a 10-year period $p = .04$	True $p = .80$	True $p = .10$	True $p = .05$	Uncontrolled leakage with no detector	$p = .004$
			False $p = .95$	Uncontrolled leakage with detector	$p = .076$
		False $p = .90$	True $p = .05$	Controlled leakage with no detector	$p = .036$
			False $p = .95$	Controlled leakage with detector	$p = .684$
	False $p = .20$			No leakage	$p = .20$

p = probability

[DA08713]

In an event tree diagram, barriers are listed in the sequence in which they would be activated should the designated event occur. In each pathway, every barrier has the potential to either function or fail; therefore, the pathway splits in two, and an estimated probability—determined by experts or other analysis—is assigned to both potentials.

For each pathway in the diagram, the probability is that all its events will occur. The frequency of the consequence of each pathway is the product of the probabilities in the pathway and the frequency of the initial event. The sum of the probabilities of the outcomes, given that the initial event occurs, should total one, and the sum of the outcome frequencies should equal the frequency of the initial event.

Like a decision tree, an event tree affords the advantage of visual portrayal of event sequences and outcomes. Specifically, it can illustrate the potential effectiveness of control systems following accidental events and account for timing, other contributing factors, and domino effects. One of the limitations of event tree analysis is that it typically provides only two options—success or failure—and thereby fails to reflect the complexity of some progressions. In addition, some factors that contribute to consequences may be overlooked.

Comparing Decision Tree Analysis and Event Tree Analysis

Decision tree analysis and event tree analysis share a similar approach, appearance, and process but differ in their purposes, information used, and information produced, among other factors. See the exhibit "Comparison of Decision Tree Analysis and Event Tree Analysis."

Comparison of Decision Tree Analysis and Event Tree Analysis

	Decision Tree Analysis	Event Tree Analysis
Function	Examines consequences, costs, and gains of decisions Compares alternative decisions	Examines the consequences of accidental events
Use	Aids in the selection of the most effective strategy to achieve a goal	Examines the need for or effectiveness of risk treatment measures Can help in identifying, recommending, and justifying improvements
Features	May analyze both negative and positive consequences (losses and gains)	Typically analyzes negative consequences (risk of loss)
Inputs	Project plan with decision points Information on possible outcomes of decisions or events that might affect them	List of possible events that could lead to loss Information about risk treatments and the probabilities of various barriers failing Understanding of how failure escalates
Process	Definition of problem Construction of pathways to outcome Assignment of probabilities to various events that could affect outcomes Assignment of value to outcome for each pathway	Identification of accidental event Construction of pathways, including barriers, to outcome Assignment of probability of success or failure of each barrier in pathway Determination of frequency of outcomes for each pathway
Outputs	Analysis of risk of each pathway with various options Calculated expected value for each pathway	List of potential problems that could arise, calculated expected values for outcomes and frequencies Recommendations regarding effectiveness of various barriers
Advantages	Presents visual portrayal of problems, sequences, and outcomes Provides a means to calculate the best pathway through a problem Provides both qualitative and quantitative information	Presents visual portrayal of potential sequences of events following accidental event Illustrates the potential effectiveness of control systems following accidental events Provides both qualitative and quantitative information
Disadvantages	May be overly complex and difficult to communicate May be oversimplified, resulting in less accurate information for decision making	May be ineffective unless all potential initiating events are identified Analysis is limited to only two options—success or failure of barriers—possibly overlooking other factors May not address dependencies that arise within a sequence, resulting in inaccurate risk estimations

[DA08714]

ANALYZING LOSS EXPOSURES

Analyzing loss frequency, loss severity, total dollar losses, and timing helps insurance and risk management professionals develop loss projections, and, therefore, also helps them prioritize loss exposures so that risk management resources can be concentrated where they are needed most.

The analysis step of the risk management process involves considering the four dimensions of a loss exposure:

- Loss frequency—The number of losses (such as fires, auto accidents, or liability claims) that occur during a specific period.
- Loss severity—The dollar amount of loss for a specific occurrence.
- Total dollar losses—The total dollar amount of losses for all occurrences during a specific period.
- Timing—The points at which losses occur and loss payments are made. (The period between loss occurrence and loss payment can be lengthy.)

If any of these dimensions of loss exposure analysis involve empirical distributions developed from past losses, the credibility of the data being used needs to be determined. Data credibility is the level of confidence that available data are accurate indicators of future losses.

Loss Frequency

Loss frequency is the number of losses—such as fires, thefts, or floods—that occur during a specific period. Relative loss frequency is the number of losses that occur within a given period relative to the number of exposure units (such as the number of buildings or cars exposed to loss).

For example, if an organization experiences, on average, five theft losses per year, five is the mean of an empirical frequency distribution. If the organization has only one building, then both the loss frequency and the relative frequency of losses from theft is five per year. However, if the organization has five buildings, then the organization still has a loss frequency of five theft losses per year, but the relative frequency is one loss per year per building. Two of the most common applications of relative frequency measures in risk management are injuries per person per hour in workers compensation and auto accidents per mile driven.

Frequency distributions are usually discrete probability distributions based on past data regarding how often similar events have happened. For example, the exhibit contains the frequency distribution of the number of hurricanes that make landfall in Florida during a single hurricane season. One way of describing the frequency of hurricanes is to report a mean frequency of occurrence, such as approximately 1.2 hurricanes making landfall per year. See the exhibit "Skewness of Number of Hurricanes Making Landfall in Florida During One Hurricane Season."

Skewness of Number of Hurricanes Making Landfall in Florida During One Hurricane Season

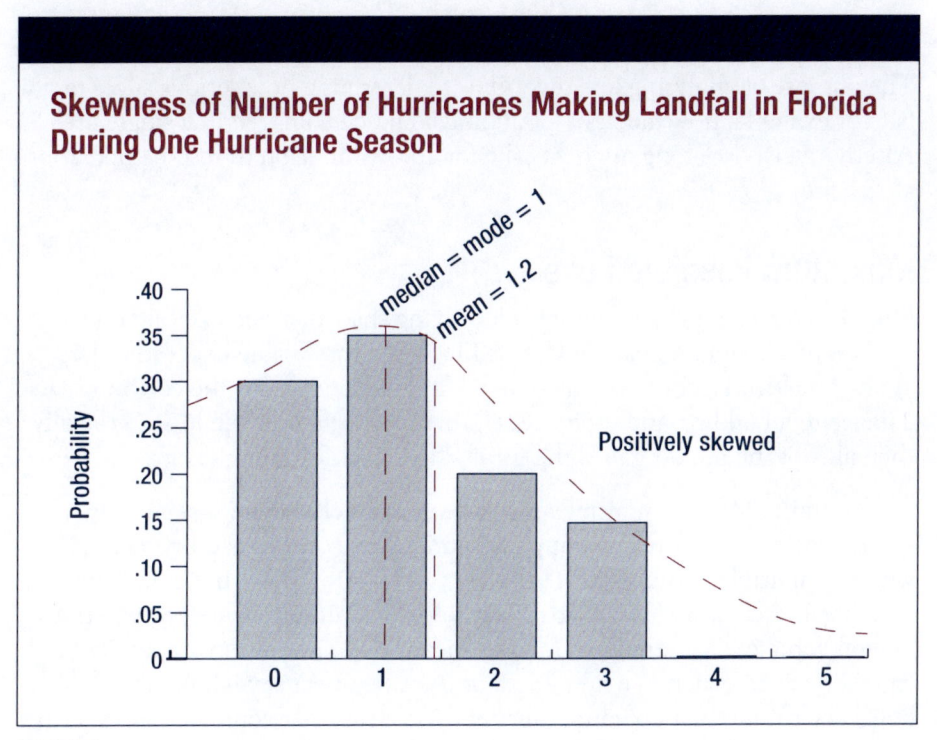

median = mode = 1
mean = 1.2
Positively skewed

[DA02586]

However, this figure does not incorporate some of the other information available from the entire frequency distribution. For example, the most likely outcome may be one hurricane per year (35.0 percent of the time). However, having zero hurricanes per year is also reasonably likely (30.0 percent of the time), but having five or more hurricanes make landfall in Florida is reasonably unlikely (0.1 percent of the time). Therefore, an insurance or risk management professional should supplement the mean of 1.2 with other information from the frequency distribution, such as the standard deviation (which is approximately 1.04) and skewness measures.

Loss frequency can be projected with a fairly high degree of confidence for some loss exposures in large organizations. For example, a company that ships thousands of parcels each day probably can more accurately project the number of transit losses it will sustain in a year, based on past experience and adjusted for any expected changes in future conditions, than can a company that ships only hundreds of parcels each month.

Most organizations do not have enough exposure units to accurately project low-frequency, high-severity events (such as employee deaths). However, an estimate with a margin for error is better than no estimate at all, as long as its limitations are recognized.

Loss Severity

The purpose of analyzing loss severity is to determine how serious a loss might be. For example, how much of a building could be damaged in a single fire? Alternatively, how long might it take for an organization to resume operations after a fire?

Maximum Possible Loss

Effectively managing risk requires identifying the worst possible outcome of a loss. The maximum possible loss (MPL) is the total value exposed to loss at any one location or from any one event. For example, in the case of fire damage to a building and its contents, the maximum possible loss is typically the value of the building plus the total value of the building's contents.

To determine MPL for multiple exposure units, such as a fleet of cars, an insurance or a risk management professional may consider factors such as whether multiple vehicles travel together (a circumstance that could cause one event, such as a collision, to affect several vehicles at once) or whether several vehicles are stored in the same location (a circumstance that could cause one event, such as a fire, flood, or theft, to affect several vehicles). This helps determine the maximum number of vehicles that could be involved in any one loss and therefore the event's MPL.

Although maximum possible property losses can be estimated based on the values exposed to loss, this estimation is not necessarily appropriate or possible for assessing maximum possible liability losses. In theory, liability losses are limited only by the defendant's total wealth. Therefore, some practical assumptions must be made about the MPL in liability cases to properly assess that loss exposure. Instead of focusing on the defendant's total wealth, a common assumption is that the maximum amount that would be exposed to liability loss 95 percent (or 98 percent) of the time in similar cases is the MPL.

Frequency and Severity Considered Jointly

In order to fully analyze the significance of a particular loss exposure, it is important to consider both severity and frequency distributions and how they interact. One method of jointly considering both loss frequency and loss severity is the Prouty Approach, which identifies four broad categories of loss frequency and three broad categories of loss severity. Another method is more statistically based and involves combining frequency and severity distributions to create a single total claims distribution. See the exhibit "The Prouty Approach."

The Prouty Approach

		Loss Frequency			
		Almost Nil	Slight	Moderate	Definite
Loss Severity	Severe	Reduce or prevent / Transfer	Reduce or prevent / Transfer	Reduce or prevent / Retain	Avoid
	Significant	Reduce or prevent / Transfer	Reduce / Transfer	Reduce or prevent / Retain	Avoid
	Slight	Reduce or prevent / Retain	Reduce / Retain	Reduce or prevent / Retain	Prevent / Retain

As shown in the exhibit, the Prouty Approach entails four categories of loss frequency:

- Almost nil—extremely unlikely to happen; virtually no possibility
- Slight—could happen but has not happened
- Moderate—happens occasionally
- Definite—happens regularly

There are three categories of loss severity:

- Slight—Organization can readily retain each loss exposure.
- Significant—Organization cannot retain the loss exposure, some part of which must be financed.
- Severe—Organization must finance virtually all of the loss exposure or endanger its survival.

These broad categories of loss frequency and loss severity are subjective. One organization may view losses that occur once a month as moderate, while another would consider such frequency as definite. Similarly, one organization may view a $1 million loss as slight, while another might view it as severe. However, these categories can help insurance and risk management professionals prioritize loss exposures.

A loss exposure's frequency and severity tend to be inversely related. That is, the more severe a loss tends to be, the less frequently it tends to occur. Conversely, the more frequently a loss occurs to a given exposure, the less severe the loss tends to be.

Loss exposures that generate minor but definite losses are typically retained and incorporated in an organization's budget. At the other extreme, loss exposures that generate intolerably large losses are typically avoided. Therefore, most risk management decisions, such as whether to adopt the risk control and risk financing techniques shown in "The Prouty Approach" exhibit, concern loss exposures for which individual losses, although tolerable, tend to be either significant or severe and have a moderate, slight, or almost nil chance of occurring.

A given loss exposure might generate financially significant losses because of either high individual loss severity or high-frequency, low-severity losses that aggregate to a substantial total. Organizations may be tempted to focus on high-profile "shock events," such as a major fire, a violent explosion, or a huge liability claim. However, smaller losses, which happen so frequently that they become routine, can eventually produce much larger total losses than a single dramatic event. For example, many retail firms suffer greater total losses from shoplifting, which happens regularly, than they do from large fires that might happen once every twenty years. Minor, cumulatively significant losses usually deserve as much risk management attention as large individual losses.

Another way of jointly considering frequency and severity is to combine both frequency and severity distributions into a total claims distribution, which can provide additional information about potential losses that may occur in a given period. Combining distributions can be difficult because as the number of possible outcomes increases, the possible combinations of frequency and severity grow exponentially. See the exhibit "Total Claims Distribution for Hardware Store Shoplifting Losses."

The "Total Claims Distribution for Hardware Store Shoplifting Losses" exhibit presents a simple example of three possible frequencies (0, 1, and 2) and three possible severities ($100, $250, and $500) that represent shoplifting losses from a hardware store. The frequency and severity distributions for a given year are shown in the exhibit, along with the total claims distribution created by considering all the possible combinations of the frequency and severity distributions.

For example, a 33 percent chance exists of a loss not occurring during the year (frequency = 0). Therefore, in the total claims distribution, a 33 percent chance exists of the total losses being $0. There is only one possible way for a $100 loss to occur: a frequency of 1 and a severity of $100. Therefore, that probability is .11 [.33 (frequency 1) × .33 (severity $100) = .11]. There are two ways that the total claims for the year could equal $500. Either the organization could have one loss of $500, or it could have two losses of $250.

Total Claims Distribution for Hardware Store Shoplifting Losses

Frequency

	Number of Losses	Probability
F0	0	.33
F1	1	.33
F2	2	.34

Severity

	Dollar Loss	Probability
S1	$100	.33
S2	$250	.33
S3	$500	.34

Total Claims Distribution

Dollar Loss	Probability*	Probability Calculation	
$ 0	.33	p(F0)	← There is only one possible way to have $0 losses: the frequency = 0. That happens 33% of the time.
100	.11	p(F1) × p(S1)	
200	.04	p(F2) × p(S1) × p(S1)	
250	.11	p(F1) × p(S2)	
350	.07	p(F2) × p(S1) × p(S2)	
500	.15	[p(F2) × p(S2) × p(S2)] + [p(F1) × p(S3)]	← There are two possible ways to have $500 in losses in a given year: two $250 losses or one $500 loss.
600	.08	p(F2) × p(S1) × p(S3)	
750	.08	p(F2) × p(S2) × p(S3)	
1,000	.04	p(F2) × p(S3) × p(S3)	← There is only one possible way to have $1,000 in losses: two $500 losses.

*Rounded

[DA02589]

Therefore, the probability of a $500 loss is the probability of one $500 loss plus the probability of two $250 losses.

A total claims distribution can be used to calculate the measures of central tendency and dispersion and evaluate the effect that various risk control and risk financing techniques would have on this loss exposure.

Total Dollar Losses

The third dimension to consider in analyzing loss exposures is total dollar losses, calculated by multiplying loss frequency by loss severity. Total dollar losses represent a simplified version of combining frequency and severity distributions and can be used when analyzing frequency and severity distributions that have multiple possible outcomes. See the exhibit "Total Dollar Losses."

Total Dollar Losses

Frequency

	Number of Losses	Probability
F0	0	.03
F1	1	.05
F2	2	.08
F3	3	.10
F4	4	.15
F5	5	.20
F6	6	.15
F7	7	.10
F8	8	.08
F9	9	.05
F10	10	.01

Severity

	Dollar Loss	Probability
S1	$100	.30
S2	$250	.25
S3	$500	.20
S4	$683	.15
S5	$883	.10

Expected value = $383.33.

Expected value = 4.9.

Expected total dollar losses = 4.9 × $383.33 = $1,878.33

Worst case total dollar losses = 9 × $883.00 = $7,950.00

[DA02590]

Expected total dollar losses can be projected by multiplying expected loss frequency by expected loss severity, while worst-case scenarios can be calculated by assuming both high frequency and the worst possible severity. For example, the "Total Dollar Losses" exhibit includes the frequency and severity distributions that were shown in the "Total Claims Distribution for Hardware Store Shoplifting Losses" exhibit if they were expanded to include more possible outcomes.

Combining the frequency and severity distributions in the exhibit would be difficult given the total number of possible combinations. An insurance or risk management professional could make some simpler calculations to determine what the potential total dollar losses may be. In this example, expected total dollar losses would be $1,878.33, and the worst-case scenario could be calculated as $7,950.00, using F9 in the exhibit. (F10 was not used, given its low probability.) These estimates could then be used in managing these loss exposures, such as evaluating whether to insure the loss exposures for the premium an insurer is quoting.

Timing

The fourth dimension to consider in analyzing loss exposures is timing of losses. Risk assessment requires considering not only when losses are likely to occur, but also when payment for those losses will likely be made. The timing dimension is significant because money held in reserve to pay for a loss can earn interest until the actual payment is made. Whether a loss is counted when it is incurred or when it is paid is also significant for various accounting and tax reasons that are beyond the scope of this discussion.

Funds to pay for property losses are generally disbursed relatively soon after the event occurs. In contrast, liability losses often involve long delays between the occurrence of the adverse event, when an occurrence is recognized, the period of possible litigation, and the time when payment is actually made. Damages for disability claims, for example, might be paid over a long period. In some cases, especially those involving environmental loss exposures or health risks, the delay can span several decades. Although this delay increases the uncertainty associated with the loss amount, it allows reserves to earn interest or investment income over a longer period of time.

Data Credibility

After analyzing the four dimensions of a loss exposure, an insurance or risk management professional then evaluates the credibility of the projections of loss frequency, loss severity, total dollar losses, and timing. The term data credibility refers to the level of confidence that available data can accurately indicate future losses. Two related data credibility issues may prevent data from being good indicators of future losses—the age of the data and whether the data represent actual losses or estimates of losses. See the exhibit "Assessing Credibility of Data."

> ### Assessing Credibility of Data
> There are several factors, both internal and external, that may influence data credibility for an organization. Internally, changes in the way that an organization operates, such as alterations to manufacturing processes or changes in data collection methods, may significantly reduce the credibility of previously collected data. Externally, events such as natural catastrophes, large liability awards, or terrorist attacks not only alter the data that are collected in that time frame, but also may cause shifts in the operating environment that render previously collected data less credible.

[DA02591]

Ideally, data used to forecast losses are generated in the same environment that will apply to the projected period. However, the environment for most loss exposures changes, even if those changes happen slowly. The changing environment renders more recent data a more credible predictor of future losses than older data. However, because of delays in reporting and paying of claims, more recent data are not always actual losses, but estimates of what the ultimate losses will be.

This leaves insurance and risk management professionals with a dilemma: Is it better to use older data, which are accurate but may have been generated in an environment that is substantially different from that of the period for which they are trying to predict, or to use more recent data and sacrifice some accuracy to maintain the integrity of the environment?

Once the projections are made along the four dimensions of loss exposures, the analysis of the loss exposures will often dictate which type of risk control or risk financing measures should be implemented. See the exhibit "Transportation Losses for a Large Shipper."

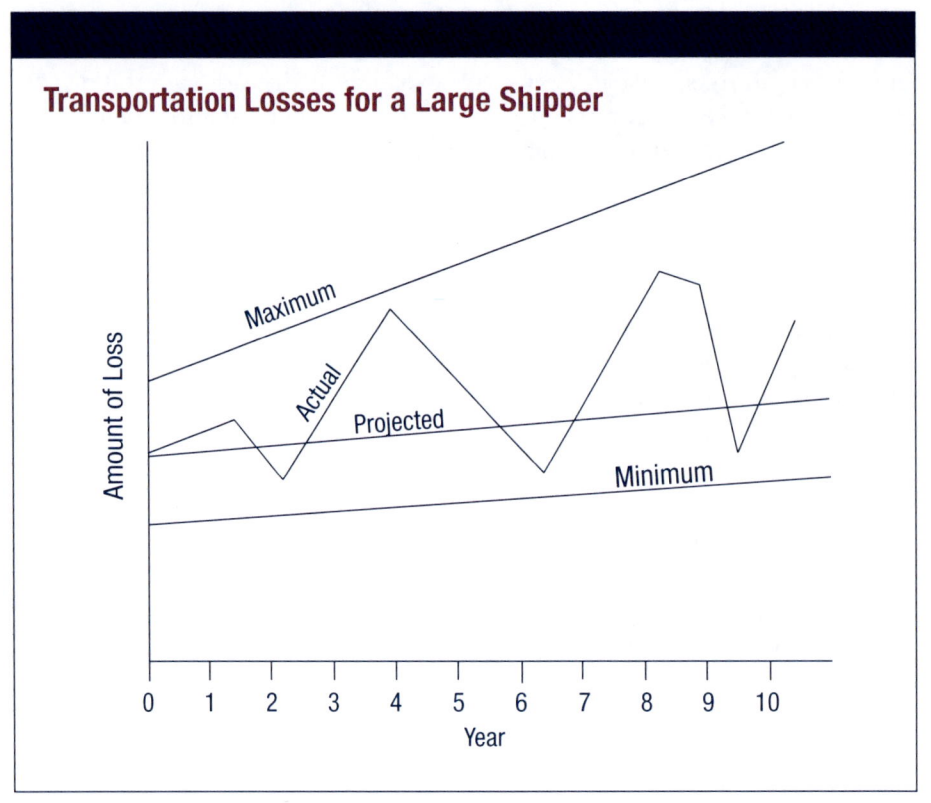

Transportation Losses for a Large Shipper

[DA02592]

For example, the pattern shown in the "Transportation Losses for a Large Shipper" exhibit illustrates the expected transportation losses for a large shipper that has been in business for ten years and that has a steadily increasing volume of transportation services.

The average losses during the coming years might be projected to fall along the line labeled "projected," and the probable maximum loss might be projected to fall along the line labeled "maximum." Probable minimum loss levels might also be projected, as shown by the "minimum" line.

If such projections can be made with a high degree of confidence in the data used for the projections, actual losses would be expected to follow a pattern like the "actual" line on the graph, deviating from the average from one year to the next but in no case exceeding the maximum or falling below the minimum. Because the shipper can reasonably anticipate the degree of uncertainty, it may choose to retain these losses instead of insuring them. See the exhibit "Product Liability Losses for a Large Manufacturer."

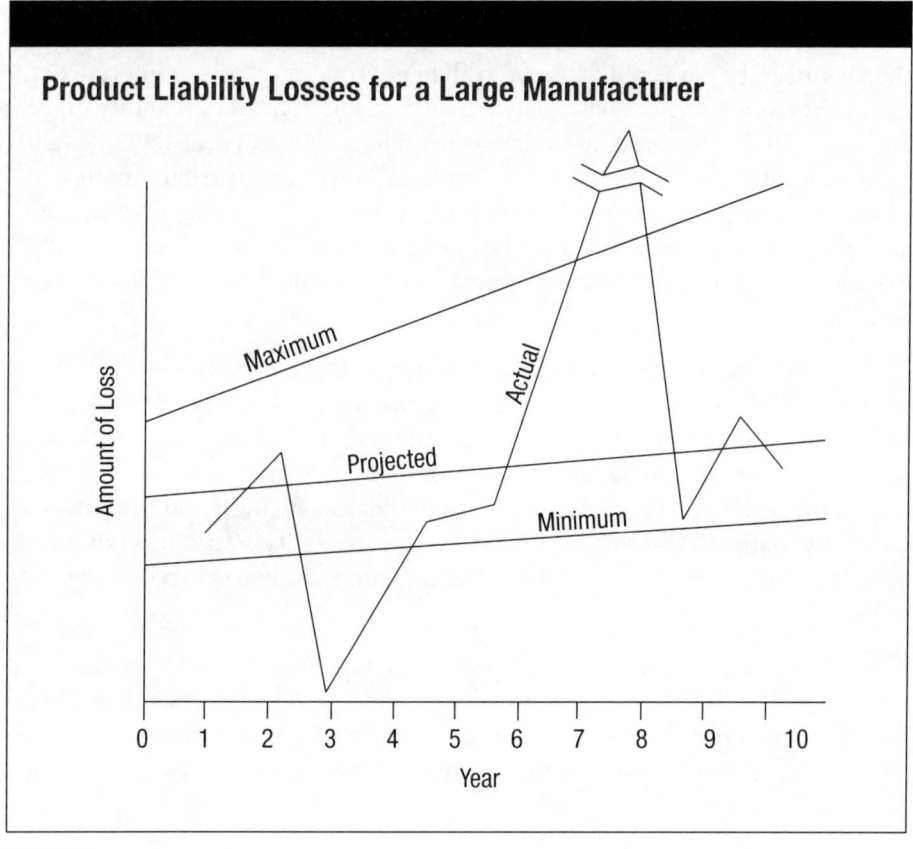

Product Liability Losses for a Large Manufacturer

[DA02593]

Similarly, the "Product Liability Losses for a Large Manufacturer" exhibit represents products liability losses experienced by a large manufacturer. A few losses usually occur each year. However, in Year 4, almost no losses occurred, whereas, in Year 8, at least one major loss occurred. (The losses in Year 8 are so high that total losses exceeded even maximum projections.) It may have been possible to project these losses to a certain extent at lower levels, but possibilities existed for substantial losses above the expected and maximum levels. It might be disastrous to attempt to finance such losses solely out of the organization's operating budget.

SUMMARY

Organizations use risk analysis to determine their levels of risk and how best to treat identified risks. A risk analysis can include qualitative assessment, quantitative analysis, or a combination of those methods. As part of risk analysis, various approaches can be used to determine the probabilities of assorted consequences of a risk. To accurately determine its level of risk, an organization must examine the effectiveness of its current risk control measures.

The probability of an event is the relative likelihood (frequency) with which the event can be expected to occur in the long run in a stable environment. An event has a range of consequences, each of which has a probability of occurring. Probability-related concepts include theoretical probability, empirical probability, and the law of large numbers. Probability distributions are used to analyze probabilities. A properly constructed probability distribution always contains outcomes that are both mutually exclusive and collectively exhaustive. All probability distributions can be classified as either discrete or continuous.

The central tendency is the single outcome that is the most representative of all possible outcomes included within a probability distribution. Expected value and mean are two measures of central tendency. Dispersion can also be used to compare the characteristics of probability distributions. Two widely used statistical measures of dispersion are standard deviation and the coefficient of variation. A normal distribution is a probability distribution that can help in accurate forecasting of the variability around some central, average, or expected value.

Trend analysis seeks predictable patterns of change in a dynamic, changing environment. Organizations use trend analysis to develop forecasts based on patterns of change. Regression analysis can increase the accuracy of an organization's forecasts by using statistical analysis to examine related variables that affect trends.

Organizations use decision tree analysis to compare the consequences, costs, and gains of alternative decisions and to select the most effective strategy to achieve a goal. Organizations use event tree analysis to examine all possible consequences of an accidental event and the effectiveness of existing measures to prevent or control those consequences.

The analysis step of the risk management process involves considering the four dimensions of a loss exposure: loss frequency, loss severity, total dollar losses, and timing.

ASSIGNMENT NOTE

1. Marvin Rausand, "Event Tree Analysis," slide presentation, Department of Production and Quality Engineering, Norwegian University of Science and Technology, October 7, 2005, slide 3, www.ntnu.no/ross/slides/eta.pdf (accessed April 3, 2012).

Direct Your Learning

Risk Treatment

Educational Objectives

After learning the content of this assignment, you should be able to:

- Describe the risk treatment process and risk treatment techniques.
- Describe risk financing and its importance to organizations.

Outline

Risk Treatment

Introduction to Risk Financing

Summary

Risk Treatment

RISK TREATMENT

Risk treatment decisions are based on the results of a risk assessment.

The assessment includes identifying and analyzing an organization's various risks. See the exhibit "Enterprise-Wide Risk Management Process Model."

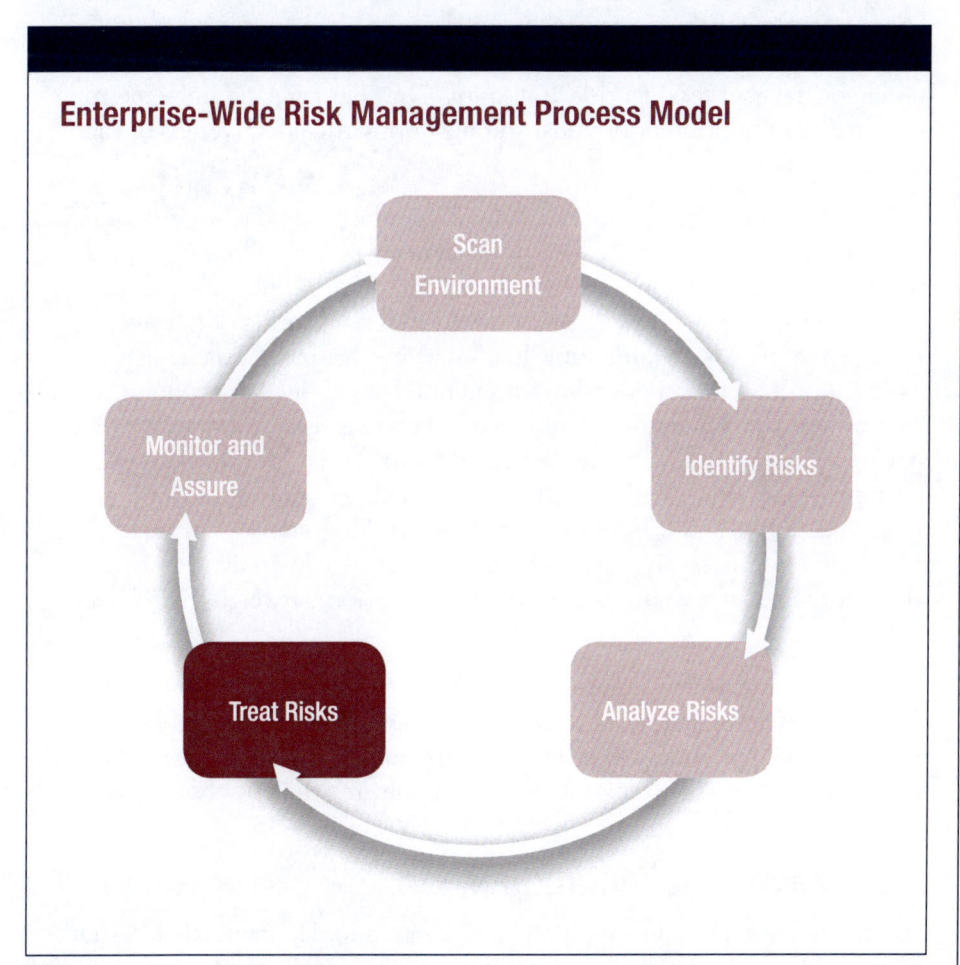

Enterprise-Wide Risk Management Process Model

[DA08717_6]

Available risk treatment techniques include these:
- Avoid the risk
- Modify the likelihood and/or impact of the risk

- Transfer the risk
- Retain the risk
- Exploit the risk

Risk Treatment Process

Risk treatment involves making decisions based on the outcome of the risk identification and analysis. For risks identified as needing treatment, specific options must be selected to modify them. Treatment options will vary, and the negative or positive effects of the uncertainty on the organization should be considered. The goal of risk treatment is to modify identified risks to assist the organization in meeting its objectives.

The risk treatment process is continuous and entails examining each risk treatment option (or combination of options) in terms of whether it leads to a tolerable level of residual risk. It also involves selecting and implementing a risk treatment option or options, and measuring the effectiveness of each option selected.

Risk treatment techniques are not mutually exclusive, and many risks require a combination of techniques. The risk treatment plan should indicate risk priorities and the order in which chosen techniques will be implemented. Review of risk treatment plans as part of overall monitoring of the risk management process is important. Risks may change based on changes in the organization's operation or on environmental factors, such as economic conditions or legal and regulatory requirements. Previous risk treatment decisions may no longer be valid, and implemented controls may no longer be effective. Furthermore, emerging risks—such as those arising from new technology or the acquisition of a new business unit—must be identified and assessed. The risk treatment process should also include a cost-benefit analysis to assess whether the benefits of the chosen treatment option outweigh the related costs.

The risk treatment plan should document the process and designate the chosen risk treatment options as well as people responsible for implementing the plan. The plan should also include a timetable for implementing the risk treatment options and for monitoring and reviewing the established plan.

Risk Treatment Techniques

Risk treatment techniques apply to hazard, operational, financial, and strategic risks. In general, available risk treatment options fall into the categories of avoidance, modification, transfer, retention, or exploitation. Because speculative risks can result in both negative and positive consequences, the organization must consider a range of risk treatment techniques or a combination of techniques to manage negative and positive outcomes. For pure risks, the focus of risk treatment is on managing negative outcomes.

For events that appear to have primarily positive potential outcomes, such as a major competitor leaving the market, treatment would focus on exploiting the risk by maximizing expected gains. Techniques would include modifying the likelihood of an event to increase the opportunity to meet objectives while also considering treatment options for potential negative outcomes.

In some cases, risk avoidance is an appropriate option; when considering it, organizations must take into account any opportunity costs of not accepting a particular risk. See the exhibit "Risk Treatment Techniques."

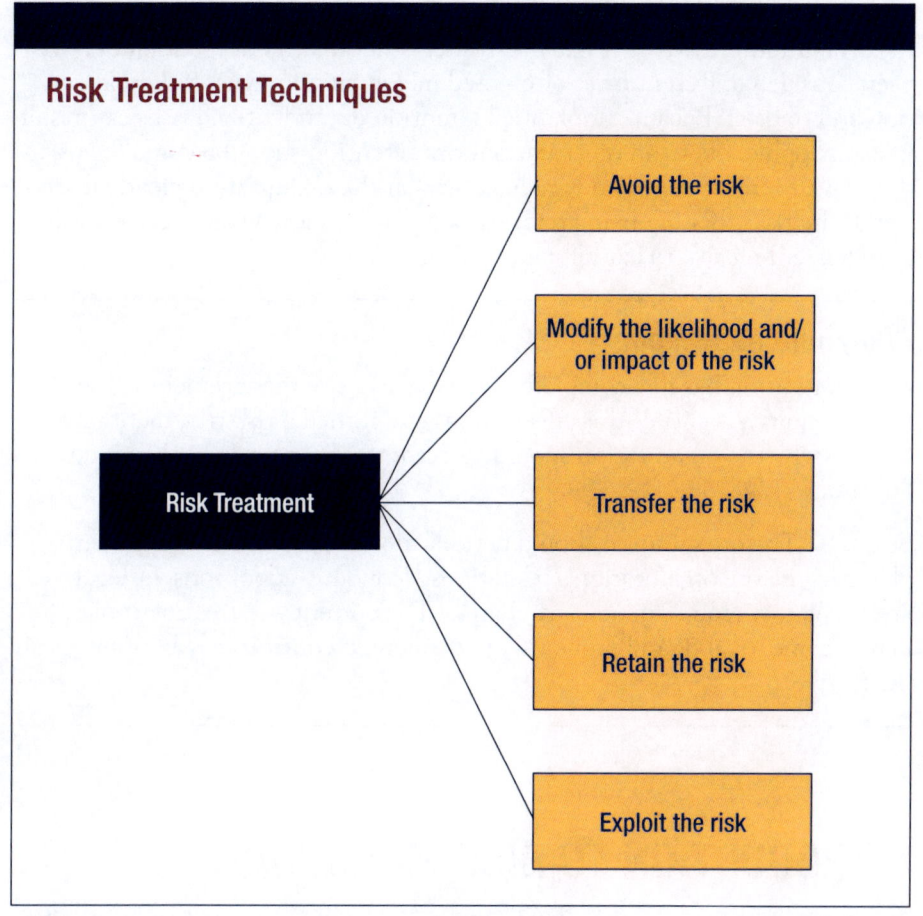

Risk Treatment Techniques

Risk Treatment:
- Avoid the risk
- Modify the likelihood and/or impact of the risk
- Transfer the risk
- Retain the risk
- Exploit the risk

[DA08744]

Identified risks can also be treated by modifying the likelihood and/or impact of events resulting in positive or negative outcomes. For hazard risks, modifying the likelihood of events focuses on **loss prevention** efforts to reduce overall loss frequency. Techniques designed to modify the impact of events recognize that not all negative outcomes can be avoided, but that the financial consequences of these events can be decreased. Techniques such as sprinkler systems in buildings or driver training for commercial truck operators are **loss reduction** efforts aimed at reducing the severity of losses. An organization can use contingency plans to modify the consequences of an

Loss prevention
A risk control technique that reduces the frequency of a particular loss.

Loss reduction
A risk control technique that reduces the severity of a particular loss.

operational risk, such as a disruption in its supply chain resulting from a permanent or temporary loss of a major supplier of raw materials.

Risks can be transferred, or shared, through contractual arrangements or joint ventures with other organizations. Outsourcing is a method of risk sharing that can be used to transfer noncritical operations and their related risks to another organization. For hazard risks, insurance is the primary technique used to transfer risk. Contractual risk transfers (noninsurance), such as hedging or other contractual agreements, can be used to transfer financial consequences of risks to another party or organization.

Risk **retention** is used for residual risk after other treatment techniques have been considered. Retention is often used in combination with risk modification and transfer. Because unplanned retention of unidentified risks can result in catastrophic loss to an organization, risk retention should be used for risks that have been identified and analyzed so that the organization clearly understands the risks that are being retained. Organizations may also actively take or increase their risk to exploit an opportunity.

Retention
A risk financing technique that involves assumption of risk in which gains and losses are retained within the organization.

Apply Your Knowledge

An organization has just completed an extensive risk management review for its operations. As part of this effort, it has established a risk treatment plan. Explain why the organization should monitor this plan periodically going forward.

Feedback: The organization should periodically monitor the risk treatment plan because the organization's operations, economic conditions, or legal and regulatory requirements may change. The current risk treatment plan may become invalid, and previously implemented controls may become ineffective.

INTRODUCTION TO RISK FINANCING

Risk financing enables a risk management professional (any person who has responsibility under an organization's risk management program) to apply techniques that can provide critical resources when needed.

Risk management professionals use **risk financing** to respond to risks that have been identified as a financial threat to the organization.

Risk financing
A conscious act or decision not to act that generates the funds to offset the variability in cash flows that may occur as an outcome of risk.

Transfer
In the context of risk management, a risk financing technique by which the financial responsibility for losses and variability in cash flows is shifted to another party.

Risk Financing as a Part of Risk Treatment

Risk financing can be categorized as either risk **transfer** or risk retention, both of which are risk treatment techniques. See the exhibit "Risk Treatment Techniques and Risk Financing."

Risk Treatment Techniques and Risk Financing

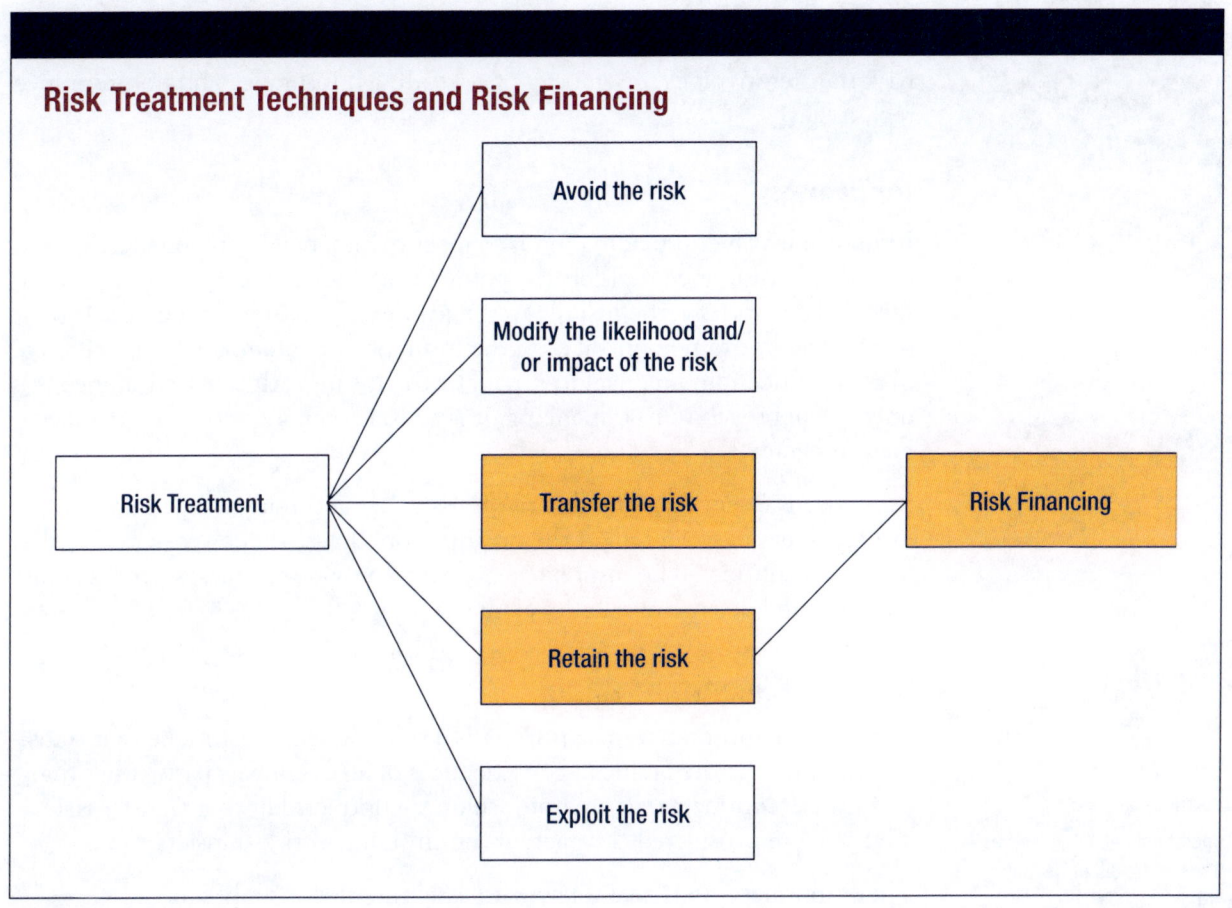

Risk Treatment branches to:
- Avoid the risk
- Modify the likelihood and/or impact of the risk
- Transfer the risk → Risk Financing
- Retain the risk → Risk Financing
- Exploit the risk

[DA08833]

Risk financing techniques are applied primarily to hazard (insurable) and financial risk. The risk financing techniques for hazard risk are insurance, insurance-linked securities, internal funds, and contracts (noninsurance). These techniques involve the transfer or retention of losses. The risk financing techniques for financial risk are futures, forwards, swaps, and options—collectively known as derivatives, or hedging techniques. These techniques involve the transfer of the downside of a speculative risk and can result in a missed opportunity for gain. (In some cases, the techniques used for financial risk have been used for hazard risk as well.)

Many risk financing techniques for hazard risk contain elements of both retention and transfer. For example, insurance with a deductible entails retention of the deductible amount and transfer of losses that are above the deductible.

Determining which risk financing techniques are appropriate requires the risk management professional to understand the organization's risk management program goals, which often may be broad and dependent on the successful implementation of both risk financing and other risk treatment techniques. Additionally, risk management professionals must finance risk within the overall context of the organization's financial goals.

Risk Transfer

Risk transfer involves the transfer of risk through insurance and noninsurance techniques.

Insurance

Insurance involves providing funds to meet the financial consequences of hazard risk. Insurance transfers the potential financial consequences of certain specified events from the insured to the insurer. The insurance buyer substitutes a small certain financial cost, the insurance premium, for the possibility of a large uncertain financial loss, paid by the insurer. Although insurance is only one approach to risk financing, it is a vital component of a risk management program.

Insurance is essentially a funded risk transfer. By accepting a premium, the insurer agrees to pay for all of the organization's losses that are covered by the insurance contract. The insurer also agrees to provide services, such as claims handling and defense of liability claims.

Contract (Noninsurance)

Contract (noninsurance) risk transfer is a risk financing technique that transfers all or part of the financial consequences of an event to a party other than an insurer. Contracts that are not insurance contracts but that transfer **risk** are therefore considered contractual (noninsurance) risk transfers.

These contracts often deal solely with assigning responsibility for an event arising out of a particular relationship or activity and are known as hold-harmless agreements (or indemnity agreements). See the exhibit "Hold-Harmless Agreement for Use in a Lease."

> **Hold-Harmless Agreement for Use in a Lease**
>
> To the fullest extent permitted by law, the lessee shall indemnify, defend, and hold harmless the lessor, agents, and employees of the lessor from any and all claims arising out of or resulting from the leased premises.

[DA08624]

Hedging

Hedging is practical when it is used to offset the consequences of risk to which one is naturally, voluntarily, or inevitably exposed. It is a form of risk financing for financial risks, which are uncertainties associated with the organization's financial activities. The activities could benefit or harm the organization. For example, currency conversion (converting one country's currency to another's), with the possibility of change in value as a result of the conversion, could either benefit or harm an organization.

Risk
Uncertainty about outcomes that can be either negative or positive.

As another example, a newspaper publisher faces the risk of newsprint price variability. To offset this risk, the publisher might enter into a **futures contract** with its newsprint supplier to purchase a fixed quantity of newsprint over the coming year at a preagreed price. If the market price of newsprint increases over the next year, the newspaper publisher has saved money by buying newsprint below the prevailing price. If the market price drops, the newspaper publisher's risk is still reduced because it has eliminated variability in the newsprint's cost.

The same can be said for the newsprint supplier. Whether the newsprint supplier would have made more or less money depends on the ultimate prevailing market price of newsprint, but, in either case, the futures contract reduces the cost's variability.

> **Futures contract**
> An exchange-traded agreement to buy or sell a commodity or security at a future date at a price that is fixed at the time of the agreement.

Risk Retention

For hazard risks, risk retention is often considered to be a form of risk financing when there is an internal fund within the organization to pay the cost of losses. Because retention can be the most economical risk financing technique, it is sometimes preferred even when insurance or contractual (noninsurance) risk transfer is available. Retention can also be the risk financing technique of last resort; the financial burden of any consequences from an event that cannot be insured or otherwise transferred must be retained.

Planned or Unplanned

Retention can be planned or unplanned. Planned retention is a deliberate assumption of a risk (and its consequences) that has been identified and analyzed. Planned retention may be chosen because it is cost-effective, convenient, or the only option.

Unplanned retention is the inadvertent assumption of a risk (and any consequences) that has not been identified or accurately analyzed. For example, many people inadvertently retain flood losses because they do not anticipate the torrential rain associated with hurricanes, against which they would otherwise insure.

Complete or Partial

Retention can also be complete or partial. Complete retention is assumption of the full cost of any consequences that are retained by the organization. Partial retention is assumption of a portion of the cost of a loss by the organization and transfer of the remaining portion.

Funded or Unfunded

Funding for retention differs in this way:

- Funded retention is a pre-event arrangement to ensure that funding is available to pay for the consequences of an event after it occurs.
- Unfunded retention is the lack of advance funding for the consequences of an event that occurs.

Apply Your Knowledge

David is a risk manager of a trucking company with a fleet of trucks that specializes in hauling gravel. Frequently, when a truck is operated on the road by an employee of the trucking company, gravel escapes from the back and cracks the windshield of a vehicle behind the truck. If no insurance or contractual (noninsurance) risk transfer is available for this risk, what risk financing techniques might David consider to pay for these losses?

Feedback: Since neither insurance nor contractual (noninsurance) risk transfer is a viable option, David's employer should consider retaining these losses. This would be a planned retention because it is a deliberate assumption of a risk (and its consequences). Because no risk transfer is available, the retention would also likely be complete, not partial. Finally, it would probably be unfunded, as the cost of repairing or replacing an occasional windshield is minor enough that no advanced funding is needed.

SUMMARY

The risk treatment process involves assessing specific risk treatment options to determine whether residual risks are tolerable to an organization. Risk treatment techniques include avoiding risk, modifying the likelihood and/or impact, transferring the risk, retaining the risk, and exploiting the risk. These techniques can be applied to hazard, operational, financial, and strategic risks.

Risk financing is a conscious act or decision not to act to provide funds to offset variability in cash flows that may occur. Risk financing can be categorized as risk retention or risk transfer, both of which are risk treatment techniques. Risk financing techniques for hazard risk are insurance, insurance-linked securities, internal funds, and contracts (noninsurance). Risk financing techniques for financial risk are futures, forwards, swaps, and options—collectively known as derivatives, or hedging techniques.

Segment C

Assignment 9
Financial Statement Risk Analysis

Assignment 10
Capital Investment and Financial Risk

Assignment 11
Monitoring and Reporting on Risk

Direct Your Learning

9

Financial Statement Risk Analysis

Educational Objectives

After learning the content of this assignment, you should be able to:

▸ Describe the purpose of financial statements.

▸ Describe the purpose and content of the balance sheet.

▸ Describe the purpose and content of the income statement.

▸ Describe the content and purpose of the statement of changes in shareholders' equity and statement of cash flows.

▸ Describe the following sources of financial information:
- Notes to financial statements
- Securities and Exchange Commission (SEC) filings
- Company annual reports

▸ Apply trend analysis to income statements over multiple periods.

▸ Explain how ratio analysis can be used to evaluate liquidity.

▸ Describe the components of the typical capital structure for a company.

▸ Explain how companies apply financial leverage to increase returns to shareholders.

▸ Explain how operating leverage determines the degree to which a business disruption will reduce operating income.

Outline

Purpose of Financial Statements

Balance Sheet

Income Statement

Statement of Changes in Shareholders' Equity and Statement of Cash Flows

Supplemental Sources of Financial Information

Income Statement Trend Analysis

Analyzing Liquidity Risk

Capital Structure

Financial Leverage

Operating Leverage

Summary

Financial Statement Risk Analysis

PURPOSE OF FINANCIAL STATEMENTS

Financial statements can be used by management and other interested parties to make informed business decisions about their areas of responsibility. They can be useful to insurance professionals in many aspects of their work. For example, financial statements can help agents and brokers assess coverage needs, help underwriters assess acceptability for coverage, and help claim representatives calculate the amount of a claim settlement.

A financial statement is a document that quantitatively presents an organization's financial activities or status. Such activities include sales, purchases, borrowings, repayments, and investments. When a financial activity occurs, the information regarding that activity is forwarded to the accounting department. Initially, the activity is recorded using a process known as bookkeeping. Once the information has been recorded, it goes through the **accounting** process. See the exhibit "Flow of Information From Financial Activity to Financial Statements."

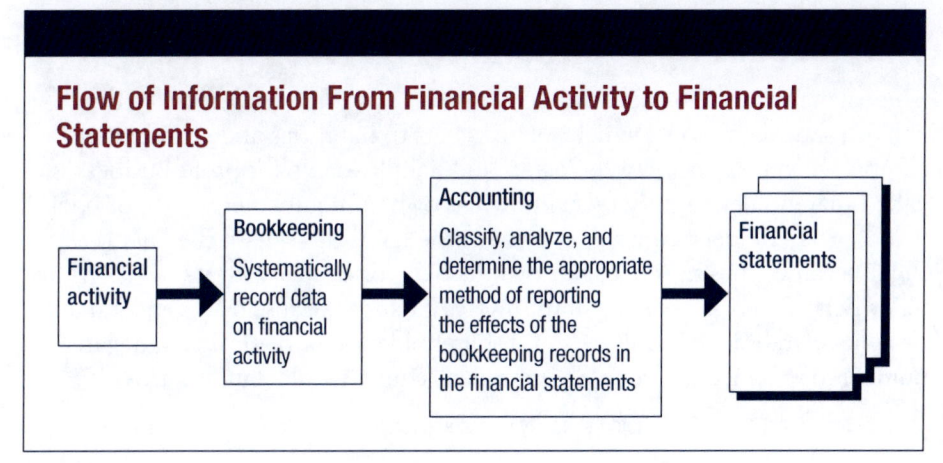

Accounting
The classification, analysis, and determination of the appropriate method of reporting the effects of the bookkeeping records in an organization's financial statements.

Flow of Information From Financial Activity to Financial Statements

Financial activity → Bookkeeping (Systematically record data on financial activity) → Accounting (Classify, analyze, and determine the appropriate method of reporting the effects of the bookkeeping records in the financial statements) → Financial statements

[DA02108]

The purpose of financial statements is to communicate information about an organization's financial activities, and the results of those activities, to individuals who need to make informed financial decisions about the organization. Such individuals can include management, investors, insurers, and employees.

There are four primary financial statements: the balance sheet, the income statement, the statement of changes in shareholders' equity, and the statement of cash flows. Individually, each of these statements provides valuable information, but because they are interrelated, they provide a more complete picture when viewed together. When considered together, they present the organization's financial condition, including its resources, liabilities, and investment decisions. To help ensure consistency among the financial statements of different organizations, these statements are prepared using standardized accounting concepts and principles.

BALANCE SHEET

A balance sheet indicates the financial position of an organization.

Financial analysts, investors, and insurance underwriters evaluate an organization's financial strength by examining its balance sheet. The balance sheet discussed in this section is based on generally accepted accounting principles (GAAP).

The balance sheet is a listing of everything that the organization owns and everything that it owes at a particular moment in time. It is a snapshot of the company's financial position as of that date. The accounting equation ties together the balance sheet's main components, which are assets, liabilities, and shareholders' equity.

The Accounting Equation

The balance sheet illustrates the accounting equation (also known as the balance sheet equation), which relates assets to liabilities and shareholders' equity. The difference between assets and liabilities in a for-profit business is called shareholders' equity (also known as owners' equity, net worth, or book value). Shareholders' equity is shown on the liabilities side of the balance sheet because a business does not own its net worth. It "owes" its net worth to its owners. The balance sheet must always balance because assets equal liabilities plus shareholders' equity, even if shareholders' equity must be a negative number for balance to occur. Shareholders' equity is calculated in this way:

Assets − Liabilities = Shareholders' equity (owners' equity)

Assets

Assets are the resources an organization owns or uses to operate its business. Assets are grouped into **current assets** and noncurrent assets. Current assets can include cash, **marketable securities**, **receivables** (accounts and notes), **inventories**, and **prepaid expenses**. Noncurrent assets are those assets that will be used over a period greater than one year, and they are grouped into tangible assets (such as land, buildings, and equipment) and intangible assets. Intangible assets include all assets that cannot be seen or touched, such as

---

Current assets

A balance sheet asset classification that includes cash and other assets that are expected to be converted into cash, sold, or exchanged within the business's normal operating cycle, usually one year.

Receivables

An asset classification that consists of the amounts owed to a company by customers and other outsiders.

Marketable securities

An asset classification that includes temporary investments that can easily be converted into cash.

Inventory

An asset classification that consists of goods available for sale to customers; for a manufacturing company, also includes raw materials and finished goods.

Prepaid expenses

An asset classification that represents the amount that has already been paid for services that have not been received or used.

leaseholds, patents, copyrights, and trademarks, and they are often categorized as intellectual property. See the exhibit "Goodwill."

> **Goodwill**
>
> Goodwill is usually classified as an intangible asset and is usually generated as part of an acquisition. Whenever the acquiring organization pays more than the book value for the acquired organization, the difference between the price paid for the organization and the book value can be listed as goodwill on the balance sheet. Goodwill is not amortized over any specific time period, like other intangible assets. If goodwill becomes impaired, it is reduced in value on the balance sheet and is recognized as a loss on the income statement.

Noncurrent assets, by definition, are used over multiple years. The value of many noncurrent assets, such as machinery, declines over time due to a variety of factors including usage, wear and tear, and obsolescence. Depreciation is an accounting term used to describe the allocation of the value of a noncurrent tangible asset over its useful life. There are many methods of depreciating assets, such as straight-line depreciation or declining balance depreciation. On the balance sheet, the historical cost of a noncurrent asset is reduced by the depreciation amount, leaving the net value of the asset (historical cost − accumulated depreciation) on the balance sheet.

Liabilities

Liabilities are the debts and obligations that represent claims against an organization's assets. As with assets, liabilities are categorized as current or noncurrent. **Current liabilities** can include accounts payable, short-term debt, or the current position of a long-term debt. Noncurrent liabilities are those that will be paid or satisfied more than one year after the balance sheet date, such as long-term notes payable.

Current liabilities
A balance sheet liability classification that includes obligations whose payments are reasonably expected to require the use of cash or the creation of other current liabilities within one year.

Shareholders' Equity

Shareholders' equity (owners' equity) is the net amount of assets after deducting an organization's debts and obligations (liabilities). It includes the capital contributed by owners and the accumulation of earnings retained by the organization (**retained earnings**) since it was started. Also, for specified assets and liabilities, it includes cumulative changes in value that were not used to calculate cumulative earnings. On the balance sheet of a not-for-profit organization, shareholders' equity is often called "surplus."

If some or all of the assets on the balance sheet are listed at the price paid for them (historical cost) rather than at current fair market value (fair value), net worth would not reflect the market value of the assets. Because historical costs may be significantly higher or lower than fair value, shareholders' equity (net

Retained earnings
The cumulative net income that an organization has retained, after payment of dividends, for reinvestment in the organization's operations.

worth) based on historical cost of assets may differ significantly from shareholders' equity (net worth) based on fair values of assets. This same concept applies to liabilities.

Shareholders' equity is negative whenever liabilities exceed assets. A business with negative shareholders' equity may be close to bankruptcy.

Balance sheets for different organizations are similar in format but may not be exactly alike. See the exhibit "Balance Sheet for Manufacturing, Inc.."

Balance Sheet for Manufacturing, Inc.

Manufacturing, Inc.
GAAP Balance Sheet
12/31/20X1

ASSETS				**LIABILITIES AND SHAREHOLDERS' EQUITY**		
Current Assets	Cash	$ 50,000		Current Liabilities	Accounts Payable	$ 1,250,000
	Accounts Receivable	125,000			Wages Payable	250,000
	Inventory	1,500,000			Taxes Payable	3,750,000
	Supplies	75,000			Short-Term Debt	5,000,000
	Marketable Securities	25,000,000				
Noncurrent Assets	Property, Plant, & Equipment			Noncurrent Liabilities	Long-Term Debt	200,000,000
	Land	100,000,000		Total Liabilities		210,250,000
	Buildings	150,000,000				
	Equipment	50,000,000		Total Shareholders' Equity (Owners' Equity)		111,500,000
	Less Accumulated Depreciation	10,000,000				
	Intangible Assets	1,500,000				
	Goodwill	3,500,000				
Total Assets		$ 321,750,000		Total Liabilities & Shareholders' Equity		$ 321,750,000

From the balance sheet, these facts are evident:

- The current assets of Manufacturing, Inc., total $26,750,000.
- The noncurrent assets total $295,000,000.
- The noncurrent assets include $1,500,000 in intangible assets; and $300,000,000 in property, plant, and equipment minus the accumulated depreciation of $10,000,000 (for a total of $290,000,000).
- The current liabilities of Manufacturing, Inc., total $10,250,000.
- The noncurrent liabilities total $200,000,000.
- The shareholders' equity (owners' equity) for Manufacturing, Inc., is calculated as assets minus liabilities: $321,750,000 − $210,250,000 = $111,500,000.

[DA06309]

INCOME STATEMENT

An income statement provides stakeholders with information regarding the profitability of an organization over a given period of time. Risk and insurance professionals can gain a better understanding of an organization and its insurance needs by reading and interpreting its income statement. The income statement discussed is based on generally accepted accounting principles (GAAP).

An income statement shows an organization's profit or loss for a stated period. It is created by comparing the **revenue** generated with the expenses incurred to produce those revenues, and then adding any gains and subtracting any losses during the reported period.

An organization's operations generate revenue, usually from sales, and incur expenses in creating such revenue. Normally revenue will exceed expenses. However, it is not unusual to find a business that shows minimal net profit or even a loss. If expenses consistently exceed revenue, an organization may eventually run out of money and be forced to close.

Gains and losses result from the organization's financial activities other than its normal operating activities. For example, the sale of assets for more than the amount at which they are recorded on the balance sheet is indicated as a gain on the income statement, while a sale for less than the amount recorded on a balance sheet would be indicated as a loss.

The income statement describes the organization's experience over time, whereas a balance sheet lists the organization's assets and liabilities at a given moment.

Revenue

An organization generates revenue from sales of its products or services. For a nonprofit organization, revenue might come from dues, memberships, or contributions. Revenue does not include gains from the sale of property, plant, or equipment.

Expenses

Expenses are measured by the assets relinquished or consumed in the process of delivering goods or rendering services to customers. The nature of these expenses depends on the nature of the organization. Every operating expense can be categorized as either a general operating expense or an expense directly related to sales. An expense directly related to sales is one that increases or decreases in direct relationship to sales, such as the cost of goods sold, commissions, or the cost of the materials used to ship goods that have been sold. If there are no sales, these types of expenses are not incurred. A general operating expense is one that is necessary to run the business but bears no direct relationship to the volume of sales, such as a retail store's cost for heating or

---

Revenue
The inflow of assets, usually cash or accounts receivable, resulting from the sale of products or the rendering of services to customers.

air conditioning its place of business. Whether sales are booming or nonexistent, the cost of heating or air conditioning is incurred each day.

The cost of goods sold is an expense that deserves special note. Although the term "cost of goods sold" applies to any business, the type of business dictates the expenses that are included. In retail operations, the cost of goods sold is usually the business's cost to purchase its merchandise and for shipping. In manufacturing operations, the cost of goods sold includes the cost of the materials to make the product, the labor involved, and the overhead to make the product. In a service operation, such as an insurance agency, the cost of goods sold is minimal or nonexistent because no physical product is being sold. The income statements of most service businesses do not include a cost of goods sold category.

Unlike most other operating expenses, the cost of goods sold corresponds directly to sales. Calculating cost of goods sold is an accounting method for appropriately recognizing as expense the cost of purchasing inventory. Inventory is an asset that appears on the balance sheet until it is sold. Directly showing the purchase of inventory as periodic lump sums to represent expense on the income statement would skew the income statement because the purchase and the resale of inventory are not perfectly timed. Businesses often stock up months before a busy sales season and may not restock as their busy sales season nears an end. The cost of goods sold formula is a method of recognizing the expense of acquiring goods to sell and coordinating it directly with sales on the income statement.

The cost of goods sold expense that appears on the income statement is calculated according to this formula:

	Beginning inventory
+	Additions to inventory
=	Amount that could have been sold
−	Ending inventory
=	Cost of goods sold

If there are no sales, the ending inventory is equal to the sum of the beginning inventory plus any additions to it. Notice that under this formula, there can be a cost of goods sold only if there has been a sale that lowers the ending inventory from the amount that could have been sold. Once an item of inventory has been sold, its cost appears as an expense on the income statement by operation of the cost of goods sold formula.

Gross Profit

The cost of goods sold expense, which is shown separately from other expenses, is subtracted from sales on the income statement to arrive at the **gross profit**. This is sometimes referred to as the trading section of the income

Gross profit
An income statement value that represents sales or operating revenue minus the cost of goods sold.

statement. Any item deducted from revenue to arrive at gross profit is said to be included in the trading section.

Gross profit expressed as a percentage of gross sales is sometimes called the **gross margin**. Similarly, the gross profit expressed as a percentage of the cost of goods sold is sometimes called mark-up.

Operating Income

General operating expenses are deducted from gross profit to arrive at an **operating income** amount.

Not all money a business spends is counted as operating expenses. To be recorded as operating expenses, expenses must be incurred in the business's ordinary operations. For this reason, capital expenditures appear on the income statement gradually over time, normally as a depreciation expense. A depreciation expense spreads out the expense of a large purchase over time and may be calculated based on the item's life expectancy or, more arbitrarily for accounting convenience, according to generally accepted accounting principles (GAAP). Depreciation is a common operating expense. As such, depreciation also lowers the business's net income for tax purposes. See the exhibit "Capital Expenditures—An Example."

> ### Capital Expenditures—An Example
> If a manufacturing business bought a piece of real estate, the money spent on the purchase would not be an expense item on the manufacturer's income statement. Instead, the purchase would appear on the manufacturer's balance sheet as a reduction of one asset, cash, and an increase in another asset, real estate.
>
> Large purchases of land, buildings, or equipment are called capital expenditures. These capital expenditures appear on the balance sheet but do not appear as one-time lump sums on the income statement. Although capital expenditures may seem to be very large operating expenses, showing such large expenditures as a one-time lump sum expense on an income statement would skew the income statement because capital investments and expenditures are not considered operations.

[DA06414]

Gross margin (gross profit margin)
The percentage of sales remaining after deducting the cost of goods sold from sales, calculated by dividing gross profit by sales.

Operating income
An income statement value that reflects income that results from the normal operations of the business during the period covered by the statement; calculated as the gross profit less selling, general, and administrative expenses.

Net Income

If expenses and losses exceed revenue and gains for the period, then the organization has a net loss and is not operating profitably. Negative net income is known as a net loss. Positive net income for a for-profit business is often called net profit. The ability to earn net income is essential to a business's continuation. Anything that decreases revenue or increases expenses threatens a business's profit and its future. Net income is calculated in this way:

Net income = Revenue − Expenses (including depreciation) + Gains − Losses − Taxes

For nonprofit organizations, a difference between revenue and expenses might be called by a different name, such as "contribution to surplus" or "excess of revenue over expenses." Just as with for-profit businesses, nonprofit organizations require an amount of income that will cover expenses in order to continue operating. Income statements for different organizations are similar in format but may not be exactly alike. See the exhibit "Income Statement for Manufacturing, Inc.."

Income Statement for Manufacturing, Inc.

Manufacturing, Inc., GAAP Income Statement
For the year ended 12/31/20X1

Sales	$400,000,000
Cost of Goods Sold	300,000,000
Gross Profit	$100,000,000
General Operating Expenses	
Advertising	$6,000,000
Office	8,000,000
Warehouse	22,000,000
Depreciation	2,000,000
Total Operating Expenses	38,000,000
Operating Income	$62,000,000
Other Income and Expenses	
Investment Income	$1,500,000
Interest Expenses	20,000,000
Total Other Expenses	18,500,000
Net Income Before Taxes	$43,500,000
Income Taxes	15,225,000
Net Income	$28,275,000

From the Income Statement:

- The income statement for Manufacturing, Inc., shows gross sales of $400,000,000, gross profit of $100,000,000, and a before-tax net income of $43,500,000.

- Net income is colloquially known as the "bottom line" because it appears as the bottom item in a listing of revenue and expenses. Manufacturing's net income after paying income taxes is $28,275,000.

Comprehensive Income

In the late 1990s, the Financial Accounting Standards Board (FASB) began requiring organizations to report not only their net income but also their comprehensive income. **Comprehensive income** is defined in Concepts Statement 6 and in Statement of Financial Accounting Standards No. 130 as "the change in equity [net assets] of a business enterprise during a period from transactions and other events and circumstances from nonowner sources. It includes all changes in equity during a period except those resulting from investments by owners and distributions to owners."[1] In other words, comprehensive income includes an organization's net income from the income statement plus other income that is not required to be reported on the income statement.

This other income that is not reported is referred to as "other comprehensive income." Other comprehensive income can include unrealized gains and losses on securities for sale, foreign currency translation gains or losses, and minimum pension liability adjustments. FASB allows comprehensive income to be reported on the income statement or as a separate financial statement, the Statement of Comprehensive Income. See the exhibit "Statement of Comprehensive Income for Manufacturing, Inc.."

> **Comprehensive income**
> A measure of income that goes beyond that reported on the income statement by including items such as unrealized gains and losses.

Statement of Comprehensive Income for Manufacturing, Inc.

Manufacturing, Inc. Statement of Comprehensive Income
For the year ended 12/31/20X1

Net Income (from income statement)	$28,275,000
Other comprehensive income (net of taxes)	
Change in unrealized appreciation (depreciation) of investments	(11,500,000)
Foreign currency translation gains (losses)	750,000
Changes in minimum pension liability	(1,250,000)
Comprehensive Income	$16,275,000

From the Statement of Comprehensive Income:
- The net income for Manufacturing is carried over from the Income Statement.
- The Statement of Comprehensive Income shows stakeholders that Manufacturing's comprehensive income was significantly lower than their reported net income.

[DA06417]

Creation of this reporting standard was driven by concerns that other comprehensive income of some organizations was materially important to the stakeholders of the organization and, therefore, needed to be reported.

STATEMENT OF CHANGES IN SHAREHOLDERS' EQUITY AND STATEMENT OF CASH FLOWS

Stakeholders often need more information about an organization than what the balance sheet and income statement can provide. Two other important financial statements are the statement of changes in shareholders' equity and the statement of cash flows.

Two key financial statements measure activity during a fixed period:

- The statement of changes in shareholders' equity explains increases or decreases in capital accounts.
- The statement of cash flows summarizes the cash effects of an organization's operating, investing, and financing activities.

Statement of Changes in Shareholders' Equity

The **statement of changes in shareholders' equity** shows changes from the beginning to the end of the period for each major component of the capital accounts that constitute shareholders' equity.

There are four major components of shareholders' equity:

- Paid-in capital
- Retained earnings
- Accumulated other comprehensive income
- Treasury stock

> **Statement of changes in shareholders' equity**
> The financial statement that explains any changes that have occurred in the organization's capital accounts during a specific period.

Paid-in Capital

Paid-in capital is the amount of money raised by issuing stock, calculated as the par value of the stock issued plus any additional paid-in capital over the par value. Par value is an arbitrary dollar value that a corporation assigns to its shares. Most new stock is issued at very low or no par value and is sold for whatever price the market is willing to pay. Par value generally bears no relationship to the market value of a share of stock.

For example, assume that during the fiscal year, Manufacturing, Inc., issued 300,000 shares of common stock, with a par value of $0.15 per share, for $20.00 per share. The issuance of the stock would be recorded as $45,000 (300,000 × $0.15) attributed to common stock at par value plus additional paid-in capital of $5,955,000 [300,000 × ($20.00 − $0.15)]. Therefore, the total paid-in capital was $6,000,000.

> **Paid-in capital**
> The total amount invested in an organization by the owners.

Retained Earnings

An organization may use retained earnings for purposes such as funding capital expenditures, research and development, or debt repayment. Dividends are the portion of an organization's profits that is paid to shareholders. Dividends are not deducted as expenses to arrive at net income; therefore, they are deducted from net income to determine the change in retained earnings from one period to the next. One of the purposes of the retained earnings section of shareholders' equity is to connect the income statement to the balance sheet by indicating how much of the net income of the company is being reinvested for ongoing and future business needs rather than distributed to the owners in the form of dividends.

Accumulated Other Comprehensive Income

Comprehensive income includes a corporation's net income from the income statement plus other income that is not required to be reported on the income statement. This other income that is not reported is referred to as "other comprehensive income." Accumulated other comprehensive income is the cumulative other comprehensive income from previous periods.

There are three components of other comprehensive income: change in unrealized appreciation or depreciation of investments (these are the same as unrealized gains and losses), foreign currency translation gains or losses, and changes in minimum pension liability.

Treasury Stock

Treasury stock
A corporate stock issued as fully paid to a stockholder and subsequently reacquired by the corporation to use for business purposes.

When a corporation buys back its own stock, those shares become **treasury stock**. The cost of treasury stock is deducted from shareholders' equity because the company used an asset (cash) to buy back stock that it had previously issued. The company initially received payment for the stock and included it in the paid-in capital section of shareholders' equity. See the exhibit "GAAP Statement of Changes in Shareholders' Equity."

Statement of Cash Flows

The purpose of the statement of cash flows is to identify the sources and uses of cash during the year, essentially reconciling any difference in the beginning and ending balances in the cash account.

Depreciation expense
An accounting method that spreads out the expense of a purchase over the life expectancy of the item.

This statement is used to determine an organization's ability to generate positive future cash flows, its ability to meet its financial obligations, and its need for additional financing. It is also used to determine the reasons for any differences between net income and associated cash receipts and disbursements, such as those resulting from loan proceeds or repayments, increases or decreases in accounts receivable, or **depreciation expense**. See the exhibit "Statement of Cash Flows."

GAAP Statement of Changes in Shareholders' Equity

Manufacturing, Inc.
GAAP Statement of Changes in Shareholders' Equity
For the Year Ended December 31, 20X1

Paid-in Capital:	
Beginning balance, January 1, 20X1	$ 19,105,000
Common stock issued	6,000,000
Ending balance, December 31, 20X1	25,105,000
Retained Earnings:	
Beginning balance, January 1, 20X1	61,845,000
Net income	28,275,000
Shareholder dividends	(3,500,000)
Ending balance, December 31, 20X1	86,620,000
Accumulated Other Comprehensive Income (Loss)	
Beginning balance, January 1, 20X1	13,525,000
Other comprehensive income (loss)	(12,000,000)
Ending balance, December 31, 20X1	1,525,000
Treasury Stock	
Beginning balance, January 1, 20X1	(1,250,000)
Repurchase of shares	(500,000)
Ending balance, December 31, 20X1	(1,750,000)
Total Shareholders' Equity as of December 31, 20X1	$111,500,000

[DA06430]

The statement of cash flows is divided into three sections: operating activities, investing activities, and financing activities.[2]

Operating Activities

The operating activities section starts with the net income figure, which reflects operating cash inflows (such as cash receipts from the sale of goods and services) and operating cash outflows (such as cash payments to suppliers and employees). However, the net income figure also reflects noncash revenue (such as an increase in accounts receivable) and noncash expenses (such as depreciation and an increase in accounts payable). Although changes in these amounts either increase or decrease net income, they do not reflect the receipt or use of cash. For example, depreciation is deducted as an expense on the income statement, but no cash payment is made by the organization. Therefore, to determine the actual cash generated by operating activities,

Statement of Cash Flows

Manufacturing, Inc.
GAAP Statement of Cash Flows
For the Year Ended December 31, 20X1

Cash Flows From Operating Activities:	
Net income	$ 28,275,000
Add (Deduct) Items Not Affecting Cash:	
Depreciation expense	2,000,000
Decrease (increase) in accounts receivable	(25,000)
Decrease (increase) in inventories and supplies	(125,000)
Increase (decrease) in payables	345,000
Cash from (used for) operating activities	$30,470,000
Cash Flows From Investing Activities:	
Additions to property, plant, & equipment	(32,750,000)
Cash from (used for) investing activities	$(32,750,000)
Cash Flows From Financing Activities:	
Proceeds from issuance of debt	0
Proceeds from issuance of common stock	6,000,000
Disposition (purchase) of treasury stock	(500,000)
Dividends paid to shareholders	(3,500,000)
Cash from (used for) financing activities	$2,000,000
Increase (Decrease) in Cash	$(280,000)
Cash, Beginning of Year	330,000
Cash, End of Year	$ 50,000

[DA06431]

noncash expenses (such as depreciation) are added back to the net income figure and noncash revenues (such as an increase in accounts receivable) are deducted from the net income figure.

Investing Activities

The investing activities section reflects the actual cash inflows and outflows that have occurred as a result of activities such as the sale or purchase of property, plant, or equipment; the acquisition or disposal of marketable securities; and the receipt of payments on loans made to others.

Financing Activities

The financing activities section reports the cash inflows and outflows that have occurred as a result of activities such as issuing or repurchasing stock, bonds, or mortgages. Financing activities include cash payments for the payment of dividends.

SUPPLEMENTAL SOURCES OF FINANCIAL INFORMATION

While the balance sheet, income statement, and other financial statements provide valuable information about an organization, a more complete financial picture of an organization is developed by examining additional sources of financial information.

Organizations provide a large amount of financial information to their stakeholders. A majority of this information is included in financial statements.

However, some information is best communicated through other reports, such as these:

- Notes to financial statements
- Securities and Exchange Commission (SEC) filings
- Company annual reports

Notes to Financial Statements

Financial statements are the central feature of financial reporting. However, in the interest of complete disclosure, some information is better provided, or can only be provided, in notes to the financial statements.

Notes to financial statements contain additional details that are disclosed to explain or amplify the information presented in financial statements. The information provided is essential to understanding the statements and has long been considered an integral part of financial statements prepared in accordance with generally accepted accounting principles (GAAP). These items are included in the notes:

- A brief description of the nature of the company's operations
- A summary of significant accounting policies and changes to accounting policies
- A detailed listing of long-term debt
- A summary of loss contingencies and other commitments (such as long-term rental commitments for leased property)
- A report of selected financial information by business segment
- Any other explanations that management deems necessary to help the user understand the financial statements

Of the information provided in the notes to the financial statements, a summary of loss contingencies is often the most directly related to the risk management and insurance issues of an organization. A contingency is defined as an existing condition, situation, or set of circumstances involving uncertainty as to a gain or a loss to a company. The contingencies note to the financial statements summarizes any material loss contingencies to which the company is subject.

Companies record accruals for loss contingencies directly to the balance sheet and income statement when it is probable that a liability (loss) has been incurred and the amount can be reasonably estimated. However, companies can also be subject to loss contingencies for which the results are not reasonably estimable at the time of the preparation of the financial statements. In such cases, the fact that the company is exposed to possible loss and liability must be disclosed in the notes to the financial statements to ensure that the statements will not be misleading. The disclosure should include the nature of the contingency, the potential damages, and a statement of the likelihood that future events will confirm the loss.

Examples of loss contingencies include these:

- Current or pending litigation
- Obligations related to product warranties and product defects
- Risk of damage to or uninsured loss of company property by fire, explosion, or another hazard
- Hold-harmless agreements

Securities and Exchange Commission Filings

All publicly traded companies are required to file quarterly and annual financial information with the SEC. They are also required to file a notice of any potential material events that might affect the company's financial condition. The filings that the users of financial statements access most often are the annual Form 10-K report, the quarterly Form 10-Q report, and the Form 8-K material event report. See the exhibit "EDGAR: Electronic Data Gathering, Analysis, and Retrieval System."

> ### EDGAR: Electronic Data Gathering, Analysis, and Retrieval System
>
> The SEC developed EDGAR to automate the collection, validation, indexing, acceptance, and forwarding of registration statements, periodic reports, and other forms that it requires all foreign and domestic companies to submit. EDGAR provides a means of disseminating time-sensitive corporate information to investors and others that increases the efficiency and fairness of the securities market. Underwriters can access most of the information collected by EDGAR through its Web site (www.sec.gov/edgar.shtml) free of charge.

[DA06763]

Form 10-K

Form 10-K, which publicly traded companies must file annually with the SEC, is similar to the company's own annual report, except that it contains more-detailed information about the company's business, finances, and management. It also includes information not contained in the company's annual report to shareholders, such as the company's bylaws and other legal documents.

The SEC recognizes three different types of filers with regard to the 10-K deadline. Large accelerated filers (companies with more than $700 million in public float—that is, companies that have a total market value of at least $700 million and whose stock is held by public investors rather than company officers, directors, or controlling-interest investors) must file form 10-K within sixty days after the end of the company's fiscal year. Companies that have at least a $75 million public float (accelerated filers) must file form 10-K within seventy-five days after the end of the company's fiscal year. Companies with less than a $75 million public float (nonaccelerated filers) must file form 10-K within ninety days after the end of their fiscal year.

Form 10-Q

Publicly traded companies are also required to file a quarterly report with the SEC on Form 10-Q. The 10-Q report is an abbreviated version of the 10-K report. The information contained in the 10-Q report includes unaudited financial statements, a Management Discussion & Analysis (MD&A) for the quarter, and a list of material events that have occurred with the company during the prior three months. The 10-Q, which provides a continuing view of the company's financial position, is filed for each of the first three quarters of the fiscal year. Companies with a public float of at least $75 million must file form 10-Q within forty days after the end of each fiscal quarter. Companies with less than a $75 million public float must file form 10-Q within forty-five days after the end of each fiscal quarter.

Form 8-K

Form 8-K is the "current report" that publicly traded companies must file with the SEC. It is used to announce major events that shareholders should know about.

Events that trigger an 8-K filing include these:

- Material definitive agreements entered into or terminated that are not in the ordinary course of the company's business, such as a definitive agreement to sell a significant operating division to an unrelated company
- Release of nonpublic information about a company's financial condition
- Creation of a direct financial obligation (such as a long-term operating lease) under an off-balance sheet arrangement—that is, an arrangement that does not have to be recorded in the financial statements

- Change of independent auditor certifying the financial statements
- Departure or election of directors and departure or appointment of principal officers

While these events are also noted in the management discussion section of the 10-Q and 10-K reports, the 8-K must be filed with the SEC within four business days of the triggering event to provide shareholders with information about important events in a timely manner so that they do not have to wait until the next 10-Q or 10-K is filed. See the exhibit "SEC Filings Comparison."

SEC Filings Comparison

Form	Filing Frequency	Purpose
10-K	Annual	• Comprehensive view of financial condition. Annual report, similar to company annual report, but with more detailed information.
10-Q	Quarterly	• Continuing view of financial condition. An abbreviated 10-K report.
8-K	Within four days of the triggering event	• Current announcement of major event for organization.

[DA06337]

SEC 2010 Rules on Enhanced Disclosure on Proxy Statements

In 2010, the SEC issued rules regarding enhanced disclosure in proxy and information statements. Two that pertain directly to the risk management of a company include these:

- The relationship of a company's compensation policies and practices to risk management, which includes whether a company has incentivized excessive or inappropriate risk-taking by employees. Also included is a requirement for a narrative disclosure about the company's compensation policies and practices for all employees, not just executive officers, if the compensation policies and practices create risks that are reasonably likely to have a material adverse effect on the company.

- Board leadership structure and the board's role in risk oversight, which includes whether the company has combined or separated the chief executive officer and chairman position, and why the company believes its structure is the most appropriate for the company at the time of the filing. Also included is whether and why a company has a lead independent director and the specific role of such director.

Securities and Exchange Commission, "SEC Approves Enhanced Disclosure About Risk, Compensation and Corporate Governance," www.sec.gov/news/press/2009/2009-268.htm (accessed March 30, 2012). [OV08731]

Company Annual Reports

An annual report is a formal report on the company's performance for the stated year. The audience for the annual report is the company's shareholders and other interested parties such as customers, vendors, and investors. Insurance professionals find the annual report a valuable source of information about the company's business purpose and philosophy, its financial results, and its directions for the future. This information helps provide a general background for making specific underwriting decisions.

The United States SEC requires a publicly traded company to keep shareholders informed of its financial state on a regular basis. The annual report is the main method of reporting how the company is performing and of explaining the scope of the business, its mission, and its management philosophy. The annual report consists of sections required by the SEC and other information the company believes is appropriate to provide. The required sections include these:

- Financial statements and notes
- Auditor's report
- Report of management
- Management's discussion and analysis of results of operations and financial condition
- Selected financial data

Additional information that companies usually provide, but that is not required, includes these items:

- Financial highlights
- Letter to shareholders
- Corporate message
- Names of the board of directors and management
- Corporate information such as the date of the annual meeting; stock trading information; and contact information for investor relations, media relations, and company news

Report of Management

The report of management is a report to the users of the financial statements in which the company's management acknowledges its responsibility for the quality and integrity of the company's financial statements, as well as for the accuracy and effectiveness of internal controls over financial reporting. It also attests that management's assessment of the internal controls has been audited by an independent accounting firm. The report is signed by the chairman of the board and the chief financial officer.

Management's Discussion and Analysis of Results

Management's discussion and analysis of results of operations and financial condition (MD&A) is essential to understanding a company's financial statements. The SEC has set forth three goals for the MD&A:

- Provide a narrative explanation that enables users to view the company from management's perspective
- Improve overall financial disclosure and provide the context within which financial statements should be analyzed
- Provide information about the quality and potential variability of the company's income and cash flow that addresses the likelihood that past performance indicates future performance

An MD&A should explain the company's operating results and condition. It should also provide insight into the opportunities, challenges, and risks faced by the company as well as the actions the company is taking to address them.

The **Sarbanes-Oxley Act of 2002** prompted the SEC to issue interpretive guidance for improved MD&A disclosure in three areas:

- Liquidity and capital resources, including off-balance sheet arrangements, contractual agreements, and contingent liabilities
- Certain trading activities involving non-exchange-traded contracts accounted for at fair market value, including buying or selling private securities
- Relationships and transactions with persons or entities that derive benefits from nonindependent relationships with the company or the company's related parties

The reasoning behind the SEC's provision of interpretive guidance in these areas was to bring greater **transparency** to financial reporting. See the exhibit "Letter to Shareholders."

Sarbanes-Oxley Act of 2002
A federal statutory law governing corporate directors in the areas of investor protection, internal controls, and penalties, both civil and criminal.

Transparency
In the context of financial accounting, the provision of sufficient detail regarding transactions to enable a prudent investor to understand the economic effect of those transactions on the company's financial statements.

Letter to Shareholders

The letter to shareholders is usually written by the chairman of the board of directors, the chief executive officer, or both. It provides a review and analysis of the significant events of the year and typically addresses any issues and successes the company experienced. One of the most anticipated letters to shareholders every year is from Berkshire Hathaway's Warren Buffett. Buffett's letters not only discuss Berkshire Hathaway's performance but also his views on a variety of topics, including finance, accounting, regulation, investments, and insurance.

[DA06338]

INCOME STATEMENT TREND ANALYSIS

Risk management professionals need to be able not only to read financial statements but also to perform trend analysis to evaluate how an organization has been performing. Trend analysis will provide a more complete understanding of an organization's financial condition.

Trend analysis studies changes in values from year to year. This technique is effective for identifying trends for items such as total assets, revenue, or net income. Two methods of conducting trend analysis are year-to-year analysis and base-year-to-date analysis. Year-to-year analysis determines the percentage change in values for statement items between consecutive years in the period under consideration. Base-year-to-date analysis uses the earliest year of the period under consideration as a base year and determines the percentage change in statement item values for each successive year relative to that base year.

Trend analysis
A comparison of financial statement data across two or more periods.

Although trend analysis techniques can be applied to the balance sheet to quantify the changes in assets and liabilities over time, this type of analysis is usually applied to the income statement to quantify the changes in a company's profitability over time. An analyst's attention is focused on the major components of the income statement: revenue, cost of revenue, gross profit, operating expenses, and net income. For example, suppose that an analyst's goal is to quantify the growth rates of revenue and net income over the most recent three-year period. This information might be used in combination with the results of a more comprehensive financial statement analysis, or it might provide a basis for projecting a company's performance for the coming year. Such an analysis begins with calculating the year-to-year percentage change for sales and net income.

Expert Data Manager (EDM) is an Internet company whose revenues are being reduced by lower advertising rates. Advertising rates are one of EDM's primary sources of income. During the same accounting period, EDM's salary expenses, some of its largest expense factors, are increasing to attract and retain essential staff members.

Overview of the Procedure

To calculate the percentage change of an amount from one year to the next, divide the change from the first year to the subsequent year by the first year amount, and multiply the result by 100 to express it as a percentage. See the exhibit "Example of Calculating the Annual Percentage Change."

The next step is to perform the same calculations on selected components of EDM's income statements over three years to produce an annual percentage change income statement. The final step is to interpret the results.

Example of Calculating the Annual Percentage Change

	Amounts in Thousands Fiscal Year Ended	
	Dec. 31, 20X5	Dec. 31, 20X4
Revenue	$25,000	$30,000
Net Income	$1,200	$1,500

Percentage change from 20X4 to 20X5:
Revenue ($25,000 − $30,000) ÷ $30,000 = (.166) = −16.6%
Net Income ($1,200 − $1,500) ÷ $1,500 = (0.2) = −20.0%

[DA08745]

Annual Percentage Change

EDM's income statement figures used to calculate the annual percentage change over three years are not included, but the results of the calculations are provided. See the exhibit "EDM's Annual Percentage Change Income."

EDM's Annual Percentage Change Income

	Income Statements Percentage Change From Prior Year		
	20X5 – 20X4	20X4 – 20X3	20X3 – 20X2
Revenue	−16.6%	−8%	2%
Cost of revenue	24	15	10
Gross profit	−10	−7	0
Expenses:			
Selling, general, and administrative	21	15	9
Research and development	−9	11	24
Other expenses	−6	14	25
Total expenses	22	17	12
Operating income	−17	−11	19
Investment income	4	5	−2
Income before income taxes	−19	−18	22
Income taxes	−21	−17	23
Net income	−20%	−18%	21%

[DA08746]

Interpreting the Results

An analyst can draw several conclusions about EDM's financial trends from these results:

- Declining revenue and operating income are consistent with lower advertising rates, one of EDM's primary sources of income.
- Higher salary costs to attract and retain essential staff members are reflected in higher cost of revenue and higher selling, general, and administrative expenses.
- Management apparently became aware of its worsening financial position as it sought to lower its research and development and other expenses in the last two years. However, the increasing salary expenses were a large portion of the company's overall expenses, and EDM's total expenses continued to rise.

The analyst could conclude that EDM must change its current trends to remain solvent. Specifically, it must diversify its sources of revenue to not be as dependent on advertising, as advertising rates may decline to a level that is inadequate to maintain long-term operations at EDM. This may not be the appropriate time to decrease spending on research and development, as this activity could create another revenue source. EDM must also find a way to contain its salary expenses, such as through contract labor or through profit sharing with employees in return for lower salaries.

Apply Your Knowledge

John is a risk management professional working for XYZ Corporation, which is experiencing rapid growth. XYZ's annual percentage change income statement shows the corporation's percentage change associated with total operating expenses closely parallels the percentage change in revenue. What should that indicate to John?

Feedback: John should recognize the parallel of total operating expenses with revenue indicates the corporation's management has maintained control over its operating expenses despite XYZ's rapid growth.

ANALYZING LIQUIDITY RISK

A risk management professional should be able to determine how well an organization can meet its obligation to pay cash to others because a deficiency in this area could signal significant financial risk for the organization.

Ratio analysis provides risk management professionals with easily comparable standard measures of performance and is one of the most popular methods of analyzing an organization's financial statements. Ratios can highlight both

> **Ratio analysis**
> A financial analysis tool used to study the financial condition of an account; two or more data items from accounting records of a company are related to one another and the result is compared to results for prior accounting periods or for similar businesses.

Liquidity
The ease with which an asset can be converted to cash with little or no loss of value.

Working capital
A liquidity measure that is calculated by subtracting current liabilities from current assets. It is used to determine a company's ability to finance immediate operations (to buy inventory, finance growth, and obtain credit).

relationships among items that appear within a single financial statement and relationships among items on different financial statements. As a result, ratios can be used to analyze a single company or to compare two companies.

One of the more useful applications of ratio analysis is measuring **liquidity** of an organization. Liquidity refers to a company's ability to convert assets to cash to satisfy its obligations. Most organizations are exposed to at least some degree of liquidity risk. Liquidity can be measured using **working capital**, the **current ratio**, and the **acid-test ratio (quick ratio)**, which are applied to values in an organization's balance sheet.

Max HR Software (MHRS) is an Internet company that sells software to help organizations perform their human resource functions more efficiently. MHRS has grown rapidly in the last couple of years. However, MHRS's management is concerned that its liquidity position may be inadequate to meet its obligations in the current year and has asked its risk management professional to assess this risk. See the exhibit "Balance Sheet for MHRS."

Balance Sheet for MHRS

MHRS
GAAP Balance Sheet
12/31/20X1

ASSETS			LIABILITIES AND SHAREHOLDERS' EQUITY	
Current Assets:			Current Liabilities:	
Cash	$ 50,000		Accounts Payable	$ 1,250,000
Accounts Receivable	125,000		Wages Payable	250,000
Inventory	1,500,000		Taxes Payable	3,750,000
Supplies	75,000		Short-Term Debt	15,000,000
Marketable Securities	15,000,000			
Noncurrent Assets:			Noncurrent Liabilities:	
Property, Plant, & Equipment			Long-Term Debt	200,000,000
Land	50,000,000		Total Liabilities	220,250,000
Buildings	100,000,000			
Equipment	50,000,000		Total Shareholders' Equity (Owners' Equity)	101,500,000
Less Accumulated Depreciation	10,000,000			
Intangible Assets	111,500,000			
Goodwill	3,500,000			
Total Assets	$ 321,750,000		Total Liabilities & Shareholders' Equity	$ 321,750,000

[DA08767]

Measuring Liquidity

The following sections show and explain the calculations for working capital; the current ratio; and the acid-test, or quick, ratio using the amounts provided in the balance sheet of MHRS.

Working Capital

Working capital is the excess of a company's current assets over its current liabilities.

> Working capital = Current assets − Current liabilities

Current assets are cash and assets that are likely to be converted to cash within one year of the balance sheet date—primarily marketable securities, accounts receivable, and inventory. Current liabilities are obligations that will need to be paid within the same one-year period, including accounts payable; the current portion of loans payable; and accrued expenses such as wages payable, interest payable, and taxes payable. Although a company may not have enough cash on hand to meet all its obligations for the next year, it usually expects to collect accounts receivable and sell inventory to provide the required cash.

> MHRS's balance sheet shows current assets of $16,750,000 and current liabilities of $20,250,000. Therefore, working capital can be calculated in this manner:
>
> = $16,750,000 − $20,250,000
>
> = ($3,500,000)

Current Ratio

Most financially sound companies have positive working capital. However, simply having positive or negative working capital does not give an analyst much information about how adequately that working capital will meet the company's upcoming obligations. The current ratio is a liquidity ratio that indicates the adequacy of a company's working capital to meet its current financial obligations.

> Current ratio = Current assets ÷ Current liabilities

To calculate MHRS's current ratio for the year 20X1, the current assets and current liabilities figures from the balance sheet are needed.

> The balance sheet shows current assets in 20X1 of $16,750,000 and current liabilities of $20,250,000. Therefore, MHRS's current ratio is calculated in this manner:
>
> = $16,750,000 ÷ $20,250,000
>
> = 0.83

Current ratio
A liquidity ratio that indicates the company's ability to meet its short-term financial obligations; calculated by dividing current assets by current liabilities.

Acid-test ratio (quick ratio)
A liquidity ratio that provides a measure of a company's ability to meet its current obligations if it cannot sell its inventory.

A result of 0.83 indicates that current liabilities are 21 percent higher than current assets. This is not a favorable financial condition, as it suggests that MHRS is unable to meet its current financial obligations.

Acid-Test Ratio

The acid-test ratio, or quick ratio, is a more conservative measure of liquidity than the current ratio because it includes only cash, marketable securities, and accounts receivable in its numerator.

> Acid-test ratio = (Cash + Marketable securities + Accounts receivable) ÷ Current liabilities

To calculate MHRS's acid-test ratio for the year 20X1, the cash, marketable securities, accounts receivable, and current liabilities from the balance sheet are needed.

> The balance sheet for 20X1 shows cash of $50,000, marketable securities of $15,000,000, accounts receivable of $125,000, and current liabilities of $20,250,000. Therefore, MHRS's acid-test ratio is calculated in this manner:
>
> = ($50,000 + $15,000,000 + $125,000) ÷ $20,250,000
>
> = 0.75

Interpreting the Results of Liquidity Ratio Analysis

MHRS's negative working capital amount of $3.5 million means it has greater current liabilities than current assets and therefore is in an illiquid financial position. This will likely cause problems with vendors when MHRS tries to buy products or services on credit or if it tries to incur additional short-term or long-term debt. A vendor may require a large deposit or prepayment before delivery. A financial institution may insist on a higher interest rate and a shorter amount of time to pay back a loan. These changes will further drain MHRS's cash resources and may make its ability to compete for customers more tenuous. However, the illiquid position may be temporary and resolved later in the year as sales of its products generate cash revenue.

When calculating the current ratio, a risk management professional should be aware that different inventory valuation methods produce different inventory values for the balance sheet and therefore can produce different values for the current ratio. For example, if MHRS uses the **LIFO method** of inventory valuation when costs are increasing, the inventory that it sells will be valued at a higher cost than the remaining unsold inventory. The remaining unsold inventory is a part of current assets and is valued lower than its current cost. That reduces the current ratio compared to what it would be if inventory were based on its current cost.

In contrast, if MHRS uses the **FIFO method** of inventory valuation, when costs are increasing, the inventory that it sells will be valued at a lower cost than the remaining unsold inventory.

LIFO method
An inventory valuing method that assumes that the last items brought into inventory are the first items taken out.

FIFO method
An inventory valuing method that assumes that the first items purchased are the first items sold.

The remaining unsold inventory is valued higher than its current cost, which increases the current ratio compared to what it would be if inventory were based on its current cost.

As with any type of comparative analysis, benchmarks are needed when one organization's results are compared with those of its industry or another organization. Without some basis for making comparisons, it is difficult—if not impossible—to determine whether a single value for a given ratio or percentage should be interpreted as superior, average, or below average. Most industry or trade organizations publish average industry ratios based on information submitted by their members.

A balance sheet provides a snapshot of an organization's position as of a certain date. The figures in the balance sheet can change significantly because of transactions entered into after that date. As the figures change, the ratios that rely on those figures also change.

Apply Your Knowledge

If MHRS can sell an additional $5 million of its products while holding the other current assets and current liabilities accounts constant, how would that affect its liquidity condition?

Feedback: It would cause the working capital to go from a negative $3.5 million to a positive $1.5 million. The current ratio would also move from 0.83 to 1.07. The acid-test ratio, or quick ratio, would move from 0.75 to 1.00. Most financially sound companies have positive working capital. So going from a negative to a positive working capital number is an indication of an improving liquidity condition. The results from the ratios should be compared to industry benchmarks to further assess MHRS's current liquidity condition.

CAPITAL STRUCTURE

The goal of financial managers is to maintain a capital structure that both meets the needs of the company and maximizes shareholder value.

Capital structure is a corporation's mix of long-term debt and equity. A company's capital structure decisions are important financial policy decisions that are made at senior levels of management. Although these decisions focus on the composition of debt and equity on the balance sheet, in effect, they create the assets a company has available and affect how the company deploys those assets. For a manufacturing company, financial policy decisions involve questions concerning the optimal mix of debt and equity.

An insurer's management makes analogous decisions when it determines the appropriate premium volume that can be supported by a given level of policyholders' surplus. In either type of organization, the capital structure either enables or restricts company growth. The mix of long-term debt and equity can significantly affect a company's value by influencing risk and return. The financial manager's goal is to maintain a capital structure that both meets the company's needs and maximizes the shareholders' wealth.

Financial managers decide how to raise and spend capital within a company. The exhibit illustrates how a company's funds flow in a cycle. The company sells common stock (equity), bonds (debt), or some other type of security in the capital market and receives cash, as shown by transaction (1) in the "Flow of Funds in a Company" exhibit. Proceeds from the security's sale are used to purchase assets (2). Cash returns from the assets can be retained in the company to finance operations or to finance the purchase of more assets (3). Ultimately, cash returns can be distributed to the suppliers of capital (4). Debt holders receive income in the form of interest payments, and equity holders can receive income as cash dividends. See the exhibit "Flow of Funds in a Company."

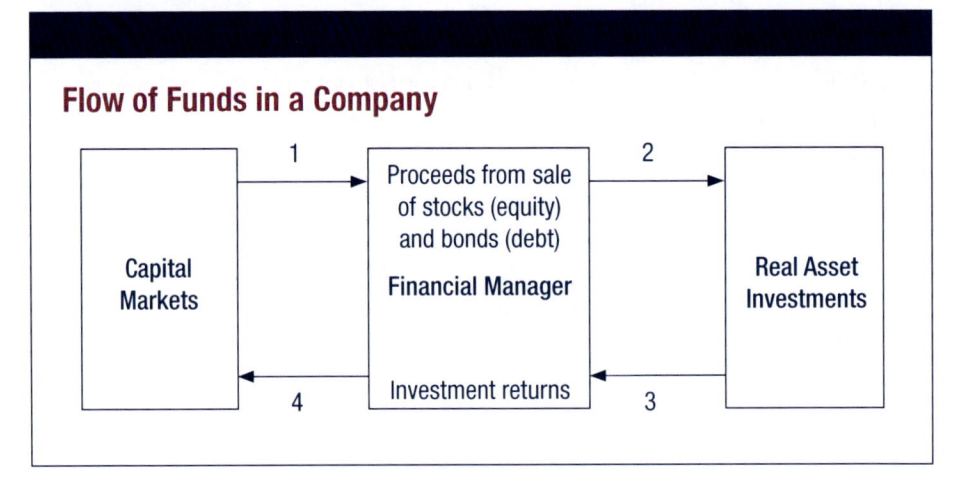

Flow of Funds in a Company

Capital Markets → (1) Proceeds from sale of stocks (equity) and bonds (debt) → Financial Manager → (2) → Real Asset Investments → (3) Investment returns → Financial Manager → (4) → Capital Markets

[DA02773]

Equity

Shareholders of the company have an equity interest, which is the right to whatever profits remain after all other expenses and creditors have been paid. The rights that shareholders have depend in part on whether they are common shareholders or preferred shareholders.

Common stock shares are the first security issued by a corporation and the last retired. Common shareholders are entitled to receive the residual earnings after bond and preferred shareholders, and consequently they bear the greatest risk. Although common shareholders are entitled to dividends, these dividends are paid only when declared.

Common shareholders are usually the voting owners of the company. With their right to vote for the members of the board, they can indirectly exercise control over company management. A company's management is supposed to act in the best interests of its shareholders and to take those actions that it believes will maximize share price—including actions regarding the appropriate capital structure of the company.

Preferred stock has features of both debt and equity. It can resemble debt if its dividend is a fixed obligation (either a stated percentage of the par value of the preferred share or a stated dollar amount per share) and resemble equity in that omission of a dividend does not result in the entire issue becoming payable immediately, as would a bond.

Preferred stock sits between pure debt and pure equity in terms of priority: preferred shareholders have priority over common shareholders but stand behind debt holders.

If the preferred stock is cumulative, any dividends that are not paid when due accumulate. Once a dividend is declared, the accumulated amount must be paid before any dividends are paid to common shareholders.

Some preferred stock, like some debt securities, is convertible into common stock under terms and conditions specified at the time of issue. This feature is used when the company desires to sell common stock to increase capital, but when selling is not economical because the company's stock price is depressed.

Debt

Under generally accepted accounting principles (GAAP), liabilities of companies are classified as either short-term liabilities or long-term liabilities.

Short-term liabilities are those due within one year and include bank loans, trade credit, commercial paper, and other sources of funds. Short-term liabilities are used to manage net working capital or to smooth variations in cash flow within an accounting cycle. The products available to do this depend on the nature of the business, although many companies use bank lines of credit. For larger and better-known companies, issuing commercial paper is a viable alternative. Long-term liabilities are liabilities that are due in more than one year and include bonds, mortgages, leases, and other variations of debt financing.

Debt capital is usually raised through the sale of bonds in the capital market. If the bonds are backed simply by the general assets of the corporation (that is, they carry no specific pledge of assets), they are referred to as debentures.

Bondholders and debenture holders have a priority claim on the company's assets ahead of preferred shareholders and common shareholders. If the collateral with which the bonds are secured is insufficient to repay the bonds, the bondholders become unsecured creditors for the remaining balance.

FINANCIAL LEVERAGE

Financial managers work to establish and maintain a capital structure that meets the needs of the company and maximizes shareholder value.

Financial leverage is the use of fixed cost funds (debt) to increase returns to shareholders. This increase is accomplished through the use of capital raised by the issue of debt to earn a rate of return higher than the fixed cost of that debt. As long as the cost of debt is less than the return on the additional capital, the shareholders benefit. Typically, the fixed financial cost amount reported on a company's income statement reflects interest payments on debt. This amount must be paid regardless of the amount of earnings available. The effect of financial leverage can be illustrated through financial leverage analysis.

Financial Leverage Analysis

Financial leverage analysis is a technique used for comparing earnings per share (EPS) under alternate capitalization plans with varying levels of debt and equity. The advantage of financial leverage analysis is that it provides a succinct portrayal of revenues and expenses under various circumstances.

Financial Leverage Analysis for Zeselle Company

To illustrate, assume that Zeselle Company has an all-equity capital structure of $5 million from 125,000 outstanding shares of stock, with earnings of $1 million. At that level, earnings per share are $8 ($1 million / 125,000 shares), and **return on equity (ROE)** is 20 percent ($1 million profit / $5 million in capital). Zeselle plans a major expansion that will require $2 million. After the expansion, with $7 million total capital, earnings are estimated to be $1.3 million, a $300,000 increase.

The company is considering raising the required funds by either selling common stock or issuing debt. An additional 50,000 common shares could be sold at $40 per share, while debt would require interest at 6 percent, or $120,000 per year. The exhibit shows EPS calculations under each of the financing plans, assuming that earnings before interest and tax (EBIT) is the estimated $1.3 million. See the exhibit "Zeselles Company Financial Results Under Two Financing Alternatives."

Zeselle's EPS is higher under the debt alternative than under the equity alternative, despite the fact that additional expense is incurred in the form of interest payable on the debt. Return on equity is also higher using debt alternative. Even though net income was reduced because of the interest expense from using debt, less equity was needed to finance Zeselle's operations. This illustrates the beneficial effects of financial leverage.

The leverage effect can also be viewed as the effect of adding equity or debt to the current capital. In the Zeselle example, the alternative that added $2

Return on equity (ROE)
A profitability ratio expressed as a percentage by dividing a company's net income by its net worth (book value). Depending on the context, net worth is sometimes called shareholders' equity, owners' equity, or policyholders' surplus.

Zeselles Company Financial Results Under Two Financing Alternatives

	All Common Stock (Equity)	All Debt (Financial Leverage)
Income Statement:		
EBIT	$1,300,000	$1,300,000
Interest expense	0	120,000[1]
Net income (NI)	$1,300,000	$1,180,000
Balance Sheet:		
Assets	$7,000,000	$7,000,000
Liabilities	$ 0	$2,000,000
Equity	7,000,000	5,000,000
Total (Liabilities and Shareholders' Equity)	$7,000,000	$7,000,000
Common Shares Outstanding (CSO)	175,000	125,000
Return on Equity (NI ÷ Equity)	18.57%	23.60%
Earnings per Share (NI ÷ CSO)	$7.43	$9.44

[1] $2,000,000 × 6% = $120,000

[DA02786]

million of equity produced $300,000 more in profit ($1.3 million − $1 million originally). The marginal ROE of the new equity is 15 percent ($300,000 / $2 million)—lower than the original 20 percent. The debt alternative produces only $180,000 additional profit after interest is paid, but the ROE on the existing shares increased because no new equity was issued.

Financial leverage can work in the opposite direction, as well. If the increase in Zeselle's net income in the example were less than $120,000, the EPS would decrease since the increase in net income would be less than the interest expense on the debt. Financial leverage analysis is used in the estimation of the optimum mix of equity and debt capital.

Tax Shield

Under federal tax law, interest on debt is deductible in calculating taxable income, but dividends paid to stockholders are not. As a result, more after-tax money is available to the company if it raises capital using debt rather than equity. The amount of income taxes saved because of the deductibility of interest expense is known as the tax shield. The tax shield effectively reduces the cost of the debt. The Zeselle leverage example ignored tax effects.

Limitations of Financial Leverage

The analysis of Zeselle suggests that it should raise capital by issuing debt because that alternative allows for an expected return on its investment that is greater than the cost of the debt. However, this strategy should not be taken to extremes.

Additional Cost of High Debt

Lenders require higher interest rates as debt increases, and additional investments by Zeselle may offer lower returns than previously earned. The higher cost of greater amounts of debt and the potentially lower returns from additional investments reduce the benefits of leverage.

Reduced Cash Flow Flexibility

Additional debt also reduces the flexibility that management has in managing cash and increases the company's liquidity risk by increasing the amount of cash flow required to pay the debt holders. These situations could also reduce the market value of the company.

Cost of Financial Distress

The concept of perfect capital markets assumes that bankruptcy costs are zero. In practice, bankruptcy involves legal and administrative costs, as well as the potential cost of selling assets at less than their true economic value. As a result, bondholders and stockholders receive less than they otherwise would. The difference between what they receive with and without bankruptcy is the cost of financial distress.

As its ratio of debt to equity rises, a company will experience an increased risk of defaulting on its debt and an increased potential of bankruptcy. The owners of the securities issued by the company, who will bear the costs associated with these events, will also assume more risk as the company's use of debt increases. Thus, increasing financial leverage has both a positive and a negative effect. The positive effect is the potential additional EPS. However, the probability of bankruptcy rises along with financial leverage. Bankruptcy has serious financial effects on both bondholders and stockholders. Under bankruptcy, bondholders are likely to see interest payments to them suspended, and there is the potential that they may not receive repayment of the full amount loaned to the company. Shareholders lose any dividends they would have received, and, since their claims are lower priority than those of all other creditors, stand to lose some or all of their investment.

At low levels of debt, the cost of financial distress is low. As the level of debt increases, the cost of financial distress increases until at some point it exceeds the EPS benefit from financial leverage. Once the cost of financial distress is greater than the EPS benefit, the value of the company will start to decline. Therefore, management must carefully consider the maximum amount of financial leverage it can use before negatively affecting the value of the company.

OPERATING LEVERAGE

It is essential that a risk management professional be able to analyze the cost structure of an organization when assessing its financial risk.

The components of an organization's cost structure should be analyzed in terms of their ability to influence operating leverage. These components and the resulting operating leverage create advantages and disadvantages for an organization, which can best be understood through an illustration of the effect of changing sales revenue on different cost structures.

Analyzing Cost Structure

How an organization structures its cost of production affects its financial risk. Cost of production has two components—fixed and variable costs. Fixed costs are incurred in the production of products or services and do not change when the amount of products or services produced changes; examples include rent, property tax, and interest. In contrast, variable costs are those expenses that do change when the amount of products or services that are produced changes, such as direct labor and raw materials.

An organization can either structure its costs of production with a high percentage of fixed costs and a correspondingly low percentage of variable costs or structure them with a low percentage of fixed costs and a correspondingly high percentage of variable costs. There are advantages and disadvantages for each structure.

If an organization chooses to structure its costs with a high percentage of fixed costs and a low percentage of variable costs, it is considered to have high operating leverage. This means the high percentage of fixed costs of the organization's cost structure will be leveraged to make its operating profit more volatile. A small increase in the amount of sales can cause a relatively large increase in operating income. However, the disadvantage of this structure is that a small decrease in the amount of sales can cause a relatively large decrease in operating income.

An organization with a low percentage of fixed costs, and therefore a low operating leverage, will have a lower volatility of operating profit. This is a disadvantage when sales increase, because operating profits will not increase as much as they would with a highly leveraged organization. The advantage is that, when sales decrease, operating profits will not decrease as much as they would with a highly leveraged organization.

The degree of operating leverage is determined by how strong an effect it has on the volatility of an organization's operating profit. The strength of the effect can be measured using this formula:

Degree of operating leverage = % change in operating profit ÷ % change in sales

Operating Leverage Example

To see how operational leverage can vary based on an organization's revenue and expense structures, the income statements for two organizations can be compared—for example, those of two lawnmower equipment companies, Atley Tractors and Zelles Tractor Equipment. The primary difference between these two organizations is that Zelles builds its own lawnmowers rather than purchasing them from a manufacturer. Both Atley and Zelles have the same level of sales, charge the same prices for their lawnmowers, and earn the same amount of operating profit. The difference between the two organizations is the way in which their production costs are structured. While Atley has variable expenses per unit equal to 80 percent of its average price ($400 ÷ $500) and fixed expenses of $1 million, Zelles has variable expenses per unit equal to 50 percent of the sales price ($250 ÷ $500) and fixed expenses of $4 million. These differences alter the operational leverage, and therefore the financial risk, of the two organizations. See the exhibit "Comparative Income Statements for Atley Tractors and Zelles Tractor Equipment—Expense Category Basis."

Comparative Income Statements for Atley Tractors and Zelles Tractor Equipment—Expense Category Basis

	Atley		Zelles
Price per unit	$500	P	$500
Quantity of units sold	20,000	Q	20,000
Variable cost per unit	$400	V	$250
Fixed cost	$1,000,000	F	$4,000,000
Interest expense	$300,000	I	$300,000
Average tax rate	40%	t	40%
	Year Ending 12/31/XX		Year Ending 12/31/XX
Net sales	$10,000,000	P × Q	$10,000,000
Variable costs	(8,000,000)	V × Q	(5,000,000)
Fixed costs	(1,000,000)	F	(4,000,000)
Operating profit	$1,000,000	OP	$1,000,000

[DA08760]

Suppose that both organizations suffer a ten-week business interruption in the wake of a hurricane. Both organizations lose 20 percent of their sales for the year because of the interruption, and the number of lawnmowers each sells drops from 20,000 units to 16,000 units. Because of Zelles's cost structure, it suffers a greater net income loss than Atley. Zelles's operating profit drops from $1 million to zero, while the operating profit at Atley drops only from $1 million to $600,000. See the exhibit "Comparative Income Statements for Atley Tractors and Zelles Tractor Equipment Following a Drop in Quantity Sold."

Comparative Income Statements for Atley Tractors and Zelles Tractor Equipment Following a Drop in Quantity Sold

	Atley		Zelles	Percentage Change Atley	Zelles
Price per unit	$500	P	$500	0.00%	0.00%
Quantity of units sold	16,000	Q	16,000	−20.00%	−20.00%
Variable costs per unit	$400	V	$250	0.00%	0.00%
Fixed costs	$1,000,000	F	$4,000,000	0.00%	0.00%
Interest expense	$300,000	I	$300,000		
Average tax rate	40%	t	40%		
	Year Ending 12/31/XX		Year Ending12/31/XX		
Net sales	$ 8,000,000	P × Q	$ 8,000,000	−20.00%	−20.00%
Variable costs	(6,400,000)	V × Q	(4,000,000)	−20.00%	−20.00%
Fixed costs	(1,000,000)	F	(4,000,000)	0.00%	0.00%
Operating profit	$600,000	OP	$0	−40.00%	−100.00%

[DA08761]

The difference in the level of reduction in operating profit is caused by the organizations' cost structures and their corresponding operational leverages. Zelles has more fixed expenses that must be paid regardless of the level of sales, and so has more exposure to financial risk from reductions in the level of sales. Atley can tolerate a larger reduction in sales (either through a reduction in price or a reduction in units sold) before its operational profit becomes zero or negative.

Note that although Zelles is more susceptible to losses in the event of a decline in sales, Zelles also generates more profit with increased sales because each dollar of sales over $8.6 million generates $0.50 toward taxable income. For Atley, each sales dollar above $6.5 million contributes only $0.20 toward taxable income. Therefore, a level of financial risk similar to Zelles's is often considered beneficial for an organization because of the potential for higher profits. However, a higher level of financial risk means that the organization must make a greater effort in its management of hazard risk exposures to alleviate the greater degree of exposure to financial risk.

Increases in the variable costs per unit sold (V) are a price risk, which is a type of financial risk. Increases in variable costs are either the result of increases in raw materials and labor costs that constitute the cost of production or of increases in the costs of wholesale products that the organization buys and then resells, either of which can reduce operating profit.

To illustrate, Atley and Zelles have different variable cost risks. Atley buys its lawnmowers exclusively from a single manufacturer, ABC Mowers (ABC), which operates three factories in Alabama, Vermont, and Oregon. Zelles manufactures its own lawnmowers. Part of the variable cost for Atley is the transportation costs of moving the assembled mowers from ABC's closest plant, which is in Oregon, to Atley's warehouse and from there to the sales showroom. But suppose that ABC's Oregon factory was damaged in a fire and had to suspend operations (a hazard risk). Atley could still buy its mowers from the remaining plants, but the average shipping cost per mower could increase. That increased cost would affect Atley's profits but not Zelles's. Atley might not be able to pass on the increased costs to its customers if it wanted to remain price competitive, which is a form of price risk. Because the variable cost per unit sold (V) would increase, Atley would suffer a loss of operational profit. The degree of the loss would depend on how long it took ABC to return to full operations at its Oregon plant.

Atley also faces a financial risk related to its variable costs—the risk that ABC could simply raise the price of its products, which is a form of price risk. While that would cause short-term loss of operating income, Atley could address that risk by switching to an alternative manufacturer, diversifying its product line, or perhaps using its marketing skills to convince customers to pay more for ABC-brand mowers.

General financial risks can be addressed through general financial risk management techniques. However, it may not be appropriate to use these techniques to address a hazard risk such as the increased transportation costs due to ABC's Oregon factory's being damaged in a fire. The line between financial risk and hazard risk is sometimes blurry, which emphasizes the need for coordinated risk management efforts throughout an organization.

Apply Your Knowledge

Tom operates a beverage manufacturing company. His company competes against George's company. Tom has structured into his cost of production a higher percentage of fixed costs than George. Sales for both companies generally increase in the warmer months of the summer and decline in the cooler months of winter. Which company will benefit more in the summer and in the winter? Explain your answer.

Feedback: The higher operating leverage of Tom's company will be an advantage during the summer months. As sales rise, the leverage will result in greater operating profit for Tom than for George. However, that same leverage and volatility of operating profit will become a disadvantage during the winter months, when the sales for both companies decline. The decrease in operating profit will be greater for Tom than for George.

SUMMARY

Financial statements are documents that quantitatively present an organization's financial activities or status. The purpose of financial statements is to communicate information about an organization's financial activities, and the results of those activities, to individuals who need to make informed financial decisions about the organization. Such activities can include sales, purchases, borrowings, repayments, and investments.

The balance sheet lists the assets and liabilities of an organization. This financial statement provides valuable information to stakeholders regarding the organization's financial condition.

The income statement provides an accounting of an organization's revenues and expenses over a given period of time. Understanding how to read and interpret the income statement enables risk management and insurance professionals to gain a better understanding of the organization and its risk management or insurance needs.

During a specified period, the statement of changes in shareholders' equity explains any changes that have occurred in the organization's capital accounts, and the statement of cash flows summarizes the cash effects of an organization's operating, investing, and financing activities.

Organizations provide a large amount of financial information to their stakeholders. While a majority of this information is included in financial statements, some information is best communicated through other reports, such as these:

- Notes to financial statements
- SEC filings
- Company annual reports

Trend analysis, a technique for analyzing financial statements, involves making comparisons across two or more years of financial statement data. Although these techniques can be applied to the balance sheet to quantify the changes in assets and liabilities over time, this type of analysis is usually focused on the income statement and quantifies the changes in a company's profitability over time.

Liquidity refers to a company's ability to convert assets to cash to satisfy its obligations. For most organizations, liquidity can be measured using working capital; the current ratio; and the acid-test, or quick, ratio.

Capital structure is a corporation's mix of long-term debt and equity. Under generally accepted accounting principles (GAAP), liabilities of companies are classified as either short-term liabilities (due within one year) or long-term liabilities (due in more than one year).

Shareholders of the company have an equity interest, which is the right to whatever profits remain after all other interested parties have been compensated. Common shareholders typically have voting rights and are entitled to dividends, although these dividends are paid only when declared. Preferred stock sits between pure debt and pure equity in terms of priority; preferred shareholders have priority over common shareholders but stand behind debt holders.

Financial leverage is the use of fixed cost funds (debt) to increase returns to shareholders. This increase is accomplished by using the capital raised through the issue of debt to earn a rate of return higher than the fixed costs of that debt. Financial leverage analysis is a technique used for comparing EPS under alternate capitalization plans with varying levels of debt and equity. Several practical considerations on the use of debt include higher interest rates at higher levels of borrowing, the tax shield advantage, and the cost of financial distress.

Fixed costs and variable costs are the two components of an organization's cost of production. Their percentages in an organization's cost structure influence operating leverage, creating advantages and disadvantages for an organization.

ASSIGNMENT NOTES

1. Statement of Financial Accounting Standards No. 130, June 1997, www.fasb.org/st/summary/stsum130 (accessed May 28, 2010).
2. Manufacturing Inc.'s balance sheets as of December 31, 20X1, and December 31, 20X0 (not included), would be needed to verify the changes in assets and non-cash revenues and expenses mentioned in this section.

Direct Your Learning

10

Capital Investment and Financial Risk

Educational Objectives

After learning the content of this assignment, you should be able to:

▸ Calculate the present value of a future payment.

▸ Calculate the present value of an annuity, given the applicable rate of return and number of periods.

▸ Calculate the present value of unequal payments, given the applicable rate of return and number of periods over which the payments will be spread.

▸ Calculate the net present value of a series of cash outflows and inflows, given the applicable rate of return and number of periods.

▸ Evaluate capital investment proposals using the net present value method.

▸ Calculate the net present value of a capital investment proposal, taking into account accidental losses and loss prevention.

▸ Calculate the effect on net income of a call option that offsets input price increases.

Outline

Present Value and Discounting

Present Value of an Annuity

Present Value of Unequal Payments

Net Present Value

Evaluating Capital Investment Proposals

Evaluating Cash Flows From Treating Hazard Risk

Using Call Options to Limit Financial Risk

Summary

Capital Investment and Financial Risk

10

PRESENT VALUE AND DISCOUNTING

Various situations exist in which a risk management or an insurance professional should know the current, or present, value of money that will be received or paid out in the future. He or she might have to determine, for example, how much needs to be invested today to generate funds sufficient to pay for loss control equipment at a specific time in the future.

Because a sum of money grows over time by earning a return (for example, interest on a bond investment), its **present value** is less than its future value. The present value of a sum of money to be received in the future depends on the rate of return it could earn if it were received today and the number of periods over which it would earn the rate of return.

Present value
The value today of money that will be received in the future.

Present Value Over a Single Period

The process of calculating present value is called **discounting**. A **discount rate** is used to calculate the present value of a future amount. This is the formula for present value:

$$PV = FV_n \div (1 + r)^n$$

where n = number of periods

r = rate of return

Discounting
The process of calculating the present value of a future amount.

Discount rate
The rate of return used in determining the present value of a future sum.

For example, assume that at the end of one year, an organization needs $10,300 to be in a savings account that pays 3 percent interest compounded annually. The financial manager must determine how much to deposit in the account today to have the required $10,300 in one year; that is, the present value of $10,300 discounted at a rate of 3 percent for one year. The answer can be calculated using the present value equation:

$$PV = FV_n \div (1 + r)^n$$

$$= \$10{,}300 \div (1 + 0.03)^1$$

$$= \$10{,}300 \div 1.03$$

$$= \$10{,}000$$

Therefore, the financial manager needs to deposit $10,000 into the savings account today in order to have $10,300 at the end of the year.

Present Value Over Multiple Periods

Discounting can also be used to determine the present value of money that will be received or paid out many years in the future. For example, assume an organization has a receivable totaling $11,910 that is due three years from today.

The financial manager must choose between receiving full payment of $11,910 in three years or accepting a reduced payment today in full settlement of the receivable. Assuming the money, if received today, could be deposited in an account that earns 3 percent interest for three years, what is the smallest amount the financial manager can accept today to make the second option an acceptable alternative? The decision can be made by calculating the present value, or discounted value, of $11,910:

$$PV = FV_n \div (1 + r)^n$$
$$= \$11,910 \div (1 + 0.03)^3$$
$$= \$11,910 \div 1.0927$$
$$= \$10,899$$

The present value of $11,910 received three years from now at a discount rate of 3 percent is $10,899. Therefore, the financial manager views receiving $10,899 today as equally beneficial as receiving $11,910 in three years. If the settlement offer to be received today is less than $10,899, the promise of $11,910 in three years is preferable. Conversely, if the settlement offer is more than $10,899, then settlement is preferable to the promise of $11,910 in three years.

Another method of determining present value is by using financial tables. The present value factors $[1 \div (1 + r)^n]$ can be obtained from the present value table in the exhibit, which shows the present value factors for several combinations of r and n. See the exhibit "Present Value Table."

To determine the present value in the previous example by using the present value table, multiply the future value, $11,910, by the factor in the 3 percent interest rate column at the third period row (0.9151).

$$PV = FV_n \times PV \text{ factor}$$
$$= \$11,910 \times 0.9151$$
$$= \$10,899$$

As an alternative to using the present value table, risk management and insurance professionals often use financial calculators and/or computer spreadsheet programs to determine present values.

Present Value Table

Period (*n*)	Interest Rate (*r*)				
	1%	2%	3%	4%	5%
1	0.9901	0.9804	0.9709	0.9615	0.9524
2	0.9803	0.9612	0.9426	0.9246	0.9070
3	0.9706	0.9423	0.9151	0.8890	0.8638
4	0.9610	0.9238	0.8885	0.8548	0.8227
5	0.9515	0.9057	0.8626	0.8219	0.7835
6	0.9420	0.8880	0.8375	0.7903	0.7462
7	0.9327	0.8706	0.8131	0.7599	0.7107
8	0.9235	0.8535	0.7894	0.7307	0.6768
9	0.9143	0.8368	0.7664	0.7026	0.6446
10	0.9053	0.8203	0.7441	0.6756	0.6139

[DA08782]

PRESENT VALUE OF AN ANNUITY

To make appropriate financial decisions for an organization, a risk management professional should be able to determine today's value of future payments.

A risk management professional must often determine the present value of an ordinary **annuity**—that is, the value today of a series of equal payments to be made or received in the future at the end of each specified period. The present value of the annuity can be determined by calculating the present value of each individual payment and then adding the results together to determine the sum of the present values. Alternatively, the present value of an annuity can be determined by multiplying the annuity payment per period by the present value of an annuity factor in an annuity table.

Suppose a manager is offered payments of $750 at the end of each year for three years in satisfaction of a current account receivable of $2,100. Also assume that the $2,100 sum, if received today, could be invested and earn a 6 percent rate of return. Therefore, the opportunity cost of receiving payments in the future rather than today is 6 percent per annum.

The exhibit illustrates the solution to finding today's equivalent value of the consecutive payments described in the example. See the exhibit "Present Value of an Ordinary Annuity."

The valuation method used in the exhibit calculates the present value of each individual payment and then calculates the sum of the present values. This is the present value equation:

Annuity
A series of fixed payments made on specified dates over a set period.

Present Value of an Ordinary Annuity

	1	2	3	Year
Present value at 6% interest	$750	$750	$750	End of year payments

$$$ 708 = $750 \div 1.06$
668 = $750 \div 1.06^2$
630 = $750 \div 1.06^3$
$$$2,006

[DA02374]

$$PV = FV_n \div (1 + r)^n$$

Applying the present value equation to the payments of $750 discounted for one, two, and three years produces an overall present value of $2,006. See the exhibit "Present Value of an Annuity of $1 Per Period for n Periods = $[1 - (1 \div (1 + r)^n)] \div r$."

Present Value of an Annuity of $1 Per Period for n Periods = $[1 - (1 \div (1 + r)^n)] \div r$

Period (n)	Interest Rate (r)									
	1%	2%	3%	4%	5%	6%	7%	8%	9%	10%
1	0.9901	0.9804	0.9709	0.9615	0.9524	0.9434	0.9346	0.9259	0.9174	0.9091
2	1.9704	1.9416	1.9135	1.8861	1.8594	1.8334	1.8080	1.7833	1.7591	1.7355
3	2.9410	2.8839	2.8286	2.7751	2.7232	2.6730	2.6243	2.5771	2.5313	2.4869
4	3.9020	3.8077	3.7171	3.6299	3.5460	3.4651	3.3872	3.3121	3.2397	3.1699
5	4.8534	4.7135	4.5797	4.4518	4.3295	4.2124	4.1002	3.9927	3.8897	3.7908
6	5.7955	5.6014	5.4172	5.2421	5.0757	4.9173	4.7665	4.6229	4.4859	4.3553
7	6.7282	6.4720	6.2303	6.0021	5.7864	5.5824	5.3893	5.2064	5.0330	4.8684
8	7.6517	7.3255	7.0197	6.7327	6.4632	6.2098	5.9713	5.7466	5.5348	5.3349
9	8.5660	8.1622	7.7861	7.4353	7.1078	6.8017	6.5152	6.2469	5.9952	5.7590
10	9.4713	8.9826	8.5302	8.1109	7.7217	7.3601	7.0236	6.7101	6.4177	6.1446

[DA06173]

Alternatively, to determine the present value of the annuity in the example by using the present value of an annuity table, multiply the payment per period, $750, by the table value in the 6 percent interest rate column at the third-period row, 2.6730:

$$PVA = A \times PVAF$$

$$= \$750 \times 2.6730$$

$$= \$2,005$$

$$A = \text{annuity payment per period}$$

$$PVAF = \text{present value of annuity factor}$$

Because the present value of the annuity is less than the present value of the account receivable, the manager should not accept the offer.

Apply Your Knowledge

Consider the case of a manager who is planning to retire and must choose between taking an immediate lump sum of $250,000 or an ordinary annuity that pays $35,000 per year for ten years. Assume that 5 percent is an achievable rate of return based on the retiree's investment philosophy. Also, although income taxes would ordinarily be a significant consideration, assume that they do not apply in this example. What should the manager decide and how should he arrive at his decision?

Feedback: To make an informed decision, the future retiree must determine the present value of the annuity and compare it to the lump sum payment. The present value can be solved by using the present value of an annuity table. Multiplying the present value of an annuity factor in the 5 percent column at the tenth-period row (7.7217) by the $35,000 payment produces a present value of $270,260. In this example, the present value of the annuity payments, $270,260, is greater than the lump sum payment, $250,000. Therefore, based on these assumptions, the retiree should accept the annuity rather than the lump sum.

The present value of an annuity may also be calculated by using a scientific calculator or a spreadsheet program.

PRESENT VALUE OF UNEQUAL PAYMENTS

Not all investment decisions involve streams of payments that are equal. In some, payments that will be made or received vary substantially from period to period.

The valuation methods required to calculate the present value of a stream of unequal payments differ from those used to calculate the present value for a stream of equal payments (an annuity). As with an annuity, the present value of a stream of unequal payments is the sum of the present values of the individual payments. However, with an annuity, the annuity present value table provides a simplified method for calculating the present value of the stream of payments. With unequal payments, the present value of each individual payment must be calculated and the results summed. For example, assume an individual is offered $250 one year from now, $300 two years from now, $500 three years from now, and $700 four years from now. The present value of this future stream of payments can be calculated using the present value table. See the exhibit "Present Value of $1 to Be Received After n Periods = $1 \div (1 + r)^n$."

Present Value of $1 to Be Received After n Periods = $1 \div (1 + r)^n$

Period (n)	Interest Rate (r)									
	1%	2%	3%	4%	5%	6%	7%	8%	9%	10%
1	0.9901	0.9804	0.9709	0.9615	0.9524	0.9434	0.9346	0.9259	0.9174	0.9091
2	0.9803	0.9612	0.9426	0.9246	0.9070	0.8900	0.8734	0.8573	0.8417	0.8264
3	0.9706	0.9423	0.9151	0.8890	0.8638	0.8396	0.8163	0.7938	0.7722	0.7513
4	0.9610	0.9238	0.8885	0.8548	0.8227	0.7921	0.7629	0.7350	0.7084	0.6830
5	0.9515	0.9057	0.8626	0.8219	0.7835	0.7473	0.7130	0.6806	0.6499	0.6209

[DA06176]

Assuming a 6 percent rate of return, the exhibit shows how the present value of this stream of unequal payments can be calculated. In this exhibit, the present value of each individual payment is calculated by multiplying it by the corresponding present value factor from the present value table and then summing the individual present values. See the exhibit "Present Value of a Stream of Unequal Payments."

Present Value of a Stream of Unequal Payments

(1) Year	(2) Payments	(3) Present Value Factor	(4) = (2) × (3) Present Value
1	$250	0.9434	$ 235.85
2	300	0.8900	267.00
3	500	0.8396	419.80
4	700	0.7921	554.47
			$1,477.12

[DA02352]

In addition to the present value table, financial calculators and computer spreadsheets also may be used to calculate the present value of a stream of unequal payments.

NET PRESENT VALUE

The net present value technique for evaluating an investment is based on discounting the related cash outflows and inflows using a required rate of return. For example, a risk management professional may want to determine whether investing today in a machinery maintenance program (a cash outflow) will save costs from machinery breakdown incidents in the future (a form of "cash inflow" based on saving expenses).

An investment's **net present value (NPV)** is the difference between the present value of its cash inflows and the present value of its cash outflows. The rate of return used for discounting (r) is the rate of return required by the investor. When making investment choices, organizations generally adhere to what is known as the NPV rule, which dictates that an investment should be made only if its NPV is greater than zero. The organization investing in a project usually sets its required rate of return equal to its cost of capital so as to only accept investments that cover its cost of funds.

Net present value (NPV)
The present value of all future net cash flows (including salvage value) discounted at the cost of capital, minus the cost of the initial investment, also discounted at the cost of capital.

The NPV calculation is represented as an equation:

$$NPV = -C_0 + (C_t \div (1+r)^1) + \ldots + (C_n \div (1+r)^n),$$

where:

C_0 = Cash flow at beginning of project,

C_t = Payment at period t for $t = 1$, through $t = n$,

r = Discount rate,

n = Number of periods

Note that the cash outflow is a negative number and the cash inflows are positive. Furthermore, the equation assumes there is a single cash outflow (investment) made today. The equation would differ if the investment called for a series of cash outflows (investments) to be made at various points in time.

For example, assume that a risk management professional is determining whether to invest $10,000 today in a three-year machinery maintenance project. The company requires a rate of return of 7 percent. Further assume that it expects to save breakdown expenses of $2,500 at the end of the first year, $3,300 at the end of the second year, and $4,700 at the end of the third year. These figures can be entered into the NPV equation to determine whether the investment should be made:

$$NPV = -C_0 + [C_1 \div (1+r)^1] + [C_2 \div (1+r)^2] + [C_3 \div (1+r)^3]$$

$$= -\$10{,}000 + [\$2{,}500 \div (1+.07)^1] + [\$3{,}300 \div (1+.07)^2] + [\$4{,}700 \div (1+.07)^3]$$

$$= -\$10{,}000 + [\$2{,}336] + [\$2{,}882] + [\$3{,}837]$$

$$= -\$945$$

The present value table also may be used in the determination of NPV. See the exhibit "Present Value of $1 to Be Received After n Periods = $1 \div (1+r)^n$."

Present Value of $1 to Be Received After n Periods = $1 \div (1+r)^n$

Period (n)	1%	2%	3%	4%	5%	6%	7%	8%	9%	10%
1	0.9901	0.9804	0.9709	0.9615	0.9524	0.9434	0.9346	0.9259	0.9174	0.9091
2	0.9803	0.9612	0.9426	0.9246	0.9070	0.8900	0.8734	0.8573	0.8417	0.8264
3	0.9706	0.9423	0.9151	0.8890	0.8638	0.8396	0.8163	0.7938	0.7722	0.7513
4	0.9610	0.9238	0.8885	0.8548	0.8227	0.7921	0.7629	0.7350	0.7084	0.6830
5	0.9515	0.9057	0.8626	0.8219	0.7835	0.7473	0.7130	0.6806	0.6499	0.6209

[DA06176]

The present value of each payment may be calculated by multiplying the payment amount by the appropriate present value factor. The present value factor lies at the intersection of the corresponding period and interest rate. In the previous example, the corresponding periods are one, two, and three, respectively, and the corresponding interest rate is 7 percent. The exhibit depicts how the present value factors may be used to determine the investment's NPV. See the exhibit "Net Present Value of Proposed Investment."

Net Present Value of Proposed Investment

Year	Payment	Present Value Factor	Present Value (Payment × Present Value Factor)
0	-$10,000	1.0000	-$10,000
1	$2,500	0.9346	$2,336
2	$3,300	0.8734	$2,882
3	$4,700	0.8163	$3,837
Net Present Value (NPV)			-$945

[DA06242]

Because this investment's NPV is negative, the NPV rule suggests that the organization should not make this investment because the present value of its cash inflows does not exceed the present value of its cash outflow. If the proposed investment's NPV were positive, the NPV rule would dictate that the investment should be made.

NPV analysis and the NPV rule should not be used as the sole determinant as to whether to make an investment. In the machinery maintenance example, the risk management professional may have nonfinancial reasons for avoiding machinery breakdowns. Alternatively, perhaps not all the costs related to machinery breakdowns were factored into the NPV analysis. Some of the limitations of NPV analysis that should be considered are these:

- The amounts and timing of cash flows may differ from those expected over the life of an investment.
- NPV analysis does not formally factor in the effect of uncertainty (risk) with respect to future cash flows, losses, discount rates, or time horizons.
- NPV analysis focuses on maximizing economic value and disregards an organization's nonfinancial goals and other stakeholders' interests.

EVALUATING CAPITAL INVESTMENT PROPOSALS

Capital investment proposals provide opportunities for an organization to spend (invest) capital with the expectation that net cash flows will increase in the future.

The method for determining net present value (NPV) frequently employs capital budgeting of long-term inflows and outflows of cash as well as cash flow analysis to determine whether an investment proposal is expected to produce net cash flows with a present value that will be greater than the amount of funds invested.

Capital Budgeting and Expenditures

Capital budgeting is used when cash expenditures or receipts are expected to span several accounting periods. Organizations have two types of expenditures: **operating expenditures** and **capital expenditures**. Capital budgeting focuses on capital expenditures that generate cash receipts or require cash disbursements over a long period of time. It typically involves situations in which an asset or activity requires immediate cash expenditures but will generate future cash receipts. For example, if a manufacturer builds a new plant (immediate cash disbursement), the cash receipts (inflows) attributable to that investment proposal will be received over the plant's entire useful life (cash receipts over a long period). To make sound decisions about purchasing capital assets, an organization must compare present values of future cash inflows and outflows with the investment proposal's initial cost.

Capital budgeting

The process of evaluating alternative capital investment proposals in terms of the cash outlays that the proposals require and the present values of the cash inflows that the proposals are likely to generate.

Operating expenditures

Disbursements for assets that will be consumed in a relatively short period, usually within one year or a single accounting period.

Capital expenditures

Disbursements for assets that will be consumed over a relatively long period, usually over multiple accounting periods.

NPV Method

The NPV method is an evaluation method used to apply cash flow analysis as a decision criterion. It calculates whether, at a specified rate of interest, the present value of a proposal's net cash flow (cash inflows minus cash outflows) is positive or negative. If the net cash flow is positive, the proposal generates a rate of return higher than the specified rate. If the net cash flow is negative, the proposal generates a rate of return lower than the specified rate.

To evaluate capital investment proposals using the net present value method, this information is required:

- The amount of initial investment
- The acceptable annual rate of return
- The amount and timing of the differential (incremental) annual after-tax net cash flows associated with the proposal over its estimated useful life
- The **salvage value** (if any) of the investment

The exhibit illustrates the information necessary for evaluating a capital investment proposal using the NPV method. The proposal involves acquiring an asset for $30,000 cash. The estimated useful life of the asset is three years, and the asset is expected to generate additional annual after-tax net cash inflows of $12,000 at the end of each year, or a total of $36,000 over three years, with no salvage value. The minimum acceptable rate of return is 10 percent annually. See the exhibit "Information for Evaluating a Capital Investment Proposal."

> **Salvage value**
> An amount that an insurer can recover by selling or otherwise disposing of insured property for which the insurer has paid a total loss or a constructive total loss.

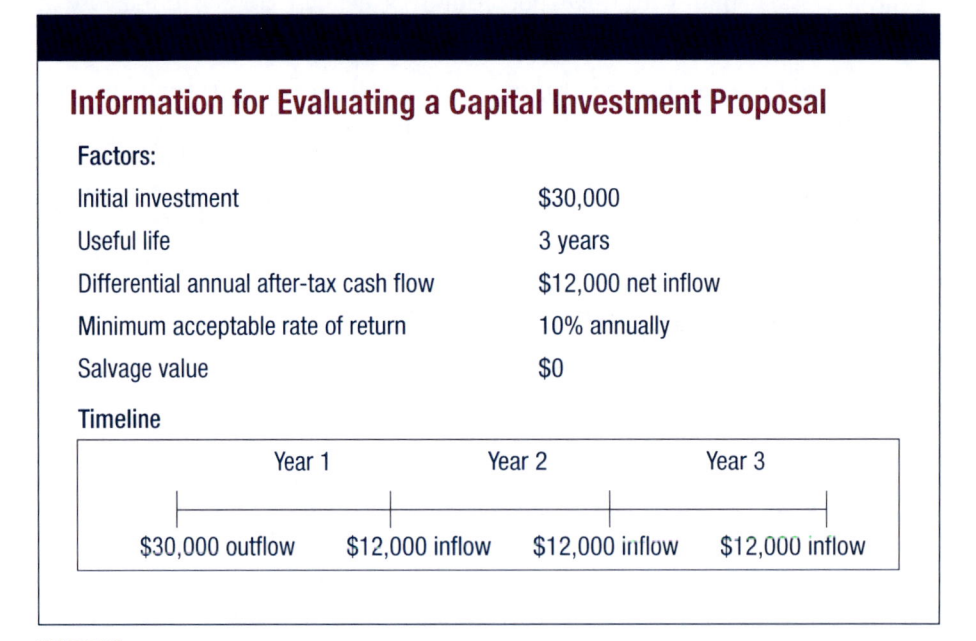

Information for Evaluating a Capital Investment Proposal

Factors:

Initial investment	$30,000
Useful life	3 years
Differential annual after-tax cash flow	$12,000 net inflow
Minimum acceptable rate of return	10% annually
Salvage value	$0

Timeline

Year 1	Year 2	Year 3
$30,000 outflow $12,000 inflow	$12,000 inflow	$12,000 inflow

[DA02034]

The NPV of an asset or activity can be expressed as this:

NPV = PV (sum of future net cash flows) − *PV* (initial investment)

For most proposals, a single investment is initially made—that is, the present value of the required investment will equal the initial required cash outlay, and no discounting is needed.

The NPV method can be used only when a minimum acceptable rate of return is predetermined. Typically, this minimum acceptable rate of return is the organization's cost of capital and generally will be given to, not established by, a risk management professional.

The cost of capital is not the only consideration when determining the minimum acceptable rate of return. A risk-averse financial officer of an organization will demand a higher rate of return from an investment proposal that has a higher risk. This is known as the **risk-return trade-off**, and it requires investors to determine the appropriate balance between assuming the lowest possible risk and achieving the highest possible return.

Once the minimum rate of return is established, any investment proposal whose projected cash inflows have a present value greater than the present value of the required outflows is acceptable according to the NPV method. The net cash flow (NCF) from a proposal in any specified time period equals the cash inflows that the proposal is expected to produce, minus any cash outflows it requires. If inflows exceed outflows, the net cash flow from that proposal is positive. If outflows exceed inflows, net cash flow is negative. The **differential (incremental) annual after-tax net cash flow** is the change in an organization's aggregate annual net cash flows resulting from implementing a proposal.

The first step in using the NPV method is to calculate the present value factor for three equal cash inflows at the end of each year for three years at a discount rate of 10 percent. The exhibit indicates that the present value factor for $1 received annually at the end of each year for three years at 10 percent interest compounded annually is 2.487. See the exhibit "Present Value of $1 Received at the End of Each Period for *n* Periods."

Multiplying the present value factor of 2.487 by $12,000 yields the present value of the differential (additional) net cash inflows, $29,844. In other words, $29,844 is the amount that would have to be invested today at 10 percent interest compounded annually to receive $12,000 at the end of each year for a period of three years. See the exhibit "Evaluating a Capital Investment Proposal Using the NPV Method."

The proposal's NPV is the present value of the additional net cash inflows minus the investment's present value. Therefore, the NPV of this proposal is a negative $156, calculated by subtracting the $30,000 initial investment that the proposal requires from the $29,884 present value of the proposal's future cash inflows. This negative result shows that the proposal will not generate

---

Risk-return trade-off
The tendency for the potential return to increase as risk increases.

Differential (incremental) annual after-tax net cash flow
The change in an organization's aggregate annual net cash flows resulting from implementing a proposal.

Present Value of $1 Received at the End of Each Period for n Periods

Number of Time Periods (n)	Interest Rate (r)									
	1%	2%	4%	6%	8%	10%	12%	14%	15%	16%
1	0.990	0.980	0.962	0.943	0.926	0.909	0.893	0.877	0.870	0.862
2	1.970	1.942	1.866	1.833	1.783	1.736	1.690	1.647	1.626	1.605
3	2.941	2.884	2.775	2.673	2.577	2.487	2.402	2.322	2.283	2.246
4	3.902	3.808	3.630	3.465	3.312	3.170	3.037	2.914	2.855	2.796
5	4.853	4.713	4.452	4.212	3.993	3.791	3.605	3.433	3.352	3.274
6	5.795	5.601	5.242	4.917	4.623	4.355	4.111	3.889	3.784	3.685
7	6.728	6.472	6.002	5.582	5.206	4.868	4.564	4.288	4.160	4.039

[DA08784]

Evaluating a Capital Investment Proposal Using the NPV Method

Evaluation by NPV method:

Present value of differential inflows	$12,000 × 2.487 = $29,844
Less: Present value of initial investment	($30,000)
Total	(156)

[DA08785]

the minimum acceptable rate of return of 10 percent. The present value of the additional net cash inflows does not outweigh the investment's initial cost. Therefore, undertaking the proposal is estimated to reduce the organization's value purely from a financial viewpoint. Nonfinancial considerations, such as legal compliance and social responsibility, should also be evaluated before an organization undertakes an investment.

Cash Flow Analysis

The NPV method is used for evaluating after-tax net cash flows associated with a capital investment proposal. How these differential cash flows are calculated needs to be explained.

In practice, capital budgeting often requires calculating net cash flows from revenue and expense data. When reviewing such data, organizations undertake a cash flow analysis that involves looking at net cash inflows rather than gross cash inflows. Therefore, buying a piece of equipment, for example, does not just involve looking at resulting increases in ongoing revenue and the initial outlay of cost. It involves both looking at increases in maintenance expenses going forward and offsetting these increases with decreases in income taxes resulting from the expenses' deductibility against taxable income. It also involves looking at the income tax reduction that is provided by depreciation over time of the equipment's initial capital outlay.

In for-profit organizations, income taxes are cash outflows and must be deducted from cash revenues to calculate net cash flows. Taxes are treated like any other cash outlay, with income taxes calculated as a percentage of taxable income. Taxable income is based on some cash and some noncash revenues and expenses. For organizations not subject to income taxes, these noncash revenues and expenses can be ignored, simplifying cash flow calculations.

In capital budgeting decisions, the main noncash item affecting income taxes is depreciation of long-term assets. Depreciation expense is not a cash outflow in the period in which the expense is recognized; it merely recognizes the outlay in a way that spreads the cost of the asset over the years that it is expected to produce revenue, matching expenses with revenues period by period.

The simplest depreciation method is the **straight-line depreciation method**. The related illustrations calculate depreciation expense by this method. Salvage value, the resale value of used property, is assumed to be zero unless otherwise specified. For example, if the initial investment in an asset with a seven-year useful life is $30,000, the annual depreciation expense is $4,286 ($30,000 ÷ 7 years). Although not a cash outflow, depreciation should be added to other expenses when calculating taxable income. For illustrative purposes, marginal income taxes (the amount of tax paid on the next dollar earned) are assumed to be 40 percent of taxable income, unless otherwise specified.

The exhibit illustrates the procedure for calculating the differential annual after-tax net cash flow from a proposal in which depreciation represents a tax-deductible expense. The exhibit also evaluates the proposal by using the NPV method. The proposal involves an organization's purchase of a risk management information system (RMIS) that costs $30,000 and that has an expected useful life of seven years. Maintaining this system will add $500 annually to operating expenses and $100 per year to the property insurance expense. Notice that maintenance and insurance expenses are differential expenses—the organization's total cash outlays for all maintenance and all insurance are far more than $500 and $100 per year, respectively. The differential cash revenues to the organization attributable to use of the risk management information system are $12,000 per year. See the exhibit "Cash Flow Analysis of Risk Management Information Systems."

Straight-line depreciation method

An accounting method of calculating depreciation by taking an equal amount of an asset's cost as an expense for each year of the asset's expected useful life.

Cash Flow Analysis of Risk Management Information Systems

Cash Flow Analysis of Risk Management Information Systems

Cash revenues		$12,000
Less: Cash expenses		
(except income taxes):		
Maintenance expense	$500	
Insurance expense	$100	($600)
Before-tax NCF:		$11,400
Less: Income taxes:		
Before-tax NCF	$11,400	
Less: Depreciation		
expense ($30,000 ÷ 7 years)	(4,286)	
Taxable income	$7,114	
Income taxes (40%)		($2,846)
After-tax NCF:		$8,554

Evaluations of Annual NCF

Factors:
Initial investment	$30,000
Useful life	7 years
Annual after-tax NCF	$8,554
Minimum acceptable rate of return	8% annually

Evaluation by the NPV method:
Present value of NCF ($8,554 × 5.206)	$ 44,532
Less: Present value of initial investment	($30,000)
Net present value	$14,532

Callouts:
- Under this proposal, the differential cash revenues to the organization attributable to use of the machine are $12,000 per year.
- Use of this machine will add $500 annually to the organization's operating expenses and $100 per year to its property insurance outlay, both of which are cash expenses.
- This calculation involves an organization's proposed purchase of a machine that costs $30,000 and that has an expected useful life of seven years.
- Here, annual depreciation expense is $4,286 ($30,000 ÷ 7 years), making taxable income $7,114 and differential income tax $2,846. After the deduction of the cash outflow for taxes, this machine's annual after-tax net cash flow becomes $8,554.

[DA08786]

The procedure for calculating differential annual after-tax net cash flows from this risk management information system starts by subtracting annual expenditures, other than income taxes, from cash revenues. The result is before-tax net cash flows ("before-tax NCF").

Although income taxes must be deducted from cash inflows to determine the net cash flow for any period, income taxes must be calculated separately because they are a percentage of taxable income. Here, annual depreciation expense is $4,286, making taxable income $7,114 after subtracting the depreciation expense from the before-tax NCF ($11,400 – $4,286), and income taxes $2,846 ($7,114 × 0.40). After the deduction for taxes, the system's annual after-tax net cash flow ("after-tax NCF") becomes $8,554 ($11,400 – $2,846).

This $8,554 after-tax NCF for a for-profit organization is equivalent to differential annual after-tax net cash flow. The NPV method of evaluation reveals that this RMIS proposal surpasses the minimum acceptable rate of return of 8 percent compounded annually. Discounted at 8 percent, the NPV of the system is $14,532.

For organizations not subject to income taxes, after-tax net cash flows are equal to before-tax net cash flows. Regardless of whether the organization must consider the effect of income taxes, the procedure for calculating net cash flow and determining the NPV provides a basis for evaluating all risk management investments.

In virtually all organizations, net cash flows are subject to uncertainty (risk). That risk should be considered when choosing the discount rate (cost of capital) that will be used to calculate the present values of expected NCF. The greater the uncertainty of future net cash flows, the greater the minimum required rate of return as organizations expect a higher rate of return for taking on more risk. Ideally, managers should attempt to quantify the effects of the risk on the organization's expected net cash flows and should incorporate the costs into NPV calculations. However, many of these costs cannot be measured with much precision. When the expected costs of uncertainty are difficult to measure, organizations might assign a "price tag," or cost, to the uncertainty. This implicit after-tax cost can then be treated like any other cost, or cash outflow, in a cash flow analysis of a risk management technique. The cost so assigned is called the cost of uncertainty and is sometimes referred to as a risk premium.

The cost of uncertainty from the net cash flows of an investment proposal being at risk will cause the discount rate to increase as the risk increases. Accordingly, the NPV of a proposal may go from positive to negative, potentially causing a proposal to be rejected despite having expected net cash flows with a present value (at the original discount rate) substantially higher than the initial investment. **Sensitivity analysis** can be used to determine whether the decision to accept or reject a proposal would change if a variable such as the amount of uncertainty were to increase or decrease. The analysis is most accurate when all variables except the one being analyzed are held constant. The NPV can then be measured to see how sensitive it is to changes in that variable.

Sensitivity analysis
A method to investigate the effect of a change in one or more variables on the results of a financial analysis.

EVALUATING CASH FLOWS FROM TREATING HAZARD RISK

Knowing how to recognize the costs associated with expected accidental hazard losses when evaluating capital investment proposals is an important skill. A risk management professional who has acquired such a skill can analyze the effects of various loss control techniques on those losses.

Case Facts

Atwell Hospital (Atwell) is considering using one of its buildings, previously leased as office space, to house the James Research Center (JRC). JRC would be run by Dr. James, who is well known for his medical research. The relevant facts of the JRC proposal are these:

- The expected life of the project and the length of the proposed contract are ten years.
- The hospital projects that its association with Dr. James will yield an additional (differential) $60,000 in annual revenues compared with its prior net revenues from leasing the building.
- In addition to providing the building for the research center, Atwell will provide Dr. James with a $200,000 grant to help establish the research facility and obtain necessary equipment.
- The $200,000 grant is depreciated over ten years on a straight-line basis.
- The chief financial officer of Atwell has told the risk management professional that the minimum acceptable rate of return is 10 percent.
- Because of the use of volatile chemicals in Dr. James's research, the primary property loss exposure attributable to JRC is the risk of physical damage to the building from fire.
- Atwell's management has asked its risk management professional to consider only the property loss exposure from fire and no other property or liability loss exposure when evaluating the JRC proposal.
- Under the terms of the JRC proposal, the hospital is not responsible for any damage to the building's contents, furnishings, and fixtures, all of which will be owned by Dr. James.

Overview of Steps

To adequately consider the financial effects on an organization of an investment or activity such as the JRC proposal, the first step is to recognize the costs expected from accidental losses in the cash flow analysis of the proposals. Once the risk management professional has recognized the costs associated with the accidental losses, the next step is to analyze the effects of various loss control techniques on those expected accidental losses.

Cash Flow Analysis Recognizing Expected Losses

Recognition of expected accidental losses and the choice of loss control techniques affect the net cash flow (NCF). Changes to the NCF can alter the net present value (NPV) of an investment proposal and, ultimately, affect the decision regarding to which proposal an organization will devote its resources. The exhibit shows the probability distribution of differential annual fire losses to the building resulting from Dr. James's occupancy, prepared by Atwell's risk management professional from a variety of data. See the exhibit "Annual Fire Loss Probability Distribution."

Annual Fire Loss Probability Distribution

Probability	Annual Fire Damage	Expected Value
.80	$ 0	$ 0
.10	$ 30,000	$ 3,000
.07	$100,000	$ 7,000
.03	$200,000	$ 6,000
1.00		$16,000 = Annual expected value

[DA02048]

The expected value of the differential fire loss is $16,000 per year. This annual expected accidental loss average reduces the proposal's annual expected cash flows. The NPV for the JRC proposal is shown in the *Annual After-Tax Cash Flows Recognizing Expected Losses* exhibit. If, when evaluating the proposal, Atwell considers the cost of retaining the expected differential annual fire losses to the JRC building, the resulting net present value is $11,388. The proposal has a lower NPV as a result of recognizing expected losses, but the NPV is positive. See the exhibit "Annual After-Tax Cash Flows—Recognizing Expected Losses."

The calculations in the exhibit recognize only the expected value of differential fire losses, not the effects that a loss control technique might have on expected losses and NCF.

The recognition of expected accidental losses ($16,000 per year before taxes) in cash flow analysis may have a significant effect on the decision to undertake a proposal. The relatively large value of the differential expected losses compared with the $200,000 investment is used to highlight the importance of recognizing expected accidental losses and risk management considerations. However, the same principles used in evaluating the JRC proposal would apply even if the amounts and effects were smaller.

The calculations in the exhibit assume that fire damage to the JRC building is the only differential loss; that is, that physical damage from causes of loss other than fire will not occur. Perhaps more important, the calculations assume that the before-tax expected value of fire losses represents the only cost of retention. The calculations do not specifically consider the potential adverse effects and costs to Atwell of annual variability in the amount of fire damage.

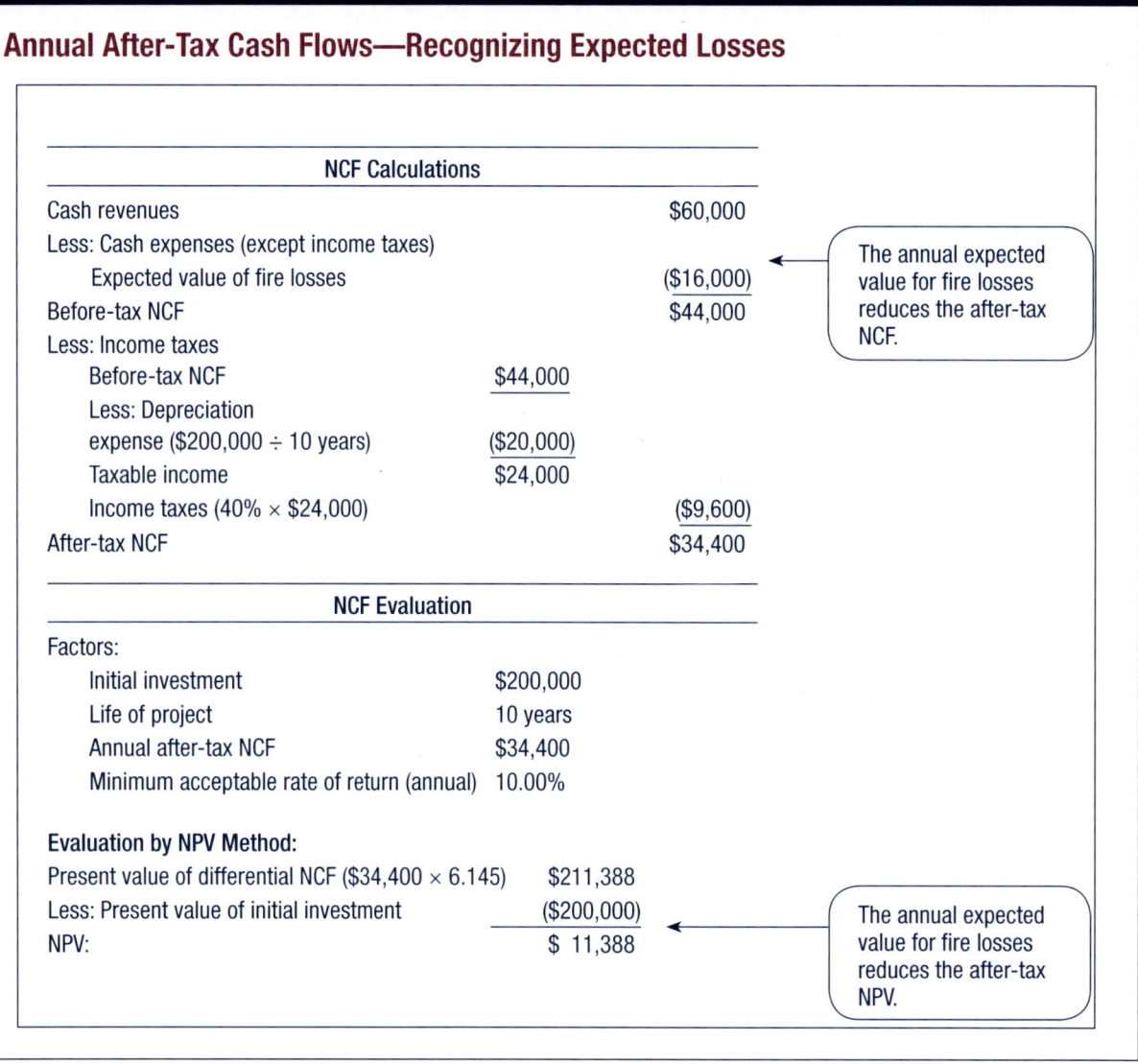

Annual After-Tax Cash Flows—Recognizing Expected Losses

NCF Calculations

Cash revenues		$60,000
Less: Cash expenses (except income taxes)		
Expected value of fire losses		($16,000)
Before-tax NCF		$44,000
Less: Income taxes		
Before-tax NCF	$44,000	
Less: Depreciation		
expense ($200,000 ÷ 10 years)	($20,000)	
Taxable income	$24,000	
Income taxes (40% × $24,000)		($9,600)
After-tax NCF		$34,400

The annual expected value for fire losses reduces the after-tax NCF.

NCF Evaluation

Factors:
- Initial investment $200,000
- Life of project   10 years
- Annual after-tax NCF $34,400
- Minimum acceptable rate of return (annual)   10.00%

Evaluation by NPV Method:

Present value of differential NCF ($34,400 × 6.145)	$211,388
Less: Present value of initial investment	($200,000)
NPV:	$ 11,388

The annual expected value for fire losses reduces the after-tax NPV.

[DA02049]

Cash Flow Analysis With Loss Prevention or Reduction

A variety of loss control techniques are available to Atwell. Therefore, its risk management professional needs to understand how cash flow analysis can be used to aid in the proper selection of the appropriate loss control techniques. By selecting the most appropriate technique, a risk management professional can prevent or reduce accidental losses associated with a particular capital investment proposal and make the proposal more appealing to senior management. For example, management may reject the JRC proposal if it requires acceptance of a $16,000 increase in expected annual fire losses. In an attempt to make the proposal more appealing, the hospital's risk management professional develops a probability distribution for differential annual fire losses if a $10,000 sprinkler system is installed when Dr. James moves in. The expenditure would be depreciated for tax purposes on a straight-line basis over the ten-year life of the contract. The sprinkler system would have a $400 annual maintenance expense and would have no salvage or residual value at the end of the ten years. The risk management professional has estimated that the system will reduce the expected value of the differential fire losses from Dr. James's occupancy, as shown in the exhibit. See the exhibit "Annual Fire Loss Probability Distribution With Sprinkler System."

Annual Fire Loss Probability Distribution With Sprinkler System

Probability	Annual Fire Damage	Expected Value
.80	$ 0	$ 0
.10	$ 5,000	$ 500
.07	$ 10,000	$ 700
.03	$100,000	$3,000
1.00		$4,200

[DA02050]

With the installation of the sprinkler system (a loss reduction measure), the before-tax expected value of annual fire losses decreases to $4,200. The addition of a sprinkler system produces these changes to the proposal's net cash flows (compared with not installing such a system):

- The sprinkler system reduces the expected value of fire losses that Atwell will retain.
- The sprinkler system's initial cost is added to the cost of the proposal's initial investment.
- The depreciation and maintenance expenses for the sprinkler system are considered in calculating after-tax net cash flows each year.

The differential annual after-tax NCF from the sprinkler-system JRC proposal is calculated in the upper portion of the *Annual After-Tax Cash Flows—Loss Reduction or Prevention Device* exhibit. The lower portion shows the evaluation of the JRC proposal's cash flow using the NPV method. See the exhibit "Annual After-Tax Cash Flows—Loss Reduction or Prevention Device."

The exhibit shows that installing a sprinkler system increases the hospital's initial investment to $210,000. The proposal's NPV is $45,878. Because the NPV is higher with the loss reduction measure than without it, the sprinkler system installation makes the JRC proposal more attractive.

Annual After-Tax Cash Flows—Loss Reduction or Prevention Device

NCF Calculations

Cash revenues		$60,000
Less: Cash expenses (except income taxes)		
Expected value of fire losses	$4,200	
Sprinkler maintenance	$ 400	($4,600)
Before-tax NCF		$55,400
Less: Income taxes		
Before-tax NCF	$55,400	
Less: Depreciation expense ($210,000 ÷ 10 years)	($21,000)	
Taxable income	$34,400	
Income taxes (40% × $34,400)		($13,760)
After-tax NCF		$41,640

- The before-tax expected value of annual fire losses decreases to $4,200 (the value of fire losses the hospital will retain).
- The maintenance expenses on the sprinkler system are considered when calculating taxable income.

NCF Evaluation

Factors:

Initial investment	$210,000
Life of project	10 years
Annual after-tax NCF	$41,640
Minimum acceptable rate of return (annual)	10.00%

- The sprinkler's cost is added to the cost of this proposal's initial investment when calculating taxable income.

Evaluation by NPV Method:

Present value of differential NCF ($41,640 × 6.145)	$255,878
Less: Present value of initial investment	($210,000)
NPV	$45,878

- Installing a sprinkler system would raise the initial investment to $210,000.

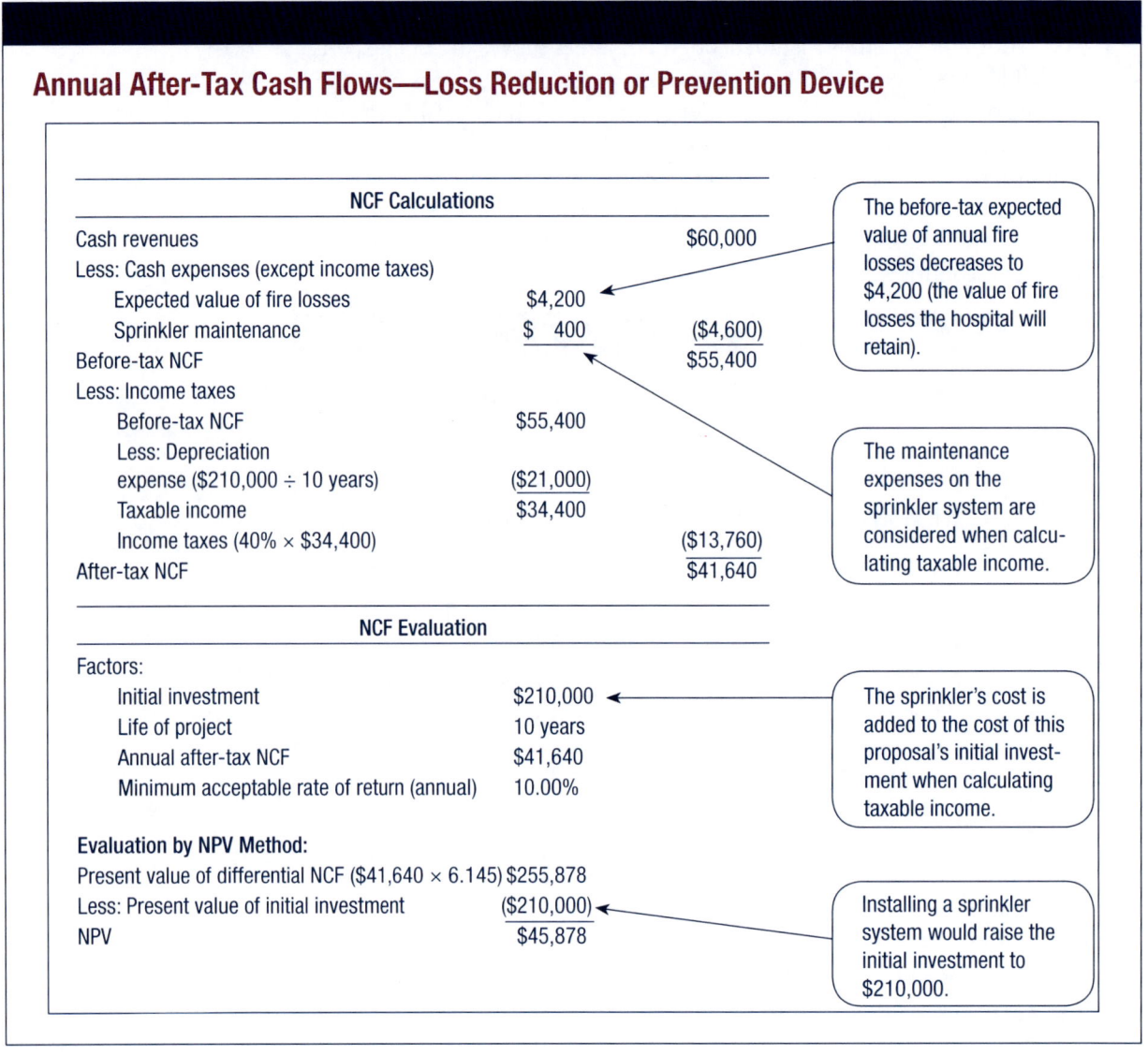

[DA02053]

Knowledge to Action

If the building has a fire in the first year that, despite the sprinkler system, causes $100,000 in property damage, explain how that would affect the project's value as a capital investment. How would the project's value be affected if business disruption were also included in the damages?

Feedback: The $100,000 loss in the first year, when the value of fire losses for the year was expected to be only $4,200, will negatively affect the project's value. The before-tax NCF will be a negative $40,400 for the first year. If the data the risk management professional uses are accurate, the probability that such a large fire will occur again during the remaining nine years of the project is low, at .03 percent. If it does not occur again, the NPV could return to a positive number overall for the project within the next two years. However, this does not recognize the additional damages that could be incurred as a result of the doctor's having to shut down his operations until the building and its contents are repaired or replaced. The income that would have been earned as a result of the doctor's work and paid to the hospital will be reduced. This increase in damages elevates the sensitivity of the project's value to losses.

USING CALL OPTIONS TO LIMIT FINANCIAL RISK

A risk management professional should be familiar with risk financing techniques that can offset the business risks from price changes. The resulting net income losses from business risks created by price changes can be just as devastating to an organization as the net income losses from a major fire or flood that strikes the organization's facilities.

Case Facts

Millwright Food Products Company (Millwright) produces baked goods that it sells around the United States. Wheat and the flour made from the wheat are necessary ingredients to make its products. Millwright's ability to earn net income depends heavily on the prices it must pay for its ingredients, especially wheat. The price of wheat changes over time. Millwright's management is uncomfortable with a swing in the company's monthly net income that results from a change in the price of wheat. To smooth the largely unpredictable fluctuations in wheat prices and its monthly operating results, Millwright is considering hedging this business risk through the use of a call option.

These are the facts needed to calculate the effect on net income of a call option that offsets input price increases for this company:

- Millwright needs an average of 10,000 units of wheat each month.
- The current market price of a unit of wheat is $3.
- The strike price (the price set in a call option contract) of a unit of wheat is $3.
- The call fee, which is the commission earned by the brokerage firm handling Millwright's purchase and sale of its call option contract, is $300.
- The purchase price of the call option contract is $5,200.
- The selling price of a call (high) is $15,200.
- The selling price of a call (low) is $0.

Underlying Concepts

A risk financing technique applicable to price changes is hedging of business risks. Unforeseen changes in prices that an organization pays for supplies, raw materials, or product components—as well as changes in the prices it receives for the goods or services it sells—are major sources of price risk, which is a form of business risk that can greatly affect the organization's operations and value.

Price increases for its inputs and price decreases for its outputs reduce an organization's cash flows and net income. Conversely, decreases in input costs and increases in selling prices increase cash flows and net income. Many organizations' managers know that input and output prices will change during the next accounting period, but they cannot reliably project the direction or size of these price changes.

Organizations that are unwilling or unable to tolerate such fluctuations in their operating results often use hedging to stabilize their cash flows. However, when hedging with **forward**, futures, or call option contracts, the organization's management must be willing to sacrifice some or all of the potential net revenue gains that could arise from favorable price changes in order to achieve protection against net income losses from adverse price changes. That sacrifice enables the organization to come closer to its projected operating results despite unpredictable price changes.

Forward contract
A contract that obligates one party to buy and another party to sell a specific financial instrument or physical commodity at a specified future date and price.

Transferring Wheat Price Increases

If Millwright pays $3 per unit of wheat, without hedging of wheat prices, the company's anticipated net income would be $11,000, per the exhibit. The exhibit provides a comparison of the effects of hedging if the price of wheat increases or decreases. The exhibit assumes that Millwright cannot pass on the changes in input prices to the end consumer. That is, Millwright would not charge more (less) for its baked goods because the price of wheat has gone up (down). See the exhibit "Monthly Income Statement With and Without Hedging Using a Wheat Call."

If, without hedging, Millwright had to pay $4 for each unit of wheat, its monthly net income would drop to $1,000, as shown in the exhibit. But if wheat prices fell to $2.50 per unit, the company's monthly net income would rise to $16,000.

It is understandable that Millwright's management would be uncomfortable with a potential $15,000 swing (from as low as $1,000 to as high as $16,000) in the company's monthly net income as a result of a change in the price of one unit of wheat of $1.50 or less. To smooth the effect of these largely unpredictable fluctuations in wheat prices and, therefore, in monthly operating results, Millwright could hedge this business risk with a forward or a futures contract, giving up a potential net income increase from falling wheat prices to protect against losses from rising wheat prices. This approach would give

Monthly Income Statement With and Without Hedging Using a Wheat Call

Without Hedging	Wheat Prices Stay at $3.00	Wheat Prices Fall to $2.50	Wheat Prices Rise to $4.00
Revenues			
Sales	$100,000	$100,000	$100,000
Other income	$3,000	$3,000	$3,000
Total Revenues	$103,000	$103,000	$103,000
Expenses			
Wheat flour	$30,000	$25,000	$40,000
Other expenses	$62,000	$62,000	$62,000
Total Expenses	($92,000)	($87,000)	($102,000)
Net Income	$11,000	$16,000	$1,000
With Hedging $3 Call			
Revenues			
Sales	$100,000	$100,000	$100,000
Other income	$3,000	$3,000	$3,000
Net income on call option	$0	$0	$10,000
Total Revenues	$103,000	$103,000	$113,000
Expenses			
Wheat flour	$30,000	$25,000	$40,000
Other expenses	$62,000	$62,000	$62,000
Call fee	$300	$300	$300
Loss on call option	$5,200	$5,200	$0
Total Expenses	($97,500)	($92,500)	($102,300)
Net Income	$5,500	$10,500	$10,700

[DA08802]

Millwright greater assurance that its monthly net income would be consistently closer to the normal $11,000 despite any change in the cost of wheat.

Instead of a forward or a futures contract, Millwright could purchase a type of option contract known as a call. The call would offset losses from any increase in the price of wheat, but Millwright would have to pay a premium for the contract analogous to an insurance premium. Consequently, even though option contracts are not insurance contracts, using them to transfer risk is sometimes called insurance.

Consider the effects on cash flows if Millwright were to purchase a call option on wheat (a "wheat call"). A wheat call is a contract that gives the holder the right to buy wheat at a given price (strike price) at any time before the contract's expiration date. Therefore, if the market price (called the spot price) of wheat is higher than the strike price, in theory the owner could use the contract to buy wheat at the strike price and then sell it for a profit at the spot price. This ability to sell the wheat at a profit gives the contract a commercial value, and the contract is called "in the money." Because the contract potentially has value, it can be traded in an organized market. Therefore, an alternative to buying and selling wheat is to buy or sell the contract.

Even if the spot price is lower than the strike price (called "out of the money"), the contract still has some value because there is a chance that the spot price will rise above the strike price before the expiration date. However, the value of the contract will be lower than if it were in the money. Therefore, as the spot price rises, the value of the call rises, and as the spot price declines, the value of the call declines.

If Millwright buys a call contract and the price of wheat rises, then Millwright could sell the call and use the profit to offset some of the additional costs caused by the wheat price increase. Alternatively, if the price of wheat declines, Millwright could choose not to sell the contract. Some of the increased net income that results from the lower wheat cost is offset by the purchase price and fee paid for the call contract.

The exhibit illustrates the effects of buying a call option on wheat, which brings Millwright's net income back to a range near the normal $11,000 level. If wheat prices climb to $4 and Millwright has purchased a call option on wheat, the exhibit gives a simplified general example of rising wheat prices and opportunities for increasing net income from the rising price of wheat call options. Assume that in a particular month, Millwright pays $5,200 for a call for enough units of wheat to produce the baked goods that the company plans to sell during the month. As the wheat price rises during the month, Millwright may be able to sell this wheat call option for $15,200, making a $10,000 ($15,200 – $5,200) net income. The brokerage firm handling Millwright's purchase and sale of its wheat call must be paid its call fee of $300. The overall result, shown at the bottom of the exhibit in the column farthest to the right, is a $10,700 net income, close to the $11,000 normal net income that Millwright would have earned had the price of wheat been $3.

Millwright's only real cost in this example is the $300 call fee. Without it, the company would have made its anticipated $11,000 net income.

The exhibit, in the lower half of the middle column, shows what happens if wheat prices fall with hedging, causing Millwright to make a greater net income producing baked goods but to lose money on its wheat call. Assume that the spot price of wheat falls below the $3 per unit price available under Millwright's call and remains below $3 until the option expires. In that case, Millwright loses the $5,200 purchase price if it holds the option until expiration. (It might reduce this loss if it sells the option before expiration.) A $5,200 expense is shown in the lower portion of the exhibit, along with the call fee of $300 for the option's purchase and sale. The loss on the call and the related call fee reduce to $10,500 the $16,000 net income that Millwright would have earned because of falling wheat prices had it purchased no call (per the middle column and upper portion of the exhibit). Again, however, this $10,500 net income is close to the $11,000 normal monthly net income.

SUMMARY

Present value is the current value of money that will be received in the future. The process of calculating the present value of a future amount is called discounting. The discount rate is the rate used to calculate the present value of a future amount, whether it is to be received after a single period or multiple periods.

An annuity is a series of equal periodic payments made or received at the end of each period. A risk management professional often must determine the present value of an annuity—that is, the value today of a series of consecutive payments to be made or received in the future at the end of each specified period. The present value can be calculated by summing the present values of each of the payments or by using a present value of an annuity table. The present value is calculated by multiplying the payment amount by the applicable present value of an annuity factor from the table.

The valuation methods required to calculate the present value of a stream of unequal payments differ from those used to calculate the present value for a stream of equal payments. One way in which to calculate the present value of a stream of unequal payments is to use the present value table to calculate the present value of each individual payment and then sum those values.

One method that may be used to determine whether an investment is sound is to determine its net present value, which is the difference between the present value of its cash inflows and the present value of its cash outflows. The NPV rule suggests that if an investment's NPV is positive, the investment should be made. However, NPV analysis and the NPV rule should not be used as the sole determinant as to whether to make an investment.

The NPV method is commonly used to make capital budgeting decisions. It involves determining whether a particular proposal is expected to produce net cash flows with a present value that exceeds the amount of funds invested using a discount rate that reflects the organization's cost of capital.

Cash flow analysis of a capital investment proposal should incorporate the estimated differential after-tax NCFs related to all the proposal's costs and benefits, including any expected accidental losses and the loss control techniques that could be implemented to control them. Cash flow analyses should explicitly recognize that the one-time costs of implementing loss control techniques should often be added to a proposal's initial investment, while continuing loss control costs should be deducted from the projected annual NCFs.

For business risks created by price changes, hedging in the form of a call option is a risk financing technique that enables an organization to transfer those risks to another party. Hedging is a financial transaction in which one asset (typically a contract—in this case, a call options contract) is held to offset the risks associated with another asset. The risk transferred is the exposure to loss from declines (or increases) in the market price of a commodity (such as wheat), which the transferor must hold for an extended period as a normal part of doing business. Hedging of business risks allows an organization to protect itself against price-level losses by sacrificing possible price-level gains.

Direct Your Learning

11

Monitoring and Reporting on Risk

Educational Objectives

After learning the content of this assignment, you should be able to:

▸ Describe the responsibilities and functions of an organization's board of directors in providing effective risk management oversight.

▸ Explain how organizational environment and internal control techniques support risk monitoring efforts.

▸ Explain how the responsibilities and functions of an internal audit differ from those of internal controls and how an internal audit provides support to an organization's risk monitoring efforts.

▸ Describe risk assurance methods that advise an organization of its risk management performance level.

▸ Identify the elements of effective risk management reports.

Outline

Board Risk Oversight

Internal Controls Support to Risk Monitoring

Internal Audit Support to Risk Monitoring

Risk Assurance to Evaluate Risk Management Performance

Risk Management Monitoring and Reporting

Summary

Monitoring and Reporting on Risk

BOARD RISK OVERSIGHT

Effective oversight of the risk management process by the boards of directors at certain key financial firms might have alleviated much of the global financial crisis of 2008 and 2009. Recognition of the consequences of this lack of effective oversight has led to more intense scrutiny of board activities by regulators, rating agencies, and financial markets.

The board of an organization is responsible for overseeing the overall risk management effort within that organization. The board must ensure that there is a working risk management planning process, that the organization's managers are actually doing the risk management planning, and that the appropriate risk management decisions are being carried out.

In addition to its oversight duties, a board provides overarching guidance regarding an organization's risk profile and the tools necessary to manage that level of risk.

Board Responsibility for Risk Management Oversight

The ultimate responsibility for an organization's risk management rests with the board. Legal and regulatory authorities are escalating boards' requirements, mandating that they demonstrate that appropriate risk management processes and adequate oversight are in place.

Some broad categories of risks that a board must oversee include these:

- Strategic risks that arise from trends in the economy and society, such as changes in the political climate in a particular country or changes in the competitive environment
- Operational risks that arise from people, processes, systems, or controls, such as information technology (IT) risk and management oversight
- Financial risks that arise from the effect of market forces on financial assets or liabilities, such as changes in interest rates or changes in the prices of inputs

A board takes an active role in determining the appropriate portfolio of risks that an organization undertakes, and it provides guidance in the prioritization of the management of key risks.

11.4 Risk Management Principles and Practices

In the wake of the global financial crisis of the late 2000s, a number of government regulations have been created to address board oversight of risk management. Board members are now required to demonstrate that they are evaluating the organization's risk management posture on an ongoing basis. These are some of the laws and regulations:

- The Dodd-Frank Act, a United States financial reform legislation passed in 2010, establishes requirements for risk committees at bank holding companies and certain nonbank financial holding companies and sets specific rules for risk oversight and reporting.
- Effective in 2010, the U.S. Securities and Exchange Commission (SEC) Rule 33-9089 requires that publicly traded companies disclose board risk oversight activities.
- The 2010 update to the UK Corporate Governance Code added a specific risk management principle that states, "The board is responsible for determining the nature and extent of the significant risks it is willing to take in achieving its strategic objectives. The board should maintain sound risk management and internal control systems."[1]
- The European Union's European Systemic Risk Board was created in 2010 to monitor and assess systemic risk. Individual countries within the European Union have established country-specific agencies to perform similar functions.

In addition to government regulations, there are requirements from world stock exchanges, credit rating agencies, banks, and insurance underwriters. Here are some examples of these nongovernmental regulations:

- The New York Stock Exchange's principles for board governance now include several direct references to a board's risk management responsibilities, including establishing effective systems and establishing suitable compensation incentives for "appropriate—but not excessive—risk-taking."[2]
- The Tokyo Stock Exchange has strengthened its requirement for boards to report on their risk management oversight activities.
- Standard & Poor's (S&P's) and other credit rating agencies have incorporated into the credit rating process an assessment of board oversight of an organization's risk management process. S&P's review focuses on how well an organization identifies its key risks and how well it makes decisions that are consistent with the organization's stated appetite and tolerance for risk.

Risk Management Reporting

Each organization tailors its risk management oversight to suit its own needs, and there is no one-size-fits-all model for risk management reporting.

Risk management information can come to the board from a number of different sources. In some organizations, risk management information is reported directly to the board or the risk committee. In others, the information is reported to the board through the chief executive officer (CEO).

Boards form special committees to address certain routine risk categories while maintaining total board oversight on selected higher-level risks. For example, risk committees are sometimes formed to oversee routine risk management processes within business units, though the entire board may still oversee risk management issues that affect the survival of the organization, such as political or economic risk.

This kind of board risk committee is becoming more commonplace with the current global emphasis on stricter board oversight of risk management processes. Some U.S. firms are now required to have a separate risk committee as part of the board.

A board audit committee is tasked with ensuring that the organization is in compliance with its stated internal procedures as well as with regulatory and legal requirements. As such, this committee provides risk-management-related information to the board. In many organizations, the audit committee is tasked with the same functions that a risk committee would normally handle.

Other board committees may also have a risk management reporting function. For example, the personnel committee is typically tasked with preparing a succession plan for senior management (which can also be construed as a risk management activity).

Larger organizations, especially in financial services, are establishing the chief risk officer (CRO) role. This is a senior management position tasked with coordinating the risk management process throughout the organization. See the exhibit "An Example of a Risk Management Organization Chart."

An Example of a Risk Management Organization Chart

A board's risk management reporting system may include reporting from the various parts of the organization to the chief executive officer, as well as reporting from the "C" offices to board committees that are responsible for specific issues, such as from the chief risk officer to the risk committee or from the chief financial officer to the audit committee.

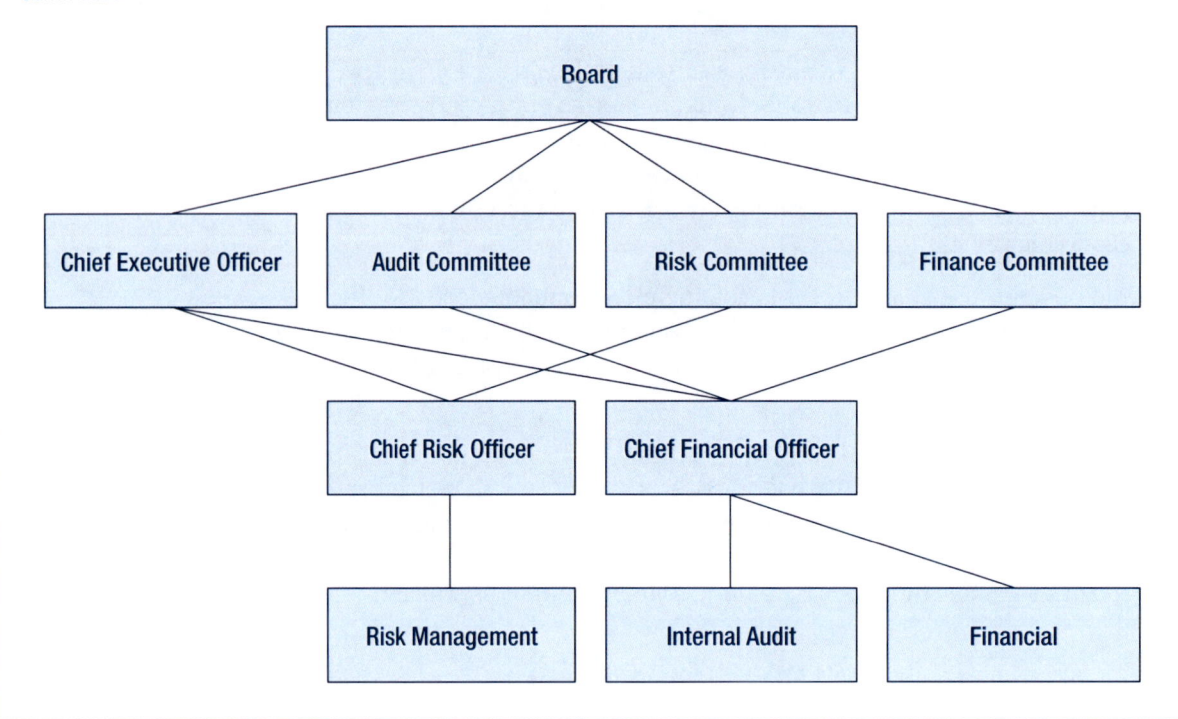

[OV08754]

Board Risk Committee

Recent trends in government regulations have instituted more formal requirements for organizations' boards, especially for the boards of financial services companies like banks. In larger organizations, risk committees are being set up to focus on their boards' risk management oversight functions. The increased focus on risk management oversight is also spreading to nonfinancial firms. Although the form and function of the risk committee differs from organization to organization, there are certain common principles that are followed:

- Ensuring that a risk management process is in place at all levels of the organization and that the risk management process is being adhered to
- Identifying and quantifying risks within the organization
- Defining the organization's risk appetite and tolerance
- Prioritizing the selection of risks to determine those that should be retained within the organization and those that should be reduced, eliminated, or transferred

Monitoring and Reporting on Risk   11.7

The risk committee receives reports from senior management and may also receive reports from other board committees or departments within the organization, such as the finance department or the risk management department.

Apply Your Knowledge

While risk committees are formed to handle routine risk management oversight, the full board retains oversight of certain types of risks that can affect a firm's survival. Which one of the following risk management oversight functions would be the most likely to be retained by the full board rather than be delegated to the board's risk committee?

a. Evaluating political and economic risk within the host country
b. Reviewing the credit limits for the ten largest customer accounts
c. Receiving reports from the CRO about planned retentions of interest rate risk exposures
d. Assessing the progress of the firm's insurance purchasing program

Feedback: a. Evaluating political and economic risk within the host country is an example of a strategic risk, and this type of risk is more likely to be evaluated by the full board rather than be delegated to a committee. Reports on interest rate risk management efforts, credit risk exposures, and the organization's insurance purchasing program are routine in nature and would be the type of oversight functions normally delegated to the risk committee.

Chief Risk Officer (CRO)

A CRO serves as the primary executive in charge of risk management throughout an organization. Although most organizations do not have a formal CRO, this position is becoming more common, especially in financial institutions and energy companies. Regardless of whether an organization has a CRO or not, the duties of the position are present in the organization. If there is no CRO, the CEO or the chief financial officer (CFO) might assume the CRO duties and functions, or those duties might be delegated to a committee.

When there is a CRO, that person typically has direct line authority over the risk management department and indirect authority over the risk management planning process in all other line units. The CRO typically reports directly to the board and may also chair the board's risk committee.

Transparency and Clear Communications

Open and constructive communications between the board and management is essential to ensuring that an effective risk management culture exists within an organization. The New York Stock Exchange governing principles suggest that there should be "constructive tension" between the board and the management team, but also indicate that both teams should still work together toward a common goal. Constructive tension should be healthy—for example, the board asking the CRO to explain the reasoning behind a particular risk management decision or policy. Although the CRO may not enjoy having his decisions questioned, the board's oversight responsibility requires it to ask that type of question.

Communications through the various C-level officers and the board committees must be coordinated to ensure effective oversight of the enterprise risk management efforts. Lines of communication between the board and senior management should be clearly delineated to ensure transparency and foster cooperation.

It is important for boards to ensure that the information received in the managerial reports truly reflects the way things are actually being managed within the organization. The board can easily become overloaded with information, but there is also a potential problem if the information that the board receives has been edited too much. Some boards seek periodic reports from midlevel managers to try to stay abreast of emerging issues within the organization.

Internal Audits

The purpose of a board's audit committee is to assess the organization's compliance with legal and regulatory requirements and its financial reporting systems. Audit committees are frequently assigned risk management oversight responsibilities, as well. To some extent, the duties of the audit committee are naturally concerned with risk management activities, as compliance with financial regulations and legal requirements is necessary to the long-term financial health of the organization. Internal auditors can also assess the extent to which an organization's managers are complying with stated risk management policies and procedures.

The primary difference between having an audit committee oversee risk management and having a separate risk committee is that the audit committee's focus is on compliance with existing standards, while the risk committee's focus should be on setting new and appropriate standards and evaluating the existing standards. A risk committee is meant to create policy, while an audit committee is more attuned to assessing policy adherence.

Internal Audit Committee Formal Reports

Formal reports on the financial condition of the organization are generated as part of the overall risk management process. An audit committee works with internal and external auditors to ensure that the organization is in compliance with governmental regulations. As part of that process, the audit committee is responsible for the annual financial reporting, as well as other internal control reports. The audit committee function in reviewing financial statements is to attest to the accuracy of those statements. Sarbanes-Oxley requires both the CEO and the CFO to certify that the statements are correct and valid under penalty of fines and imprisonment.

Section 404 of the Sarbanes-Oxley Act requires public companies in the U.S. to report on their operational risks and on the adequacy of their organizations' internal controls to monitor those risks. This expanded transparency of companies' financial reporting helps ensure that an organization's risk appetite and risk posture are communicated to stakeholders.

Internal Audit Committee Informal Reports

An internal audit may also complement the work of the risk committee by producing informal reports on the scope and nature of risks within the organization. For example, the risk committee may develop guidelines on counterparty risk that limit the organization's exposure to any single counterparty to $10 million, which would establish a risk management standard for credit risk exposure. The audit committee, as part of the process of reviewing compliance, would check the organization's internal records to determine whether there were any noncompliance issues with this standard. As part of its audit process, the auditors might also find evidence that the existing standards are either too stringent or too lax, and that information could then be forwarded to the risk committee for its consideration.

INTERNAL CONTROLS SUPPORT TO RISK MONITORING

Diamond Foods recently fired its chief executive officer (CEO) and chief financial officer (CFO), following a restatement of its earnings, because revenues were reported in the wrong periods. The restatement prompted additional regulatory scrutiny, threatened its credit rating, and damaged the firm's reputation. The root cause for the earnings restatement was poor internal controls within the organization's financial reporting system.

A strong risk management culture coupled with effective internal controls strengthens an organization's risk monitoring efforts. The term "organizational environment" refers to the attitudes and values in an organization that make up its culture. A culture that emphasizes effective risk management at all levels helps to ensure that all members of the organization are continually monitoring risk. Internal controls are the processes an organization uses to systematically review its operations and to monitor its compliance with its own risk management value system.

Internal Controls Defined

In 1992, the Committee of Sponsoring Organizations of the Treadway Commission (COSO) drew up a framework of internal controls. COSO classifies internal controls as all of the systems and processes that an organization uses to achieve its operational goals, internal and external financial reporting goals, and legal and regulatory compliance goals. The COSO framework has become a global standard for the design, implementation, and evaluation of internal control systems.

Purpose of Internal Controls

The purpose of internal controls is to maximize the effectiveness of the organization. With respect to risk monitoring, internal controls help the organization define and monitor objectives that contribute to effective risk management.

COSO groups internal control objectives into three categories:

- Effectiveness and efficiency of operations objectives—Management determines these as part of its overall strategy. These organizational-level objectives define how the organization intends to go about its business. Examples of these types of objectives include quality standards, cost-control objectives, and production levels. Individual operating units use these objectives to develop lower-level objectives, which support the organizational-level objectives. Risks that might prevent an organization from achieving these objectives must be evaluated and monitored.
- Reporting objectives—These produce accurate and effective financial reporting to outside parties. Reliable financial statements are essential to the firm's ability to borrow funds and to maintain good relations with investors. The organization also relies on accurate and timely internal reports to effectively manage itself. The reporting objectives support the effectiveness and efficiency objectives by providing the information necessary to determine whether the organization is meeting those objectives.
- Compliance objectives—These arise because organizations are subject to numerous local, national, and international laws and regulations. Examples include financial reporting standards for publicly traded corporations, environmental compliance reporting requirements, and worker safety requirements.

Benefits of Internal Controls

Internal controls reduce uncertainty within an organization in several ways. First, internal controls establish clear lines of authority and responsibility for risk management at all levels of the organization. Internal controls generate communication among all levels of management and within departments, which promotes a better understanding of the effect of risk across departmental lines. Effective internal controls promote a risk management culture and help the organization to efficiently allocate internal risk management resources.

COSO's Five Components

The COSO framework lists five interrelated components of internal controls. See the exhibit "COSO's Five Components of Internal Controls."

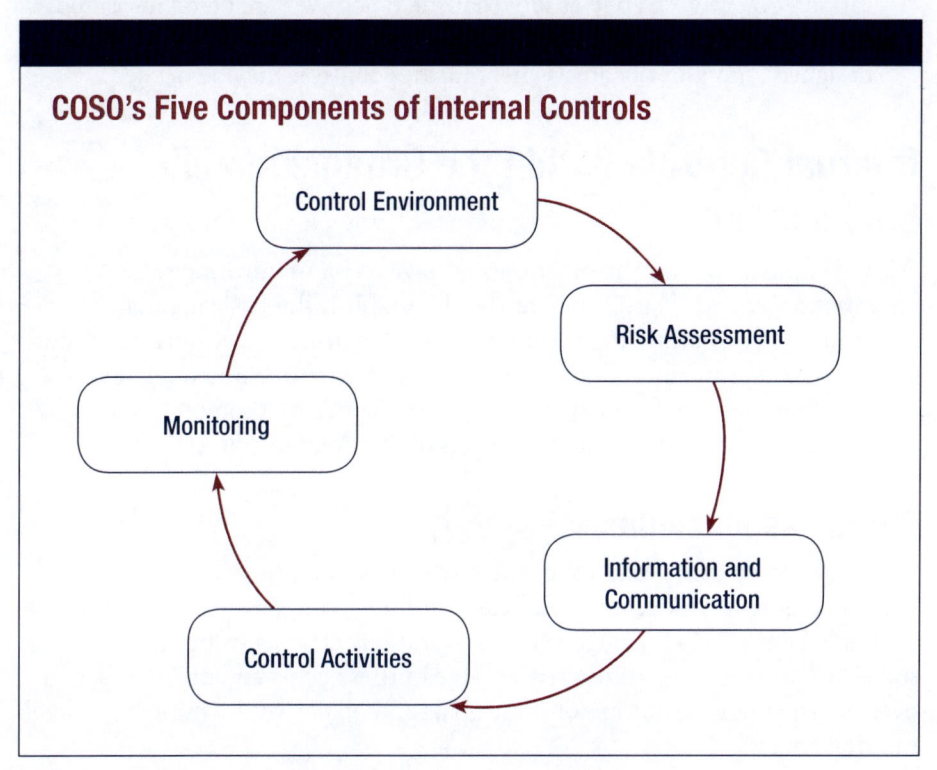

COSO's Five Components of Internal Controls

[Diagram: A circular flow showing five components connected by arrows in sequence: Control Environment → Risk Assessment → Information and Communication → Control Activities → Monitoring → (back to Control Environment).]

Committee of Sponsoring Organizations of the Treadway Commission (COSO) [OV08756]

These are the components:

- Control environment—This component forms the basis for carrying out all of the organization's other functions. The control environment establishes the lines of authority within the organization, individual and departmental responsibilities, lines of reporting, accountability, and ethics.
- Risk assessment—This component defines the manner in which the organization measures and manages risk. The organization must identify and quantify risk, establish its risk appetite, choose the type of risks it wishes to retain or diminish, prioritize those risks, and determine the best methods for monitoring them.
- Control activities—Control activities are all the actions that the organization takes to implement its objectives in accordance with its risk appetite. Control activities are the steps that the organization takes to actively manage its risk.
- Information and communication—Appropriate information must be disseminated within the organization and externally to stakeholders and regulatory authorities. Relevant and accurate information is necessary to

establish appropriate risk management objectives. That information must be communicated to the appropriate parties in order to be effective.
- Monitoring—Monitoring activities measure compliance with the organization's objectives. They ensure that the objectives are being measured, ascertain whether the various internal controls are functioning as designed, and identify areas where further controls may be needed.

Internal Controls Within the Organizational Environment

All stakeholders within the organization have a risk monitoring role. An organization's control environment should establish the basic approach to risk management by defining the organization's risk culture and its attitude toward risk and risk monitoring. That culture must be communicated to all levels of the firm from the top down. A risk management culture promotes awareness and continuous improvement at all levels of the organization.

Board Responsibilities

The board of directors establishes the risk management profile for an organization, including its risk tolerances. The board sets policy, assigns responsibility for implementing risk management goals and objectives, ensures that all stakeholders in the organization are aware of these goals and objectives, and oversees the implementation of these goals and objectives by using high-level internal controls.

Management Responsibilities

Management is responsible for establishing effective internal controls to monitor risk. The internal controls implemented at lower levels must support the internal controls implemented at higher levels. The internal controls in different departments or divisions should be mutually supportive and should contribute to the organizational-level internal control systems.

Employee Responsibilities

Employees support risk monitoring efforts by participating in internal control processes. Employees should communicate suggestions to improve systems and report any breaches of internal controls to the appropriate managers.

Auditor Responsibilities

Auditors are responsible for monitoring compliance with internal control systems. Internal auditors collaborate with external auditors when necessary. Auditors also recommend new internal control processes and standards when existing standards are inadequate or when new, unexpected risks arise.

Transparent Communications

Transparent communications between individuals at all levels of an organization are necessary to implement effective internal controls to monitor risk. Employees should be encouraged to report problems without fear of repercussion. Communications should emphasize the comprehensive nature of an organization's risk monitoring efforts. See the exhibit "Internal Controls with the Organizational Environment."

Internal Controls with the Organizational Environment

Although everyone in the organization is responsible for risk monitoring to some extent, certain groups of individuals have specialized roles and responsibilities in developing and implementing internal controls for risk monitoring.

Roles and Responsibilities	
Board	Provide guidance on appropriate risk management goals and objectives and oversee management's implementation of internal controls
Management	Design and implement effective internal controls at all management levels and coordinate the controls to ensure they are mutually supportive
Employees	Support the risk management effort at all levels by reporting problems, proposing solutions, and supporting a culture of effective risk management
Auditors	Measure the effectiveness of existing internal control systems and propose new and improved systems when necessary

[OV08757]

Internal Control Techniques

Internal controls are classified as either hard controls or soft controls. Hard controls are tangible items that are easily audited; soft controls are intangibles that deal with people's attitudes and beliefs.

Examples of hard controls include process checklists, corporate policies and procedures manuals, lines of authority, physical controls like fire alarms and safes, performance reports, and equipment condition reports. These controls can be measured directly. For example, organizational policy may require that all employees involved in an accident involving a company vehicle submit to a drug screening within twenty-four hours of the incident. The written policy can be observed directly, and compliance can be measured by reviewing the organization's accident report records. Similarly, a distillery may require that random samples of its product be quality tested at least once per shift. When a sample falls outside the established quality standards, other control processes are implemented to identify and correct the problem.

Soft controls include an organization's core values and ethics, risk management philosophy, collegiality among its stakeholders, and commitment to excellence. Soft controls are difficult to audit because they are intangible, but they can be measured. For example, an employee questionnaire may uncover perceived problems with customer service. Employee meetings or open forums with senior management or board members may turn up employee dissatisfaction issues. Organizations can use surveys to measure employee attitudes toward risk and risk management.

Internal Control Linked to Risk Monitoring

Internal reporting systems provide information to managers to help them better achieve the organization's objectives. Assessing and monitoring risk, which is defined as the effect of uncertainty on those objectives, is an integral part of the internal controls process.

For example, suppose customer feedback reports reveal quality problems with an organization's electronics products. Other internal control reports may supply additional information that can be used to pinpoint the problem. For example, an increase in the number of hours worked may suggest that worker fatigue is the cause. Equipment service reports that show additional maintenance requirements on plant machinery may suggest a mechanical cause. Polling the various internal control reports may help isolate the problem before it becomes a serious threat to the organization.

Internal controls may also indicate positive changes in risk. Accounts receivable delinquency reports may show an overall drop in the number of late payments in several of an organization's subsidiaries. This may signal management that economic conditions are improving, allowing the organization to begin to loosen its credit standards to improve its sales.

Apply Your Knowledge

Courtland Limited sells its products and services in several countries. While sales are recorded in the host country currency, commissions paid to sales agents are based on the equivalent value of the sale in euros. Courtland's accounting department must manually code each sales associate's monthly commission expense into the accounting system, based on the currency exchange rate in effect on the fifteenth of each month. There are twenty sales associates operating in fourteen countries, and each associate generates approximately 10,000 euros in commissions each month. Courtland wishes to implement internal controls that will reduce the potential for currency translation errors, which could result in a material misstatement of the company's financial results. Which one of the following internal controls would best support the organization's risk monitoring process to ensure accurate financial reporting of its monthly commission expenses?

a. Courtland should set corporate policy to allow only one employee to enter commission expenses in its accounting system.
b. Courtland should buy currency translation insurance to protect itself from errors.
c. Courtland should limit its sales operations to countries that use the euro in order to eliminate its currency translation risk.
d. Courtland should have a second employee verify each monthly calculation.

Feedback: d. By having two employees verify each monthly calculation, Courtland reduces the potential for errors. If Courtland set corporate policy so that a single employee did all entries (a.), it would still be exposed to that one employee's errors, and it could also increase its risk of employee dishonesty. Purchasing currency translation insurance (b.), if such insurance were available, would not address all of the potential regulatory and compliance risks to which the company would be exposed in the event of a material misstatement in its financials. Finally, limiting sales to countries that use the euro (c.) would eliminate the currency translation risk, but it might also significantly reduce the firm's revenues and profits.

Benefits of Risk Monitoring

Effective risk monitoring detects risk while it is still small and manageable. An effective system of risk assessment can build internal control systems that are able to identify emerging problems at early stages.

Limitations of Risk Monitoring

Internal controls cannot identify every risk in existence and may not detect emerging risks before they create problems. Internal control systems rely on people, and people are sometimes prone to hide problems rather than solve them. In some organizations, a silo mentality forms, in which business units and departments fail to communicate with one another and reduce the effectiveness of risk monitoring controls. Finally, deliberate fraud and employee dishonesty are inherently difficult to detect.

INTERNAL AUDIT SUPPORT TO RISK MONITORING

The Latin phrase "*Quis custodiet ipsos custodes*" loosely translates to "Who watches the watchers?" In the context of oversight of an organization's risk management process, one appropriate answer is, "The internal auditors."

Internal controls are the systems and processes that an organization uses to achieve its operational goals, internal and external financial reporting goals, and legal and regulatory compliance goals, including risk monitoring objectives. Internal controls are set up by managers. An internal audit is the system that checks on whether the internal controls managers have implemented are actually working as planned.

Defining Internal Audit

An internal audit department is an independent department within an organization that evaluates how well an organization is achieving its business objectives. The auditors are employees of the organization, but they operate independently of the management teams that they audit. The internal audit process may be supplemented by external auditors (nonemployees), or an organization may outsource its internal audit functions to an external audit firm. However, external auditors would not be as familiar with the internal workings of an organization, which limits their effectiveness in this kind of situation. External auditors are primarily used to comply with statutory requirements by certifying that the organization's financial statements present an accurate representation of its financial situation.

Functions and Responsibilities

The functions of an internal audit are evaluation and assessment. Internal auditors evaluate processes and systems to ensure that they are meeting the desired business goals and objectives. To do that, internal auditors determine what information is available to evaluate those processes, then gather that data and assess it.

Use of Internal Controls

An internal audit validates that internal controls are in place, functioning, and meeting design objectives. Internal auditors also review existing internal controls to identify potential weaknesses and recommend additional internal controls to improve operations.

Independent Status

Internal auditors must be independent to remain unbiased and objective in their evaluations. If the internal auditors were evaluating a control system that they had themselves designed, they would have an obvious conflict of interest.

Benefits to the Organization

An internal audit benefits the organization by ensuring that financial reports are accurate and that the appropriate risk disclosures are reported. Traditionally, the primary goal of the internal audit process has been to ensure accurate reporting in an organization's financial statements. Newer regulatory requirements have increased financial reporting mandates so that an organization's primary risk factors must also be disclosed in the financial statements. The major stock exchanges around the globe have increased their disclosure requirements, as well. The internal audit is evolving away from being primarily a financial controls evaluation process; it's becoming a more holistic system of reviewing an organization's overall objectives and evaluating the risks that challenge the organization's ability to meet those objectives.

Report Assurance

An internal audit provides assurance that reports are accurate and that internal controls are in place that will ensure the accuracy of the financial statement data. An internal audit also assesses the inherent risks in processes and systems, which increases the accuracy of risk reporting.

Report Certification

Many organizations are required to have an external auditor certify that financial statements represent a true and fair view of an organization's financial situation. External auditors test financial reporting systems and internal controls to ensure that the systems are reporting transactions correctly. Internal auditors may work with external auditors to provide the information necessary for audit certification.

Risk Management and Internal Audit

Risk management and internal audit are separate but complementary functions. Both areas increase the efficiency of the organization's risk monitoring efforts, but they do it in different ways.

Role of Risk Management

The risk management team first identifies and prioritizes risks, based on guidance from the board of directors about the organization's risk appetite and tolerances. Risk management professionals then design a plan to meet the risk management objectives, design internal controls to manage the risks, and implement the plan. After the risk management plan has been implemented, the risk management team monitors the plan and looks for new risk management opportunities and threats. The risk management team is held accountable for the proper design and implementation of the risk management plan, internal controls, and overall success of the risk management effort.

Role of Internal Auditor

Internal auditors are responsible for auditing the internal controls implemented by the risk management team. As part of that effort, internal auditors first check to see that the risk controls have actually been implemented and that they are being used properly. Then the internal auditors evaluate the effectiveness of the controls to determine whether the intended risk management goal is being achieved. Auditors also look for risks that might have been overlooked in the design process. Auditors might provide alternatives and recommend solutions, but the implementation of risk management solutions is left to management. See the exhibit "Risk Management and Internal Audit Roles."

Risk Management and Internal Audit Roles

The board of directors establishes the risk management policy and risk appetite. It also determines the amount and types of risk that the organization wants to pursue, retain, reduce, or avoid.

Risk Management	Internal Audit
• Designs and implements the risk management plan, including the choice of appropriate tools and responses to risk, in accordance with board guidance	• Reviews and critiques the implementation of the risk management plan
• Establishes internal risk management controls	• Audits internal risk controls to ensure that they are in place and working as designed
• Monitors risk levels within the organization	• Monitors risk levels within the organization to determine whether the risk management plan and internal risk controls are effectively managing risk as expected
• Identifies and quantifies new, emerging risks and recommends appropriate responses	• Identifies and quantifies new, emerging risks
• Is accountable for whether the risk management plan is effective	

[OV08755]

Apply Your Knowledge

Camp Hill Transport's financial results for the most recent quarter show that its operating expenses have increased dramatically following a series of traffic accidents involving its fleet of delivery trucks. The problem seems to be a result of poor vehicle maintenance, but there have been no changes to the maintenance schedule that would explain the rash of accidents. Several of Camp Hill's customers are threatening to move their accounts to other delivery firms because of shipping delays. Which of the following activities would be the most appropriate action for Camp Hill's Internal Audit Department to take in response to this situation?

a. Internal Audit could allocate the loss costs and the maintenance costs among the various divisions and departments so that the costs are spread more evenly.
b. Internal Audit could design new driver training procedures to reduce the number of accidents.
c. Internal Audit could review the accident costs and then choose alternative insurance limits and deductibles that minimize the overall cost of risk.
d. Internal Audit could review the company's internal risk controls, such as vehicle maintenance schedules and maintenance reports, to determine whether the appropriate controls are in place and are being followed.

Feedback: d. Internal Audit should review the company's internal risk controls and evaluate whether the established procedures are being followed, as well as whether those procedures are effective controls. Allocating costs to various departments (a.) is outside of the scope of the auditors' evaluation of internal controls. Similarly, the implementation of risk management solutions such as driver training programs or insurance levels (b. and c.) is not an Internal Audit function. Such solutions might be part of the department's recommendations, but Internal Audit does not implement solutions or perform a management function.

Risk-Based Auditing

Risk-based auditing prioritizes the use of an organization's limited internal audit resources in the areas that pose the greatest risk to the organization. Successful risk-based auditing focuses on these three principles:

- Audit to business objectives
- Focus on the materiality of the risk
- Identify the threats to the achievement of the business goals and objectives

Adhering to these three principles increases the efficiency of the internal audit process.

Audit to Business Objectives

The risk-based audit begins by examining the business objectives of the process or control being audited. To understand whether a control is working properly, the auditor must first establish the business objective that the control is trying to achieve. Internal auditors are rarely experts on the detailed managerial aspects of the function being audited, but they are experts on evaluating processes and systems in general. Auditors, with the help of managers who are functional experts, can help to determine solutions that achieve the business objective.

Focus on the Materiality of the Risk

Risk-based auditing focuses its efforts on those systems and processes that pose the greatest threat to the organization. For example, in a financial advisory firm, employee dishonesty could pose a much more significant threat to the reputation of the firm than potential misstatements of expenses on employee travel vouchers. Although it is important for the expense vouchers to be accurate, risk-based auditing recognizes that a scandal involving employee embezzlement of client funds could destroy the organization's reputation and threaten its very survival. Similarly, risk-based auditing focuses its effort on financial reporting issues that could result in material misstatements of its financial position, requiring the organization to issue restatements.

Identify the Threats to the Achievement of the Business Goals and Objectives

Risk-based auditing starts with an evaluation of the business objective, which means that it can help to identify threats to the achievement of that objective. By the time risk-based auditing has begun, managers have identified the key threats to the successful achievement of their business objective; however, an internal auditor brings in a fresh perspective. As auditors examine processes, they may see threats that have been overlooked or tie in threats to a particular process that are related to another part of the organization.

RISK ASSURANCE TO EVALUATE RISK MANAGEMENT PERFORMANCE

Confidence in an organization's ability to manage risk creates a host of financial benefits for the organization. Measuring that level of confidence is therefore a very important aspect of board oversight.

Risk assurance refers to the level of confidence in the effectiveness of the organization's risk management culture, practices, and procedures. There are a number of sources for that assurance, both within the organization and with outside stakeholders. Many organizations benefit from using the Control Risk Self-Assessment (CRSA) model, which relies on risk management assessment from business unit managers and employees. High levels of risk assurance result in lower costs to the organization, enhancing its long-term value.

Risk Assurance

A high level of risk assurance gives an organization these characteristics:

- The board of directors is certain that key risks that could affect the organization's successful attainment of goals and objectives have been properly identified, quantified, prioritized, and managed in an effective and cost-efficient manner.
- Managers have implemented a system of effective risk management controls; they also have an effective risk monitoring system in place and are using it.
- Risk reporting systems are providing information up the management chain to the board of directors, as well as down the management chain to the operating units.
- A culture of risk management prevails within the organization. Internally, employees recognize this culture; externally, customers, suppliers, lenders, and shareholders are aware of the organization's risk management culture as well.

Risk Assurance Sources

Risk assurance can be provided through many different sources within the organization. Here are some examples:

- Policy and procedures documentation, which include safety manuals, training plans, disaster recovery plans, product recall procedures, and data privacy protection plans
- Normal business unit and department operating reports such as profit and loss statements, expense reports, equipment utilization reports, and staffing and payroll reports
- Internal audit reports of operations and processes, internal controls, and risk monitoring
- Risk management reports and documentation, including business continuity plans, incident documentation reports, and strategic planning documents indicating strengths, weaknesses, opportunities, and threats to the business units and the organization as a whole

External sources also provide risk assurance. External audits confirm that the financial statements represent a true and fair depiction of the organization's financial position. Favorable press reports may bolster the organization's reputation and can demonstrate a favorable public perception of the organization.

The willingness of lenders to supply funds at favorable rates is an indication of the organization's relative standing among its peers. Reports and rankings from legal and regulatory authorities can provide evidence of risk assurance. Surveys of customers and suppliers may provide evidence about the organization's risk assurance level as well.

Apply Your Knowledge

Westfork Mutual's board of directors is seeking assurance regarding whether the risk management program is being carried out throughout the organization. The board wants to determine whether the organization's risk culture properly reflects the organization's board-established risk tolerances. Which one of these sources would be the best source of documentation about employee attitudes to risk?

a. The risk manager could supply the board with a summary of incident reports from the past two years.
b. The Internal Audit Department could survey a sample of employees using a risk questionnaire.
c. The board could ask senior management to provide a report on employee attitudes.
d. Outside auditors could be hired to perform an employee satisfaction survey.

Feedback: b. Tasking internal auditors to survey employees could provide information about compliance using intangibles like employee attitudes to risk, which are hard to quantify. A summary report of incident reports could measure past compliance with standards (a.), but it does not really provide much information about attitudes. Reports from senior management (c.) provide the board with the managers' perception of employee attitudes, but not the actual attitudes themselves. Finally, although an externally produced survey might provide the necessary information (d.), external auditors are less attuned to the internal culture of an organization and may be less effective in eliciting information about the true risk management culture.

Risk Management Effectiveness

The ability of the organization to manage risk effectively contributes to the level of risk assurance. The organization's risk management culture and its dedication to risk management are difficult to measure objectively, but they can be assessed through surveys, internal discussions with management, and interactions with employees. An internal audit can provide evidence that risk controls are in place and functioning as designed. Self-assessment done by business units and management can demonstrate adherence to risk management standards as well as risk tolerances. Many of these reports are part of the normal risk monitoring and reporting systems, but they can be supplemented or examined in greater detail in special quarterly or annual management retreats.

Control Risk Self-Assessment

CRSA is a process in which managers perform an annual self-audit of the risk assurance within their own particular area of responsibility. The Committee of Sponsoring Organizations of the Treadway Commission (COSO) developed standards for United States companies in the early 1990s. Similar standards were developed in the United Kingdom by the Cadbury Committee as the UK Corporate Governance Code. These two frameworks set the foundation for CRSA as it is practiced today.

The purpose of CRSA is to evaluate the effectiveness of business processes. The managers who actually perform the processes and focus on the business unit's goals and objectives are the ones who do the evaluation. CRSA evaluates the risk management process, risk controls that are in place, risk controls that may be needed, weaknesses in controls, problem areas, and overall effectiveness.

CRSA focuses on business objectives and the threats to meeting those objectives. CRSA can be conducted using questionnaires or score sheets, or it might be conducted as workshops or facilitated sessions among line managers and workers. CRSA workshops can focus on specific business processes, such as inventory expense control, or they might cover a broad array of topics within the business unit. An advantage of the face-to-face workshop approach is that information is disseminated quickly among individuals. A disadvantage is the cost.

CRSA helps managers, through the process of explaining the risks they face in detail to others, to better understand those risks. CRSA illuminates problem areas within a business unit, but it also identifies strengths that may be exploited.

CRSA does not replace an internal audit, but it does supplement the process. Using the CRSA model gets unit managers directly involved in the evaluation process, allowing risk management control lapses to be recognized and rectified more quickly and promoting unit manager ownership of the risk management process.

CRSA provides assurance that managers know the key risks that must be managed in their areas and confirms that proper risk controls are in place and functioning. Managers identify, quantify, and discuss significant strengths, weaknesses, opportunities, and threats within their sphere of control. The information CRSA provides discloses risk management successes and failures. This information serves as a basis for internal auditor review.

Risk Assurance Benefits

Risk assurance reduces the potential for financial surprises, enhances the organization's reputation, and breeds greater confidence in the long-term health and vitality of the organization. There are a number of benefits to internal and external stakeholders:

- The board of directors has greater confidence in management effectiveness.
- Employees have greater job security, which itself reinforces a culture of risk management as employees feel an even greater stake in maintaining and enhancing the organization's risk assurance.
- Tensions are reduced within the organization, resulting in greater cooperation and communication among departments and divisions.
- Customers and suppliers are more confident in the financial health and well-being of the organization, which may generate more favorable business terms.
- Lenders and equity shareholders have greater confidence in the organization, which reduces the organization's capital costs.
- Insurance premiums and other hazard risk management costs are reduced.
- Regulatory authorities have greater trust in the organization, which reduces the organization's regulatory compliance costs and enhances its reputation.

RISK MANAGEMENT MONITORING AND REPORTING

Renowned management theorist Peter Drucker emphasized, "What gets measured gets managed." Incorporating risk information into the management information system is essential to meeting the organization's goals and objectives.

A board of directors needs risk management information to properly oversee an organization. Managers need risk management information, as well, to be effective. Risk management monitoring and reporting must incorporate several key design features:

- Risk reporting should direct the essential information necessary to managing strategic, financial, and operational risks to the appropriate people.
- The information being reported from the lowest levels, whether it is quantitative data or qualitative data, must be consolidated and integrated as it flows up to the board level.
- The information must be in an appropriate and easy-to-use format at every stage of reporting.

Risk Reporting

An effective risk reporting system provides efficient information flow up and down the lines of authority, from the board of directors to the most entry-level employee. The board sets risk management policy, which must be communicated down. Then managers report on compliance with that policy through the risk monitoring and reporting system. These kinds of reports include risk response plans, financial reports, and incident reports. These reports allow the board to assess the overall risk management process within an organization.

Characteristics

Risk reporting should be focused on key risk indicators. The risk information must be timely and detailed, but also concise. The board needs to get a sense of how well the organization is meeting its risk management goals and objectives without being overwhelmed with information. Reports should include objective measurements and subjective assessments and perspectives so that management's views and insights are clearly expressed. Reports should show trends, comparative performance measures, and compliance with standards. Both internal and external sources of information should be included in the reports.

Functionality

Risk reports should be focused on business objectives as well as compliance with regulatory requirements. Reports should identify risks that are increasing or decreasing, risks that need immediate attention, and risks that require further analysis to determine their eventual effect on the organization.

Managing Data

A board can quickly be overwhelmed by the flow of data if that data is not managed properly. Individual reports take time to analyze, compare, and be put into perspective. Individual reports do not describe the organization's overall performance to objectives. Here are two of the kinds of choices to be aware of in managing the data reporting process:

- Integrated reporting versus silo reporting
- Quantitative data versus qualitative data

Integrated Reporting Versus Silo Reporting

The silo reporting approach has each department producing its own risk report. But risks often affect a number of departments at the same time, and as those individual department reports go up the chain, they must be integrated and summarized to be useful at the senior management and board level. On the other hand, an integrated risk report, which aggregates all of the information and then describes its effect across all departments within the organization, gives the board a much more concise and useful picture. The board can then use that information to form policies and procedures to handle risk at all levels.

Quantitative Data Versus Qualitative Data

Both types of information—quantitative and qualitative—are important in a risk management monitoring and reporting system because some metrics lend themselves to one type of data over the other. For example, credit default rates, profit ratios, and equipment utilization rates are quantitative metrics that are used to measure how well a business is managing its operating risks. Threats to an organization's reputation, on the other hand, do not lend themselves to quantitative measurement.

Often, both types of information are contained in a report. For example, customer satisfaction surveys may produce quantitative scores that can be measured over time; but those surveys might also allow for customer comments, providing qualitative information that can help to explain the scores themselves.

Apply Your Knowledge

Which of the following risk reporting processes would be most useful in reporting management's compliance with the board's credit risk policy standards?

a. Each department or division manager prepares a monthly memo about his or her perception of credit exposures in the department, and those reports are placed into a folder so that the board of directors can read them prior to the next board meeting.

b. The organization's credit analysts prepare a thoughtful annual analysis of the current credit conditions in the market.

c. Management prepares a quarterly summary report that relates the credit default rates in each division to the organization's target default rate, along with management commentary on trends in the metrics.

d. The internal auditors brief the entire board at each meeting on how well they feel the organization is handling credit risk.

Feedback: c. A summary report to the board should include high-level information and should include both quantitative and qualitative analyses. Having each department manager provide a separate report (a.) would deluge the board with information that has not been collated, analyzed, or measured against the organization's overall business objectives. A credit analysis report (b.) may provide useful information on the business environment, but it would not provide information regarding whether the organization is meeting its own goals and objectives. A briefing by internal auditors (d.) might also be useful, but it may also include too much detail and not enough management perspective.

Report Formats

There is no single standard for report formats. Each organization designs its own reporting system based on its needs. The most important characteristic of the report format is that it be useful to the user.

Best Concepts

Here are some features and concepts that some organizations find useful in a report format:

- Drill-down capability, which allows the user to view data at increasing levels of detail
- Current and updatable information, so that the user knows what is happening right now
- Room for analysis and commentary from the users at each level so that additional information can be shared immediately

Dashboards and Scorecards

Dashboards are electronic reports that use graphs and charts to summarize large amounts of data in a compact form. The main purpose of a dashboard is to summarize high-level information. Users are able to view trends, heat maps, and bar charts that provide high-level summary information; however, details of the summary information, often down to transaction level, can be made accessible as well by using drill-down functions.

Scorecards provide measurements against a set of specific objectives. For example, a scorecard on inventory control risk management might show the inventory levels during the quarter against the expected levels or show the level of inventory shortages in each business unit compared to the historic norms. Scorecards may feature visual graphics as well, but the main function is to show whether performance metrics are being met.

SUMMARY

A board determines an organization's risk management policy and is responsible for oversight of the risk management process within the organization. Recent changes in regulatory requirements across the globe have expanded boards' responsibilities in terms of ensuring that organizations' risk management policies are transparent and that organizations are in compliance with those policies. While there is no one-size-fits-all model of board oversight, there is a trend toward the establishment of board risk committees to direct the risk management oversight process. Additionally, the position of chief risk officer is becoming more common.

Internal controls are used to maximize the effectiveness of the organization. Internal controls help an organization define and monitor objectives that contribute to successful risk management. Risk is the effect of uncertainty on objectives; therefore, risk controls directly support an organization's risk management efforts by providing a form of risk assessment and monitoring.

Organizations use internal controls to monitor risk. Internal audit is the system that checks whether the internal controls are actually working as planned and identifies any necessary additional internal controls. An internal audit department performs a complementary function to the risk management function and adds another dimension to the risk monitoring process. Risk-based auditing focuses the internal audit process on the risks that pose the greatest threat to an organization.

Risk assurance regarding the effectiveness of an organization's risk management reduces costs and increases value. A number of internal and external sources can provide risk assurance information. Some organizations use the CRSA model to directly involve business unit managers and employees in the risk assurance process.

A risk management monitoring and reporting system should be designed so that it forwards the correct information both up and down the lines of authority within the organization. The right information must reach the right people in the organization and must be in an appropriate form and format. Timeliness is also important so that management can be responsive to threats and opportunities.

ASSIGNMENT NOTES

1. Financial Reporting Council, The UK Corporate Governance Code, June 2010, p. 7, www.frc.org.uk/press/pub2282.html (accessed May 21, 2012).
2. Report of the New York Stock Exchange Commission on Corporate Governance, September 23, 2010, www.nyse.com/pdfs/CCGReport.pdf (accessed May 21, 2012).

Index

Page numbers in boldface refer to pages where the word or phrase is defined.

A

Accounting, **9.3**
Accounting equation, **9.4**
Accumulated Other Comprehensive Income, 9.14
Acid-Test Ratio, **9.26**, 9.28
Actual cash value, **3.18**
Additional Cost of High Debt, 9.34
Advantages and Disadvantages of Economic Capital Analysis, 4.30
Aircraft Insurance, 3.24
Align and Integrate, 5.6, 5.24
Allocate Resources, 5.6, 5.24–5.25
All-risks policy, **3.18**
Analyze Risks, 5.17, 5.27
Analyzing Cost Structure, 9.35–9.36
Analyzing Event Consequences, 7.23–7.26
Analyzing Liquidity Risk, 9.25–9.29
Analyzing Loss Exposures, 5.19, 7.28–7.37
Annual Percentage Change, 9.24
Annuity, **10.5**
Applying the Enterprise-Wide Risk Management Framework and Process, 5.22–5.30
Applying the Risk Management Framework, 5.23–5.25
Applying the Risk Management Process, 5.25–5.30
Assessing Controls, 7.5
Asset Exposed to Loss, 3.8–3.9
Assets, 9.4–9.5
Audit to Business Objectives, 11.20
Auditor Responsibilities, 11.12
Auto Insurance, 3.21–3.22
Avoidance, **3.5**, 8.5

B

Background, 2.9, 2.14
Bailees' customers policy, **3.18**
Balance sheet, **6.23**, 9.4, 9.4–9.6
Basel II and III, 2.19–2.22
Basic Risk Map, 6.17
Basic Risk Measures, 1.19–1.23
Benefits for an Organization, 1.9–1.13
Benefits for the Economy, 1.13–1.14
Benefits of Internal Controls, 11.10
Benefits of Risk Management, 1.9–1.14
Benefits of Risk Monitoring, 11.15
Benefits to the Organization, 11.17
Best Concepts, 11.27
Board Responsibilities, 11.12
Board Responsibility for Risk Management Oversight, 11.3–11.4
Board Risk Committee, 11.6–11.7
Board Risk Oversight, 11.3–11.9
Breach of contract, **3.21**
Builders' All-Risk Insurance, 3.19
Business Continuity, 1.17
Business income insurance, **3.18**–3.19

C

Call option, **4.16**, 10.24
Capital, **4.21**
Capital budgeting, **10.11**
Capital Budgeting and Expenditures, 10.11
Capital expenditures, **10.11**
Capital Structure, 9.29–9.31
Case Analysis Tools, 6.30
Cash flow, **4.16**
Cash Flow Analysis, 10.14–10.17
Cash Flow Analysis Recognizing Expected Losses, 10.18–10.19
Cash Flow Analysis With Loss Prevention or Reduction, 10.20–10.23
Cash matching, **4.15**
Cause of Loss, 3.9–3.10
Central tendency, **7.11**
Characteristics, 11.25
Characteristics of Probability Distributions, 7.11–7.17
Chief Risk Officer (CRO), 11.7
Claims-made coverage form, **3.23**
Claims-made coverage trigger, **3.23**
Classifying Commercial Insurance Policies, 3.16
Coefficient of variation, **7.13**–7.14
Coinsurance clause, **3.18**
Commercial Insurance Policies, 3.16–3.25
Commercial property insurance, **3.18**
Commitment of Resources, 5.12
Commodity futures contract, **4.16**
Commodity price risk, **4.16**
Common Elements of Risk Management Standards, 2.4–2.5
Communicate and Report, 5.6, 5.25
Communication, 5.13
Communication and Reporting, 5.12–5.13
Company Annual Reports, 9.21–9.22
Comparing Decision Tree Analysis and Event Tree Analysis, 7.26

Comparing the Enterprise-Wide Risk Management Process With the Traditional Risk Management Process, 5.15–5.22
Complete or Partial, 8.9
Compliance Review, 6.28
Components of a Risk Management Framework, 5.4–5.6
Comprehensive income, **9.12**–9.13
Conditional value at risk, **4.19**
Contract (Noninsurance), 8.8
Contracts, 6.24–6.25
Control Activities, 2.16–2.17
Control Indicators, **4.10**
Control Risk Self-Assessment, 11.23
Correlation, **1.22**
COSO Enterprise Risk Management—Integrated Framework, 2.13–2.17
COSO's Five Components, 11.11–11.12
Cost of Financial Distress, 9.34–9.35
Cost of risk, **1.9**
Credit risk, **1.24**, 1.27, 4.3, 4.17
Currency Price Risk, 4.15
Current assets, **9.4**, 9.27
Current liabilities, **9.5**, 9.27
Current ratio, **9.26**, 9.27–9.28

D

Dashboards and Scorecards, 11.27
Data Credibility, 7.35–7.37
Debt, 9.31
Decision Tree Analysis, 7.23–7.24
Defining Internal Audit, 11.16
Definition of Hazard Risk, 3.3–3.4
Definition of Risk Identification, 6.4
Delphi Technique, 6.9
Demographics, **4.33**
Dependent property exposure, **3.19**
Depreciation expense, **9.14**, 10.15
Designing and Implementing an Enterprise-Wide Risk Management Framework and Process, 5.9–5.14
Differences, 5.21–5.22
Differential (incremental) annual after-tax net cash flow, **10.13**
Direct physical loss, **3.18**
Directors and Officers Liability Insurance, 3.23
Discount rate, **10.3**
Discounting, **10.3**
Dispersion, **7.11**
Diversifiable and Nondiversifiable Risk, 1.26
Diversifiable risk, **1.26**
Diversification, **3.5**
Document Analysis, 6.21–6.28
Duplication, **3.5**

E

Earnings at risk, **4.18**, 4.19–4.20
Earnings Stability, 1.17
Economic Capital, 4.26–4.31
Economic Capital for Insurers, 4.28–4.29
Economic Environment, 4.32–4.33
Economy of Risk Management Operations, 1.18
Elements of Loss Exposures, 3.8–3.10
Empirical probability (a posteriori probability), **7.6**
Employee Responsibilities, 11.12
Employment Practices Liability, 3.23
Enterprise Risk Management, 1.29–1.34, **4.30**
Enterprise-Wide Risk Management Framework and Process Model, 5.3–5.4
Enterprise-Wide Risk Management Process, 5.15–5.18
Entity coverage, **3.23**
Environmental Insurance, 3.25
Equipment Breakdown (Boiler & Machinery) Insurance, 3.19–3.20
Equity, 9.30–9.31
Equity capital, **4.22**
Equity price risk, **4.16**
ERM Definitions, 1.29
Evaluating Capital Investment Proposals, 10.11–10.17
Evaluating Cash Flows From Treating Hazard Risk, 10.17–10.23
Evaluation of Internal and External Environments, 5.10–5.11
Event Tree Analysis, 7.24–7.26
Examining the Feasibility of Risk Management Techniques, 5.20
Expected value, **7.12**
Expenses, 9.8–9.9
Expertise Within and Beyond the Organization, 6.29
Exposure, **1.20**
Exposure Indicators, **4.9**
External Environment, 5.11
External Events, 4.7–4.8

F

Facilitated Workshops, 6.8–6.9
Fair value, **4.26**
Fair Value Accounting, 4.26–4.27
Fair Value of Insurers, 4.27–4.28
Fidelity and Crime Insurance, 3.20
Fiduciary Liability, 3.24
Fiduciary liability insurance, **3.24**
FIFO method, 9.28
Financial Consequences of Loss, 3.10
Financial Crises, 4.33
Financial leverage, **9.32**–9.35
Financial Leverage Analysis, 9.32–9.33
Financial Leverage Analysis for Zeselle Company, 9.32–9.33
Financial Risk, 4.13–4.18
Financial Risk in General, 4.14
Financial statement, **9.3**
Financial Statements and Underlying Accounting Records, 6.23–6.24
Financing Activities, 9.17
Flowcharts and Organizational Charts, 6.26–6.27
Focus on the Materiality of the Risk, 11.20
Form 8-K, 9.19–9.20
Form 10-K, 9.19
Form 10-Q, 9.19
Forward contract, **10.24**

Framework, **2.3**, 2.9–2.11, 2.14–2.15
Frequency, **3.4**
Frequency and Severity Considered Jointly, 7.30–7.33
Functionality, 11.25
Functions and Responsibilities, 11.16
Funded or Unfunded, 8.10
Futures contract, **8.9**, 10.24

G

Gap Analysis, 5.9
GDP, 4.32
General Liability Insurance, 3.21
Generally accepted accounting principles (GAAP), **4.27**, 9.17
Gross margin (gross profit margin), **9.10**
Gross profit, **9.9**–9.10

H

Hard controls, **11.13**
Hazard, **3.9**
Hazard analysis, **6.29**
Hazard risk, **1.6**, 8.7
HAZOP, 6.10
Hedging, **4.14**, 8.8, 8.8–8.9, 10.24
Hold-harmless agreement (or indemnity agreement), **6.25**, 8.8
Holistic Approach to Risk Identification, 6.6–6.8
Holistic Risk Management, 1.12

I

Identify Risks, 5.17, 5.26
Identify the Threats to the Achievement of the Business Goals and Objectives, 11.20
Identifying Loss Exposures, 5.18, 6.21–6.29
Identifying Risk, 6.29–6.34
Identifying Risks—Team Approach, 6.30–6.31
Illustrating Risk Treatment Decisions, 6.20–6.21
Impediments to ERM, 1.33–1.34
Implementing ERM, 1.33
Implementing the Selected Risk Management Techniques, 5.21
Improved Allocation of Productive Resources, 1.14
Income statement, **6.23**, 9.8–9.13
Income Statement Trend Analysis, 9.23–9.25
Indemnification, **6.25**
Indemnify, **3.21**
Independent Status, 11.16
Indicators by Operational Risk Class, 4.9
Industrial All-Risk (Special Risk) Insurance, 3.19
Inflation, 4.32
Inherent risk, **2.15**, 6.19
Insurance, **3.5**, 8.8
Insurance Policies, 6.25–6.26
Insurance-to-value provision, **3.18**
Insuring agreement, **3.21**
Intangible property, **3.11**
Integrated Reporting Versus Silo Reporting, 11.25
Integration Into Existing Processes, 5.11–5.12
Intelligent Risk Taking, 1.11–1.12

Interest rate risk, **4.15**–4.16
Internal Audit Committee Formal Reports, 11.8–11.9
Internal Audit Committee Informal Reports, 11.9
Internal Audits, 11.8–11.9
Internal Audit Support to Risk Monitoring, 11.16–11.20
Internal Control Linked to Risk Monitoring, 11.14–11.15
Internal controls, **11.10**, **11.16**
Internal Controls Defined, 11.9–11.12
Internal Controls Support to Risk Monitoring, 11.9–11.15
Internal Controls Within the Organizational Environment, 11.12–11.13
Internal Control Techniques, 11.13–11.14
Internal Environment, 5.10
International Trade Flows and Restrictions, 4.33
Interpreting the Results, 9.25
Interpreting the Results of Liquidity Ratio Analysis, 9.28–9.29
Introduction to Regulatory Capital, 4.21–4.23
Introduction to Risk Analysis, 7.3–7.5
Introduction to Risk Financing, 8.6–8.10
Introduction to Risk Identification, 6.3–6.8
Introduction to Risk Indicators, 4.8
Introduction to Risk Management Standards and Guidelines, 2.3–2.6
Inventory, **9.4**
Investing Activities, 9.16
ISO 31000 Risk Management—Principles and Guidelines, 2.8–2.13

K

Key performance indicator (KPI), **5.5**
Key risk indicator (KRI), **4.8**, 5.5, 11.25

L

Law of large numbers, **1.20**, 7.6, 7.6–7.7
Lead and Establish Accountability, 5.4–5.5, 5.23–5.24
Legal and Regulatory Compliance, 1.16
Legal and Regulatory Requirements, 1.13
Legal hazard, **3.10**
Leverage, **4.23**
Liabilities, 9.5
Liability, **3.16**, 3.21
Liability Loss Exposures, **3.12**
LIFO method, 9.28
Limitations of Financial Leverage, 9.34–9.35
Limitations of Risk Monitoring, 11.15
Line of business, **3.16**
Linear regression analysis, **7.18**
Liquidity, **9.26**
Liquidity risk, **1.27**, 4.17, 9.26
Loss Exposures, **3.8**–3.16
Loss Frequency, 7.28–7.29
Loss Histories, 6.28
Loss prevention, **8.5**
Loss ratio, **4.10**
Loss reduction, **8.5**
Loss Severity, 7.30–7.33

M

Manage the Downside of Risk, 1.11
Management Liability Insurance, 3.23–3.24
Management Responsibilities, 11.12
Management's Discussion and Analysis of Results, 9.22
Managing Data, 11.25–11.26
Market risk, **1.27**, 4.3, 4.14–4.17
Market value margin, **4.27**
Market value surplus, **4.27**
Marketable securities, **9.4**
Maximize Profitability, 1.12
Maximum Possible Loss, 7.30
Mean, **7.13**
Measuring and Managing Hazard Risk, 3.4–3.5
Measuring Liquidity, 9.27–9.28
Modeling, **2.18**
Modeling an Enterprise-Wide Risk Management Framework and Process, 5.3–5.7
Monitor and Assure, 5.18, 5.30
Monitoring and Improvement, 5.14
Monitoring Results and Revising the Risk Management Program, 5.21
Monoline policy, **3.18**
Monte Carlo simulation, **4.19**
Moral hazard, **3.9**
Morale hazard (attitudinal hazard), **3.9**

N

Named peril, **3.18**
Nature of Hazard Risk, 3.3–3.8
Nature of Probability, 7.5–7.7
Nature of Risk Analysis, 7.4
Nature of Standards and Guidelines, 2.3
Net Income, 9.10–9.11
Net Income Loss Exposures, **3.14**–3.16
Net Present Value, **10.9**–10.11
Nondiversifiable risk, **1.26**
Normal distribution, **7.14**–7.15
Notes to Financial Statements, 9.17–9.18
NPV method, 10.12, 10.12–10.13

O

Objective risk, **1.25**
Obligee, **3.20**
Occurrence, **3.21**
Occurrence coverage form, **3.23**
Ocean Marine Insurance, 3.24–3.25
Operating Activities, 9.15
Operating expenditures, **10.11**
Operating income, **9.10**
Operating Leverage, 9.35–9.39
Operating Leverage Example, 9.36–9.39
Operational Risk, 4.3–4.8
Operational Risk Definitions, 4.3–4.4
Operational Risk Indicators, 4.8–4.12
Operational Risk in General, 4.3
Optimum risk, **6.19**

Organizational Policies and Records, 6.26
Organizational Relationships, 1.31
Organizational Risk Register, 6.15
Overview of Steps, 5.23, 6.30, 10.18
Overview of the Procedure, 9.23

P

Package policy, **3.18**
Paid-in capital, **9.13**
P-D-C-A Cycle, **5.14**
People, 4.5–4.7
People, Process, Systems, and External Events, 4.5–4.8
Perils of the sea, **3.25**
Personal Inspections, 6.28–6.29
Personal loss exposure, **3.13**
Personal property, **3.11**
Personnel Loss Exposures, **3.13**
Physical hazard, **3.10**
Planned or Unplanned, 8.9
Political Environment, 4.34
Political risk, **4.34**
Practical Application: Normal Distribution, 7.16–7.17
Prepaid expenses, **9.4**
Present value, **10.3**
Present Value and Discounting, 10.3–10.4
Present Value of an Annuity, 10.5–10.7
Present Value of Unequal Payments, 10.7–10.9
Present Value Over a Single Period, 10.3
Present Value Over Multiple Periods, 10.4
Price risk, **4.18**, 10.24
Principal, **3.20**
Principles, 2.9
Probability analysis, 7.5–7.11, **7.6**
Probability distribution, **7.7**
Probability Distributions, 7.7–7.11
Process, 2.11–2.13, 4.7
Professional Liability or Errors and Omissions Insurance, 3.22
Profitability and Growth, 1.17–1.18
Property, **3.16**
Property Insurance, 3.18–3.20
Property Loss Exposures, **3.10**–3.11
Property-casualty insurance, **3.16**
Pure and Speculative Risk, 1.23–1.24
Pure risk, **1.23**, 3.3, 8.4
Purpose of a Risk Management Framework, 5.3
Purpose of Financial Statements, 9.3–9.4
Purpose of Internal Controls, 11.10
Purpose of Risk Registers, 6.12–6.13
Put option, **4.16**

Q

Quadrants of Risk: Hazard, Operational, Financial, and Strategic, 1.27–1.28
Qualitative Assessment and Quantitative Analysis, 7.4
Quantitative Data Versus Qualitative Data, 11.26

R

Ratio analysis, **9.25**
Real property (realty), **3.11**
Receivables, **9.4**
Reduce Cost of Hazard Risk, 1.9–1.10
Reduce Deterrence Effects of Hazard Risks, 1.10
Reduce Downside Risk, 1.10–1.11
Reduced Cash Flow Flexibility, 9.34
Reduced Systemic Risk, 1.14
Reduced Waste of Resources, 1.14
Regression analysis, **7.17**, 7.18–7.20
Regression Analysis Example, 7.20–7.23
Regulatory Capital, 4.20–4.26
Regulatory Risk Capital Under Basel II, 4.23–4.26
Reinvestment risk, **4.16**
Relating Indicators and Outcomes, 4.11–4.12
Replacement cost, **3.18**
Report Assurance, 11.17
Report Certification, 11.17
Report Formats, 11.27
Report of Management, 9.21
Reporting, 5.13
Residual risk, **2.15**, 6.19, 8.4
Retained earnings, **9.5**, 9.14
Retention, **8.6**
Return on equity (ROE), **9.32**
Revenue, **9.8**
Risk, **1.3**, **8.8**
Risk and Risk Management Defined, 1.3–1.5
Risk appetite, **6.17**
Risk Assessment, 2.12
Risk Assessment Questionnaires and Checklists, 6.22–6.23
Risk Assurance, 11.21–11.22
Risk Assurance Benefits, 11.24
Risk Assurance Sources, 11.21–11.22
Risk Assurance to Evaluate Risk Management Performance, 11.20–11.24
Risk Classifications, 1.23–1.28
Risk control, **5.20**, 7.5
Risk criteria, **2.11**, 5.5, 5.16
Risk financing, **8.6**
Risk Financing as a Part of Risk Treatment, 8.6–8.7
Risk financing techniques, **5.20**
Risk governance, **2.5**
Risk Identification Tools, 6.4–6.5
Risk management, **1.5**
Risk Management and Internal Audit, 11.17–11.19
Risk Management Effectiveness, 11.22
Risk Management Environment, 1.3–1.7, 1.6–1.7
Risk management framework, **2.9**, 5.3, 5.9
Risk Management Goals, 1.15–1.18
Risk Management Monitoring and Reporting, 11.24–11.27
Risk Management Objectives, 1.15
Risk Management Objectives and Goals, 1.14–1.19
Risk Management Policy, 5.7
Risk Management Reporting, 11.5–11.8
Risk management standard, **2.3**
Risk map, **6.17**
Risk Mapping, 6.32–6.34
Risk Maps, 6.17–6.21
Risk Map Variations, 6.17–6.19
Risk Monitoring and Review, 2.13
Risk optimization, **4.14**
Risk owner, **5.5**
Risk profile, **1.6**
Risk Registers, **6.12**–6.15, 6.17, 6.32
Risk Reporting, 11.25
Risk Retention, 8.9–8.10
Risk Transfer, 8.8–8.9
Risk Treatment, 2.12–2.13, 8.3–8.6
Risk Treatment Process, 8.4
Risk Treatment Techniques, 8.4–8.6
Risk-based auditing, **11.19**–11.20
Risk-based capital (RBC), **2.18**, **4.28**
Risk-return trade-off, **10.13**
Role of Insurance, 3.5–3.8
Role of Internal Auditor, 11.18–11.19
Role of Risk Management, 11.17
Root cause, **4.8**

S

Salvage value, **10.12**
Sarbanes-Oxley Act of 2002, **9.22**
Scan Environment, 5.26
Scan the Environment, 5.15–5.16
Scenario Analysis, 6.9–6.10
Scope, 2.9
Securities and Exchange Commission Filings, 9.18–9.20
Selecting the Appropriate Risk Management Techniques, 5.20
Sensitivity analysis, **10.17**
Separation, **3.5**
Severity, **3.4**
Shareholders' Equity, 9.5–9.6
Similarities, 5.21
Social Responsibility, 1.18
Soft controls, **11.13**
Solvency II, 2.18–2.19, 4.31
Solvency II and Basel II and III Regulatory Standards, 2.18–2.22
Speculative risk, **1.23**, 8.4, 8.7
Standard deviation, **7.13**
Statement of cash flows, **6.24**, 9.14, 9.14–9.17
Statement of changes in shareholders' equity, **9.13**–9.14
Statement of Changes in Shareholders' Equity and Statement of Cash Flows, 9.13–9.17
Statutory accounting principles (SAP), **4.27**
Straight-line depreciation method, **10.15**
Strategic Risk, 4.31–4.34
Subjective and Objective Risk, 1.25–1.26
Subjective risk, **1.25**
Summary of the Major Standards and Guidelines, 2.5–2.6
Supplemental Sources of Financial Information, 9.17–9.22
Surety, **3.20**

Surety Bonds, 3.20
Survival, 1.16–1.17
Swap, **4.15**
SWOT, 6.11–6.12
Systematic risk, **4.14**
Systemic risk, **1.9**, 1.26, 4.23, 4.31
Systems, 4.7

T

Tangible property, **3.11**
Tariff, **4.33**
Tax shield, 9.33, **9.34**
Team Approaches to Risk Identification, 6.8–6.12
Theoretical and Empirical Probabilities, 7.5–7.6
Theoretical Pillars of ERM, 1.29–1.30
Theoretical probability, **7.5**
Time horizon, **1.21**
Timing, 7.35
Tolerable Uncertainty, 1.16
Tort, **3.21**
Total Dollar Losses, 7.33–7.34
Trade-Offs Among Goals, 1.19
Traditional Risk Management Process, 5.18–5.21
Transfer, **8.6**
Transferring Wheat Price Increases, 10.24–10.26
Transparency, **9.22**
Transparency and Clear Communications, 11.7–11.8
Transparent Communications, 11.13
Treasury stock, **9.14**
Treat Risks, 5.17–5.18, 5.28–5.30
Trend analysis, **7.17**–7.23, **9.23**
Types of Loss Exposures, 3.10–3.16

U

Underlying Concepts, 10.24
Use of Internal Controls, 11.16
Use of Risk Registers With Scenario Models, 6.13
Using Call Options to Limit Financial Risk, 10.23–10.26

V

Value at risk, **1.16**, 4.18, 4.19, 4.24
Value at Risk and Earnings at Risk, 4.18–4.20
Volatility, **1.20**

W

Workers Compensation and Employers Liability Insurance, 3.22
Working capital, **9.26**, 9.27

Z

Zero-coupon bond, **4.15**